THE GRANITE MEN

THE GRANITE MEN

A History of the Granite Industries of Aberdeen and North East Scotland

JIM FIDDES

The
History
Press

The publication of this book would not have been possible
without the generous support of the following:

Leiths (Scotland) Ltd
Rigifa
Cove
Aberdeen

Robertson Granite
Silvertrees Drive
Westhill
Aberdeenshire

Cover illustations: *Front, Top*: Frontage of Marischal College. (Courtesy of
Ian Jackson); *Bottom*: The huge stone blasted from the face of Kemnay
Quarry in September 1956. The men on the stone are Robbie Thomson,
Bill Law and James Clark. (Used by kind permission of D.C. Thomson &
Co. Ltd); *Rear*: Kemnay Quarry today.

First published 2019

The History Press
The Mill, Brimscombe Port
Stroud, Gloucestershire, GL5 2QG
www.thehistorypress.co.uk

© Jim Fiddes, 2019

The right of Jim Fiddes to be identified as the Author
of this work has been asserted in accordance with the
Copyright, Designs and Patents Act 1988.

British Library Cataloguing in Publication Data.
A catalogue record for this book is available from the British Library.

ISBN 978 0 7509 9001 1

Typesetting and origination by The History Press
Printed and bound in Great Britain by TJ International Ltd

CONTENTS

ACKNOWLEDGEMENTS

The heyday of the granite industry has long since passed, as have many of the men who worked in it. It is particularly sad that three of my main informants for this book passed away in 2016 but I owe a considerable debt to Michael O'Connor, Fred Cargill and my uncle Robert Taylor. I hope I have done justice to their industry. I would also like to thank the following, who either worked in the industry or had family members who connected to the industry: the late Sandy Argo, Michael A. Grant, Brian Innes, Roy Lyall, Ron McKay, Judy and Bill Mackie, Mary Macrae, Ron Michie, Alistair Sutherland, Mary Williamson. Several people who are still connected with the granite industry have given me help and encouragement. These include Hugh Black, owner of Rubislaw Quarry, Alan Bruce of Fyfe Glenrock, Ian Leith of the Leith Group, Graeme Robertson of Robertson Granite, and the redoubtable Bruce Walker, sculptor. Special thanks to Craig Godsman of Breedon Group who gave me exhilarating tours of Craigenlow and Tom's Forest quarries on a working day.

Duncan Downie provided invaluable help on all things related to Kemnay Quarry, including reading and commenting on various parts of the manuscript relating to Kemnay. Sir Archibald Grant of Monymusk gave me information on the various quarries on his land, information that would have been difficult to obtain elsewhere.

When I first started out on this work one of the first people I spoke to was Jenny Brown, lead curator at Aberdeen Art Gallery and Museums. As well as sharing her knowledge of the granite industry, Jenny accommodated me in the Maritime Museum while I ploughed through the many volumes of the Aberdeen Granite Association. She also read some of the first chapters of my text and encouraged me to believe that I was producing something worthwhile. Her colleagues in the Aberdeen City and Aberdeenshire Archives were also of considerable help as were those in Aberdeenshire Libraries. David Main of Aberdeen Central Library very helpfully coordinated my request for photographs. Penny Hartley from Robert Gordon's College found information on the stone used in the building of the school in its archives. Fiona Riddell of Peterhead Museum was generous in sharing her information and photographs relating to Cairngall Quarry. Staff at Durlston Country Park and Swanage Museum helpfully provided information and photographs of the Granite Globe.

Other who have helped and encouraged along the way were Bill Brogden, George Cheyne, John and Marion Donald, John Glover, Alan Holmes, Ian Jackson, David Miller, and John Reynolds.

I would also like to thank Professor Gokay Deveci for his support and comments, and Amy Rigg and team at The History Press for their help and support.

I am very grateful to *Lallans: The Journal of the Scots Language Society* and to Frances Mackie, daughter of Alistair, for allowing me to use Alistair's wonderful words on the end of the granite industry.

Finally I would like to thank my wife Jenny, my daughter Kerry, and son Stephen for their support in the long haul to produce this work.

I would like to thank the following individuals and institutions for kindly giving me permission to reproduce their images:

Aberdeen and Aberdeenshire Archives
Aberdeen Art Galleries and Museums
Aberdeen City Libraries
Duncan Downie, Kemnay
DC Thomson/Aberdeen Journals
Steve Dunn (USA)
Illustrated London News Ltd/Mary Evans
Ian Jackson, Drumoak
Lebanon County Library, Fredericksburg, Pennsylvania
Roy Lyall, Lyne of Skene
Bill and Judy Mackie
Ellen Massie, Skene
Ron Michie, Torphins, Grandson of James Macdonald
The late Michael O'Connor and his family
Fiona Riddell, Arbuthnot Museum, Peterhead
Robertson Granite
Skene Heritage Society and John Milne
Swanage Museum
Bruce Walker. Sculptor, Kirriemuir

To Fred Cargill, Michael P.S. O'Connor and
Robert Taylor.

Granite men all in their different ways.

INTRODUCTION

Whit did ye bigg, granda? The sillert mansions o Rubislaw and Mannofield; the twistit crunny and orra stink o Crooked Lane, the brookit tenements o Black's Buildings, the Denburn, the Gallowgate, East North Street and West North Street … . The offices and shops and banks o the touns steery hert, its mile-lang monument to the grey skinkle and mica een o the quarry hole, a pavit river that took the jossle and stour o fowk and traffic aa bent on their ain ploys … Granite for Edward the Seventh's statue, the fat clort, wi doos' shite on his brou … Granite for Union brig wi its metal lions black and kenspeckle … Or were you in Canada when the Marischal gaed up, oor Kremlin to college lear. And made aa the weather-cocks jealous? The masons' hemmers dung oot reels and strathspeys on the keys o granite squares and bumbazed steen spieled fae the foonds. Its tormentit diamante bleezed grey in the wink o its million een; and abeen aa, wee gowd-yella pennants were stuck like a stray notion at the hinner-end, never to flame in ony wind that blew … A year or twa back the quarry stoppit for good. Nae mair the hubber and rattle-stanes o the muckle crusher; nae mair the dirlin o the dreels, nae mair the grey smoor o stew; nae mair the blondin's pulley-wheels breel on their iled road ower yon howkit hole.

Alistair Mackie 'My Grandfather's Nieve'[1]

Apologies to those who don't understand the north-east version of the Scots language, commonly called Doric, but this piece of prose graphically captures the granite industry and the granite city of Aberdeen that was created from that industry. Alistair Mackie, teacher and makar (poet), was well qualified to write about it is as his father Frank, his grandfather Alexander (Sandy), and other members of his family all worked in the granite quarries. He describes the mile-long monument to granite (Union Street in Aberdeen), granite that came out of the gleaming mica opening of the quarry hole; the masons' hammers beating out reels and strathspeys on the stone; some of the celebrated creations from those hammers – Union Bridge, Edward VII's statue at the corner of Union street and Union Terrace; and above all Marischal College; finally the end of the quarry with an end to its dust (stew), and noise from the drills, the stone crusher, and the blondin's pulley-wheels.

Granite, the hardest of all building stones, had been used for buildings in the north-east long before the opening of the quarries of Rubislaw, Kemnay and Dancing Cairns from where the granite came for the silver mansions and king's statues. One such, for example, is Craigievar Castle which rises up from Craigievar Hill, and looks down on the valley of the Leochel Burn. The castle dates from the 1580s to 1620s and was built from rough pink granite, field gatherings of the local stone (what *The Architect* magazine in 1872 called outlier or surface stones), relatively unworked. The lintels and jambs of the doors and windows, as well as the stairs, have been treated with more care, doubtless with better quality stone. To the east of the castle, across the Leochel Burn there is a range of hills, running roughly north–south. The central hill is marked Red Hill on Ordnance Survey maps, and that is the name locals use for the whole range. At the north-east end of this line of hills is the Corrennie Quarry, source of salmon pink granite since the second half of the nineteenth century. The stone for building Craigievar came from the surrounding area, including the Red Hill, with the dressed work possibly coming from the area around Corrennie. However, there would not have a been a quarry in the modern sense at the time the castle was built, the stone for dressing would have been taken from outcrops that would later become the quarry.

Craigievar, almost certainly the work of one of the Bel family of masons from Midmar, was one of the last of the great north-east tower houses, the final flowering of a long tradition. All over the north-east, tower houses were built from the local stone, sometimes granite and sometimes sandstone, taken from as near as possible to the site of the building because transporting it would have been too difficult at a time when there were few roads and few wheeled vehicles. The great tower at Drum, which the most recent archaeological work now assigns to the early fourteenth century, is perhaps the earliest surviving castle built from granite field gatherings, reputedly from the Cowie Hill above the castle, the quarry site there was apparently still visible in Knight's day in the early 1830s.[2] Even before Drum was built, local granite was used in the building of the late twelfth- or early thirteenth-century Augustinian Priory at Monymusk, which later became the parish church. Although much altered and restored, Romanesque details can still be seen at Monymusk and most authorities would accept that it is the earliest surviving granite building in the north-east. Pink granite was used with sandstone dressings, sandstone being much easier to work than granite. The parish minister in 1895 recorded, 'The granite used in the building is not the same as the common blocks in the fields or in recently-opened quarries.' The tradition is that it was taken from Tombeg Farm, and that the stones were passed from hand to hand down the hill, which seems unlikely.[3] Historian W. Douglas Simpson had the granite geologically examined and he concluded that the lower courses were similar in colour and grain to pink granite quarried in the Cunningar Wood near Cluny Castle, a mile and a half south of the church. Above that level he suggested that the walls were of porphyritic granite, fine-grained and pale pink with large crystals of feldspar and smoky quartz. This rock he identified with the later quarry on Pitfichie Hill. The Tombeg quarry itself produced a grey-yellow granite, not pink.[4]

In Old Aberdeen parts of the nave of St Machar Cathedral, particularly the west front, including the towers, are also of granite, making it the only granite cathedral in the country. Why this part of the cathedral was built of granite in the first half of the fifteenth century is not clear, perhaps the supply of red sandstone, used earlier in the cathedral, was interrupted for some reason. The towers with their machicolated parapets originally had cap-houses instead of the freestone spires that were added 100 years later. It would therefore have looked even more castle-like than it does today. Perhaps the mason who built it was more used to working on castles and towers, or maybe there were practical reasons for this military look. Lairds and clan chiefs were in the habit of bringing their feuds and war-like practices to the environs of the cathedral, hence the defensive nature of the

Chanonry with its ports. In a similar way there were stout defensible churches built in various parts of France during the Hundred Years War. Whoever the mason was his skill in working granite created, for example, a moulded doorway that architect William Kelly compared with one in sandstone at Elgin Cathedral.

In Aberdeen itself the earliest medieval granite structure that survives is the much altered St Mary's Chapel at the east end of St Nicholas Kirk, probably dating from the 1440s. The chapel helped support the extension of the Mither Kirk where the ground fell away to the Putachie Burn. The chapel also includes some granite carving, inevitably cruder than those from sandstone.

A tradition recorded by the parish minister at Monymusk was that the mason who built the church there 'looked from the Tombeg hill on the finished tower and exclaimed that if he had received a few merks more he would have been properly paid.'[5] A similar story is told of Corse Castle near Craigievar where, after he had finished, the mason washed his hands in the burn and said 'gin I'd had anither tippence I'd hae been weel aff.' Medieval masons were immensely skilled men, they were architects as well as masons and these stories suggest that they felt that they didn't receive true remuneration for their work.

Much earlier than all these medieval buildings, granite blocks and stones were used by our pre-historic ancestors to build their monuments and homes– stone circles, burial cairns, round houses etc. In the centre of Aberdeen the Langstane is an example of this, but they can be found

St Machar Cathedral.

throughout the north-east. Granite does so much to define our landscape. Our finest novelist, Lewis Grassic Gibbon, wrote that 'nothing endures but the land' and granite is the most enduring of the materials found in our land.

This book is the story of how the descendants of these Neolithic farmers and medieval masons blasted the granite from the depths of the earth creating huge holes that can be found all over the north-east; how they worked that granite at the quarries and in the granite yards and turned this hardest of materials into buildings and objects of beauty, shaping and polishing the material; it is the story of the tools and technology they used to bring the material to the surface, to work the granite and create an industry; and it is also the story of how Aberdeen, in particular, became the Granite City, both in terms of the built environment of the city but also in the minds of its population and of people beyond the city.

THE BEGINNINGS
OF AN INDUSTRY

The early burgh of Aberdeen was surrounded to the north, south and west by abundant outcrops of granite, but the first stone house built in the burgh was said to have been for Provost Menzies of Findon in 1530, his previous timber house having burnt down the year before. It stood at the south-west corner of the Castlegate and such was the novelty of a stone house that a local is recorded defiantly stating that he 'cared not for the provost or his stane hoos'. The house passed to the Provost's son, Thomas Menzies of Pitfodels and became known as Pitfodel's Lodgings. A few years later another important figure in the north-east, the Earl Marischal, built himself a town house alongside it. Both houses survived until the late eighteenth century. These houses, as with the castles and tower houses, would have been built of rough gathered stone, but they also had dressed work around the windows and doors in sandstone, as can be seen in the surviving houses of Provosts Skene and Ross in the Guestrow and the Shiprow respectively. With field-gathered granite you get walls that have a variety of colours and grains in the stones, the stones themselves being rough and difficult to fashion as a result of being exposed to the action of the elements, including the movement of ice, over the millennia. This is one of the reasons why many early granite buildings were harled, for aesthetic reasons. Nineteenth-century writers used the word rude (i.e. crude) to describe this stonework and any early attempts to carve granite.

The Burgh records for 2 June 1539 record that 'the sayd day, the prowest and balzes consentis and ordains, wytht the awse of the hayll towne, that thair be ane cassay maker feyit and conducit for daly wagis, to mak, reforme, and mind all streyttis and calsayis of the sayd burght.'[12] This cassay maker was a forerunner of the settmakers who would provide road and pavement material not just for Aberdeen but also for London and other cities in the kingdom. The sett trade with London provided one of the most important stimuli for the infant granite industry.

The first record we have of an attempt to actually quarry granite comes in 1603 when the Council Registers records that a John Meason (mason) be 'permitted to open a quarry within the freedom lands, in order to supply the inhabitants with stones for doors, windows and rigging, and no person to be at liberty to open any other quarry for that purpose for five years'.[3] It is usually stated that this quarry was at the Hill of Rubislaw, but no location is given in the council records and Cairncry, Rosehill and Loanhead are also possibilities. Despite his monopoly, Meason's quarry does not seem to have been successful, and it wasn't until the early eighteenth century that granite quarrying can really be said to have begun in earnest in the burgh.

By the early eighteenth century, the town was far from being the 'Granite City', and the Council tried to encourage and then insist on building in stone (though not necessarily granite). In June 1731 they reported on the:

> Dangerous consequences re-building their house of timber after they become ruinous and like-wise building their chimney with plaster and lath and covering houses with heath or thatch or divot. Ordain that no individual or proprietor of tenements do presume to build the forepart of their houses (such as forestairs) with any sort of timber, but only with stone or brick and that they do not build any of their chimneys of plaister or lath, commonly called staik and ryce or cove, the roofs of their houses with heath, thatch or divot but altenerly with slate or tyle. Or their building will be pulled down and each transgression fined 50 pounds Scots.[4]

This encouragement met with only limited success and a further Act of 1741 admitted that the 'previous Act of 1731 has not had the desired effect'. The Council acted quickly because this Act of 17 August 1741 came about after 'the many dreadful and fatal instances that have happened within the burgh by fire, more particularly the late dismal that happened 4th August when several houses in the west side of the Broadgate were brunt down.'[5] Not only was it difficult to extinguish a fire in timber buildings but the extension of wooden forestairs in front of properties caused lanes such as the Guestrow and the Narrow Wynd to become too narrow for adequate access. Building in stone, the Council further argued, would also 'add to the beauty and policy of the Town.'[6] The act compelling houses to be built of stone extended as far as the Bow Brig to the south, all the houses on the north side of the Denburn from the Bow Brig to the Infirmary, up to Mounthooly and on the east to the Justice and Fittie Ports. This time the Council had more success, particularly in the new streets that began to be built from the 1760s onwards. By 1782 Francis Douglas would report that as far as the Town House and the Mason Lodge were concerned:

> The fronts of the wings are uniform, and built of a fine whitish granite, squared and well-smoothed. The Exchange [or the Plainstones as it was more commonly known] is a pavement of granite, squared and well-smoothed, raised two steps above the street, and terminated on the east by the cross. Though in the by-streets there are some brick buildings, the houses in general are built of granite, cut square, and smoothed, some of them better than others.[7]

How had this transformation come about?

James Elmslie of Loanhead (1683–1764): The Man Who Began it All

The *Council Register* records on 7 May 1722 that 'William Menzies of Pitfodels granted some years ago to the Town of Aberdeen to make a quarry on the Hill of Pitfodels for repairing the Bridge of Dee'. This was for granite as part of the repairs to the bridge carried out in the early 1720s, though most of the work was done in freestone and there is no record of significant amounts of granite coming from the Pitfodels Quarry. It is really James Elmslie, later described as a merchant and ardent Jacobite in both the 1715 and 1745 rebellions, who can really be considered the man who started the granite industry in the north-east.

Elmslie is buried in St Machar churchyard, the earlier stone of his first wife, Barbara King, having been placed on top of his following his death. She died in 1725 and on her stone he is described as stonecutter in Loanhead of Aberdeen, just beside the then Skene Road. The likelihood is that he carved the lettering on her stone himself. It wasn't until 1730 that he began quarrying near Loanhead. In present day terms the quarry ran from the top of Craigie Loanings (where it joins Rosemount Place). From there the quarry ran in a south-westerly direction through the east end of Hamilton Place and Craigie Park, and down to the Gilcomston Dam. The year after Elmslie opened his quarry stone from the quarry was used to begin building Robert Gordon's Hospital (or school), though the school itself wasn't opened until much later. The Hospital records for 1731 show the following account: 'Item payed to James Elmsly Quarrier for winning 1760 stones at one hundred pounds Scots the eleven hundred … £160.' Unlike later quarries, Elmslie's does not seem to have delivered or dressed the stone, as there are payments to others for horses and carts and to John Thain and Andrew Edward for dressing these stones. The records also name the masons for the actual building works as John Aikenhead, William Sangster, and Alexander Riach who were paid £2,481 4s 10d for their efforts.[8]

Robert Gordon's Hospital would be followed in later decades by several other important buildings in the town built from Loanhead stone – notably the first Royal Infirmary on the Woolmanhill site, the Grammar School on Schoolhill and the Waterhouse on Broad Street. These three are no longer in existence, although a gable and bellcote from the Grammar School survive within the current school. It has also been suggested that

The tombstones of James Elmslie and his wife in St Machar's Kirkyard.

Gilcomston Chapel of Ease was built from Loanhead granite and, given its location not far from the quarry, this may well have been the case. It is difficult to tell today because it was substantially rebuilt in the nineteenth century. Diack[9] states that it was in fact built for the quarry workers at Loanhead and this suggestion was also picked up by Fenton Wyness.[10] However, I think it more likely that it was built for the large weavers' colony around the Gilcomston area. Robert Gordon's itself, then, was probably the earliest building in the Granite City to be built from dressed and quarried granite and thankfully it survives today.

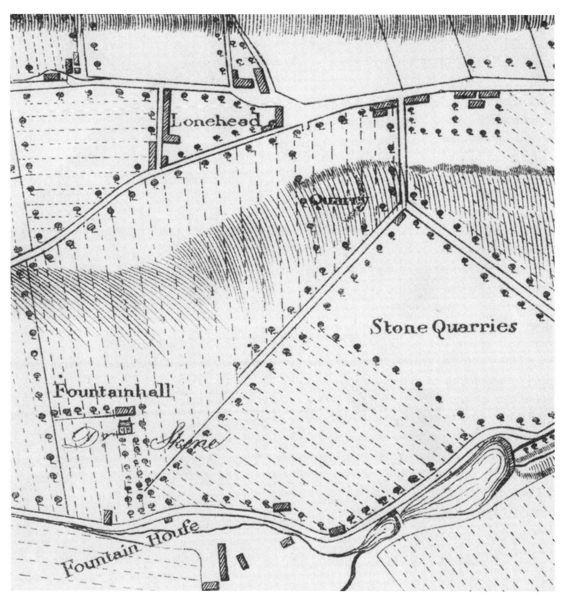

Taylor's map of 1773 shows Loanhead itself just where Rosemount Place branches right to become Mid Stocket Road and left Beechgrove Terrace. The quarries run south east from there down to the Gilcomston Dam.

The Bow Brig carried the main road into the town from the south over the Denburn, and there had been several bridges prior to the eighteenth century. A replacement Bow Brig was agreed by the Town Council at their meeting of 9 May 1747, to be funded by money from the Bridge of Dee fund. It was built by John Jeans, mason, from dressed granite, with each parapet adorned by a tapering obelisk also of dressed granite. According to James Rettie it was 'said by some one to be the first of the kind used'.[11] I presume that Rettie means the first bridge to be built of dressed granite and the likelihood is that it was Loanhead granite.

Several writers on granite (including Diack, Kelly, Donnelly, McLaren and others) have claimed the Town House in Old Aberdeen as being built in 1721 and therefore possibly the oldest ashlar granite building in Aberdeen. However, the Town House was actually built in 1788. The confusion arose because the notable local architect William Kelly gave a lecture to granite workers in 1898 during which he gave the date of Old Aberdeen Town House as 1721. William Diack was at that lecture and used the date in his later writings. Other writers on granite took the date from Diack. However, Kelly was mistaken. The Town House includes an armorial panel dated 1721 taken from the previous town house, hence the confusion. When Aberdeen University published a series of Kelly's essays in his honour in 1949 the error was corrected, but this correction wasn't picked up by later writers.

Loanhead granite was also used as the town began its first phase of planned street layout with Littlejohn Street, Queen Street and adjacent Longacre, the streets of the Lochlands, and above all Marischal Street, which is the best place to see Loanhead granite today, though there may be Loanhead granite in one or two buildings in Belmont Street and also a few in Upperkirkgate. Partly because of growing traffic, and partly to stimulate growth, the city needed easier and more direct access to the harbour, rather than the steep and winding Shiprow. Marischal Street, planned from the early 1760s, was to be more direct and with a more gradual incline, and it would include one of Scotland's first flyovers in Bannerman's Bridge. It was probably the first street in Aberdeen to be paved with granite blocks. The first phase of Marischal Street, north of Bannerman's Bridge, dates from 1767–89. Most of the buildings here are of Loanhead granite, a light beige colour and softer, more open in texture than Rubislaw. In fact there is a building on the west side of Marischal Street where some of the granite has actually crumbled. As Rubislaw Quarry began to be developed it replaced Loanhead in the buildings in Marischal Street built from the 1790s onwards, up to the very early years of the nineteenth century. You can trace this transformation simply by walking down Marischal Street where the changeover to the superior Rubislaw stone is clearly visible. Nos 1–3 Marischal Street at the top, formerly the Royal Oak and now the Old Blackfriars, was actually built of Loanhead granite in 1763, just before the street itself. It was designed to stand on the planned new street, as well as on Castle Street itself. Across on the north side of the Castlegate, No. 17 (Portals Bar) is even earlier, dating from 1760 and also built of granite from Loanhead.

Loanhead survived as a quarry into the early years of the nineteenth century but by then its best days had long passed. Francis Douglas in his description of Aberdeen in 1782 describes Loanhead thus: 'This place was formerly wholly possessed by labourers who wrought in the adjacent quarries, or was the occasional residence of beggars, who were not permitted to settle in the town. There are now many decent houses in it, and the fields around are in high culture.'[12] This perhaps suggests that

Loanhead was already in decline as other quarries came into production. George Keith, writing of the Fountainhall Estate in 1811, does say that it had a valuable stone quarry and this is presumably one of the Loanhead quarries.[13] An advertisement from 1805 for the remainder of the lease of 6 acres of improved ground at Loanhead estate optimistically describes inexhaustible stone quarries, near to the town with all the stone selling rapidly. The advert states that 'the ground may be left in quarry pits at the end of the lease; and as many quarries opened as may be thought proper.'[14] I think it highly likely that at the end of this lease period the quarry would have been all but finished. In the late nineteenth century houses were eventually built in the area of the quarry, one unfortunate legacy of the quarry would appear in the form of subsidence. For example, the building numbered 7, 9 and 11 Hamilton Place suffered from subsidence and in the late 1980s it was taken down with each stone numbered. 360 tons of rubble were removed from the site and thirty-five piles sunk round the footprint of the building. At the front of the building they went down 2m, at the back 6m, before they hit bedrock. The whole process took three years. Further west along the street a bay window was taken out and the foundations filled with concrete. Similarly Hamilton Lodge at the east end of the street had part of the west wall of the rear wing had to be taken down and rebuilt. Someone who worked there when it was a doctor's surgery told me of feeling nauseous in certain rooms and of pencils rolling across the floor. Properties in nearby Beechgrove Terrace have also suffered subsidence in the past.

Rubislaw: the Early Years

As we have seen there may have been a quarry at Rubislaw in the seventeenth century. However, it wasn't until the eighteenth century that quarrying really got going on the Hill of Rubislaw, and it was to be an inauspicious start. In the 1740s the Council hoped that granite from Rubislaw could be used to rebuild the old church i.e. the West Kirk of St Nicholas. Some years before this they had bought the potential quarry from George Skene of Rubislaw for £160 Scots. Evidently some stone was dug out from Rubislaw, because in January 1741 the Register records that:

> The Council agrees that the masons desist from digging more in Rubislaw Quarry until they hew the stone already quarried by hewing a few of each kind of the work – esler [ashlar], pillars, cornices, ribbets, arches, and that they hew the esler both after the best manner they can be dressed and another sort of rough esler, and after they are hewen the Council with other knowing persons to vest the said quarry and the stones so hewen. And the masons then to fix a price on the foot of each kind of hewen work, and contract to furnish all stones shall be necessary for the old church at the price agreed upon.[15]

Presumably the Council were not happy with this first group of masons because in June:

> The said day the Council agreed that David Barrie, mason in Montrose, with John Jeans and other masons shall instantly take down the westernmost pillar both south and north of the old church, in order to know the quality of the pillars and arches, and also take down part of the west gavel [gable].

Likeways to employ labourers for redding the face of the westernmost part of the quarrie of Robslaw so that the above masons may work some days therein to know how the same will work.[16]

The venture was not a success. The West Kirk was eventually rebuilt, to plans by James Gibbs, perhaps the greatest architect Aberdeen has produced, but apart from a base course in granite, it was built from sandstone.

Rubislaw Quarry seems to have produced very little thereafter and then the Council and its 'knowing persons' made a colossal blunder. In June 1788 it was recorded that:

The said day Baillie Adam and the Treasurer reported that in consequence of the Council's remitt to them the 10th May last they had inspected the piece of ground in the Den of Rubislaw bought for a quarry from the present Mr Skene's grandfather, and that it appeared to them that the stones found in it are of a very bad quality and unfit for any public buildings, of which they produced a specimen. That from the appearance of the ground itself they could not see any useful purpose to the community to which it could be turned. And as the public had never reaped any advantage from it since the purchase they were of the opinion that the Council should redispose of it to the present Mr Skene at the price paid for it by the Town which they found to have been one hundred and sixty pounds Scots.

At the Council's next meeting the sale was accepted.[17]

Presumably Baillie Adam and the Treasurer had not examined the rock beneath the tirr or the bar, and one wonders if they lived long enough to realise their error because within a few years buildings in the lower half of Marischal Street would be built from Rubislaw granite, stone of a quality far surpassing that of Loanhead. Rubislaw granite would go on to be used in the city that developed from the town once Union Street had been built and the Denburn crossed. Just three years after buying the quarry back James Skene and his agents were advertising in the *Aberdeen Journal* in May 1791:

That upon Friday 27th inst. between the hours of five and six in the afternoon within the house of Peter Wilkie, vintner, there will be set in tack by public roup for the space of seven years – the whole stone quarries upon the estate of Rubislaw in one lot – the tenant will have immediate access to the quarries with the benefit of a new road to be made out by the proprietor, leading towards Hirpletillum.[18]

The Trade with London

Writing in 1811 George Skene Keith wrote that granite had brought gold to Aberdeen.[19] What he went on to write about was the real stimulus for quarried granite in the eighteenth century, which came not from the Granite City but from London. In 1791 the parish minister for Nigg, including Torry, just across the River Dee from Aberdeen, reported that:

In 1766, the granite quarries by the sea and in the hills were opened for making causeway stones to pave some streets in London. This granite is of a remarkably close texture, and of great hardness. To this new work some 600 men were collected from different places. It led many families to settle for a time in the parish, and employed some horses in drawing the stones, where water conveyance could not be obtained. Decreasing rapidly from 1772, it now engages only 17 inhabitants with a few strangers.

He goes on to say that trade continued but with more shaped stones with 3,000 tons being exported annually to London, Maidstone, Ramsgate and other places.[20]

The trade in cassies or setts for London began around 1760. According to Dr Knight 'it had to undergo a severe ordeal, and many reports were spread against it.' He goes on to say that it wasn't until 1766 that the Paving Commissioners at Guildhall gave a formal preference for Aberdeen granite over blue whin and entered into large contracts for its supply.[21] Initially it was simply rounded stones from the shore, such as had been used in Aberdeen for centuries, and also stones cleared off the land in this era of agricultural improvement. Very soon this source either ran out or was not supplying sufficient quantities to meet the demand and quarries were opened in Torry and elsewhere. Among those involved in the trade was John Adam, oldest son of William, and brother to Robert, James and William. John was also an architect who took over the family business on the death of his father in 1748. Gradually his more talented brothers joined him and John increasingly looked after the business side of the enterprise. This included several quarries in Scotland. In Aberdeen on 26 March 1766, 'The Council having heard a memorial laid before them from Mr John Adam architect in Edinburgh craving a tack of the stones in the Bay of Nigg. They recommend to the magistrates to commune with Mr Adam who is presently in town and to report.'

The following day the Council considered the memorial from Adam which said that:

Your memorialist has in view to make use of such stones as are in your Honours' property from the Timberhead on the southside of the river to the Cove, he will take a lease for a term of twenty one years, upon an adequate rent with a break in his option at the end of the first year by way of a trial, in case it should not answer, and at the end of every third year thereafter.

Adam got his lease for those quarries lying 'between the Town's Quarry in the Grey Hope and the Cove'. He was to pay a rent of ten pounds sterling per annum with the Town:

To retain their present quarry at Grayhope and what lyes to the north thereof for the purposes of building in or about the Town, and not to let the same to any person whatever who shall prove a rival to the said Mr Adam in the business he intends to carry on.

The Town also reserved for themselves 'any of the loose stones lying on the shore or to any of the pebbles that are usually carried to London'.[22]

The Town, then, was already operating a quarry at Greyhope and carrying on a trade with London before Adam came along. Despite what they said initially they did allow Adam a year's trial to quarry stones at Greyhope as well, after which he was to desist. Adam was subsequently allowed to expand the area in which he quarried. The Lands of Torry in which he was quarrying had been granted to the town by a mortification of the Menzies of Pitfodels family who owned the lands. In previous centuries the Menzies family had been very powerful in the affairs of the burgh, providing numerous provosts, particularly in the fifteenth and sixteenth centuries. Although their influence waned after the Reformation because they remained Catholics, they were still major landowners, the last Menzies laird, John, gifting his property at Blairs to the Catholic Church in 1827. Despite the mortification of the Torry lands in favour of the burgh, the Menzies family continued to have some say in how they were managed. In August 1770 David Menzies complained to the Council about the way in which John Adam was managing the quarries. His complaints included Adam paying far too low a rent; that he had extended his quarrying without permission; that he should be obliged to 'leave the Quarries he has brock up into the country to throw all the rubbige into the hols, which will make them less dangerous than they are at present'; that Adam's workers should not be allowed to dig up pasture land for turfs or sods (presumably for roofing their houses); and that his option, allowed in the original tack, to re-assess the lease every year be withdrawn otherwise Adam would 'work as much in one year as he coud carry of in three.' Clearly Menzies was not happy at the way the quarries were managed and this was a common complaint by landowners in the early days of quarrying. Adam's lease was changed in 1771, with some of Menzies's recommendations being included. The Town did retain the right to quarry stone for use in the town and Adam was obliged to make and pay for a carriage road leading to the shipping places at Torry, as well as tidy the area once he had finished quarrying.[23]

Quarrying at the End of the Eighteenth Century

By the latter years of the eighteenth century, Aberdeen was ringed with quarries to the west, across the River Dee to the south, and especially on the hills to the north and north west. Evidence of the site of many of these quarries has to a great extent been obliterated as the town grew in size and housing was built over or around former quarries. London was still the main destination for quarried stone and evidence of the growth in quarrying since Elmslie opened Loanhead earlier in the century comes from the *Statistical Account*. Although usually written by the parish minister, for Aberdeen and Old Machar the account was taken from 'the communications of several gentlemen of that city'. Old Machar Parish included much of the area just outside the town itself, and the account for the parish, written in 1796-97, reports that:

> Granite abounds in the parish. There are excellent quarries at Rubislaw, Loanhead, Pitmuxton and other places, beside plenty of outlayers in the Hill of Grandhome. About 100 men are constantly employed in working them. Many of these stones are used for building in Aberdeen and its neighbourhood, but by far the greater part are sent to London. Nor is this trade likely to fail; for not withstanding the uncommon durability and hardness of these stones, such is the prodigious intercourse of carriages in that immense metropolis, that a street paved with them will in a few years be so broken as to require great quantities of new pavement. Some houses in and about London have also been built of Aberdeen granite.

The author estimated that at that point around 12,000 tons were being sent to London annually, presumably just from the quarries in the parish.[24]

Also in the *Statistical Account* the minister for Dyce recorded that about twenty-four years before he was writing, *c.*1766, a quarry had been opened there for dressing stones for paving the streets of London, and that it was still continuing. At Newhills, written in 1792, quarrying and preparing stones for the London market was listed as the principal trade of the parish. Here there were four quarries on the Auchmull Estate exporting 45,000 sq.ft of litter stones (for building), and some years more than 15,000 tons of cassies, to London. There was a fifth quarry on another estate in the parish also supplying London. The minister of Newhills described the granite as being of a 'very good kind, exceedingly durable, capable of a fine polish'. He estimated that around fifty men were employed in the trade, which also benefited local farmers who carted the stones. As with later workers, the men were paid piecemeal, though in different ways as the masons who dressed the litter stones were paid twopence the square foot, while those who made the cassies (later called settmakers) were paid 1*s* 6*d* per ton.[25]

The four quarries on the Auchmull Estate were probably those that later made up the famous Dancing Cairns Quarry, with Auchmull House no doubt being built from stone from the quarry. In a visit to the quarry in 1906 the Aberdeen Association of Civil Engineers were told by the manager, William B. Wight of A. & F. Manuelle, that it was probably the oldest quarry in the area, being shown on a chart dated 1415![26] This may possibly refer to a very old estate map and, if true, it would be remarkable. Just to the west of the other quarries there was also the Froghole Quarry. In these early days of quarrying the quarry was not one large hole as it would become later. Rather there was a series of smaller surface quarries, often worked by different quarriers, and we will see this again when we look at the development of Rubislaw in the nineteenth century. In a vague way Patrick Morgan states that sometime towards the end of the eighteenth century Dancing Cairns Quarries were opened by Messrs Snell, Rennie and May. May was Alexander May who he says had quarried at Greyhope before moving to Auchmull. Rennie may be John Rennie, the engineer and Snell may have been related to Alexander Snell who operated a quarry there in the 1830s.[27] The other quarry in Newhills at this time was probably the nearby Sclattie Quarry between Bankfoot and Bucksburn.

Immediately to the north of the town a further series of quarries were opened on the Middlefield Estate and on the lands of Sir William Johnston, James Forbes of Seaton and Sir Archibald Grant of Monymusk. These would include the Cairncry Quarries, Rosehill Quarries and Hilton Quarries, which have left their mark in the place names in the Northfield area of the city with Quarryhill School, Granitehill Road etc.

James Forbes of Seaton and his son-in-law, Lord James Hay, owned a number of quarries including Dancing Cairns and Sclattie, the latter probably purchased from Dr John Chalmers, Principal of King's College, in 1803. In their archives some letters survive which give details of the use of granite from their quarries in London. In December 1794 the Scottish architect Robert Mylne, famous for designing Greyfriars Bridge, London, wrote to Forbes that he had 'spoken to Mr Hamilton, pavior of Broad Street, Cheapside, London, and recommended your Aberdeen stone quarries. He is a large consumer and desires you will state in writing the situation of the quarries exactly, and whether they are now worked, and by whom, and of what sort of stone.'[28] As we will see in the next chapter, Dancing Cairns granite was to be used at some prestigious sites in London.

Across the River Dee at Cove it is not entirely clear that one of the quarries operated by John Adam, as noted above, was actually at Cove. However, the parish minister writing the Statistical Account for Nigg in 1793 does state that quarrying began at Cove in 1766 which would tie in with Adam's dates, quarrying being carried out at the coast and in the hills. The minister also states that between then and 1772 around 600 workers were attracted to the area to work in the quarries, an incredible figure if true. From 1772 he says that numbers have declined to just seventeen, mainly locals, when he was writing.[29] The minister describes 12in x 6in setts, 9in deep, tapering by 2in to the base, being made at the quarries. One man would make a ton in two days, and 3,000 tons were exported annually to London, Maidstone and Ramsgate.

The Opening of Quarries in the Peterhead Area

In the era before the improvement of the transport infrastructure of the north-east the other area that could take advantage of the growing need for good quality granite in the late eighteenth century was around Peterhead. This was because here the quarries are relatively near the coast and the harbour of Peterhead. Here again the parish ministers reported on quarrying activities in their area. The Peterhead minister, writing in 1794, states that there are:

> inexhaustible quarries of excellent granite of which all the houses in Peterhead are built, and great quantities exported to the London market, and for different parts of England; the granite admits of the finest polish, and lapidaries are frequently employed in forming it into various shapes for different pieces of furniture. From 600-800 tons of kerb and carriage-way stones are annually sent to London and other places.[30]

Peterhead is, of course, famous for its dark red granite. Nearby in Longside, the minister wrote in 1792-93 that two types of granite were produced in the parish – a dark blue one which had been used in Cairness House nearby in Lonmay parish; and a beautiful lighter coloured granite produced at Cairngall, 'frequent specimens of which are to be seen in London and other parts of England.'[31] Blue stone was also quarried on the estate of Cairness itself and this had also been used at Cairness House. The account books for the overseer of Cairness in 1796 record wages for estate workers working at the quarries in Cairness and Rora.[32]

FACTORS IN THE DEVELOPMENT OF THE INDUSTRY 1790–1850

Three key areas influenced the subsequent development of the granite industry from the 1790s onwards: firstly, improved transport in the shape of turnpike roads, the Aberdeenshire Canal and then the coming of the railways; secondly, the further growth in trade outside Aberdeen, particularly in London, with the use of north-east granite extending from paving stones to civil engineering and architectural use; thirdly, the building of Union Bridge and Union Street which eventually led to the creation of a New Town in Aberdeen west of the Denburn Valley, with streets and squares lined with granite buildings many of them built by Aberdeen's two great granite architects, John Smith and Archibald Simpson.

Transport

The turnpike roads were instrumental in the growth in granite quarrying. The pre-turnpike roads had grown up by common usage in an age when there were few wheeled vehicles in Scotland. Despite attempts, especially by landowners, to improve the roads the lack of continued maintenance meant that where roads existed they were of poor quality. Moreover they tended to follow the high ground to avoid boggy areas. The gradients involved were a major obstacle to the movement of granite blocks. The worst example of this was the Tyrebagger where the original road went much higher up the hill than the subsequent turnpike.

The idea of the turnpike roads was that 'gentlemen' would subscribe to help fund them and recoup their investment through tolls. Many of the subscribers also hoped that the roads would help develop their estates thus making them more profitable – taking rural produce to markets and enabling improving material such as lime and fertilisers to be more easily transported inland. Following pressure from landowners the Turnpike Bill was introduced to Parliament in April 1795 and passed shortly thereafter. By far the largest subscriber to the Skene Road was James Skene of Rubislaw. He hoped that the proposed road would make it easier to transport granite from the quarries on his land and that the road would eventually link up with the new Union Street at its west end, once that street had been finished. Granite from Rubislaw might then be made more accessible for the buildings gradually being erected on the new street. As early as 1802 Skene and his factor, Charles Gordon, were drawing up plans to develop high class housing in what became Albyn Place, though it took a number of years before their plans really came to fruition. Skene used his position to ensure that the road did pass the Hill of Rubislaw, fighting off a counter proposal from Provost More who tried to get the new road to follow more closely the old road, and thereby pass near his own property of Raeden. The Inverurie Road would also pass near to a number of quarries including Dancing Cairns, Slattie, and quarries near the Tyrebagger.

Traffic from granite quarries would inevitably be heavy on these early roads, some of which were not that well constructed. The Inverurie Road was opened in 1800, but by 1808 the heavy loads from Dancing Cairns Quarry were already taking their toll. A notice in the *Aberdeen Journal* announced that the Trustees had determined to exact the full tolls on the weight of stone carts using the road after the expiry of the present leases. Apparently by Act of Parliament every cart having wheel rims of less than six inches, drawn by two horses, was allowed to carry 1½ tons in weight in summer and 1 ton 7cwt in winter, including the weight of the cart. If it was drawn by one horse it was allowed 1 ton in summer and winter. Anything over this was charged extra for every cwt.

The Aberdeenshire Canal also helped granite to be transported to Aberdeen when it opened in 1805. Several of the quarries to the north of the town were within reach of the canal. It had the advantage that it could take the stone right into Aberdeen and near to the harbour where initially much of it was to be used. From there it could also be transported by ship outwith Aberdeen.

The advantages of improved transport links began to be used in the advertisements for sale or lease of quarries. For example, in June 1800 Cairncry Quarry was said to be a 'small distance to canal and turnpike' making it 'an object of great value to any persons dealing in granite.'[1] This was despite the fact that the canal was only begun in 1801 and not opened until 1805. Similarly advertised in March 1811 was 'an excellent quarry at Overtown of Dyce belonging to Sir Alexander Bannerman. Situated within ¼ of a mile of the canal by which stones may be conveyed to the Harbour.'[2] The influence of the canal on granite transportation was to be relatively short-lived because it was largely replaced by the coming of the railways.

The railways had a profound effect in allowing the opening up of quarries in the Don Valley. Kemnay was opened by John Fyfe due to the construction of the Alford Valley railway, with granite from the quarry being used to help build the railway as will be detailed in the next chapter. Tillyfourie, and later Corrennie, followed and they both used the railway and were useful for it. The railway up to Peterhead was also important for the industry in that area, with one line to Cruden being built as late as the 1890s.

In the later years of the nineteenth century traction engines were also used to transport granite, though perhaps more as an intermediate transport, taking it to the nearest railway station.

Export of Granite

The initial trade in granite between the north-east and London had been for road and paving mate-rial. From the late eighteenth century onwards this grew to include granite for civil engineering projects, granite for architectural work and finally monumental granite. This was the period when the quality of north-east granite became established in London. It is recorded than when the Duke of Wellington consulted an engineer on the relative merits of Scottish and Cornish granite he was told that 'Cornish granite lasts for ever, Scotch a little longer.'[3]

William Diack, in a story that probably came from the Fyfe archive, tells how when John Rennie was about to build the bridge he had designed over the River Thames at Southwark (1813–19) he needed some massive blocks of granite, 15, 20 and 25 tons, larger than any that had been han-dled in Aberdeen before. The Aberdeen granite masters said it was impossible to transport such large blocks so Rennie went up to Peterhead. There he found a 25-ton block which was scabbed and dressed using the picks that were the mason's main tool at the time. There being no carriage able to carry such a huge block Rennie was not to be beaten and he had a carriage specially made. Diack even records that the toll keeper was unsure as to the appropriate toll for such a load. Rennie then had to persuade a captain to carry it London, most of them being reluctant to allow such a block on to their ships for fear it would sink them. However, one adventurous soul did agree to take it and the stone was loaded with the whole of Peterhead turning out to see it leave. The block was successfully conveyed to London and placed in position to provide a foundation for the bridge piers.[4]

Various notable engineers came to Aberdeen towards the end of the eighteenth century. The first was John Smeaton who drew up a report on the harbour in 1770, recommending the building of the North Pier. Smeaton wrote a second report in 1788 and granite was extensively used in the work following these reports. The *Aberdeen Journal* that year carried an advertisement to masons and quarriers for 12,000 to 16,000ft of stones, from 3ft to 6ft in length, 14in to 18in in height, with the beds and joints dressed.[5] John Rennie surveyed the harbour in 1797 and was also the designer and engineer for the Aberdeenshire Canal, opened in 1805. The most notable engineer of the time, Thomas Telford, also reported on the harbour in 1801, while carrying out a survey for the Treasury of the harbours of Northern Scotland. Telford also surveyed the harbour again in 1810. These engi-neers knew the qualities of granite and would use it in their many engineering projects as we have seen with Rennie in London. As early as 1795, Aberdeen granite was ordered by the Admiralty for building the docks at Portsmouth. In 1800 tenders were invited for supplying 60,000ft of granite for the West India Docks in London, the stones to be delivered to the Isle of Dogs.[6] And in 1818 *The Times* announced that His Majesty's Navy was receiving tenders for supplying His Majesty's Yard at Sheerness with 685,000 cu.ft of Aberdeen granite.[7]

One of the early civil engineering works to be built in granite outside Aberdeen was the Bell Rock Lighthouse, designed by John Rennie but with Robert Stevenson as his assistant. The *Caledonian Mercury* reported in 1807 that a lighthouse was to be built on the Bell Rock by Mr Rennie. Aberdeen granite was to be used 'as the most durable stone with which to construct the foundations and outside course of the building.' The stones were to be landed at Arbroath and then transported to the rock.[8] A subsequent advertisement appeared in the *Aberdeen Journal* for granite blocks for building the lighthouse to be delivered at the iron crane at the pier in Aberdeen. The agent for the granite was Alexander Gildawie, road and bridge building mason. Granite from Rubislaw, Tyrebagger and Cairngall was used in the lighthouse.[9]

The early use of Aberdeen granite in England went beyond London. For example the *Ipswich Journal* reported in 1810 that Aberdeen granite was to be used in the kerbs in Great Yarmouth and the *Caledonian Mercury* in 1818 stated that Hillesden Bridge in Norwich was to be faced with Aberdeen granite.[10]

With the example of Aberdeen's Union Bridge being available, granite also began to be used for bridge balustrades as with Waterloo Bridge around the year 1817. According to John McLaren 1,200 moulded circular balusters were supplied, made by hand using Rubislaw granite. When the bridge was being demolished one of the balusters was sent back to Aberdeen and placed at Hazelhead Park.[11] A further boost to the sett trade came in 1820 when Telford recommended to the Institution of Civil Engineers an improvement in road surfaces. The earlier setts had been fairly roughly finished. Telford now recommended a firmer substructure into which squared, more uniform setts would be laid. This was more expensive but lasted longer.

Evidence of the continuing growth in the export of granite to London can be seen in figures quoted by Harris where he states that, in 1817, 22,167 tons was exported to London; in 1821 it was 34,678 tons; and in 1868, 50,000 tons.[12] Harris's figure for 1817 comes from William Kennedy's *Annals of Aberdeen* published in 1818, and Kennedy goes on to add the value of the trade with London, including freight, was £23,275. That figure was actually lower than it had been for a number of years.[13]

The Beginning of the Granite City

In the new century granite continued to be in demand for harbour work in Aberdeen itself. In 1802 Alexander Carnegie, Advocate in Exchequer Row, advertised for 'several thousand feet of Aberdeen granite in blocks of sound quality, of an oblong form, from 3½ to 4½ long, by 2½ feet broad, and 14 inches thick. All to be laid down on the Quay at Aberdeen. The whole must be straight-sided, scabbled or rough-picked such as those lying at the Pocra Pier for building the quays at Aberdeen.'[14] This type of work, as with the large volume of granite being exported for similar dock and harbour work, required large blocks of relatively undressed granite. This certainly encouraged the development of quarries around the town. However, moves were also afoot that would eventually gain Aberdeen the title of 'The Granite City' for the actual number of buildings built in the city from dressed granite.

There is a very real sense in which Aberdeen, during the late eighteenth century and into the early nineteenth century, was moving from being a town with a medieval layout and environmental conditions, to a more modern one, and that the inhabitants of the time were aware of and encouraged this transformation. We have seen in the previous chapter the beginnings of a more planned street layout and 1795 saw an Act of Parliament being passed:

For the better paving, lighting, cleansing, and otherwise improving the streets, lanes, and other
public passages of the city of Aberdeen, and the roads and avenues within the royalty thereof; for
the better supplying the inhabitants with fresh water, and for the removing and preventing of all
obstructions and annoyances within the said city and royalty.[15]

A major part of this process was the building of Union Street and King Street and this gave a substantial stimulus to the granite industry.

The Act to allow the building of two new streets, giving better access to the town from the north
and the west, was given Royal Assent in April 1800. The need for improving access had been realised and discussed by various parties in the town for several years and various schemes produced,
the details of which do not concern us here. Along with the levelling of St Katherine's Hill, centred
on where the Adelphi is now, the key construction feature of the project was the building of a series
of arches along the line of what was to become Union Street, the most important being Union
Bridge. This latter would bridge the valley of the Denburn and allow the town to expand to the
west. In retrospect the earlier Marischal Street can almost be seen as a trial run for Union Street,
Marischal comprising a planned street, lined with granite buildings, and including a bridge over
Virginia Street. With Union Bridge John Rennie, the canal builder, was once again involved, as
consulting engineer. He recommended Thomas Fletcher as superintendent of the bridge, having
worked with Fletcher on the Lancaster and Aberdeenshire canals. The bridge designer was Glasgow
architect David Hamilton, but Fletcher soon found that there were mistakes in Hamilton's levels,
such that new plans were required for the bridge. The Trustees turned to Rennie, who produced
three plans, not all of them in granite, and Fletcher also produced a plan. After consulting with
Thomas Telford, who happened to be in the city on other business, Fletcher's plan was chosen.
It was to be of granite and it is suggested that Telford supported this as it would act as a show-case
for the structural abilities of granite and he 'had no doubt of its practicability, strength and durability.' The *Aberdeen Journal* at the time of the laying of the keystone in 1803 praised the work of Messrs
Fletcher, the engineer, and Ross, the bridge builder:

This stupendous arch, both in its design and execution, is an honour to the town, unequalled in
any part of the United Kingdom. Built entirely of Aberdeen granite, it furnishes an additional
proof of the excellency of this stone, that it is capable of sustaining the enormous pressure of an
arch of this extent. It is 130 feet span, and the arch rises only 29 feet from the spring. The breadth
of the bridge is 44 feet. The arch stones are from 3½ to 5 feet deep; and the whole weight of
materials is not less than 2000 tons.[16]

The early granite buildings in Marischal Street and elsewhere were all relatively simple in design,
a local vernacular style with little in the way of decoration. The first building to have any form of
real decoration, worked by hand, was the bank building on the Castlegate at the top of Marischal
Street, now part of the High Court. Designed by James Burn from Haddington in 1801, it
boasted a cornice, frieze and pillasters in granite. Usually described as the first fully dressed
granite ashlar building in Aberdeen, it shows outstanding workmanship given the tools available

Union Bridge under construction c.1804. The figure with the tall hat may well be engineer/designer Thomas Fletcher. It also shows some of the techniques used by the masons at the time. (Aberdeen City Libraries)

Former Aberdeen Banking Company on Castle Street, Aberdeen, now an annexe to the High Court.

at the time and the relative simplicity of the buildings that had been built before it. A curious story is related by Dr Knight and repeated in *The Saturday Magazine*, March 1844, that the masons couldn't undertake the dressing of the balusters in granite, and they were done in sandstone painted to look like granite.[17] If that was the case then within three years techniques had been developed such that the balustrade of Union Bridge, which Burn also designed, was done in granite. Burn's bank set the tone for the buildings that would eventually line Union Street, the baton being picked up by both Smith and Simpson.

There was certainly an awareness among the leading inhabitants that a new age was dawning in the architectural development of the town. Walter Thom in his *History of Aberdeen,* published in 1811, commented:

> Of the architectural taste of the private buildings in Aberdeen little is to be said in commenda-tion. We seem, however, to be of late emerging from that chaos of distinguishable bad taste which predominated for the last thirty years. It is in the interests of every man to obtain a good design from one who has studied architecture as a science.[18]

Aberdonian Andrew Robertson, one of the leading miniature painters of the age, joined in the debate from London. In a series of articles published in the *Aberdeen Chronicle* in 1818 he wrote that the best architects were in the Metropolis (London) and that their design for leading buildings might be sought as well as those from Aberdeen and Edinburgh architects. He particularly wanted to see good public buildings: 'Public buildings are generally solid in their nature and are intended to last for ages, as the pride and ornament of a city, on which they confer honour or disgrace, accord-ing to the good or bad taste displayed in their architecture.'

In a quote that is relevant today he also said, 'If public buildings are erected on a temporary narrow principle of expediency, posterity might find it necessary to rebuild them.' Robertson was particularly critical of the siting of the new Court House along Lodge Walk and behind the then Town House:

> It seems to be considered a matter of indifference at Aberdeen whether the public edifice now to be erected, its Court House, should become an ornament to the Town, or should be concealed from view. A total indifference to the beauty of our native town or county is not easily conceived, it would be worse than Gothic barbarism.

Robertson argued that 'a suite of Assembly or Concert Rooms offered another opportunity of embellishing the town; and it is now in contemplation, it is said, to erect an appropriate building, the want of which has long been felt.'[19]

This referred to the Assembly Rooms which would later be known as the Music Hall, with its huge portico of Dancing Cairns granite. This was, in fact, to be the first public building built on the Union Street, but it wasn't built until 1820, fully fifteen years after Union Bridge had been opened.

Crimonmogate House, by John Smith, was the first building built west of Union Bridge in 1807 but Union Street did not become the 'Granite Mile' overnight. Development was piece meal along the whole length of the street, including the eastern part near the heart of the town. In fact development occurred more quickly west of Union Bridge rather than east. It may have been slightly easier to build away from the heart of the town. In a letter to the Deacon of the Hammermen quoted by G.M. Fraser, Provost Leys said:

> for some time past the New Street Trustees and their Committee have had under consideration what plan would be most appropriate to be laid down for the buildings to be erected along both sides of Union Street west of the Denburn, and in doing so it has occurred to them that it will be for the interest of all concerned that the restrictions to be imposed upon the different proprietors and feuars should be as few as possible.

However, he went on to say of such buildings, 'the whole shall be built of well dressed granite stone.'

Another reason for faster development west of the Denburn was that there it was driven by the commercially minded Incorporated Trades. The latter were keen to develop their land around Diamond Street and Golden Square (The Hammermen), beginning in 1807, though not finished until 1820, Crown Street was also on Hammermen's land; Bon Accord Street was on the Wrights' and Coopers' land; and Bon Accord Square leading to Simpson's magnificent Bon Accord Crescent, on The Incorporated Tailors' land.

There is no doubt that the Trustees for the building of Union Street intended, from the outset, that it be lined with granite buildings. As part of the competition for designing the bridges that carried the street there were several grand schemes for a more unified design to the buildings lining the street. One elevation for the buildings along the street, by James Young, has survived. David Hamilton may also have provided one as part of his competition entry. This has led Frank Farmer to suggest that the use of granite on the buildings along the new street was one of the rules of the design competition.[20] Although the buildings as built were not in the more uniform style shown on Young's plan, the stipulation for granite was carried out. Thus when Alexander Brown, in 1819, took out the expensive double feu adjacent to the house at the corner of Shiprow and Union Street built by Archibald Simpson for Baillie Galen, the Trustees stipulated that Brown's building should be 'built of granite stone, dressed at least as well as the front wall of the house in Castle Street at present used as the Atheneum' (the old Atheneum).[21] The west end of Brown's building, facing the Castlegate, and another Simpson design, would become the New Atheneum.

It is well known that the Union Street project virtually bankrupted the city in 1817. However, by this stage feus had started to be taken out very quickly and at a high price. By September 1824 the town was solvent again. This building activity, from the beginning with Union Bridge and the other bridges built as part of the new street, along with the expansion of the city to the west and to the south along King Street, undoubtedly acted as stimulus to the granite quarrying industry.

The interrelation between the quarries, architects and masons is illustrated in the story of one of the finest Aberdeen granite buildings from the first half of the nineteenth century, Archibald Simpson's masterpiece at the corner of Castle Street and King Street for the North of Scotland Bank, later the Clydesdale Bank. The *Aberdeen Constitutional* reported in 1840 that:

There are now lying at the North of Scotland Bank Buildings, two blocks of granite 14½ft long, for the doorway; together with a quantity of large blocks from 5 to 5½ft square, for the columns, portico etc. They are from Rubislaw quarries, and are of a very superior description. There are also a number of large stones, from 10 to 12ft long, for the ornamental part of the front, from the Dancing Cairn.[22]

The Architect, in 1872, described this as an exquisite building, the granite dressed by hand with the patent axing technique:

Entirely in the Corinthian style, has a magnificent portico, supported by four magnificent pillars. Modelled after the Temple at Tivoli. The capitals are most wonderfully cut; in fact from the beautiful dressing and perfect jointing of the stones, the building looks like it is cut out of the rock.[23]

One of the Corinthian columns at the bank was carved by Francis Christie, then a young mason barely 20 years old. He had been born in 1820 in Banff where his father was working on Telford's harbour alterations. His father was subsequently the contractor for work at Cluny Castle where Francis also worked, but Francis's finest work was the chapel, library and staircase at Dunecht House, designed for Lord Lindsay by the famous London architect George Edmond Street. Francis was followed in his trade by a son, also Francis, senior partner of Christie, Greig & Co., and then by grandchildren. Francis died in 1901. His father had been the foreman on Union Bridge, so this one family of masons spanned the whole century.

Detail of capital on the North of Scotland Bank by Archibald Simpson.

Former North of Scotland Bank.

Aberdonians grew to love their granite and feel that it was the natural stone for the city. On the subject of the Court House and Tolbooth alterations of 1820, Joseph Robertson wrote in *The Book of Bon Accord*, published in 1839, 'it is to be regretted that the basement of the spire was not refaced in the same style and manner; the dull red sandstone of which it is built, ill harmonises with the white and glittering granite below it.'[24] Some years later the pioneer photographer George Washington Wilson is said to have been so appalled when he heard that Rubislaw Parish Church was to be built of yellow sandstone diagonally opposite his own house at Queen's Cross that he offered to pay the difference in cost if granite was used. Alas it was too late and the contracts had been signed. The church was built without a spire in 1874–75 and such was the contrast when the rival Free Church built the granite masterpiece of Queen's Cross Church across the road, with its soaring spire, that the established church felt they had to add a spire to their own church. It is said that Washington Wilson determined that no further sandstone should appear in the area and bought the feu opposite his own house and had a granite house built there (No. 2 Queen's Cross).

THE STORY OF THE QUARRIES
1790–1914

For virtually all its history as an industry in the north-east, granite was very much subject to peaks and troughs, something that is common in all parts of the construction industry, an industry that tends to mirror the general economy. In the nineteenth and early twentieth century at times of growth, as cities were enlarged, they needed granite for road setts and kerb stones. Likewise there were growth periods when granite blocks were needed to build or rebuild harbours. In Aberdeen itself good times often meant an increase in housebuilding, or building generally, and that, for most purposes, meant granite. Any of these demands could dry up quickly leaving quarries and quarry workers vulnerable to periods of inactivity. For that reason it is quite difficult to piece together the active history of each quarry. For example, you might read a church minister writing at the time of the Second Statistical Account stating that a certain quarry had been closed some years ago. However, that does not mean it was closed for good, since changes in economic and technological circumstances might mean someone else taking it over and reopening it.

We have already seen with John Adam and his quarries at Torry that landowners were concerned to limit the amount of stone quarried. They wanted to maximise their income by agreeing a lease over several years rather than have quarriers take as much stone as possible in as short a time as possible. In 1783 Skene of Rubislaw, for example, placed a restriction on the number of men one of his quarries could employ. A way round the potential for overworking would have been for the estate to receive royalties for the amount of material taken. This does not seem to have happened until much later in the development of quarrying, and it is still happening today with, for example, the Craigenlow Quarry at Dunecht paying royalties to the Dunecht Estates on all the material taken out of the quarry.

The quarries themselves, at least until the middle of the nineteenth century, were not the huge, oval shaped holes in the ground that we can still occasionally see today. Some of our major quarries, such as Rubislaw and Dancing Cairns, were really a series of very small quarries, covering quite a large area, and let and even sub-let to various individual quarriers. A cart road would lead to the quarry face and there was very little machinery used in the quarrying process. From around 1830 onwards this began to change as individuals and companies with more capital began to take over quarries, invest in machinery and new technology, and enlarge the quarries to meet the growing demand. The first to do this was civil engineer John Gibb and he was followed by English companies, notably A. & F. Manuelle and John Mowlem & Co., also known as Mowlem, Burt & Freeman. Already by 1866 Mowlem were operating four of five quarries, the main ones being at Dancing Cairns, Persley and Sclattie, employing 220 men and exporting between 12,000 and 14,000 tons of causeway and kerbstones annually. At the same date Manuelle employed 200 men at Dancing Cairns, Cairncry and Dyce, exporting 18,000 tons of paving stones, mainly to London.[1] Finally, in the 1850s, the granite king and supreme innovator John Fyfe took over a small quarry at Kemnay and completely transformed the industry.

In 1859 the British Association visited Aberdeen and Alexander Gibb of Rubislaw Quarry took a group of member to Rubislaw where they saw a blast with 20lb of gunpower dislodging 100 tons of rock. Gibb also gave the Association a lengthy talk on the granite industry. He gave the following list of quarries in operation at that time, with their distance from Aberdeen and the colour of granite they produced. These were in addition to Rubislaw, Dancing Cairns and Peterhead which he described in more detail in his talk:

Pitfodels	3 miles	Blue granite
Hilton	2 miles	Blue granite
Peterculter	8 miles	Blue granite
Cove	5 miles	Blue granite
Sclattie	5 miles	Blue granite
Persley	4 miles	Blue granite
Dyce	8 miles	Blue granite
Tyrebagger	8 miles	Light red granite
Clinterty	8 miles	Light red granite
Huntly	40 miles	Blue granite
Boyndlie	40 miles	Soft grey granite
Cairngall	40 miles	Blue granite
Benachie	27 miles	Red granite
Balbithan	10 miles	Blue granite
Kemnay	17 miles	White granite
Tillyfourie	23 miles	Blue granite
Cluny	22 miles	Blue granite
Tullynessle	30 miles	Light red granite
Balmoral	50 miles	Light red granite
Alford	28 miles	Blue granite

Aberdeen Journal, 21 September 1859

The one listed at Alford is probably what became known as Sylavethie. Some of the others, such as Balbithan, might not be too familiar today and were relatively short-lived, with a number being all but worked out by the time of the First World War.

Rubislaw

As an example of the fact that there were a series of quarries at Rubislaw we find that on 27 April 1808 the *Aberdeen Journal* carried an advertisement announcing that 'the granite quarries in the Stonyhill of Rubislaw will be let by public roup, in different lots.' In 1845 a quarry was advertised as part of the sale of the Angusfield Estate, with good access from both the Old Skene Road and the Rubislaw Turnpike.[2] This is probably the small quarry shown on the first OS map, surveyed around 1865, on the Hill of Rubislaw just north of the main Rubislaw Quarries. The sale notice also says that there was also very extensive and valuable rock in a field adjoining the Turnpike Road. This may be the small quarry shown on the OS map just north-west of Rubislaw Quarries, though without an estate map for Angusfield it is difficult to be sure. At Rubislaw itself, by the time of the OS Map, the one major quarry was beginning to take shape, but even in the 1880s Rubislaw still consisted of more than one quarry, with John Gibb and Sons working one, and Macdonald, Field & Co. the other.

At the beginning of the century, James Skene of Rubislaw and his advisors obviously had concerns regarding how the quarries at Rubislaw were being worked. In one letter to Skene from Charles Gordon, his agent or factor, on 9 February 1805, Gordon reports that he had spoken to several people who agree, 'that your quarries have been exceedingly ill-managed, and that they are in a very bad condition at present, all pitted and potched, rubbish laid down improperly, and no proper plan laid down for carrying off the water.'[3]

Gordon enlisted the aid of Alexander Gildawie, a mason very much involved in building the turnpike roads and bridges at the time. At this date a John Smith was working two quarry pits, John Webster another, and there was a further pit. Because of the state of the quarries Smith was only willing to offer a rent of £50 or £60. Then, as now, water was a big problem, with Smith's quarry being below the level of the turnpike road and the water not being carried off. Gildawie made various suggestions to improve the drainage but this was expensive and also involved clearing away a lot of the old rubbish. Presumably Gildawie's drainage plan was carried out because Smith increased his offer to £80 for a three-year lease. He was not allowed to open any new quarries, or have more than one sub-tenant, prior to that he had three. According to Gordon, 'they have been in the practice of working here and there thro' all the hill which spoils the quarry ground.'[4]

Another problem that Skene seems to have faced is that the Council, despite selling the quarry back to him in 1788, were claiming mineral rights to granite from the quarries. Skene took legal advice which led Charles Gordon to believe that the Council's claim, based on the original charter feuing the lands of Rubislaw, was limited to material to be used for public works in the town not for selling to London, which is where Gordon says most of the granite was actually going at this time.[5]

The problems of multi-tenancy continued into the 1820s, when the engineer John Gibb was one of the tenants. In a letter to Skene's then factors C. & A. Gordon, in 1829, Gibb complained that despite all the trouble he had taken at Rubislaw he had gone out on the hill and found that a Mr Forsyth's worker was about to fire off a shot half an hour before the allotted time. Having stopped him, Gibb was subsequently abused by Forsyth. Another tenant, Mr Saunders, also fired off early, pretending he had mistaken the time. That same year, Gibb made an offer to take over all the quarries at Rubislaw. At this point the quarries needed to be worked deeper, and machinery was also required to drain off the water, at a considerable expense. Gibb therefore wanted a ten-year lease so that he could re-coup his investment. In this he was successful, and his descendants continued to work the quarry until the end of the nineteenth century.[6]

John Gibb was a civil engineer, born at Gartcows near Falkirk in 1776. His father was also a civil engineering contractor, having finished the Forth and Clyde Canal, but he died when John was only 12 years of age. John subsequently worked for both John Rennie and Thomas Telford on a variety of canal and dock works, and Telford subsequently recommended him for the post of resident engineer for Aberdeen Harbour. Here he restored Smeaton's South Pier Head, which had been destroyed in 1807, and then he extended the North Pier and built the breakwater on the south side of the harbour entrance. Gibb was a founder member of the Institution of Civil Engineers in 1820 and he continued to work all over the country on projects such as the repairing

One of earliest illustrations we have of Rubislaw Quarry taken from *The Illustrated London News* of 28 March 1857. Although possibly slightly exaggerated, in the foreground it does show stones being split; wagons waiting to be loaded in the distance; and perhaps some kind of crane or pulley. Settmakers skathies are also shown and there was also a more detailed illustration of those. (see Chapter 6). (© Illustrated London News Ltd/Mary Evans)

of the Crinan Canal for Telford and the building of Glasgow Bridge. He also repaired harbours at Peterhead, Cullen, Banff and Nairn for Telford. These and other projects brought him into the granite industry, and around the year 1820 he supplied granite to Jolliffe and Banks, contractors for building the docks at Sheerness to a plan by John Rennie. To quote Gibb's obituary in the Institution of Civil Engineers, 'his scientific knowledge and practical skill were applied to the introduction of a more improved system of quarrying granite.'[7] When he died in 1850 Gibb was buried in St Nicholas Kirkyard in Aberdeen.

As well as Rubislaw Gibb also worked quarries at Dyce and Peterhead. He was subsequently joined by his son Alexander in the firm John Gibb & Sons. Alexander had been apprenticed to Telford and he also became Superintendant of the Aberdeen Harbour Works. He married the eldest daughter of City Architect John Smith, friend and colleague of his father.

Dr William Knight, writing in 1832, though published in 1835, says that formerly Rubislaw Quarry was only worked to a depth of 30ft but that at the time he was writing Gibb was already working at a much lower level, aided by having spent £800 over two years on drainage, a huge amount for the time.[8] With all the other work that he was involved in Gibb was probably more able than smaller-scale quarriers to finance development of the Rubislaw site.

The estate of Rubislaw was bought from James Skene by Sir Alexander Anderson in 1862, just two years before Skene's death. Anderson, Aberdeen's first official Lord Provost, and perhaps its most important and controversial one, subsequently went bankrupt, his estate was sequestered and the Rubislaw Estate was bought by the City of Aberdeen Land Association (CALA). John Gibb & Sons, then under Alexander Easton Gibb, second son of Alexander, were able to buy most of the Hill of Rubislaw in 1870. They retained ownership until 1889 when the sole partner William Gibb, as a result of his own ill health and consequent prolonged absences from Aberdeen, floated the Rubislaw Granite Company. The initial board of directors of the company included the architect Robert Gordon Wilson and the contractor Roderick McKay. The flotation prospectus stated that 'the objects of the company are to acquire, work and extend the well-known and old established business of quarry owners and quarry masters so long and profitably carried on by Messrs John Gibb and Son at Rubislaw. The deposit of rock is practically inexhaustible.'[9] The Rubislaw Quarry site at the time of the flotation was 20 acres, with a further 6¾ acres of vacant land leased from CALA.[10]

Contractor William Tawse was later added to the board of the Rubislaw Granite Company in 1919, and its last directors in 1967 were John R. Mutch, granite merchant; Joseph E. Farr, granite merchant; Peter Tawse, Associate Director of William Tawse Ltd; Victor M. Ross, Quarry Manager; Andrew Mutch, Granite Merchant; and John K. Hall, Building Contractor.

In the prospectus mentioned above William Gibb had quoted the amount of rock said to be obtainable within eight acres of the centre of the site. This figure came from two surveys that were carried out for Gibb by surveyor James Beattie. They were done because Gibb had used the quarry as security for loans. In 1873 Beattie estimated that there was 3,692,400 tons of granite in the quarry and that this would last 120 years at the then current rate of extraction. That survey showed that the quarry employed sixty quarrymen, three mechanics and eight carters. The latter had fifteen carting horses, fifteen single-horse carts and eleven strong double-shafted wagons. The annual output was 30,000 tons.[11]

The survey was repeated in 1886 with the following list of plant and equipment at the quarry at that time:

Four cottages on Rubislaw Road
A horseman's cottage
Quarry office
A blacksmith's shop with three hearths, powder magazine, portable tool house
A wooden boiler house and wooden coal house
Causewaymens' shelter
Two ten ton steam cranes, two steam quarry engines, a 3-ton steam crane, a marine boiler and two vertical boilers
A large wrought-iron water tank, a smaller iron water tank and cast-iron water tank
A Parker & Weston steam pump, a Tengye pump and a large donkey pump
Eight tips wagons [12]

The following year, the Association for Improving the Condition of the Poor organised work for the unemployed clearing tirr at Rubislaw Quarries. One enterprising worker, Hugh Barron, put a proposal to William Gibb to do the work at a fixed rate with the company providing all the plant except the shovels. He must have been successful because an invoice survives paying Barron, including a deduction for sharpening picks. [13]

According to George Harris, writing in 1888, every time the quarry was deepened the stone at Rubislaw became a slightly richer grayish blue, making it valuable for monumental and polished work. By 1898 the depth of the quarry was 240ft, but there were already plans for an additional 40 or 50ft. That same year, a particularly busy one, 250 men were employed at the quarry and there were ten cranes, four blondins, and two pumps to drain water. There was also another quarry known as the 'new quarry', which had reached 40ft that year.

The year 1899 saw the installation of a new Lancashire boiler to provide additional steam power, a new swing crane was also built at the west end of the quarry. At the same time a powerful new steam crane was being built, wholly of steel. It cut the time taken to raise stone from the quarry floor by half and was capable of lifting 20 tons. [14]

The Institution of Mechanical Engineers reported on the quarries in 1907. At that time the excavations covered 7 acres and they were employing about 260 men. The output was 300 tons a day, thus about 100,000 tons a year – a third of all the granite quarried in Aberdeen. The cranes and blondins mentioned above, which had been worked by steam, were now worked by electricity and the drills by compressed air. There were, in fact, four blondins, as well as ten electric cranes, the latter with a capacity of 10–20 tons. Pneumatic tools were being used for cutting up smaller stones. The report describes small stones being raised in boxes by the blondins, the boxes deposited on bogies and taken to the settmakers by a railway. [15]

Just four years later, when Professor Matthew Hay gave evidence to the Royal Commission on Mines and Quarries, the workforce at Rubislaw had gone down to 110. The reduction may have been caused by a decline in building work at that time. The breakdown of the workforce given by

Hay was twenty-one drillers, fifteen settmakers, nineteen carters, twelve enginemen, four black-smiths, and thirty-nine labourers.

The story of Rubislaw Quarry in the interwar years and beyond will be continued in later chapters.

Cove, Altens, Kincorth, Torry

We have seen in earlier chapters that some of the earliest quarries supplying stone to London were across the River Dee from Aberdeen. These lay in Kincardineshire. The *Aberdeen Journal* of 27 May 1788 advertised that there were several quarries producing stone fit for London pavements. They were near to the pier of Torry and to the harbour of Altens. There are no quarries at Altens shown in the first OS map, but the ones mentioned here might be those nearby, marked on the map as Stoneyhill Quarries, between Altens and Caiesdykes. Two groups of quarries are marked at the north and south ends of the Stoneyhill and they lay just south-west of the farm that gave the area its modern name of Kincorth. James Forbes of Waterside Cottage, Bridge of Dee, is listed in the 1899 Aberdeen Post Office Directory as the owner of the Kincorth Quarry. In the 1920s James Leith operated it. The Kincorth Quarry actually survived until fairly recent times. In 1951, when new plant was about to be installed to further develop the quarry, the proximity to the quarry of the rapidly growing housing estate was raised as an issue. The quarry was eventually closed in 1967, by then it had become impossible to use explosives so near to housing. A local commented at the time that 'it's like living on the edge of a volcano. We can't get breath with the dust and the blasting shakes the house up.'[16]

As we have seen, Cove quarries were very old, among the earliest to be worked in the north-east. Harris described the granite as being 'very hard, and owing to the presence of a great quantity of black mica the stone is of a dark hue, much more so than the ordinary granites of the district'.[17] The first OS map shows several small quarries at Blackhill and right on the coast at Hareness. Larger quarries were situated further north, on Cove Farm nearer to Cove itself, again with quarries right on the coast. At both locations the railway, when it came, ran between the inland quarries and those near the shore. An advertisement for the lease of the quarries in 1869 said they were within five minutes walk of Cove Station and that there was a siding beside the quarries. Here, as at some of the Peterhead quarries, the waste was dumped straight into the sea.[18] By the time of the second OS map, in 1899, the quarries at Blackhill and the ones on the coast at Cove Farm are described as old quarries, though Douglas Gray says that the quarry at Hareness was leased in 1902 and only finally abandoned in 1920.[19] Part of the quarry at Blackhill or Blackhills as it is now known, has been subsumed into the huge quarry now operated there by Leiths (Scotland) Limited.

The inland quarry at Cove Farm was the main Cove Quarry, which survived into the twentieth century. During the nineteenth century Cove was worked by Manuelles, and later by John Fyfe, producing paving setts and road metal. It closed in 1899 but was subsequently reopened, possibly by John McAdam & Sons, who had the lease for a few years before John Fyfe's acquired it again. In 1910 Fyfe's entered into a five-year agreement with the Caledonian Railway Company to supply 25,000 tons of granite ballast from his quarry at Cove. This was specified to be of good quality, machine broken to such a size as to pass through a 2in circular-meshed screen and be retained by 5/8in mesh.[20]

According to Gray,[21] Fyfe's retained the lease until 1952, but in the 1920s Cove was run by Kincardine County Council for road material. In February 1927 they approved expenditure on the quarry to install a travelling crane to handle the rubble and as a double line of railway track, with two travelling bogies to be laid down between the quarry face and the crushing plant. An electric crane was also installed.[22] In the Second World War, Cove Quarry was actually used to store stocks of radon gas, to protect it from bombing. An emergency laboratory was built at the quarry to supply hospitals in Scotland and the north of England with radon, used at the time in cancer treatment. Radium, which was used to produce the radon gas, was stored in a 12ft-deep hole at Rubislaw Quarry. Following its final closure in 1952 Cove was used by the local authority as a tip.

Dancing Cairns

Before John Gibb consolidated the various quarries at Rubislaw, Dancing Cairns (originally known as Dancing Cairn) was the biggest quarry in the Aberdeen area. Patrick Morgan says that at an unspecificied date quarries were opened at Dancing Cairns by Thomas Catto and James Harper, mason, with Harper being succeeded in June 1824 by Alexander Low (but see below).[23] As already noted Dancing Cairns was on the estate of Forbes of Seaton. By the 1820s Dancing Cairns granite was being considered for the new London Bridge. The Royal Society was involved in recommending granite for the bridge and in December 1823 Alex Low, who then leased the quarry, wrote to Forbes that 'this will give our blue a good chance of getting fair play.' Low went on to appeal for a lowering of his rent by claiming there was a great mass of chippings lying upon the rock and this would be expensive to remove. If the rent was moderated he would take a lease for nineteen years.[24] The following February George Tritton of Wandsworth, High Sheriff of Surrey, wrote to Lord Hay that 'Dancing Cairns stood first in the list for the new London Bridge.'[25] Some sources say that the granite used for London Bridge came from Haytor on Dartmoor. In fact, Haytor was used for one side and Dancing Cairns for the other, with red Peterhead granite also used in the arch. The bridge was designed by John Rennie, who had worked on the Aberdeen Canal; his son, John, was involved in supervising the work following his father's death in 1826. Opened by the King in 1831 the bridge itself was sold and moved to America in the 1960s.

An advertisement in the *Aberdeen Journal* in 1830 was for one of the quarries at Dancing Cairns. It stated that there was for let:

an extensive range of granite rock, at Upper Buxburn in the parish of Newhills, only about three miles from Aberdeen. The rock was lately examined by competent judges and found to be of the best quality of granite, and very easily wrought; being quite close to the surface and having sufficient declivity for carrying off any water that may arise in the quarry. These are advantages, the want of which, it is well known, are now felt in a high degree in most of the old quarries. Application to Mr Gordon at Upper Middlefield, the proprietor, or to James Wallace, mason, at Dancing Cairns.[26]

Dr Knight, writing in 1832, agreed that because Dancing Cairns was on the side of a hill it did not have the same problem with drainage that other quarries had, but he also said that this had caused the early quarriers to work the top part of the quarry and dump the rubbish lower down. The latter was now too expensive to remove.[27]

Presumably Alex Low did continue at the quarry since he still had the quarry in 1841 when it supplied the block of stone for the Duke of Gordon's statute. The *Aberdeen Journal* for 4 November 1840 says that the quarry at Dancing Cairns was worked by Macdonald & Leslie. According to Robert Fergusson, Macdonald's long-time employee, Low was the quarrier at the time the stone for the statue was supplied, with Low also providing the wagon to carry it. The wagon was subsequently sold to Macdonald's, but according to Fergusson, Low gave up the quarry shortly after.[28] However, there were obviously a number of quarries at Dancing Cairns and Macdonald may have operated one at the same time as Low. A notice from the *Aberdeen Journal* for 19 April 1837, advertises the let of the 'Dancing Cairn Quarries at Auchmull occupied by Alexander Snell, George Ritchie, Charles Adam and Alexander Petrie'. These men may have been in a consortium because the advertisement said the quarries would be let separately or together. Petrie, along with an Alexander Birnie, was still listed in the 1846/47 Post Office Directory as quarriers at Auchmull.

From about the late 1840s, Manuelle's also operated a quarry at Dancing Cairns. The *Aberdeen Journal* in 1837 carried an account of a dinner given to the quarriers at Dancing Cairns by Mr Manuel (as the *Journal* spelled it), described as a stone merchant from London who was on a visit to the area. The dinner was held in a tent and around 130 attended including Mr Manuelle and his friends as well as the proprietor of the quarry, Lord James Hay of Seaton. Contrary to what William Diack says, I don't think this means that Manuelle's ran the quarry at that time. Charles Manuelle first appeared in the Post Office Directory in 1836–37, described as a stone merchant at Waterloo Quay. The account of the dinner doesn't say that he was entertaining his workers, nor that he operated the quarry. It does say that he was on a visit – this may have been the start of Manuelle's coming into the area – and that he was entertaining local granite men as well as workers at the quarry, perhaps men he had already had dealings with from the company base in London.[29] In 1865 there was a notice in the *Journal* for the let of a quarry at Auchmull known as Duncan's Quarry, which had previously been let to Manuelle's.[30]

In the middle of the nineteenth century another quarry at Dancing Cairns was leased to John Mowlem & Co. or Mowlem, Burt & Freeman. In 1866 Mowlem's gave a dinner at the Lemon Tree Inn for workers from their quarries at Dancing Cairns, Persley and Tillyfourie.[31]

When Harris was writing in 1888 the older quarries at Dancing Cairns had been abandoned and were filled with water. Manuelle's were working newer ones, some just 100 yards from the original one. However the posts of granite were small and irregular with large blocks suitable for polishing only occasionally being found. At that time most of the stone was used for setts or rubble for building purposes.[32] The quarries were then closed for a number of years, reopening around 1895. The operations were at two different levels, an upper and lower quarry. At the reopening Manuelle's installed a large blondin at Dancing Cairns, on high ground at the quarry. This was the second blondin on the site. Around 1903 they also erected a powerful steam crane manufactured by Henderson's the engineers. However, by 1915 the quarry had closed again with sixty men affected. The War was blamed with local authorities only doing a minimum of roadworks.

One success at Dancing Cairns in the early years of the twentieth century was that it became the centre for the manufacture of adamant paving material, paving slabs made from granite chips. In the 1920s an experiment was tried with unemployed men given work at Dancing Cairns, mainly clearing stone from the spoil banks. The move was controversial because of the conditions they were working in and their poor clothing, as well as the ability of unemployed men to do such heavy work.[33]

In the period after the Second World War the abandoned quarry hole at Dancing Cairns was the scene of several fatalities. As housing in the city expanded nearer to the quarry there were several instances of adults and children falling into the hole and either being killed by the fall or drowning. An 8-year-old died at the quarry in 1947, and a 10-year-old in 1952. At that time the hole was thought to be 230ft deep. In 1953 the *Evening Express* reported that work had begun on draining the hole with a view to dumping material in it to fill it up. The *Express* stated that there had been three lives lost in the previous four years.[34]

Just to the west of the main Dancing Cairns Quarries was the Froghole Quarry, just off what today is known as the Howes Road. Patrick Morgan says it was operated by a James Gunn (he gives no date) but that in 1831 the lease was taken over by James Small, mason, and William Reid under the name of James Small & Co. Later he says it was taken over by a family named Birnie (again he gives no date).[35]

There was another quarry near Auchmull, known as the Oldtown Quarry, which was reopened around 1896 by John McAdam and Sons after it had been closed since the beginning of the century. This produced large blocks for monumental work but also setts and building stones. McAdam closed the quarry in 1908.

Dyce

There were several small quarries at Overton as well as the main Dyce Quarry just to the south west of these, nearer Kirkhill. We have already seen that a quarry was opened here in the 1760s to supply paving stones to London. Dr Knight reported that a quarry at Dyce, on the estate of Charles Bannerman, was opened in 1815, supplying blue granite. It is unclear whether or not this was the same quarry as the earlier one. The quarry supplying the blue granite was at Overton and was well placed for using the canal for transport. Despite that John Gibb, who had worked it for around seven years from 1816–23, lost money on it because of the transport costs involved in getting the granite to Aberdeen.[36] After a few years of it being closed the *Aberdeen Journal* recorded that Gibb had reopened it again in March 1826 on an extensive scale. At that time it was sending building material and paving setts by canal to Aberdeen.

Dyce was another quarry taken over by A. & F. Manuelle when they came to Aberdeen. They operated it in 1866 and still had it in 1900. The *Journal* for October 1907, reporting on the serious outlook for the quarries, stated that the Dyce quarries were closing.[37] Whether or not it reopened after that is unclear, but Dyce Quarry was marked disused on the 1928 OS map. When G.M. Fraser visited it for the first time just before this in October 1925 he found it neglected with the house and offices in ruins and the massive quarry hole full of 40–50ft of water. 'A really frightful place', he commented.[38]

For most of the 1880s Overton Quarry was unwrought, but it was opened up again by Whitehead & Sons in the 1890s. The quarry was one of the assets of Whitehead's that went up for sale in 1897 when they closed. It was listed as unwrought in the 1907 Valuation Roll.

Sclattie

Sclattie is one of the forgotten quarries of the Aberdeen area, but it was a large and important quarry, worked for a very long period. The date for the opening of the quarry is uncertain but it was probably in the late eighteenth century. It was certainly in existence in 1803 when it was for sale, being described as a valuable granite quarry.[39] It was for sale along with the mansion house and other lands on the estate of Sclattie following the death three years earlier of the owner of the estate, Dr John Chalmers, Principal of King's College. The house had been rebuilt by Chalmers after he bought the estate in 1772. After the sale the quarry must have been enlarged because in 1805 Sclattie House was taken down because the quarry workings had encroached on it. G.M. Fraser visited it in 1925 and was told that while tirring stone for an extension of the quarry they had come across the site of Sclattie House. Fraser commented on the immense size and depth of the quarry when viewed from the top.[40]

Harris described it as producing fine-grained granite, slightly lighter than Rubislaw, mainly used for building work and sett making rather than polishing. The quarry was 130ft deep at the time Harris wrote. Patrick Morgan lists it as having been worked at various times by William Thom, William Glennie, George Smith, George Milne, Mr Calder, John Glennie, Messrs John Fraser & Son, and A. & F. Manuelle, who were operating it at the time her wrote in 1886.[41]

Two adjacent quarries are shown on the first OS map. In 1860 A. & F. Manuelle were operating one, and David Glennie seems to have operated the other, because when it was for let in 1862 it was described as currently worked by Glennie. John Ritchie remembered David Glennie and his fleet of beautiful horses, working the quarry with hand cranes and handcarts. In his words, 'the place fairly hummed.' When he died David Fraser & Son took it over.[42]

In 1897 the depth of the lower dip of the quarry was 1,00ft and one blast that year produced 3,000 tons of stone. One enormous block, which virtually formed the tip of the dip, measured 30ft in height and breath, 12–15ft deep. Weighing over 1,000 tons, it was thought to be the largest block of granite ever quarried in Scotland and it created quite a spectacle as it came crashing down on to the floor of the quarry.[43]

At the end of the century the second OS map shows that the two quarries had become one and it was still operated by Manuelle's. Around 1903 Manuelle's erected at Sclattie one of the most powerful blondins yet seen anywhere. Diack[44] says that investment was begun at Sclattie before The First World War and this continued after the war. Shortly after, in 1906, the Aberdeen Association of Civil Engineers visited the quarry and they were shown the new blondin, still steam-powered, which had a very impressive 15-ton lift on a 700ft span.[45] In 1915 an electric cable was laid up to the quarry to power the pneumatic plant at the quarry. By the 1920s the quarry was fully modernised and providing building and sett making stone. The Adamant Works at Bucksburn used up the waste material from Sclattie.

The quarry manager's house for Sclattie Quarry still stands at 55 Bankhead Road.

Tyrebagger and Clinterty

These particular quarries have been difficult to trace because there were a number of them and they changed names for time to time. Tyrebagger or Stoneywood Quarry was on the Lands of Stoneywood Estate belonging to James Hay of Seaton. This was operated by John Fyfe's father, and then by Fyfe himself following his father's death. When Fyfe moved to Kemnay it was taken over by David Fraser of D. Fraser & Son. In 1879 it was operated by Alexander Gordon, and by 1892 by Pringle & Slessor. By the end of the nineteenth century the second OS map shows a series of quarries, some marked as old quarries. There are also two smithies shown. From around 1911 Tyrebagger was operated by James King, builder, of Fraser Place.

Clinterty or Little Clinterty Quarry seems to have also been called Caskieben Quarry and was on the Caskieben Estate of Alexander Henderson. At least as early as 1859 it was operated by D. Fraser & Son who still had it into the 1870s. By 1879 it had been taken over by Pringle & Slessor. Although it produced setts and kerbs it was primarily used for building stone and a large number of houses in Aberdeen are partly built from this stone. It closed in 1911.

At Tyrebagger and Clinterty the quarries produced pink granite.

Quarries in the Hilton, Cairncry and Rosehill Areas

These quarries were amongst the earliest to be worked on what was then the periphery of Aberdeen. In 1770 the *Aberdeen Journal* carried an advertisement from advocate Thomas Mosman for the roup of a nineteen-year tack of a stone quarry on the lands of Middlefield, 'close by the high road leading towards Aberdeen by Hilton.'[46] Presumably this was on behalf of his brother, the artist William Mosman, who owned the estate of Upper Middlefield. It is not exactly clear which of the quarries in that area this is referring to; perhaps one of the Hilton ones. Cairncry was on the estate feued to Sir Archibald Grant of Monymusk, and Rosehill/Hilton was on the estate of Sir William Johnston. They must have existed from at least 1780 because in the original feu charters from the 1780s the Council had reserved the right to use stone from the quarries for the benefit of the town. And, in fact, these quarries supplied stone for the paving of Union Street, a process that took a number of years because a subcommittee of the Council, accompanied by John Gibb, engineer and John Smith, architect, inspected the quarries in preparation for paving the street west of Union Bridge in 1826.[47] In fact Cairncry seemed to be mainly used for road and pavement material. When quarrier William Fleming died in 1794 the *Aberdeen Journal* announced a sale of his stock of carriageway and paving stones from the Hill of Cairncry. In 1798 when the turnpike road to Inverurie and beyond was being proposed Sir Archibald Grant wrote to the *Aberdeen Journal* saying that great quantities of granite chips for the first section of the road, from the Gallowgate Head to Tannfield, could be got from Sir William Johnston's quarry at Hilton, and his own quarry at Cairncry. For the next section to Mugiemoss

Bridge stone could be got from Cairncry or Dancing Cairn.[48] When advertised for sale in June 1800, the Cairncry Quarry was said to be 15½ acres 'on which at a very small expense a face of quarry of not less than 40ft perpendicular may be opened with sufficient fall to render it dry.'[49]

In 1826 when the Council subcommittee visited what had been North Cairncry, but which they commented was now called Back Hilton, they found three quarries being worked, two only just opened, by three different contractors. Some of these quarries dated from 1764 when the land was feued to Sir William Johnston, as they are mentioned in the feu document. The committee commented that they were producing an abundance of good-quality granite and that the whole of the back of the hill was one bank of granite. The committee also suggested that stone from these quarries could be used in the new Bridge of Don.[50]

The picture here is of numerous small quarries, worked by individual contractors, each of whom must have worked on a small scale. Dr Knight, writing just a few years after 1826, confirms this. His description of the granite is that it was white with a reddish hue, considered inferior to blue varieties.[51] The first OS map shows a proliferation of small quarries in this area, with the Hilton and Rosehill ones already disused, though Cairncry was still in operation.

In the 1860s Cairncry was worked by Manuelle's, but from the mid 1870s it was owned by quarrier James Leith. Leith lived at Lower Middlefield House, Woodside until 1895 when he bought Clifton House. That same year Leith was described in the *Aberdeen Journal* as being one of the largest granite merchants in Aberdeenshire, a contractor as well as a quarrier. Leith opened a new quarry at Cairncry in 1901 but the quarry must have been closed for a time because he reopened it in 1906, mainly for setts, transferring much of the workforce from Persley which he had just closed.[52] Cairncry closed in 1911.

The site of Hilton Quarries can be seen across Hilton Road from Stewart Park.

Carnie/Gask

The *Aberdeen Journal* of 8 January 1902 reported that James Leith had leased a quarry at Carnie in the parish of Skene. The report stated that a Mr McIntosh had operated a quarry there a few years previously but that Leith was going to be working further down the hill where a small opening had been used for building stone many years before. The stone was said to be dark grey, hammered well, could take a high polish and was very suitable for setts. This description presumably refers to Gask Hill, but I am not aware that this quarry ever provided sufficient quality stone for much building or polishing work, though it was used extensively for road material. Until quite recently the quarry site was used as a council store.

Persley

There seem to have been various quarries at Persley, sometimes known as upper and lower. John Gibb & Son of Rubislaw Quarry operated a quarry here in the mid nineteenth century, an advertisement for its let in the *Free Press* in 1861 stated that it was operated by Gibb at that time.[53] It may have been at around that time that it was taken over by John Mowlem & Co. A description of it from 1866 says that it was then a comparatively new quarry producing very fine granite, in large blocks, capable of taking a very high polish.[54]

In 1890, when it was leased by James Leith, there were three steam cranes and a blondin, one of the cranes capable of lifting 20 tons. Around 200 men were employed at the quarry in 1890. It was a light-coloured stone, good for dressings and sometimes used as a contrast to the darker Rubislaw. Leith closed the quarry in 1906, transferring many of the workers to Cairncry. By 1912 Persley belonged to George Hall, Builders of Back Hilton Road. Hall was using the stone for his own building work, but he was also providing stone for monumental work and for polished building fronts.[55] According to Diack, Persley stone was used for council houses in the 1920s and '30s.[56]

Pitfodels and Cults

Mentioned early in the eighteenth century, these quarries on the Hill of Pitfodels, the property of Menzies of Pitfodels, were still going when Knight wrote in 1832. As late as 1855 they were advertised for let with their granite said to be the equal of Rubislaw and Dancing Cairns! They never seem to have produced large quantities of granite at any time. They are presumably the small quarries on the first OS map around Woodland Cottage (possibly later renamed Rocklands Cottage) and Arnlee, some of which were then marked as old quarries.

The redoubtable Rev. George Morison, parish minister of Banchory-Devenick who would later build a bridge over the River Dee, wrote in the first Statistical Account, 'the kind of stone which prevails blue granite, of which several quarries are wrought for the purpose of sending to London, as well as building at Aberdeen'.[57]

Which quarries he was talking about is not clear, but they may have included Pitfodels and Cults, though there were also quarries elsewhere in his parish. When he wrote for the second Statistical Account in 1838 he commented that the stone 'is of so hard a quality that it is not quarried to any great extent, and is chiefly formed into causeway stones, for home consumpt, or for the London market'.[58]

Cults Quarry is shown on the first OS map, just to the west of Mains of Cults Farm. In 1859 it was operated by the owner of the Cults Estate, George Shirra Gibb. By the second OS map, the original Cults Quarry was marked as disused, but a smaller one is shown just to the north. In modern terms their location was just to the east of Cults Nursery and Primary School, with Quarry Road taking its name from them. Some of the quarriers lived at the cottages known as Hillhead, since demolished. One source states that stone from Cults Quarry was exported to pave the street of Odessa in Russia, and that one quarry worker, Moses Leiper, actually went to Russia.[59] I have not been able to corroborate this story, and it would be unusual if setts from a small quarry such as Cults were sent to Russia, unless as part of a consignment from other, larger quarries. Moses Leiper certainly lived in the area, at Burnside, Bieldside, where he was described in the 1851 Census as a crofter and labourer, aged 58. He also owned or rented a property at Powdeggie, Bieldside, which was advertised as formerly being possessed by the late Moses Leiper when it was up for let in August 1864. Did he precede James Bissett, the story of whose visit to Odessa is told in Chapter 6, or are the two men being mixed up?

Pitmuxton, Ferryhill and Auchlee, Kingcausie

According to Diack,[60] these quarries all operated from the late eighteenth century. I have found very little documentation about them. Pitmuxton must have been in operation quite early because the Dean of Guild and the Town Treasurer visited the quarry 'near the Parks of Pitmuckstown' in 1767 when two masons, Richard Craig and James Begg, wanted to lease it.[61] It was also mentioned in the first Statistical Account. Stone quarries on the hill of Auchorthies, on Irvine of Kincausie's estate, were advertised for let in 1788. The stone was described as 'of the finest granite, uncommonly beautiful, of great length and fixes, bears fire extremely well and admits of a high polish for chimneys.' Their location was described as being near the highway from Aberdeen to Stonehaven and near the harbours of Skateraw, Portlethen, Cove and Findon.[62] When the Hole-in-Wall Farm of Auchorthies was advertised for let in 1810, more than twenty years later, it stated there was 'an inexhaustible quarry of the best granite with good roads to it.'[63] These are probably the same quarry, usually marked on the OS map as Auchlee Quarry on Auchlee Hill, and the quarry is there on both the first and second OS maps. Perhaps Boswell's Monument on Auchlee Hill was built from this granite. There are also other small quarries in the area, including at Badentoy. These are on the edges of Clochandighter Hill, and the one marked Badentoy on the second OS map is probably the one that became known as Clochandighter and was operated by granite merchant James Leith in the years after the First World War.

Murtle

Knight reported that a small quarry had recently been worked for a short time on the estate of John Thorburn.[64]

Hill O' Fare

Named as Raemoir Quarry on the second OS map, but more commonly known as Hill O' Fare, it produced a red granite, popular for monumental work and widely used for building in the Banchory area. It was opened in around 1884 by a company that had James Hutcheon as chairman. Hutcheon later took over the whole quarry and in 1894 he reorganised the quarry – adding a large steam boiler plant, and moving the position of the steam cranes. On his death his son, Henry, took over and the firm became known as Henry Hutcheon Limited. Under Henry, a pneumatic plant for drilling and cutting was introduced in the first few years of the twentieth century, according to the *Quarry Managers' Journal* – making it the first quarry in Aberdeenshire to use compressed air.[65] Its granite was exported widely to America, Australia and elsewhere. Henry Hutcheon took over a granite yard in King Street and renamed it Hill O'Fare Granite Works. He subsequently bought the Hill O'Fare Granite Company and the famous firm of Alexander Macdonald & Co. The quarry manager's house still survives as does the explosives store.

The other quarry at Hill O'Fare was run by Mr Littlejohn in 1899, probably the one named as Craigton Quarries on the second OS map; two quarries and two smithies are marked. It was on the estate of Burnett of Leys and Crathes. The *Free Press* in 1894 records that John Ogg had been successful in obtaining some good stone from his Craigmyle (Hill of Fare) Quarry. It is unclear what quarry this refers to.[66] At the end of the nineteenth century, traction engines were used to cart granite from these quarries to the station at Banchory. This led to a dispute in 1890 when the Deeside District Committee levied an additional charge for road use according to tonnage. Hill O'Fare accepted the charge and gave details of their tonnage whereas Craigton refused and the matter went to court.[67]

Sundayswells

A fairly short-lived quarry operated by James Anderson in the early 1900s. In 1900 the *Aberdeen Journal* commented, 'a local industry is being developed in the shape of a quarry on Sundayswells Hill. The stone is a fine warm-coloured blue granite and takes an excellent polish.'[68] It was used to build many of the buildings in the village of Torphins and there must have been some sett making at the quarry as well as the company advertised for a settmaker in June 1907. The quarry company became members of the Aberdeen Granite Association in 1907 as the Sundayswells Grey Granite Quarries Ltd. However, the Association had problems getting them to pay their membership fees and they were taken off the Register of Adherents in December 1911. William Grant also gives James Fraser as the operator of the quarry, though he doesn't specify at what date he is referring to.[69]

Campfield, Glassel

Edgar Gauld, builder, opened a quarry here in 1898, though there was also an older quarry there. He used granite from the quarry to build the chapel at Mar Lodge.[70]

Tillyfourie

Early quarries worked on a small scale around Tillyfourie were located near Jubilee Cottage and behind Thistle Cottage, both operating in the late seventeenth and early eighteenth centuries. There was a significant borrow pit near Granite Villa when the turnpike road was built. The quarry above Tillyfourie Farm was in use during the eighteenth century. The three shaft quar-

Surviving chimney stack at Tillyfourie Quarry.

ries in the Ginashart Hillocks part of the lower Tillyfourie were in use in the late eighteenth and early nineteenth centuries, with stone from their spoil heaps later used in the construction of the railway embankments for the Kintore to Alford branch line in the 1850s.[71] These original quarries were very close to the railway; on the first OS map around five are shown in this area, on the estate of Sir James Grant of Monymusk. They were mentioned by Alexander Gibb in his lecture to the British Association in 1859. By the time of the second OS map these quarries were disused and had been replaced by a quarry much further up the hill, opened around the mid 1880s. This was originally operated by Mowlem, Burt & Co., hence the name, Mowlem Cottages, of the dwellings built nearby for quarry workers; the cottages are still there today.

Mowlem gave up the quarry in 1891 and it was closed for a number of years before being reopened in 1896 by John Fyfe. Fyfe initially signed a three-year lease from Sir Arthur Grant at a yearly rent of £50 per annum. A plan at the time shows the smithy near the main road, quite a distance from the upper quarry. It also mentions rough dressing sheds, a chimney stack at the upper quarry (still there today), a tramway road, railway and sidings. Sir Arthur retained ownership of the workers' cottages and agreed to convert the smithy and the old engine shed into further housing, while Fyfe would build a new smithy at the upper quarry.[72]

The quarry had to be drained of 40ft of water to reopen it. Fyfe employed two Tangye pumps to drain the water, powered by a vertical boiler with furnace, and water from one of the disused quarries lower down was pumped up to supply the boiler. After the water was drained the boiler powered a steam crane. Both Tillyfourie and Corrennie Quarry, situated just across the valley, made use of a loading bank at Tillyfourie Station. Both quarries also had rail lines running up to them with very steep gradients. For part of the incline Tillyfourie was able to have a double line and use the weight of the carriage coming down from the quarry to pull the empty carriage back up. Corrennie did the same, the line there coming more or less straight down, but Tillyfourie was longer because the loading bank was 250 yards from Tillyfourie station and the line from the quarry curved round between some of the older quarries.[73] Granite chips from Tillyfourie were used for lining the railway line to Alford, using V-shaped trucks with a hole in the bottom where the chips could be released as it travelled along. Tillyfourie granite is grey and it was used for sett making as well as engineering and building work. For many years Tillyfourie was the main centre of the Aberdeenshire sett-making industry. The quarry continued until the 1930s.

Today the water-filled quarry hole is a peaceful, picturesque place in among the trees on Tillyfourie Hill.

Corrennie

Corrennie was not shown on the first OS map in 1865 and seems to have been opened in 1872, though Harris, writing in 1888, said that it had been opened within the last few years. However, in 1861 a stone from Corrennie was included in a collection of Aberdeenshire granite provided by Macdonald's yard for the Museum of Practical Geology in Jermyn Street, London (later incorporated in the Natural History Museum). This may simply mean that a stone from the hill was included in the museum, not that there was a working quarry at that time. Corrennie was originally on the Cluny Estate and is situated high up the hill with wonderful views over the Vale of Alford and back towards Monymusk. Corrennie produced one of the loveliest stones in the north-east, salmon pink granite, used for building and ornamental works, as well as some grey for crushed stone. The quarry was operated by John Fyfe and in 1896 employed between sixty and

seventy men, including settmakers. At that time it was 100ft deep.[74] The incline here is very steep and, as with Tillyfourie, it used a double railway track up the slope, with a pulley system whereby full trucks going down pulled empty ones up to the various quarry faces.

Corrennie is still in operation today and unlike Tillyfourie it is not surrounded by trees, so you can appreciate the view from it.

Kemnay and Tom's Forest

There were several quarries in the Kemnay group, two at Kemnay itself, plus nearby Tom's Forest as well as quarries at Whitestones and Leshangie (see below). Tom's Forest produces a similar stone to Kemnay but a little darker. At Kemnay itself what today is one

Portrait of John Fyfe by John Singer Sargent. (Aberdeen Art Gallery and Museums Collection)

large hole was, in fact, two until well into the twentieth century, though one of them was classed as the main one. Knight recorded in the 1830s that there was a good quarry at Kemnay producing grayish blue granite belonging to the Earl of Kintore, and therefore presumably not the same as the one made famous by John Fyfe. It was not being worked at the time he was writing.[75] As pointed out by Alexander George Burnett of Kemnay in a letter to the *Aberdeen Daily Journal* in 1902, his father John, as early as the 1830s, opened a small scale granite quarry on Paradise Hill for rebuilding work at the mansion house of Kemnay.[76] The architect for this was Aberdeen City Architect John Smith, and Burnett employed a mason, James Taylor from Midmar, to work the quarry. However, the real development of Kemnay had to await the arrival of the railway and the entrepreneurial skills of perhaps the greatest of the quarry masters, John Fyfe.

The Alford Valley Railway was authorised in 1856 and opened in March 1859. John Fyfe was born at Bucksburn in 1830, his father running a quarry at the Tyrebagger. Fyfe's father died when John was only 16 and John took over the business. In 1858 he was supplying stone for the bridges being built for the Alford railway and Adam Mitchell, uncle of the great master mason John Morgan, was the builder for the bridges. Mitchell told Fyfe that he could save a considerable amount in cartage if he had a look at the possibilities of a quarry at Kemnay. Fyfe and his engineer liked what they saw and immediately signed a nineteen-year lease and the Fyfe story really began. John Ritchie recounts a story told him by Fyfe that shortly after opening the quarry while waiting for a train he got into conversation with a local farmer:

'Are you Mr Fyfe.'
    'Yes'
    'You've taen that quarry?'
    'Yes'
    'Oh, man, gang and gie it up'
    'Why?' Said Fyfe
    'Oh, man, look roon aboot you there, and nae a fairmer for twall mile roon bit his got up a new hoose. There winna be a stane wintit oot o' yer quarry for the next nineteen years.'[77]

Little did he know the vast amount of granite that would come from the quarry and find a ready market in Aberdeen and all over the country.

Fyfe's technological innovations are dealt with in the next chapter but by 1869, just eleven years after he opened the quarry, *The Scotsman* was reporting that Fyfe was employing 250 men; was the first to introduce steam power to quarrying; and had the contract for supplying the principal stones for the Thames Embankment in London.[78] In 1888 Harris wrote that the larger of the two quarries at Kemnay was the largest granite quarry in the UK. At that time it was 300ft deep and as well as a blondin, there was a huge crane at the top with several more on the quarry floor. There was also a large steam granite cutter; the only other one in the area was at Fyfe's works in Aberdeen, testimony to Fyfe's willingness to invest in up-to-date machinery.[79] Fyfe even had a telephone at this early date to connect the quarry with the office in Aberdeen.

In August 1878 Fyfe undertook a massive blast into the quarry face where he was sure there was a large amount of excellent granite. He employed a miner from Cornwall to tunnel into the rock face, 15ft up from the base. This miner drove a tunnel, 4ft by 2½ft, 60ft into the rock face. This took him a staggering fifteen months. He then made a right turn for another 20ft. At the end of this tunnel two chambers were created, one holding two tons of gunpowder, the other 17½cwt. The powder was specially made for Fyfe at Tighnabruaich Gunpowder Manufactory, Argyllshire. Thereafter several men laid the charges and the two chambers were fired simultaneously by electric battery. Fyfe invited colleagues from the building industry and elsewhere to witness the event – men such as builders John Morgan, Thomas Donaldson, Pringle & Slessor, A. & C. Christie of the Seaton Brick works, as well Mr Charles, the banker from Inverurie and W. Maitland, the merchant from Kemnay. This one blast successfully dislodged up to 50,000 tons of rock, enough to keep the quarrymen busy for two years.[80]

The quarries at Kemnay were connected to the rail line by a siding, and rail trucks were originally drawn up the incline to the loading banks by steel chains around a drum. When the GNSR railway, in 1896, substituted granite chips for sand or gravel as ballast along their tracks this created extra business for Kemnay. It also led to an extension of the siding. It could already cope with sixty trucks, but was extended at the east and west ends to hold 100. The bottom ballast was being filled at the east end of the quarry and a new narrow gauge railway was laid from the quarry to a new loading bank, which extended from that end of the quarry to the railway bridge. Side-tip steel wagons were used, light and easily handled. They were filled at the quarry and allowed to run down the incline on the service railway to the loading bank where they were easily tipped into the trucks on the siding. At this date Fyfe introduced two Baxter stone crushing machines. Driven by a 20h.p. steam engine, they were capable of producing 1,000 tons a week. This additional work employed a further 50 or 60 men and was basically using what had previously been waste.[81] An unusual addition to the work force was described in various articles in the 1880s and 1890s including this comment in the *Aberdeen Journal*: 'amid the noise of steam engines, steam pumps, steam hammers, steam cranes, steam drills, and the clatter of stone crushers, it is a relief to see wagons being shunted along the siding by the primitive agency of a work-ox'.[82] The ox or bullock actually pulled the wagons across the public road to the siding as well as pulling the heavy chain down the incline from the quarry to be connected to the empty wagons. According to an account from 1882 the work was not very arduous for the ox and it was found to thrive and fatten on it.[83] A photograph has survived of the ox at work.

In a visit to the quarry in 1889, quoted in the *Aberdeen Journal*, the Aberdeen Mechanical Society described seeing the largest quarry, No.1, which at that time was 200ft deep. They were planning the next drop at that point:

the plan is to start in one corner of the bottom of the quarry and go down a shaft or well of perhaps 40 feet, and then work outwards horizontally; boring, blasting and bringing down the 40 feet thickness until the original walls of the quarry are reached, when a new depth has to be commenced.

They also describe the line of tracks at the bottom of the quarry as carrying a 10-ton locomotive steam crane along the work face, moving stone to within reach of several other 10-ton steam cranes and, of course, the famous blondin described in Chapter 4. At that date there were also smaller quarries, Nos 2 and 3.[84]

At the end of the nineteenth century business was doing well and they were working day and night at Kemnay, using electric lighting. At the same time, perhaps the most powerful blondin anywhere was installed. This stretched 860ft across the main quarry and had a lift of almost 400ft.[85] When the Institution of Mechanical Engineers visited a few years later, in 1907, the quarries at Kemnay employed around 400 men, including the blacksmiths' and engineering workshops.

Fyfe built housing for his workers, which is detailed in Chapter 6. However, quite a number also lived in Woodside. An account in the *Aberdeen Journal* for 1898 tells that in that year, when there was an upsurge in demand for setts at Kemnay, composition rail tickets had been granted to settmakers from Woodside so they could travel every day to Kemnay, a distance of 16 miles.[86] These may have been more casual workers who travelled to where the demand was. It may also explain why Woodside Fountain was given to the burgh of Woodside by John Fyfe and the quarriers and carters of the area.

Tom's Forest was described in 1895 as employing thirty masons, twenty settmakers and drillers, quarrymen and labourers.[87] In 1906 a blondin capable of lifting 10 tons was installed, greater than existed at Kemnay at the time.

Leschangie and Whitestones

These two quarries, or series of quarries, lie between Kemnay and Kintore. Whitestones was on the Kemnay Estate and is thought to predate Kemnay Quarry, though it is not on Gibb's list of 1859 given at the start of this chapter. It is shown with a smithy on the first OS map of 1864–67, just west of the aptly named Stony Hill. An advertisement for lease of the quarry appeared in the *Aberdeen Journal* in 1861, the stone being described as superior to any yet opened on the estate, suitable for all kinds of building purposes. The quarry was advertised as being 2 miles from the railway with access to a good turnpike road.[88] In 1870, one quarry was leased to William Birse and the other to the Aberdeen Lime Company. According to Alexander George Burnett of Kemnay House, stone from Whitestones was used in the building of London and Waterloo bridges.[89] By the second OS map, Whitestones had become a series of quarries.

Following a long period of disuse, in 1954 these were due to be reopened by R.M. Dallas, a Glasgow quarrymaster. Dallas owned a portable crushing plant at Longside and this is what he planned at Whitestones. However, his plans received a setback when a major fire occurred at the quarries. The fire destroyed a house being used as a store and caused £10,000 of damage, including damage to thirty-five rolls of rubber belting each 200 yards long, fifteen electric motors, four jack hammers and a large quantity of elevator conveyors.[90] The quarries were subsequently worked until recent times, latterly for road material. They are all still visible today, used for storage and dumping by Hunter Construction. There are some signs of the remains of buildings and machinery, including the weighbridge. The quarry spoil tips are also visible, though overgrown.

There is no quarry shown on Leschangie (or Lochshangie) Hill on the first OS map. It opened in around 1868 and in 1870 it was being operated by Alexander Diack and others. By the end of that decade it was operated by the Aberdeen Lime Company. By the time of the second OS map, one quarry at Leschangie had already been worked out and was marked as 'old quarries'. Burnett says that there were two or three quarries at Leschangie, extinct by 1902, and that he had worked one himself for building a lodge at the end of the west avenue at Kemnay House in 1876. His contention was that had the railway line taken the more gentle curve round the back of Leschangie Hill, then John Fyfe would have found a better source of granite at Leschangie and Whitestones. Had Burnett not been in England at the time he would have advocated this course for the railway.[91] Fyfe bought the waste tips at Leschangie and crushed them at Kemnay.[92]

A smaller quarry at Sunnyside, just north of Leschangie, operated from the mid 1920s to after the Second World War.

Kintore and Burnside

The quarry on the Hill of Tuach overlooking Kemnay was reopened in 1898 by John Smith, a builder in Kintore, who also owned the Burnside Quarry. Quarries are shown there on the first OS map and by the second there are a few small ones with one marked 'old quarries'. Various people – Mr Petrie, Mr Birse and Messrs Sutherland – had operated the quarry in earlier years but it had been closed for a number of years before Smith reopened it.

Burnside, to the south of Leylodge, is not shown on the first OS map, but in 1870 was being operated by Robert and Peter Donald. James Thain was also involved with it at some point. Sometime in the 1870s it was taken over by the well-known Aberdeen granite yard Bower & Florence. The latter had it for a number of years, but it was certainly closed by 1892. John Smith reopened it in 1896, ordering pumping apparatus, a boiler and a 10-ton steam derrick crane with a 60ft jib from John A. Sangster's St Clair Street Engineering Works.[93] The grey stone from Burnside was said to be suitable for building and for sett making, as was the stone from Tuach. Burnside was also used for monuments and when polished it was said to resemble Rubislaw.[94] Burnside was one of the old quarries reopened after the Second World War by James Leith to help with the shortage of granite at the time.

Craigenlow/Dunecht

There is no mention of the quarry in the second Statistical Account, but tradition has it being opened to provide stone for the building of Dunecht House. Whether this was the original building of 1820 or the major additions carried out by Lord Lindsay in 1845 is unclear. Certainly it was operated by Francis Christie and used for work he carried out later in the century, particularly the chapel and library designed by London architect George Edmund Street for Dunecht House. After Christie, James Leith, who quarried at Cairncry and Persley, leased Dunecht from around the early

1890s. It was then closed for a few years before Leith reopened it in 1897, investing in a steam crane, boring machine, blacksmith's shop and powder magaznie. Despite high optimism, Leith closed it again the following year, reopening it again in 1899. This quarry was down near the base of the hill, his earlier quarry and the one that provided stone for Dunecht House was further up the hill. Leith appointed James Dawson, his manager from Cairncry, as manager at Craigenlow. Leith closed the quarry in 1907. Craigenlow was reopened and used for subsequent building work on the estate especially under Lord and Lady Cowdray. According to Diack, shortly after Lady Cowdray's death it was leased to W.J. Brown & Son, a building contractor in Aberdeen, and stone from the quarry used was for council house schemes in Aberdeen.[95]

Bennachie and Monymusk

Knight wrote that the granite from Bennachie was reddish and that there were several quarries around the base of the hill, at Pittodrie, Balquhain and elsewhere.[96] However, the granite weathered quickly and was dull compared with other reds. The minister of Chapel of Garioch wrote in the second Statistical Account of 1841 that 'the principal stones used for building mansion-houses and farm steadings in the neighbourhood are obtained from the hill of Benachie, and also at its base in this parish. The chimney-pieces in the two drawing rooms of Logie Elphinstone are of Benachie granite,' the latter being able to take a good polish.[97]

There were two quarries actually on the hill, one known as the lintel quarry and one known as the English Quarry. The latter, situated on the south side of the hill, seems to have begun around 1820. The minister of Oyne at the second Statistical Account recorded that it had operated from around eighteen years before the time he was writing in 1839. He also recorded that it supplied granite for the docks at Sheerness, as did several other quarries in the north-east. The granite blocks were taken by road to Port Elphinstone and then by the canal to Aberdeen for shipping.[98]

The lintel quarry was a small one on the north of the hill at Little Oxen Craig. It seems to have two phases of operation. Professor Ian Carter quotes a pre-1859 source as saying that 'an extensive business was done by George Sim and William Mare in the supply of granite stones of all shapes and sizes. The granite was of the best quality, and was in demand for corner stones and lintels, or whatever strength and durability were required.'[99]

Andrew Fordyce seems to suggest that the access road for this quarry was washed away in around 1830, causing the quarry to cease production. As a young man his father later reopened the quarry, his grandfather rebuilding the road. Once again a water spout washed the road away around 1890, and he comments on the curiosity of this happening twice in sixty years.[100] Some of his father's lintels can still be seen at the site, where there is also an interpretation panel as well as a sign-posted quarry trail.

There were various other small quarries in the area, also producing red stone. These included a quarry on the Gallowhill above Delab; three quarries on Pitfichie Hill, one above Ordmill marked on the second OS map, one above Milldowrie, and one above Ardneidly marked on the first OS map but noted as 'Old Quarry' on the second OS map; a quarry in a field above Blackhillock; a quarry above Ramstone.[101] One of these, possibly the one above Milldowrie, operated after the Second World War and into the 1950s.

Sylavethie

The writer of the 2nd Statistical Account for Tullynessle and Forbes parish described 'a quarry on the Forbes property, near the river, of excellent quality, which has been wrought for several years and in the immediate vicinity of a town would yield a handsome revenue to the noble proprietor.'[102]

This probably refers to Sylavethie, just 2 miles north of Alford. It is shown on the first OS map of 1866 as a very small quarry with one crane. Around that time it was worked by James Wright of the Royal Granite Works in Aberdeen, which company used it a lot in their polished ornamental work. For example 1,400cu.ft of polished Sylavethie was supplied by Wright for a building for Charles Skipper & East, wholesale stationers at Tower Hill, London. In the early years of the twentieth century it was still worked by James Wright & Sons.

In the 1870s its granite was considered more striking than Rubislaw stone, but expensive because of higher transport costs since it was some distance from the railway. Quite often in building and monuments it was used in combination with Kemnay to provide a contrast with the much whiter Kemnay stone. One of the polished granite columns in Aberdeen Art Gallery is of Sylavethie granite.

The quarry survived until the late 1970s.

Inverurie

Messrs Burnett Brothers reopened it in 1898 after it had been closed for fifty-five years. The earlier quarry had supplied stone for several buildings in the town including the Parish and Episcopal churches.

Birsemore

This quarry was on Birsemore hill, across the River Dee to the south of Aboyne. It was not shown on the first OS map. It is mentioned by Harris, operated at that time by Burgess & Son, so must have been opened sometime between 1865 and the 1880s, when Harris was writing.

Cambus O' May or Tomnakeist

The *Aberdeen Journal* in 1877 described a picnic for the workmen at these quarries and their families. At that time they were operated by Burgess & Son, and had recently been opened on the land of the Marquis of Huntly.[103] A new road had been built from the quarries to the station at Cambus

O'May. They are shown on the second OS map with a magazine also marked. In 1895 there were two quarries, one operated by Burgess, the other by Mr Stewart. Although some of the stone came to Aberdeen most of it was used for buildings in the town of Ballater. Stewart built the public hall in Ballater using grey granite from his quarry for the dressed work, with red granite from the Pass of Ballater for the ashlar. The Granite Chips column in the *Aberdeen Journal* described the granite as being like Kemnay and stated that a large number of masons and quarrymen were employed at the quarries.[104] William Grant lists James Fraser as another operator of the quarry, though at what date is not clear.[105] The remains of a Scotch Derrick from the quarry were restored in 2014 and it is on display at the entrance to the village of Ballater.

Peterhead Area

The minister of the parish of Peterhead wrote in the first Statistical Account of 1794 that there were:

> inexhaustible quarries of excellent granite, of which all the houses of Peterhead are built, and great quantities exported to the London market, and for different parts of England; the granite admits of the finest polish, and lapidaries are frequently employed in forming it into various shapes for different pieces of furniture. From 600 to 800 tons of kerb and carriage-way stones are annually sent to London, and other places, and are generally sold there at 13 Shillings per ton.[106]

Peter Buchan, in his *Annals of Peterhead* published in 1819, lists the quarries in the Peterhead area: Stirlinghill, Salthouse-head, South-head and Ive, all of which were producing large amounts of dressed granite for the London and other markets. He then says that in the neighbourhood of Peterhead there are the quarries of Cairngall, Rora and Blackhill. Buchan said that examples of granite from all three can be seen at the gate pillars of Pitfour House which were 16ft high, exclusive of base and capitals, 8ft in circumference at the lower end, and with a 17ft lintel on top.[107]

It is little wonder that William Grant, much later, told John Fyfe that there were once twenty-three quarries working in the Buchan area. Stirlinghill alone had numerous quarries often worked by different companies.[108] Grant began his working life in the Buchan quarries and he also told William Diack that during his time twenty-three red granite and eight grey granite quarries in the Buchan area had ceased production. In his own memoirs he lists thirteen in the Peterhead area, which included Longhaven, eleven in the Stirlinghill area and five grey granite quarries in the Buchan area, which he listed as Cairngall, Aikey Brae, Hill O Knock, Dens O Crichie and Rora, the latter four operated by Heslop & Wilson of Peterhead.

The Peterhead quarries were operated at various times by companies and yards from Peterhead and Aberdeen, the latter included Alexander Macdonald, Bower & Florence, James Wright & Sons, as well as Heslop & Wilson from Peterhead itself. Each quarry at Stirlinghill and Blackhill had its own name and, with their being so many, it can be difficult to pinpoint them all today.

The main areas for the famous red granite of Peterhead were at the Stirlinghill (often written as Sterling in old accounts, including the first OS map) and the nearby Blackhill, south of Longhaven.

Both of these are shown as a series of quite small quarries on the 1868 OS Map. At the time that Knight was writing, John Gibb was renting the Blackhill quarries from Mr Erskine. From 1817 Gibb had also worked the Stirlinghill quarries for a period of ten years but then gave up the lease because of the then depressed state of the industry.[109]

In 1826, when the quarries were up for lease either as whole or as individual quarries, they were described as inexhaustible; the rock was up to the surface and there was no tirr or rubbish to be removed; there was no risk of water because of their elevation; and with better stone the further down they were quarried.

When John Pratt was writing his Buchan in the 1850s there were about eighty men employed in 'transporting blocks to the work-sheds, blasting and splitting the rock, rude dressing of the stones, others carting them to the wharfs'. He also mentions that there were tram-roads in use.[110]

John McGlashan operated a quarry, possibly from 1859. In that year he advertised for various items of second-hand machinery, including a double-power quarry crane capable of lifting 4–5

Surviving quarry building at Stirlinghill, Peterhead.

tons, a wagon for driving stones capabaple of taking 3–4 tons, as well as other tools necessary for quarrying. His address was given as the Invernettie Brewery.[111] Two years later he also started a polishing business (see Chapter 5).

Macdonald & Leslie/Alexander Macdonald and Co. Ltd operated a quarry at Stirlinghill for their own use rather than for the trade. They had acquired the quarry as early as the 1830s and still operated it at the end of the century. Alexander Gordon, an old stonecutter interviewed by the *Buchan Observer* in 1903, joined Macdonald's in 1837. He stated that Macdonald acquired the quarry at Stirlinghill in 1833, and that as early as 1817 it had been operated by an English firm looking for stone suitable for the Sheerness Docks and Blackfriars Bridge in London. It was then taken over by Gibb & Low, and then an Andrew Duncan from Peterhead, before Macdonald's took it over. Gordon was sent to manage the quarry in 1845 and remained there until he retired in 1893.[112] However, several granite companies simultaneously operated quarries at Stirlinghill. In 1859 James Wright & Sons also operated a quarry there. These two quarries were on the Boddam and Sandford Estate, which was advertised for sale in 1865. The granite then was described as inexhaustible with a considerable portion of the potential quarry area still being unlet.[113]

By 1870, in addition to these two quarries, John Cameron, quarrier, was operating a quarry at Stirlinghill, though by 1879 he had been replaced by the Peterhead Granite Polishing Company of Heslop & Wilson. In the 1890s Alexander Macdonald, James Wright, and Robert Lawrence all had quarries at Stirlinghill. Also operating there at various times were James Davidson & Co., James Rennie, J. McKessor, William Stuart of Peterhead and the Great North of Scotland Granite Company.

Diack records how granite columns for the London Stock Exchange came from the Rocksley Quarry at Stirlinghill in 1882. They were 13ft 6in, and Diack says they were the last stones taken from that quarry, not because the granite was exhausted but because the post went right under the road and for safety reasons quarrying had to stop, otherwise the quarry owner would have to build a new road at his own expense.[114] However in 1894 Heslop & Wilson quarried a block at their Guite and Rocksley Quarry described as being the 'most notable block of granite ever taken from Peterhead quarries'. It was 40ft x 22ft long x 13ft thick, and without a flaw or vein.[115]

In September 1894 the first sod was cut for a new branch of the Buchan Railway running from Ellon to Boddam. One of the main reasons for building this rail line was to connect up with the quarries on Stirlinghill and Blackhill. It was estimated at the time that on average 12,400 tons of granite was carted from the Blackhill and Stirlinghill quarries to Peterhead.[116] Even before the first sod was cut Heslop & Wilson applied to build a horse tramway between their works at Stirlinghill and the proposed railway. At Blackhill there were eight quarries worked by Whitehead & Sons, Aberdeen; The Aberdeen Quarrying Company; Robert Lawrence of Aberdeen; the Great North of Scotland Granite Company; and Heslop & Wilson. Most of the quarries were owned by Aberdeen companies, and therefore most of the granite was intended for Aberdeen, although Macdonald's did some polishing work in Peterhead. The stones for Aberdeen were taken to Peterhead where they were transferred to trains for Aberdeen. The cost of transport meant that lower-value stone which would have been suitable for setts was actually thrown into the sea. At the Longhaven Quarry, owned by Charles Macdonald of the Froghall Granite Works, William Grant described a 7-ton crane positioned so that it could swing the rubbish straight into the sea[117]

– no environmental agencies to stop this in those days! When the railway began running past the quarries the quarry owners hoped to make more use of these inferior stones. The railway could also deliver coal to the quarries on its return journey, 1,205 ton of coal annually being used in the quarries in the area in 1894.[118]

Cruden Quarry was opened 1897 by James Wright & Sons. In 1899 three steam cranes were in operation and a depth of 100ft had already been reached. Once again the quarry waste was dumped directly into the sea.

Heslop & Wilson owned the Rora Quarry, 6 miles from Peterhead, in 1898, and the main quarry in the Peterhead area for providing grey granite. It was a blue/grey colour, very suitable for polishing and monumental work, but also for architectural. In that year it was 50ft deep and about 120ft square, with stones of 120 tons dislodged from the face, and numerous 10-ton blocks prepared for the granite yards. It had up-to-date machinery including a steam crane, three steam-powered drilling machines, a steam pump and also a granite-cutting saw, unusual at a quarry at that time. It also had an engine house and smithy. A further crane was soon to be added. They also operated a quarry at Longhaven producing red granite.[119]

Convict Labour at Stirlinghill Quarry

In the 1880s the Government was looking to build several harbours of refuge along the east coast where shipping could shelter in times of severe storms. One was to be in Scotland and in 1883 the Parliamentary Select Committee assessing the various possibilities supported Peterhead as the appropriate site, echoing the views of an earlier Royal Commission.[120] The abundant supply of granite nearby was one of the factors that led to Peterhead being chosen. The proposed harbour would be built using convict labour at a new prison.[121] At the time from 700-800 Scottish prisoners were being sent to England to engage in what was thought to be useful employment. Peterhead Prison was begun in 1886 and finished in 1891. As well as building their own prison, the prisoners were also used to work the quarry to provide stone for the prison and the breakwater. From 1888 onwards the Lords Commissioners of the Admiralty appear in the Aberdeenshire Valuation Roll as owners of one of the quarries at Stirlinghill. According to William Grant the stone for building the prison came from the Bog Quarry, but he doesn't say if this was the one the Admiralty subsequently bought.[122] In 1889 a 2½-mile railway was built to the quarry. The south breakwater was finished in 1912 and work began on the north breakwater. This lasted into the 1930s when much of the granite was crushed and made into concrete blocks, averaging 35 tons, for the main part of the breakwater. Granite ashlar was used for steps and coping. In 1923 the International Prison Congress went by special train from Peterhead to Boddam to view the prisoners at work in the quarry.[123]

By 1928 the numbers of prisoners working the quarry, which at one time had reached over 400, was down to 100–200.[124] Prisoners were still working in the quarry until around 1956. People can still remember seeing prison guards with rifles standing guard over the prisoners working in the quarry (as seen in the illustration). The rifle was a .303, and the guards were instructed to shoot anyone attempting escape in the ankle. In earlier times the guards had also carried cutlasses.

Prisoners, watched over by guards, some armed, board a train at one of the quarries at Stirlinghill, Peterhead. (Used by kind permission of D.C. Thomson & Co. Ltd)

The Admiralty Quarry at Stirlinghill was the last in the area to close. At the time of the publication of the third Statistical Account (1956, though written a year or two before this) it was reported that £55,500 of granite had been extracted in the previous eight years. This comprised 6,258 tons of monumental stone, 8,118 tons of building stone, and 2,478 ton of chips.

Cairngall

The minister of Longside, at the time of the Statistical Account in 1792, wrote that the parish abounded in granite, with a dark blue stone being produced in the north-east of the parish used at Cairness House in the parish of Lonmay, though most of the stone for Cairness came from a quarry on the Cairness Estate. He also mentioned that another 'of a lighter colour, but also very beautiful, is found in Cairngall, frequent specimens of which are to be seen in London and other parts of England.'[125]

Cairngall deserves a section on its own separate from the other quarries in the Peterhead area for two reasons. Firstly, despite being only a few miles from Peterhead, the granite from Cairngall was not red like most of the other granites from the Peterhead area, rather it was classed as blue or bluish grey. Secondly it was probably the finest of all the north-east granites for polished monumental work. Notably, it was used for the Royal Sarcophagus for Prince Albert and Queen Victoria at Frogmore.

The Reverend John Pratt in one of the appendices to his *Buchan*, published in 1858, quotes a description of the Cairngall quarry given in a letter from John Hutchison, landowner of the Cairngall Estate:

These quarries lie five miles west of Peterhead in a hill which rises about sixty feet above the adjacent ground. They are worked into the hill from that level, and the largest and finest blocks are got farthest down. The joints generally are perpendicular, varying in thickness from six inches to upwards of eight feet: here from five to six feet is the common thickness of a frost or joint. Blocks have been obtained above twenty feet square and eight feet thick; indeed much larger than could be removed by any machinery used in the quarry, which consists merely of two cranes capable of raising eight tons each. The large blocks must therefore be cut into smaller ones before they are removed. The quarry was not wrought to any great extent previous to 1808. In that year, when the foundations of the Bell-Rock Lighthouse were laid, it was selected by Mr Stevenson. It is very like the Aberdeen granite, although closer in grain and harder, and is often built along with it, where larger sizes are wanted than can easily be obtained at London. Thus mixed it was used in the foundations of London Bridge, and in the pier walls of the new Houses of Parliament. The contrast may be seen in the Duke of York's Monument, where the lintel over the door is of this granite – the rest of the blue or lower part being mostly from Aberdeen. The greater part of the pillars in Covent Garden Market are from this quarry. It may also be seen round the fountains at Charing Cross; and the finely axed kerb-stones in the inside of the Victoria Tower, in the new Houses of Parliament, are from Cairngall. This granite is also much used as pedestals for statues; as an example the pedestal of the Duke of Wellington's statue, Glasgow. But perhaps the most splendid specimen of the Cairngall granite yet produced is at the new County Buildings, Liverpool, where, in St George's Hall, eight pillars are erected – the shafts being eighteen feet in height, and each of one polished block.[126]

John Hutchison was born in 1760 at Boddam. As well as quarrying, his business interests included farming, shipbuilding and merchant shipping. Along with James Arbuthnot, he introduced whaling to Peterhead. In 1784 he married Elizabeth Morrison and bought the Cairngall Estate, which included Monyruy. He and his descendants either worked the quarry themselves or let it out to quarriers.

The quarry, as has been stated, produced some of the finest granite in the north-east. It was opened on a small scale in the second half of the eighteenth century, when it was involved in the London trade. An 1803 sale advertisement said that it had formerly supplied large amounts of granite to London.[127] Cairngall granite was also used in the columns and cornices of Cairness

House, largely designed by James Playfair and built from 1791–97. Knight describes this granite as the smallest-grained white granite he had yet found.

John Pratt says that it had been worked by the owner, Mr Hutchison of Monyruy, but at the time he was writing in the 1850s it was leased by John Hutchison to Macdonald & Leslie and they worked it for much of the nineteenth century.[128] As noted above, in the 1840s it provided eight pillars for St George's Hall in Liverpool, each of one polished block 18ft high.

The quarry subsequently closed and was reopened in December 1894 by Smith & Co. of Fraserburgh for the production of setts, kerbs, building stones and 'polishers'.

When the mansion and quarry were put up for sale in 1931, the quarry was described as recently having been worked by the late Colonel William Hutchinson and his son Major William Ernest Hutchinson, the owners of the estate. William had actually died in 1881 and William Ernest was only 12 years old when he inherited it. He himself died in 1929, hence the quarry being for sale in 1931. At that time the quarry was mainly used for setts and paving material.[129]

Cairngall and Monyruy were bought by James Rollo Duncan of Tillycorthie, who had made a fortune in tin mining in Bolivia. A few years later the quarry ceased to operate, but in 1939 the *Press & Journal* reported that the Aberdeenshire County Road Board proposed to acquire it for road material.[130]

New Pitsligo

This quarry was situated on Peathill just a few hundred yards immediately south-east of the village; indeed many of the buildings in the village are built from stone from the quarry.. It is shown as two quarries on the first OS map, with a rectangular building on the edge of the larger quarry. In 1884 it was being operated by builder William Davidson. In a court case at about the same time W. & A. Murray are described as quarry owners at New Pitsligo working the quarry without steam cranes.[131] Possibly Murray operated one quarry and Davidson the other. By the time of the second OS map there were three or four more buildings shown at the larger quarry.

THE DEVELOPMENT OF TOOLS AND TECHNOLOGY IN THE NINETEENTH CENTURY

In modern times granite can be cut, shaped, polished and lettered all relatively quickly, with much of it done by computer-controlled machinery. For most of us it is very difficult to imagine the sheer physical nature of much of the work before the twentieth century. The hand-wielded tools used in the industry were incredibly heavy, requiring great physical strength, far more than was needed for softer stone such as sandstone. In the quarries even the manual boring of a hole to take the charge for blasting was a lengthy process requiring laborious hammering of the jumper. Stone was raised from the quarry floor by horse and cart. Sawing a large block of granite could take months and polishing was equally time-consuming, if not quite so physical. Little wonder that in the mid-nineteenth century polished granite monuments and headstones took six months and more to complete and were, therefore, largely bought by the wealthy. Mechanisation came in various ways. From the 1830s there was Macdonald's experiment with the use of steam power for polishing and then other aspects of the manufacturing process. Technology was also borrowed, sometimes with modifications, from other industries such as mining. John Fyfe was a leader in this, while also developing some ideas of his own. When the American granite industry got off the ground the scale of the industry encouraged technological development, some of it developed by men from Aberdeen, and this was imported to the north-east. By the last two decades of the nineteenth century steam-powered derrick cranes, blondins, turning lathes and other machinery had been introduced and at the very end of the century pneumatic tools appeared, transforming the ease by which granite could be carved into elaborate shapes.

Early Tools and Techniques

In early times granite blocks were split by carving a line of rectangular grooves along the line that the mason wanted the block to split. Wooden wedges were driven into these grooves and they were soaked. As the wood swelled overnight the effect was to split the block. James Anderson gives a description of the working of granite by Aberdeen masons when he was writing in 1794:

When they mean to split it, they begin by drawing a straight line along the stone in the direction of its greet (grain); they then dig a row of little groves along that line by means of a weighty tool like a hammer drawn to a blunt point at both ends, and highly tempered at the point. This they call a pick, it being of the same nature with the tool employed by millers for picking their mill-stones. Into each groove they fix a wedge, the point of which is cut over square, so as to leave a triangular cavity below it. They then strike the wedges with a very weighty hammer. This operation is then repeated as often as necessary till the whole stone be cut into slabs as thin as are wanted.[1]

This method of splitting the block would continue, more or less the same, up to the present day. Known as the plug and feathers, it comprises a row of steel wedges or plugs driven between two semi-circular steel pieces (the feathers) along the line where the block of granite was to be split. One thing that did change was the method of drilling small holes into which the plug and feathers were inserted. By 1892 Andrew Wilson wrote that smaller drills, less than half the diameter of the older ones, were in use. The drilling was faster and was also done by one man instead of three as previously (presumably similar to the three man team using the jumper to create a drill hole to take the explosive charge). This meant that there was less wastage of the stone, less work involved in puncheoning out the drill holes for the finished block and less manpower involved in the drilling.[2]

Anderson went on:

afterwards these are divided across into the dimensions wanted at the time. In this way stones for ordinary building are shaped into the forms of bricks about two feet in length, and one foot in other dimention. These stones are called litter stones because, before the roads were formed, they used to be carried on a litter to the builders, and were sold at four-pence each delivered at the foot of the wall. It is in this manner the long stones are shaped that are sent to London for the edges of the foot pavements. For ordinary mason-work the stones are used without any further dressing; but for the fronts of houses and finer work, they are usually smoothed so as to form what they call aslar work. This is done by picking their surface, and then smoothing them by a tool in shape like a small hatchet. When thus dressed, these stones are perfectly straight and truly squared; and they join in building with such nicety that the point of a knife could scarcely find access into the jointing.[3]

Anderson saw it as a virtue that it was difficult to carve granite since it produced neat and elegant buildings, as he saw it. Easy to smooth, it is difficult to 'dress into small mouldings; and to cut into dentils, modillions, and foliage: for which reason these taudry ornaments, so often attempted upon softer stone by rude artists must here entirely avoided.' This would change in time but it would be the second half of the nineteenth century before tools became available to make it easier to create intricate decoration in granite.

An assortment of mason's tools, hammers, axes, chisels etc. are illustrated in the record book of the Aberdeen Masonic Lodge, which dates from 1670. However, at this date these would mainly be for use on sandstone rather than granite. The early work on granite was done by the scabbling pick and the lighter dressing pick as described by Anderson. Union Bridge is said to be one of the last major building projects in the city on which the old-fashioned mason's pick was used. Sometime in the early 1820s Provost James Hadden of Persley brought back a tool from New York called a 'patent axe' or 'bush hammer'. He gave the axe to a local builder called Milne who was working on building the Music Hall. Milne's workers could make nothing of the new tool but sometime later it came into the possession of Alexander Macdonald. The more far sighted Macdonald could see the potential of the axe and had a couple more made. It became the main tool for dressing granite for many years thereafter. The axe consisted of several strips of steel bound together and fastened to a handle. The surface of the granite was then fine axed by a series of taps.[4] Knight in 1832 commented, 'The degree of fineness of dressing has been carried much further of late years by what is termed axe dressing, with a hammer or iron having a blunted edge approaching to the form of tool after which it is named.'[5]

Chisels and puncheons were reputedly first used on granite at the building of the Music Hall in the early 1820s. According to the story recorded a number of years later, some freestone masons, temporarily out of work, undertook to work in granite and they took their own tools with them. *The Leisure Hour* in 1860 said that steel chisels (possibly steel tipped) were introduced in 1820 and this may have been at the music hall.[6] Knight describes how small chisels and hammers have been used to create the flutings of Doric columns and the deep volutes of Ionic columns. He said that these had been used for the last 12 years and although his account was published in 1835 it was written in 1832 and so he may well have been talking about these tools originating at the time the Music Hall was begun.[7]

A type of pick was still used, however, in the early 1830s. This is described by Knight, who calls it a hammer–chisel, though he says the workmen call it a pick, as being:

> a pointed chisel, armed with steel and assisted by a considerable weight of metal, held in both hands like a hammer, but so managed as to allow of a rapid succession of blows. These blows descend upon the slope of the inclined plane at which the stone is placed, so that not only are pieces struck off projected away from the labourer, but the impulses are given in directions most favourable for effect, as his body bends over the stone in which he is working.

His description was repeated word for word in the *Saturday Magazine* ten years later.[8] Knight also describes unusual shaped hammers with a blunt faces being used to break off large pieces in the first stage of dressing, he calls it scappling, equivalent to what was later called scabbling.

The Builder in 1866 describes granite blocks being worked with thick, heavy conical punches and a wedge-like chisel (it comments that these were nothing like those used in freestone or limestone). These were struck with heavy iron hammers or used like picks. The article comments that the laborious process was 'very different indeed from the easy operations one may see going on in the yard of a London mason.'[9] By the 1890s, when Andrew Wilson was writing, heavy steel faced iron tools had given way to lighter ones made wholly of steel which needed no facing.[10]

Quarrying and Blasting in the Early Years

Knight gives us a description of the method of blasting stone in the early 1830s. Blasting was by gunpowder with copper points to the steel borers and prickers, copper being used so as to prevent a spark which might cause a premature explosion, something he said was still a frequent occurrence. Other types of high explosive had been tried but they produced an explosion that was too violent, thereby damaging the stone. Explosives such as dynamite and gelatine could be used to break up or remove bars but for monumental stone the blast had to be controlled in such as way as not to shatter or fragment the stone. Later quarrymen would say that you could use a hard explosion for building stone and road stone, and a soft one for monumental stone, where you need larger blocks. For that reason gunpowder, working along the natural seams of the stone, continued to be used long after other types of explosive had been developed for other purposes.

One improvement that John Gibb carried out was in the depth and width of the bore for the charge. Knight says that prior to 1819 the only jumpers or boring chisels used were no more than an inch in diameter, with the holes 3 to 5ft in depth. Gibb successfully used tools of 2½in diameter, and bored holes of not less than 10 to 12ft in depth. These improvements meant that much larger rocks could be dislodged, so that the stones supplied for London Bridge were much larger than those used for Union Bridge in Aberdeen, at the beginning of the century. For normal operations 10 to 20lb of powder were used, with up to 100lb used on occasion to move larger amounts of stone. Of course with larger stones being produced there needed to be improvements in the machinery for moving them and Knight wrote that around 1820 only one type of crane was used, and that of poor quality. By the 1830s there were much improved cranes and screw-jacks capable of lifting these larger stones. He gives the example of stones of 2 tons in weight being used by Smeaton in his work on the pier and harbour in Aberdeen in 1779, and that with some difficulty. By 1830 stones weighing 15 ton were regularly passing through the streets of Aberdeen with little comment.[11]

A court case in 1886 gives a good description of how the bore was drilled out manually to take the explosive. One man sat down on the rock and held the jumper or boring rod. When he was in place and ready two other men took it in turns to hammer the jumper into the rock, the hammer being a very heavy one. Periodically one of them would change places with the man holding the jumper. From this case it appears that there was no recognised signal given for the men to begin hammering, other than an easy first stroke, but that a signal was given when they were about to stop.[12]

Various types of steam and pneumatic drills had been in use in England, Germany and elsewhere since the middle of the nineteenth century but were only gradually introduced to granite quarries in the north-east. The court case mentioned above shows that manual drilling of holes for blasting powder was still being done in 1886, yet Andrew Wilson states that the steam drilling machine had been invented around 1876 and one can be seen in a photograph of Tillyfourie Quarry dated 1879. By 1892, when Wilson was writing, steam drills were being used for drilling small holes for splitting the stone (using the plug & feathers) and for large holes to hold powder for blasting.[13] For the latter in the early years of the twentieth century Jeffrey gave the example of the steam reciprocating drill boring 20ft per day with holes 3in in diameter, followed a little later by the hammer drill boring 20ft per hour.[14] By 1924 the *Press & Journal* carried the following description of the working of Rubislaw Quarry:

Tillyfourie Quarry c.1879 showing an early pneumatic rock drill.

By means of pneumatic drills, eight or ten holes, each perhaps 20 feet deep and three inches broad at the surface, are bored. Charges of black powder, varying from 100 lb. to 600 lb. in weight are pushed home, the holes are tamped up and the explosion is caused by a current of electricity. Gunpowder is preferred because it loosens rather than shatters the rock. The amount of granite broken off depends upon the formation of the rock; it may be 50 tons, or it may be 500 tons.[15]

At that time they were pumping water out of the quarry for perhaps two hours a day in dry weather, three or four hours in wet weather, and occasionally day and night during heavy winter snow. In the 1930s a quarry manager, interviewed for a radio programme, was asked how much explosive they used. The laconic reply was 'its jist a maitter o' experience.' He went on to say that they bored holes for the explosive with compressed air. The holes were 10–20ft deep. Gunpowder was used with an electronic detonator. A tape fuse was added in case the detonator failed to explode. The stone then went to the drillers who used pneumatic drills called plug-drills (known locally as 'mannies'). The stone was split into size with these. Holes were drilled along the line for splitting and small steel wedges inserted. A few blows with a hammer did the rest.[16]

John Fyfe, the Blondin and His Other Innovations in Quarrying

It is fair to say that John Fyfe transformed granite quarrying in the north-east. Fyfe seemed to realise that resources committed to technological development would pay off in the end and he always seemed to find resources to develop new technology. Not every innovation he introduced was his own invention, some were simply adapted to granite quarrying from existing technology, but he did also have original ideas and in this he was aided by a number of engineering companies, both local and national.

John Fyfe's first machine innovation came with the introduction of the steam derrick crane, commissioned from Andrew Barclay of Kilmarnock in 1868. Hand-powered derrick cranes were already in use but this one used steam power and had a moveable jib. John Ritchie gives a good description of how this crane worked:

> The boiler and engine shed was at some distance from the crane. Engine Sandy was an oracle in the eyes of us youngsters. Then there was a steam winch worked by another man. The jib and burden chains came off the barrels of this winch and ran along a platform to the bottom of the crane. Another man stood on this platform armed with a hook and as the chain came off the barrel his duty was to pull it along until the crane could take it up through a casting in the bottom of the mast, and , as there was no slewing gear, another man was required with a guy rope to pull round the stone to the cutting bank. This meant four men to work the crane, and any heavy stone took from six to eight men to pull to its destination. I might also mention that the crane had handles, and when a stone of any consequence had to be handled, steam was shut off and men put on to the handles.

This was very labour intensive and Ritchie's final comment sums it up: 'steam was pretty low about that time.'[17] An example of a restored hand-cranked derrick crane can be seen at the entrance to the town of Ballater. This incorporates part of the machinery from a crane that was actually used in the Cambus O'May granite quarry.

One of the greatest inventions in granite quarrying was the aerial cableway or blondin, first developed by Fyfe in 1872. There are various stories as to how John Fyfe came by the idea of the blondin, including that he was inspired by the tightrope artist of that name. Certainly the name came from Charles Blondin, but G.M. Fraser, city librarian and local historian, was told by a former employee of Fyfe's that Fyfe got the inspiration from the 'cradle' which once crossed the River Dee at Abergeldie Castle, running on a rope suspended from posts or trees, and used by the postman to send mail across to the castle. Fyfe had seen it when he was returning by coach from Braemar one day. Fyfe's son also confirmed that his father had seen the cradle at Abergeldie. Apparently he was so modest that he never patented the invention.[18] Hence, perhaps, why one website claims it was first used in a Welsh slate quarry in 1913! Although Fyfe came up with the idea of a suspension cableway with a travelling carrier, there is no reason to doubt, as Diack suggests, that the Aberdeen engineering firm of John M. Henderson developed the idea into a working machine, and Henderson's may well have patented the idea. John M. Fyfe credited quarry engineers with the actual construction and fitting up of the first blondin, though he also stated that local engineering companies had provided some of the equipment and cables.[19]

Harris, writing in 1888, describes the operation of the blondin at Kemnay. At that time the quarry was 300ft deep, with a huge crane at the top of the quarry and other cranes on the floor about two-thirds of the way up the quarry. He describes the blondin as:

> Running right across the chasm to the floor. The blondin is made of two wheels, one above the other, and a tray for carrying the granite is fastened to the lower one. The whole machine runs down an inclined steel wire-rope stretched across the quarry, and the engineman can so regulate it as to cause it to stop at any part of the course, and then the lower wheel and tray are let down the quarry. When the tray is filled up it is hauled up again and the machine is pulled up the wire-rope and its burden landed on top of the quarry.[20]

The advantage of the blondin was its ability to run across the quarry opening, rather than being fixed to one side like a crane. Its disadvantage was that it was very limited in the amount of stone it could carry, typically 3-5 tons. It wasn't until the early twentieth century that blondins were built which could carry 10 tons. The blondin was therefore used to lift smaller stones and to remove waste from the quarry. This was possibly one of the reasons why it was slow to be adopted, though Donnelly suggests that another reason might have been that the quarrymasters had invested considerable sums of money in Scotch Steam Derrick Cranes.[21]

The cableway idea was further developed for other uses such as bridge-building and in the shipyards. Henderson's themselves supplied five aerial cableways for the building of the Nag Hammadi Dam across the Nile in Egypt, spanning 3,500ft.[22] They also supplied one for the demolition of the old bridge over the Thames at Kew and the building of the new bridge. The span was 525ft, travelling across the span with a load of four tons at 600ft per minute, raising or lowering at 300ft per minute.[23]

Fyfe was the first in the area to use electricity for firing the charge during blasting. The *Aberdeen Journal* of 17 July 1872 reported his first attempt. Fyfe wanted to fire four shots at once to shift a huge amount of rock. His men made four holes, 13ft deep and 6–8ft apart. D. Wright, an electrician from George Street fired the four shots at once, something that had already been tried by another electrical 'expert' at the quarry with no success, leading to the death of a quarryman sent to extricate the failed charge. This experiment was repeated on a larger scale the following March when Wright again fired the charge. This time there were 11 bores, 20ft deep and 6ft apart. The blasting was done over two days in snowy conditions and 5,000 tons of good-quality granite were displaced.[24] Twenty years later Andrew Wilson described the process as it was used in his day:

> No fuse is required, but instead an insulated copper wire is used to connect all the charges with each other, and is attached to a cap or detonator in each charge. This wire, which is called the service wire, is then connected to two large wires or cables which are in turn connected with the two poles of the battery. When all is clear, the operator has only to turn the handle of the battery so many times (according to the number of charges to be fired), and then make a quarter turn in the opposite direction, when all the charges will be exploded simultaneously, and the mass of rock removed with far less breakages than results from blasting with single bores.[25]

The process was not only safer but also led to a considerably saving in time. Under the old method the buring fuse might take ten minutes to reach the charge.

Polishing in 1856

Some twenty years after he began experimenting with the use of steam power to polish granite Alexander Macdonald had two high-pressure steam engines in his yard, each of 20hp. For polishing the block or slab was placed on a four-wheeled carriage, adjusted so that it was level and fixed in position. The carriage was then moved under the polishing machine (known as a 'rubber'), which turned an iron ring or block rapidly via a perpendicular shaft. Water mixed with sand was used to keep the stone moist and act as an abrasive. The carriage was moved slowly on rails so that the entire surface was gradually brought into contact with the rubber. After several hours the carriage was then moved to another polisher where the process was repeated with a finer abrasive such as emery. The third part of the process involved the carriage being moved under a wooden polishing ring covered with a thick type of flannel known as 'lapp' and a soft powder or paste was applied instead of emery. This finally gave the surface of the stone a glass-like finish. Mouldings and columns used different processes, the former polished using a cast-iron plane with the stone remaining fixed, and columns using a turning lathe.[26]

Sawing in 1866

In 1866 *The Builder* described the lengthy and tedious process involved in sawing blocks of granite. The saws were of soft iron set in an iron framework, as many as 18 saws could be used on one block. Several blocks were being sawn at the same time. The article described one 10ft block being cut into six or eight slabs, the saws being driven by a steam engine, and sand being washed into the cut as an abrasive. It was painfully slow, taking a whole day to cut 2/3in into the block. This also made it it extremely expensive.[27]

Description of Working Granite in 1877

John Morgan credits Alexander Macdonald's company with introducing every labour saving device, the first major one being J. D. Brunton's granite turning lathe for dressing columns, balusters, pedestals, vases and all kinds of circular work.[28] The lathe was acquired in 1873, although the company already had a smaller one of similar design. In fact a turning lathe is described in use as early as 1856.[29] The new lathe was 26ft long, weighing 16 tons and capable of turning a column 17ft in length by 3¾ft in diameter. The stone revolved at 50ft per minute and the cutting disks moved along its surface at a rate of 2 to 2½ft per hour.[30] In 1877 *The Builder* magazine visited Macdonald & Field's Aberdeen Granite Works in Constitution Street. The resulting article gives us an excellent description of how the work involved in cutting, shaping and polishing granite had changed from the time when James Anderson was writing, and from Macdonald's early experiments with mechanisation. It is therefore worth quoting in some detail, some of the techniques remained unchanged until well into the twentieth century and the description of the yard will undoubtedly be familiar to some readers:

Over a considerable portion of the area occupied by the works, we find the raw material piled in roughly-shaped cubes of granite in horizontal layers one over another, and capable of being lifted about by a travelling crane. These blocks are first very roughly shaped at the quarry in a sufficiently regular form to be convenient for stacking; after that everything is done at the works.

The stone is got into approximate shapes by blows of short heavy-headed axes, which might be better described as hammers with the striking portion worked into a sharp edge, the instrument having to be weighted with much heavier metal than is the case with an axe, in order to give the weight and momentum required to make any impression on the material. After this operation, it is 'axed granite' and is in the state in which it is used for rusticated work in architectural design; and indeed occasionally for the entire facing of buildings. There is a terrace of houses on the way out to Rubislaw quarries, treated in this way, and which looks very well [possibly Albyn Terrace].

The next stage in the mason's work is the further shaping and finishing of the surface with the cold chisel and mallet; the chisel being again a thicker and heavier implement, and rather more blunt in shape that that used for ordinary mason's work. Mere sharpness of metal will hardly touch granite; it requires weight and force in the blow to break up the particles at all. There is something in the sound of the blows upon the stone which is most peculiar, and conveys to the ear the notion that the task of shaping a material which gives such a dull iron sound as that when struck must be one requiring an unlimited stock of patience, and a very strong frame to stand the perpetual jar of the blows on the apparently unyielding surface.

After the chisel comes the fine-axe, which is another implement of hammer-headed appearance and shape, but in which the head carries half a dozen or so of parallel steel blades with a little space between them; and with this implement the surface is dressed to the finest finish it is capable of, short of polishing.

In dealing with circular columns the turning lathe, in a modified and purely mechanical form, is used. The block which is to made into a shaft is got as near into a true circular form by hand as can be, and is then fixed in a lathe, and operated on by a kind of plate-shaped circular blade on either side, placed in a vice so as to present its cutting edge at about an angle of 45% with the shaft; water is kept dripping on the granite at the point where the cutters work, and the frame or vices in which they are fixed move automatically along the length of the shaft at a very slow, and after reaching the end are set fresh for another journey along the shaft, till it is brought to the dimensions and the surface to be ready for the polisher. With this exception, the working of the granite up to the polishing point is almost entirely by hand; there is little or nothing of cutting and planing surfaces by machinery, for the material is too stubborn for these rapid methods of working, and only yields to time and patient labour. As an instance of its stubbornness under the action of machinery, we may mention an operation in which machinery is necessarily employed, sawing a block into thin slabs to be subsequently polished for use in a decorative manner. This is done by a frame full of parallel bands working backwards and forwards on the edge of the block to sawn up, and we were shown a slab, some 4 or 5ft in width, the sawing through of which had occupied twelve months. (The article comments that marble would take half this time). Contrary to what most persons would expect, the iron bands used for this sawing process are not of the hardest iron or steel; the special object is to have them as soft as possible, and the iron is even softened by a special process, the result of which is that the blade takes up the particles of quartz which are disintegrated by its first attack, which form the hardest ingredient of the granite, and which become imbedded in the blade and in reality do most of the cutting. The granite, which would be impervious to mere iron or steel, however hard or sharp, is thus made literally to cut itself, and the iron blade becomes merely the medium for carrying for carrying the friction of the quartz particles backwards and forwards.

When we come to polishing we pass almost entirely from the manual labour to the mechanical. It is aprogressive use of more and more delicate materials on the surface so as to bring it up by degrees to a glass-like finish. The blocks piled up in the yards of the works, just as they come from the quarry, have none of that sharply distinctive colour and character, by which, when polished, everyone can see the distinction between Rubislaw and Peterhead, Cairngall and Kemnay; and so different is the tone assumed by the material under different treatment that you may see an apparently polychromatic effect in three tints, all produced from the same granite in its several stages of axed, fine-axed and polished. The principal medium in polishing is emery, and the final finish in delicate work is given by oxide of tin. The polishing of large flat slabs is carried on by a series of concentric iron rings turned round horizontally upon the surface of the granite, the turning power being applied to a vertical axle rising from them. As the rings turn rapidly the slab at the same time is moved slowly backwards and forwards to the extent of 2 or 3ft each way on a timber framework, the whole reminding one of an old–fashioned mangle at work. As in the case of the cutting-bands for sawing, the rings which do the work are made of soft iron, and emery powder in water is liberally served on the surface of the stone. This mixture runs off by degrees into a trough at the side of the stone, and is then carefully collected and served on to the stone again; the economizing of the emery being of some importance in the conduct of the operation, and affecting the gains of the workman who is paid piece-work. Polishing reduced the surface by about 1/10th of an inch which is allowed for in preparing sizes for polished work. The polishing machines will not work into angles which have to be polished up afterwards by hand, but this is so thoroughly done that it is impossible, as far as we observed, for the minutest inspection to tell where the machine polish ends and the hand polish begins.[31]

Developments in Polishing in the Late Nineteenth Century

As the industry grew in the second half of the nineteenth century and the number of yards and businesses increased so did the drive for improved machinery and techniques. Some of these developments, as with quarry technology, were products of the local industry. Once the American industry developed from the 1870s onwards, new ideas also came from across the Atlantic.

Sand was the first abrasive used in granite, both for polishing and sawing. In 1872 an American inventor, Benjamin Tilghmann, famous for inventing sandblasting, also patented the use of chilled iron shot as an alternative to sand for sawing. Andrew Wilson, in 1892, described this as one of the greatest improvements known in the industry. He gave the example of a block of granite 8ft long by 4ft across and 21in thick. To cut it into six slabs each 3in thick would take a minimum of four months using sand. Using chilled shot this was reduced to no more than ten days.[32] Initially Aberdeen granite yards imported this material but eventually the Aberdeen Iron Grit Company was formed. At the opening of their new premises in Ruthrieston Road in 1896, the process was described as:

> melting old iron in a cupola. When the molten metal arrives at the foot of the cupola it is driven by a powerful blast, initiated by a fan worked by a 12 horse power steam engine, into a chamber in which is situated a concrete tank, where it falls in a shower of spherical globules. The chilled shot is then passed through apertures in the building to the drying pans. Thence it is lifted by elevators to an upper floor, and riddled in wire cylinders, graduated to regulate the fineness'[33]

Aberdeen companies went on to export iron grit overseas. By the time of the Empire Exhibition in Glasgow in 1938 two of the seven UK factories producing grit were in Aberdeen. They sent more overseas than was used at home, exporting several thousand tons annually in twelve mesh sizes.[34]

The process of polishing described in the 1870s by *The Builder* in the previous section was eventually replaced in the 1880s by the Jenny Lind, one of several types of polishing machine. This machine was named after the popular Swedish opera singer who is commemorated in Poet's Corner in Westminster Abbey, the sound of the machine said to resemble her voice! The Jenny Lind was an American invention and William Grant recounts how it came to be re-created in the north-east. According to Grant, the person responsible was George Rose, a young man from Fyvie. Rose was apprenticed to Alexander Macdonald's yard and then spent a couple of years in America before studying medicine at Aberdeen University. While pursuing his studies he worked as a buying agent for an American firm and while up at Heslop & Wilson's Peterhead Granite Polishing Company he described this newer type of polishing machine that he had seen in America. From an advertisement of the machine Heslop & Wilson, aided by the foundry in Peterhead, were able to make a copy of the machine. John M. Henderson of the famous engineering works in King Street, Aberdeen, saw the machine in Peterhead and began to manufacture in a big way from 1886 – no mention of the patent laws![35]

The principle of the Jenny Lind was to move a rotating iron or steel disc across the surface of the stone, grinding the surface down with iron grit and water, then finer carborundum or emery. In essence it was Macdonald's process, described above in 1856, turned on its head. Modified versions of the Jenny Lind were still in use in the 1970s. It is perhaps fitting that Jenny's grave in Great Malvern, Worcestershire, is marked by a monument carved in an Aberdeen granite yard. It was manufactured in 1888 from Swedish granite by Garden & Co. at the Victoria Granite Works in King Street and stands over 9ft high with the top part being a Celtic cross.[36]

Jenny Lind at Excelsior Granite Works c.1910. (Aberdeen Art Gallery and Museums Collection)

Pneumatic Tools

Writing in 1892 Andrew Wilson, of Heslop & Wilson, commented that apart from the fact that modern tools were made of better-quality material, for carving and hewing granite there had been no real improvements in methods since the days of the ancient sculptors.[37] That would all change within three years. Pneumatic hammers or chisels were first used on granite by Arthur Taylor at his yard in Jute Street. The tools were introduced in 1895 with their first real use being by Taylor in 1896 to carve the statue of Hygeia and the four lions at its base, commemorating Elizabeth Duthie's gift of the Duthie Park to the City of Aberdeen. In 1900 Taylor presented these original hammers to the Aberdeen Mechanical Society. According to what Diack had been told Taylor's first tools were cast metal, later replaced by steel. Diack was told the story of the introduction of pneumatic tools in America by a former granite worker, William Christie. This was due to the efforts of Aberdeen man, George Mitchell.

Mitchell had been a letter cutter with Garden & Co., before moving to America. While working there he was hired by the American Pneumatic Tool Company of New York and by demonstrating the capability of these tools he had few problems getting the granite workers of Barre, Vermont, to adopt them. Christie himself then became an agent for the Clement Pneumatic Tool Company of Philadelphia and came to Aberdeen to demonstrate them, the demonstration being carried out on 9 October 1895 as detailed in the *Aberdeen Free Press*. The tools had been used for twelve years in America but the main problem in Aberdeen was lack of proper air compressors and for his first demonstration they improvised and Christie carried out the demonstration at the Lemon Street works of William Thomson, soda water and lemonade manufacturer. Christie used gas from two of Thomson's carbonic acid chargers. Among those present at the demonstration were William Boddie, Robert Gibb, Arthur Taylor, J. Stewart of Garden & Co., John M. Henderson, engineer, Mr Still of Garstin & Son, and Mr Arthur of Bower & Florence. The demonstration was carried out on a large piece of Corrennie stone, one of the hardest granites. The demonstration was a great success with carving, lettering and filleting all being carried out to the apparent satisfaction of the watching granite men. It was claimed that using these tools, 'a skilled workman will turn out the work of 4 to 10 men in a more perfect and efficient manner than is accomplished by the old methods.'[38] Right away, Henderson's gave an undertaking to manufacture the tools. Though not listed as being at the initial demonstration, Alexander Macdonald's almost immediately ordered one.

Taylor operated his first tools with an engine and belt. By the end of November he was using his newly installed Crossley gas engine which also had an air-compressing chamber. This engine drove his ordinary machinery but was also being used in his experiments with pneumatic chisels. Taylor had initially carved a passion flower ornament on a small cross in Rubislaw granite and was experimenting with English and American cutters of different sizes; he found the English ones superior as regards starting and stopping, and fixing and adjusting. He had already calculated that a cutter could produce two or three times as much work using these tools. While commenting favourably on this new technology the *Aberdeen Journal* also suggested that as wage costs were lower in Aberdeen than in America, and the technology needed a considerable capital investment, then its introduction would be limited to those yards which carried out a great deal of fine carving.[39] However, Macdonald's had their plant fitted up in February 1896 and already by 1899 the press was commenting on the transformation that pneumatic tools had made. Intricate work could be carried out in much less time, and this greatly reduced the cost, but there was also less danger that weeks of work could be undone by an error in the use of a hammer. Very delicate work was now possible and many of the yards had introduced this new tool by 1899. That same year, for example, Stewart & Co. had installed an air compressor manufactured by Clayton of Brooklyn. This machine had a storage cylinder capable of maintaining a pressure of 100lbs to the square inch, piping the air the 420ft length of the finishing shed, and with twenty-four taps for working the 'Kotten's pneumatic hammers'. The piping was supplied and fitted by local engineering company John A. Sangster.[40] The extent of the transformation can clearly be seen in photographs taken inside the granite working sheds before and after the introduction of these tools. As early as 1900 adverts appeared in the press for stonecutters experienced in working pneumatic tools. Two years later there were said to be about 600 Kotten pneumatic hammers in use in the city.[41]

Sculptor Bruce Walker contends that you actually need more skill to operate pneumatic tools than traditional tools.[42] Within just a few years, local granite men were using them to carve pieces such as the Aberdeen Coat of Arms on the Electricity Works in Millburn Street and the even more impressive Royal Coat of Arms on the Crown Street entrance to the new Post Office building.

James Taggart's yard 1907, showing pneumatic tools. Image from an advertisement in a supplement to the Bon Accord 1907.

Three men using pneumatic tools on a Celtic cross. (Aberdeen City Libraries)

At the same time as he was testing pneumatic chisels the forward looking Taylor was also experimenting with the use of sand blasting for incised scroll work, lettering etc. The technology came from the glass trade in Manchester and, once again, a local engineer was also involved, in this case William Grant of Fraser Lane. The process involved was described as follows:

> The pattern is first cut out in ordinary paper in the usual way. Then it is transferred by pressure to a specially prepared adhesive film, composed of thin blotting paper, glue and glycerine. This adhesive film is then stuck on to the face of the die, and the parts to be cut are removed with a steel pencil. The face of the die may now be compared to a sheet of drawing paper on which stencil plates have been laid.

Fine sand (or chilled shot) was then blasted through a flexible tube fitted with a nozzle, the operative wearing a helmet like a divers to protect him from the sand. The application of the template film took three hours, but overall the time saved was considerable, an example being given of an ornament being incised in four minutes, work that would previously have taken a stonecutter two days.[43] The materials may have changed and improved but the process as described here is more or less as it was shown in the 1965 film 'Sculpture in granite'.

In 1902 it was announced in the press that a factory for the manufacture of pneumatic tools was to be established in Fraserburgh. Operational two years later, this became the well-known Consolidated Pneumatic Tool Company (CPT), manufacturing tools and machinery for a variety of industries including the shipbuilding granite industries. The same year William Jennings, of H.G. Kotten of New York, acquired a 2-acre site on Merkland Road East to build a workshop to manufacture and repair all kinds of granite tools and to be the British centre for Kotten's tools.[44]

The 'Dunter'

Allardyce, writing in 1905, dates the introduction of the surface cutting machine, worked by compressed air, to 1901.[45] By the following year there were seven of them in use in the city.[46] In the north-east it became known as 'the dunter', with the operator known as 'the dunterman'. It was capable of 70–80sq.ft per day, one eighth of the time a mason would take to do the same work.[47] A chisel with four blunt prongs shaped like a molar, known as the 'tooth tool', was attached to an armoured pipe, delivering an 80lb punch across the surface of a rough block of stone as one of the first stages in the preparation of the block. Allardyce also states that there was another surface cutting machine or planer that came in the same year. It was operated by belt power and could produce 100 sq.ft per day. At the time he was writing there were only two of the latter in Aberdeen. The introduction of the dunter led to a dispute between the Aberdeen Granite Association and the workers' union, over who could operate the machine (see Chapter 12). It also raised concerns over the amount of dust it generated (see Chapter 11). Charles Macdonald's was one of the first to introduce the dunter, described in 1909 as being made by Brunton and Triers and the result of many attempts and failures to produce such a machine.[48]

Local Engineering Companies

Several local engineering companies became involved in supplying tools and machinery for the granite industry. As early as 1873 Alexander Knowles, engineer, of Shuttle Lane, was involved in constructing and running a huge Brunton circular lathe at Macdonald & Field's yard. When pneumatic tools first came into use they were imported from America but local companies were quick to move from repairs and maintenance of these tools to manufacturing them. Diack gives the examples of Consolidated Pneumatic Tools (CPT) of Fraserburgh and the Bon Accord Pneumatic Tool Works.

John A. Sangster was an engineering firm who manufactured polishing machines, saws and cranes. Sangster also exported granite machines, especially to South Africa where he had an agent. In 1891 Sangster patented a stone sawing machine which greatly speeded up the process. Because of the huge cost the machine was not widely adopted but a simplified version was successful.[49]

John M. Henderson was one of the Aberdeen firms most closely associated with the granite industry. Henderson was apprenticed to Abernethy's in Ferryhill and then worked for Barry, Henry & Co., before spending some time in London. On returning to Aberdeen he worked for granite company Macdonald, Field & Co., where he gained experience of working with granite machinery. Using this experience he set up in business himself in Jopp's Lane, first appearing as Henderson & Adam, engineers and blacksmiths, in the Aberdeen Post Office Directory in 1869. Henderson's

Turning lathe *c.*1900. From a supplement to the Bon Accord 1907.

initially specialised in building machinery for the granite industry before expanding and moving to the site they occupied for many years on King Street.[50] Such was Henderson's importance to the industry that on the occasion of his son's marriage in 1901 (to a daughter of prominent granite man James Taggart) granite merchant Robert Gibb described the late John M. Henderson as 'the father of the granite trade in Aberdeen because of the ingenuity he had displayed in inventing and manufacturing machinery by which the trade had been perfected to such an extent that Aberdeen had become famous for the cutting and polishing of granite.'[51] Henderson's built many of the blondins, and under the founder's son they supplied these for companies in England and abroad. They went on to build the huge blondin at Rubislaw Quarry in 1929. In 1896 Henderson's built what was thought to be the largest granite-turning machine in the country. It was for the Aberdeen Granite Turning Company and was capable of turning columns up to 4½ft in diameter, and 20ft in length.[52]

McKinnon's and George Cassie & Son were other local companies who supplied machinery for the granite industry as well as repairing existing machines and tools.

The Future

Throughout the twentieth century the industry continued to develop, not so much new machinery as improvement and refinement of existing technology with new materials etc. Many of the machines and techniques used at the beginning of the twentieth century were still in use towards the end of the granite industry in Aberdeen. This can be seen in Nan Taggart's film *Sculpture in Granite*, filmed in 1965, which shows plug and feathers, dunters and Jenny Linds all still being used.

ALEXANDER MACDONALD, GRANITE POLISHING, AND THE BEGINNING OF THE MONUMENTAL INDUSTRY

Alexander Macdonald is widely credited with introducing polishing into the granite industry, but does he deserve that credit or are there other contenders for this honour? And how much of the traditional story regarding how he came to develop granite polishing is actually true?

Sir Archibald Grant seems to have tried granite polishing in the 1740s, the lapidary workshop was still standing in Monymusk in 1896.[1] This was almost certainly confined to small articles. At the time of the first Statistical Account in the 1790s the minister for Peterhead wrote that the granite there 'admits of the finest polish, and lapidaries are frequently employed in forming it into various shapes for different pieces of furniture.'[2] The minister of Newhills also commented that the granite from that parish was capable of a fine polish.[3] Then there is the oft-quoted advertisement that appeared in the *Aberdeen Journal* in 3 December 1770, from Coline Allan, jeweller and goldsmith in Aberdeen. He was advertising his factory where he was sawing and polishing granite for slabs, tables and chimney pieces, as well as polishing marble tables and gravestones. Allan went on to say that 'it has been found, by repeated experiment, that our common hill-stones are capable of receiving the highest polish, and are as beautifully variegated as any foreign marbles.' In comparison to marble, his granite tables were not affected by wine or vinegar, and he suggested that they were not inferior to Egyptian granite. Whatever the scale of Allan's operation it does not seem to have survived for long, Allan probably died shortly after the advertisement appeared but these examples show that polishing granite was not unknown even before 1800.

One later newspaper account said that a Mr Nelson polished granite by hand on a small scale in Union Place in the 1830s. Dr William Knight of Aberdeen University wrote in the early 1830s that polished granite at that time was confined to the very wealthy and gave the example of the Stanze de Papyri in the Vatican which he said contained as many polished granite vases, tables, columns etc. as the rest of Europe put together. Knight described the process of hand polishing carried on at that time in Aberdeen, sand being rubbed on to smooth the surface then emery to apply the gloss. Rubbers of iron were no use because the oxide of iron stained the stone and was

Alexander Macdonald's headstone in Nellfield
Cemetery, Aberdeen.

impossible to remove. Knight thought that
the first piece of blue granite polished was
in the County Record Office, dating from
the 1770s, a building later demolished. He
also said that the first tombstone in granite was a small slab of blue stone put up in
St Nicholas Churchyard in 1809, and that he
himself erected a red Peterhead headstone
in the same churchyard in 1819, with a few
other headstones having been added since
then. In the context of what he was writing
it can be inferred that these were polished
stones, but that is not definite.[4] Knight's
account, although published in 1835, was
written in 1832 and he seems unaware of
what Macdonald was experimenting with at
around the same time.

One further example, overlooked by
other writers on the subject, comes from
the *Aberdeen Journal* of 1824. The *Journal* reported that a rectangular tomb or monument had
recently been finished the previous year by Mr Milne's yard in King Street. It had been designed
by Aberdeen's premier architect, John Smith, and was made from red granite from the Stirlinghill
Quarry of Low and Gibb. It was described as being one of the finest specimens of masonry in
granite and 'executed and polished in the most correct and elegant manner.' The tomb had been
commissioned by Joseph Hume, MP for the Montrose District of Burghs, and was in memory of his
father, a shipmaster in Aberdeen. So here we have an example not only of a polished granite tomb,
but also the name of another granite yard, a contemporary of Alexander Macdonald. No suggestion
in the *Journal* that this polished granite monument was in any way unusual.[5]

The weight of the evidence is that granite was being polished before Macdonald, but by hand
on a limited scale and for expensive articles. It was not until the arrival in the city of Alexander
Macdonald that the granite polishing and monumental industry really began on a substantial scale
and that Macdonald's contribution was to mechanise the process.

Macdonald was born in Perthshire in 1794, his obituary says at Rannoch but on his gravestone
Foss, just south west of Loch Tummel, is given as his place of birth.[6] Trained as a freestone mason,
he came to Aberdeen around 1820 to carry on that craft and he set up a small yard, somewhere
near the canal basin in the Canal Terrace area, making hearthstones, chimney pieces and Turin
headstones. Macdonald then moved to a bigger yard on the site later occupied by the North Parish
Church (now the Arts Centre). Thus he appears in the first Aberdeen Street Directory of 1824/25

as a stone and marble cutter at 23 King Street and 83 Queen Street (presumably he was at the corner of these two streets. When the church acquired that site in 1829 he moved diagonally across King Street to the corner of East North Street, his address listed as 60 King Street. The commonly cited story is that in the late 1820s he got to hear about polished granite pieces from Ancient Egypt that the Italian explorer Giovanni Battista Belzoni had some years earlier sent to the British Museum. Whether or not Macdonald actually visited London and saw these statues in the Museum, or read about them in published accounts, is open to question. The story of him visiting London may well be a later addition to the legend. One of his early workmen, William Mearns, still working in 1894 after sixty-two years with MacDonald's, told the *Aberdeen Journal* in that year that he knew nothing of a visit to the British Museum.[7] However, the speed with which Macdonald soon won commissions in London suggests he may have had contacts there and did indeed visit the capital. In any case Macdonald is said to have drawn inspiration from the early Egyptians and began experimenting with polishing granite by hand on a small scale. According to William Mearns, 'when the master went up to London he took some granite columns with him and that put him on his feet'. As early as 1832–33 he supplied a polished granite headstone for the newly opened cemetery at Kensal Green in London.

A correspondence in the *Aberdeen Free Press* in 1873 between Macdonald's son and David Stewart, whose father had operated the Aberdeen Combworks, helps clarify the story of Macdonald and machine polishing of granite. John Stewart had addressed a dinner of his tenants at Banchory and in his speech he said that when he moved to Aberdeen in December 1830 he had supplied a belt from his steam engine to allow Macdonald to produce the first polished granite ever produced in Aberdeen. Clearly this was not the case and Macdonald junior wrote to the *Free Press* to correct him. From company records he could show that his father had been polishing granite well before 1830. In fact one workman, James Nicolson, had begun with his father in 1823 and worked on a polished granite pedestal for a statue of Earl Grey, the polishing business having already been in operation for two or three years. In a subsequent letter David Stewart, later Sir David Stewart, Lord Provost of Aberdeen, wrote that his father had meant to say that he had supplied power for the first granite ever polished by steam power.[8]

John Stewart of Stewart & Rowell, the Aberdeen Combworks, was a fellow Perthshire man. The works they established in 1830 were in Mealmarket Lane, quite close to the site that Macdonald had moved to in 1829. Stewart had a steam engine which, in the spirit of the time, he allowed Macdonald to utilise in his granite polishing experiments, using sand from the nearby beach as an abrasive. William Mearns described it slightly differently:

At the time I first went to Mr Macdonald's I was a little loonie (boy or young man). There was no machinery, but two old soldiers ca'd a big wheel, and I was pittin' on the stuff (sand). That was in Rodger's Walk. After a while Mr Macdonald got power off Rodger's engine.

Mearns was getting confused, I think, because the combworks itself later moved to Rodger's Walk near Gilcomston Steps, right beside one of the John Street granite works, James Wright & Son, the second major granite works established in Aberdeen.

Clearly Macdonald was polishing granite from his early days, although he was not the only one. He was, however, using hand powered machinery, but polishing granite by hand was very laborious and expensive and the key to future development was mechanisation, especially for turned work such as columns. According to Roderick Gray, Peterhead granite columns supplied for the British Museum and the Fishmonger's Hall in London were supplied in a rough state and polished in London at great expense.[9]

As regards the British Museum, these were presumably the columns of red stone supplied for the King's Library at the Museum, built from 1823–27, the columns being supplied in 1824. There were meant to be twelve columns but the first four were so expensive that no more were bought. Two modern accounts on the Museum, both published in 2002, differ on the detail and cost of these columns. Marjorie Caygill writes that there are four columns of polished Aberdeen granite, the rough columns costing £60 (each?) but that polishing brought the cost up to £1,000 (for four?) and therefore eight of the projected twelve were turned into pilasters.[10] David M. Wilson doesn't state where the columns came from but says there are four polished brown granite columns which cost £2,400 and these are flanked by grey granite wall-shafts (pilasters?).[11] Both agree that the capitals for the columns are in Derbyshire alabaster. According to Knight, writing just eight years after the columns were supplied, the stones came from the Blackhill Quarry near to the Bullers of Buchan and owned by a Mr Erskine. Each block was 21ft 4in long and weighed 10 tons. The price for each, delivered to London was £120. The polishing cost was 30s per square foot, adding £216, to give a total cost for each column of £336, a huge amount. He says there were also four square pilasters of blue Aberdeen granite, with each pilaster being of three pieces.[12]

Who supplied these columns is not clear, though Macdonald did lease a quarry at Blackhill from Erskine if not at that exact time then certainly a few years later, and it seems likely that he supplied the Museum columns as well as the ones for the Fishmonger's Hall in the 1830s. Nor is it clear whether or not London workmen polished the stones or Aberdeen men were sent down to do the polishing. If the latter then possibly Macdonald did after all visit the British Museum and see the Egyptian statues, but as yet this is unproven, and in any case both he and others were already polishing granite without the need to see examples from antiquity.

Polished granite column in British Museum, c.1824.

No doubt by the time William Mearns entered Macdonald's employment around 1832, Macdonald was still experimenting and the headstone supplied to Kensal Green would, at best, have been polished by hand powered machinery. The *Bon Accord Repository* of 1842 stated that:

> In 1834 Mr Alexander Macdonald invented machinery for polishing granite, by which he was able to produce articles, at a moderate price, and of a much finer polish than anything of the sort ever manufactured before in this country. He also erected machinery for sawing and polishing, which still further reduced the price of labour.[13]

By 1836 Macdonald still advertised as a marble and stone cutter at 60 King Street, but also as a steam power manufactory at the east end of Constitution Street, the beginning of his Aberdeen Granite Works there. This is confirmed by the recollections of Alexander Gordon, published in the *Buchan Observer* of 6 January 1903. Gordon had joined Macdonald in 1837 and at that time Macdonald had the freestone and marble works in King Street but had opened his polishing works in Constitution Street. Gordon recalled that apart from house masons there were only himself, three other journeymen masons and an apprentice in the whole of the city. Gray, writing in 1839 or just before, more or less confirms this account when he wrote that Macdonald had been polishing granite manually but that around two years before he was writing he had invented steam-powered polishing, built the new premises at great expense and that the business had been even more successful than he had expected.[14]

Macdonald was soon in partnership with William Leslie, the *Bon Accord Repository* says 1835, some sources giving the date 1834 and others 1839, the latter was certainly the date when they first advertised as Macdonald & Leslie in the Street Directory. They continued to have two premises, now 71 King Street, as well as 42 Constitution Street. Leslie is sometimes described as an architect, but was perhaps more of a mason (in fact John Morgan describes him as a mason and a railway contractor).[15] He had, in fact, been the builder for architect John Smith's North Parish Church before going into business with Macdonald. I would imagine that Macdonald took care of the growing monumental side of the business, and Leslie looked after the construction side. The latter involved some significant construction projects with Macdonald & Leslie being responsible, in 1846, for the railway viaducts between Aberdeen and Devanha and over the Dee at Polmuir. They also rebuilt Dunrobin Castle to the designs of Sir Charles Barry.

Granite quickly proved to be a much sought-after material for monumental work. Once it could be polished by mechanical means it could compete with other materials on appearance and to some extent cost, but was also far more durable than marble or any other polished material. Initially the monumental work was mainly for flat pieces such as gravestones and pedestals for statues. There was also early use of non-polished granite in monumental work. In 1832 a precursor to the McGrigor obelisk was erected near Crieff. Modelled on Cleopatra's Needle, this was to commemorate General Sir David Baird and it originally stood over 80ft high (a lightening strike knocked a few feet off in the 1870s), and was described as being of Aberdeen granite. No manufacturer is given but at this early date it may well have been Macdonald & Leslie. Two years later Aberdeenshire quarries also provided the stone for the base and column on which stood the Duke of York's bronze statue. The stone was fine-axed rather than polished, the total height of the column and base around 124ft, the column being designed by Benjamin Wyatt. By the time that Queen Victoria and Prince Albert first came to Aberdeen in 1848 Macdonald & Leslie's fame was such that Albert left the royal yacht the day before the Queen and one of the places he visited in the city was their granite yard.

The company received numerous prestigious commissions both during and after the life time of the two founders. These included the pedestal for the Duke of Wellington's statue in London in 1844, a near-run thing to get it in position before the anniversary of the battle; in 1846 the massive recumbent tombstone, 7ft long by 6½ft wide and weighing nearly five tons, in red Peterhead granite from their quarry at Stirlinghill, for Sir Walter Scott's grave at Dryburgh Abbey;[16] the recumbent figure on the tomb of General Sir Charles Napier at the Royal Garrison Church at Portsmouth in 1853; the tomb in Rubislaw and Peterhead granite of James Kershaw, MP and mill owner in West Norwood Cemetery, designed c.1864 by the famous Victorian architect Alfred Waterhouse and now Grade II listed. This latter is one of eight known Macdonald monuments at Norwood.[17] In the late 1840s, polished granite columns were supplied for St George's Hall in Liverpool. In *Granite Chips* in 1895 these were described as small columns, said to have occupied nearly the whole workforce for about eighteen months.[18] Presumably these were the red Peterhead columns, some of which were moved shortly after, c.1852, to accommodate the organ in a remodelling and finishing of the building by C.R. Cockerel in the early 1850s, following the death of the original architect, Harvey Elmes, in 1847. There are reputedly also some red Isle of Mull granite columns in the building. Four of the columns were sent to Sefton Park, where they are still part of the Aigburth Road entrance. St George's Hall also has eight polished granite columns in Cairngall granite, still *in situ*, and definitely not small, each being 18ft high.[19] I imagine that Macdonald must have supplied these as well since there would have been no other granite manufacturer in Aberdeen who was capable of such work at the time, though Wright's later acquired a reputation for turned granite columns. Nearer home, in 1863 they provided the base for the bronze statue of Prince Albert originally sited at the junction of Union Street and Union Terrace in Aberdeen. The under base was of finely dressed grey granite, with the pedestal of polished red Peterhead stone. Macdonald's also erected a travelling crane to raise the statue on to the pedestal.

The *Aberdeen Herald* wrote in 1854 of an unnamed wealthy nobleman who had ordered a complete mausoleum in polished Aberdeen and Peterhead. Egyptian in stye, it contained considerable amounts of carved ornamentation. The *Herald* was somewhat critical of this extravagance, even labelling it absurd, and stated that the amount spent on it was five or six thousand pounds (a phenomenal amount if true). However, as the *Herald* commented, the stonecutters of Aberdeen weren't complaining.[20] More modestly, in 1861 Macdonald's were preparing a sarcophagus for the Royal Mausoleum at Frogmore. This was for Queen Victoria's mother, Princess Victoria of Saxe-Coburg-Saalfield, also known as the Duchess of Kent. The *Aberdeen Journal* described the sarcophagus as being of blue granite; it may have been Cairngall:

some six tons in weight, hollowed out to the requisite depth entirely by the chisel, after the surface polishing had been finished. The top is a splendid slab nearly four tons in weight, the upper surface bevelled from the edges upward. Under the body of the sarcophagus are four moulded supports resting on a sub-plinth. The length is about eight feet by four feet in width, five in height. In style the sarcophagus is chaste and simple, with nothing in the way of ornament save plain mouldings.

The *Journal* also commented that polished granite columns and pillars were now being used to a considerable extent on Gothic buildings and, as if to emphasise the point, Macdonald's were also also working on around twenty polished red Peterhead granite columns for the extremely prestigious memorial to the Great Exhibition, unveiled in 1863 and originally sited in the Royal Horticultural Society Gardens, it was later moved to just beside the Royal Albert Hall. The finished monument contains eight columns with eight corresponding pilasters or alae behind them. Parts of the pedestal are also of polished Peterhead granite, the monument itself being topped by a bronze statue of Prince Albert. The geographical range of Macdonald's commission can be shown by the fact that they were also completing a 25ft-high memorial cross which was to be sent as far as China to mark the grave of William de Normann, a young attaché to the Earl of Elgin, who was killed

Royal Sarcophagus at Macdonald's yard c.1861. This illustration appeared in *Aberdeen: Century of Change*, by architect and local historian Fenton Wyness. Wyness states that the photograph shows Macdonald Jnr, and foreman Robert Fergusson. Unfortunately he doesn't say which one is which. Macdonald would just have been 30 years of age at this time so it seems likely that he is the young man in the dark jacket at the back and that this was before he ended up in a wheelchair. The older Fergusson would therefore be the man in the top hat with the wonderful facial hair. (Aberdeen and Aberdeenshire Archives)

while being held prisoner by the Chinese during the Second Opium War. Between their quarries and the granite works, Macdonald & Leslie were employing around 200 men in 1861.[21]

Perhaps the single most prestigious commission the firm undertook was the Royal Sarcophagus at Frogmore following Prince Albert's sudden death, also in 1861. According to the Royal Windsor Website the single block of Cairngall granite used for the sarcophagus was said to be the largest block of flawless wrought granite in existence and was the fourth one to be quarried at Cairngall, the first three being rejected because of flaws in the underside. The block for the sarcophagus weighed over 33 tons and measured 10ft x 8ft x 4ft.[22] According to Diack it needed twelve Clydesdales to pull from the quarry to Aberdeen. He quotes Robert Fergusson as saying that after being shaped the stone weighed 18 tons, and once hollowed out and polished it was reduced to 9 tons, with the lid also a single stone of Cairnagall, weighing 4½ to 5 tons.[23] Diack makes no mention of there having been three aborted attempts at providing an unblemished stone.

Macdonald & Leslie exhibited at the Great Exhibition in London in 1851, winning the Prize Medal there for granite vases. In 1855 Macdonald's were selected by the Privy Council to exhibit pedestals and an obelisk at the Paris Universal Exhibition, where he was also awarded a Silver Medal. In the Building, Decoration and Memorial section of the International Exhibition, held in London in 1862, Macdonald's exhibited a polished red granite column, a polished red pedestal with vase, a grey granite headstone, fine axed showing the difference between fine axing and polishing, a polished red and blue granite gothic illuminated baptismal font (the first experiment in contrasting colour and gilt with polished granite), a polished blue granite tomb (made from the same stone as their sarcophagus for the Duchess of Kent's tomb at Frogmore i.e. probably Cairngall), and a polished red granite chimney piece. Elsewhere in the exhibition they also displayed a polished red granite drinking fountain. The granite column demonstrated how Macdonald's built a column in pieces, with flush joints using a process which they patented in 1857.[24] They subsequently, as Macdonald & Field, exhibited in Paris in 1867 and 1878, as well as Philadelphia in 1876 and Melbourne in 1880. In 1867 they were the only Aberdeen granite yard to exhibit at Paris and they sent five pieces, among them a polished runic cross of Peterhead granite, 11ft high, and a classical column of Cairngall granite, 10ft 6in in height. They also exhibited two moulded balusters similar to ones they had supplied for the new Opera House in Paris, designed by Charles Garnier.[25] Eventually the company received the Royal Warrant from Queen Victoria, 'following which commissions poured in from nearly every country in Europe.' – a point later made by Fenton Wyness in a caption to a photograph of the tomb of Napoleon III in Macdonald's yard at Constitution Street: 'Queen Victoria was undoubtedly the monumental industry's most valued patron.'[26]

In William Leslie accompanied Harriet Beecher Stowe, author of *Uncle Tom's Cabin*, and her husband during their visit to Aberdeen. As part of the visit they went to Macdonald's yard which was described by Stowe:

We went to the marble yard, where they work the Aberdeen granite. This granite, of which we have many specimens in America, is of two kinds, one being gray, the other of a reddish hue. It seems to differ from other granite in the fineness and closeness of its grain, which enables it to receive the most brilliant conceivable polish. I saw some superb columns of the red species, which were preparing to go over the Baltic to Riga, for an Exchange; and a sepulchral monument, which was going to New York. All was busy here, sawing, chipping, polishing; as different a scene from the gray old cathedral as could be imagined.[27]

At this stage in the company's development all their work was manufactured to order and around the time that Harriet Stowe visited the yard they employed 120 men.[28]

One of Macdonald's last commissions, completed just before his death in 1860, was the McGrigor obelisk. Now in the Duthie Park, it was designed by architect Alexander Ellis and artist James Giles and originally stood in the quad of the old Marischal College. It commemorated Sir James McGrigor, pioneer of the army medical department and one of the founders of the Aberdeen Medico-Chirurgical Society, and it really is a monumental piece of granite. It stands 72ft high and is mostly of polished Peterhead granite with an inscription panel in Cairngall granite. Above ground it was estimated to contain 250 tons of granite, with another 50 tons for the foundations. In 1896 a newspaper article commented 'to shift the obelisk to another site would, therefore, cost several hundred pounds.'[29] That, of course, is exactly what was intended to happen to it around that time when Marischal College was rebuilt.

Leslie retired from the business in 1853 or 1855, and he subsequently became a councillor and eventually Lord Provost in 1869. Macdonald carried on the business on his own until his death, always very much hands-on. John Morgan recounted a tradition in the profession that Macdonald never allowed an inscription to go to the letter-cutters until it had received his personal revision.[30] Obituaries were not common at that date but the comments of journalist William Carnie, written at the time and later published in his *Reporting Reminiscences*, show the importance of Macdonald to the city:

> It would be difficult indeed to calculate the amount of labour and money the deceased gentleman and his partner in business brought (and may be said to be still bringing) to this quarter. Macdonald and Leslie soon became known world-wide for the artistic excellence of their granite productions, and the lasting beauty of the stone employed. Rich, costly, elaborate memorials for places of sepulture; pillars and columns of vast size for important public buildings; fountains; cemetery head-stones, and for other purposes. Their adoption of the beautiful Peterhead granite proved a great success.[31]

After Macdonald's death the business was run by trustees for three years before his son, also Alexander, took over and ran it for the rest of his life. This was despite Macdonald junior being paralysed and in a wheelchair for the last twenty years of his life. The younger Alexander Macdonald, usually known by his property of Kepplestone, eventually took as his partner a London architect, Sidney Field, and they became Macdonald, Field & Co. Field is credited with the design of the many of the monuments that the yard produced. Field retired in 1883 and Macdonald carried on alone under the name Macdonald & Co. Macdonald of Kepplestone became a noted art collector and, after his death in 1884 at the early age of 47, his art collection became one of the corner stones of Aberdeen Art Gallery.[32] John Morgan described him as a shrewd businessman who amassed a fortune reputed to be £45,000 at his death, a third of this going to the Art Gallery.[33]

A visiting American journalist gives us a description of Macdonald's premises in 1875:

> The first thing that struck me on entering the premises was the arrangement of the front. Here were a number of specimens of the firm's workmanship, and about them were finely-gravelled walks, pretty little hedges, and beds of blooming flowers. In front of this bright spot was a paved street and rumbling traffic; back of it were clinking hammers and stone dust. What on earth do you suppose the firm went to that expense for? I am speaking to you American cutter of marble, with your crowded yard and disordered premises.[34]

He goes on to describe the polishing process and the kind of monuments the firm were producing at that time. While wandering round the yard he was even attacked by the firm's watch dog, coming bounding out of an unnoticed kennel. Luckily it was actually chained but it did cause him to leap over an obelisk that he later found was valued at £125!!

After the death of Macdonald of Kepplestone, his trustees sold the firm to a limited liability company for £40,000. Among the original directors of the company were John Morgan, James Matthews, architect and provost, and Robert Fergusson, Macdonald's long serving foreman and manager. Fergusson was a key figure in Macdonald's, but one who is often overlooked. He came from Blair Atholl in Perthshire, his father being a distant relative of Macdonald senior. After spending a year in the polishing trade, in 1842 Fergusson began to serve his apprenticeship as a mason. Scarcely two years into his apprenticeship he was sent with another young mason, one Adam Mitchell later to be a major building contractor in Aberdeen and uncle of John Morgan, to dress the prestigious pedestal for the Duke of Gordon's statue. Mitchell and Fergusson had, in fact, started as apprentices on the same day. Fergusson, along with Mitchell, was also sent to work on Dunrobin Castle and then on the Polmuir Railway viaduct in 1849, ending the year as foreman mason. On the death of the polishing foreman at Macdonald's Fergusson took charge of both departments, running the business himself during the period of the trustees. Fergusson played an important role in the helping the company's technological innovations. When Field came into the company as partner Fergusson was made a junior partner, and again ran the company after Macdonald of Kepplestone's death in 1884. When it became a limited company he was made managing director, finally retiring in 1893 after fifty-two years in the granite trade.[35]

The history of the company gives an indication of the enormous growth in the granite industry from the middle years of the nineteenth century onwards. Macdonald senior began the business with just himself in the 1820s and, by the time of his death they employed around 200 men in in their quarrying and polishing works.[36] At their high point they are estimated to have employed around 400 men. They took on their own quarries, mainly in the Peterhead area, including Cairngall, but they also operated one of the quarries at Rubislaw at one time. Eventually they were floated as a public company with Lord Provosts Matthews and Jamieson on the board. They even had offices in Euston Road, London and in Glasgow in the 1890s. In 1907 their site covered about 4 acres. However, in 1911 they went into liquidation and were taken over by Henry Hutcheon. Hutcheon's father had actually served his apprenticeship with Robert Fergusson under Macdonald senior.

Early Development of the Granite Yards

Macdonald's work in polishing granite really created an industry and numerous other firms, large and small, sprung up in Aberdeen and Peterhead. In 1861 the *Aberdeen Journal* wrote that other firms, though on a smaller scale than Macdonald's, were doing a steady and prosperous business.[37] James Wright was probably the first to follow Macdonald. He established his business in 1850, though Wright had been working as a stonecutter earlier than this (see Appendix 1). Wright joined Macdonald in exhibiting at the Great Exhibition in 1851, earning an honourable mention for a granite headstone. He also joined Macdonald at the International Exhibition in London in 1862, where he exhibited a red granite hexagonal monument and a column with an ornamented vase on top.[38] The *Granite Chips* column 1898 reported on one of Wright's long-serving workers, John Gillies. Gillies had been born in Glendaruel in 1825 but at the age of 25 he moved to Glasgow to work as a marble polisher. He came to Aberdeen at the request of James Wright to work on marble, and more than forty-six years later he was still working for the company at the age of 73. According to Gillies, when he joined Wright's in 1852 Macdonald's and Wright's were the only firms in the area who had machinery and although Wright's did a considerable amount of work in marble, they only had three granite masons. As the marble work declined Gillies transferred to granite work and he was responsible for polishing all the mantelpieces for Balmoral Castle, the company itself later becoming the Royal Granite Works.[39] Wright's advertised in 1856 that their granite monuments were priced low because they were using steam power for sawing, rubbing and polishing. They also claimed to be the largest and most varied supplier of chimney pieces in Aberdeen, not just in Aberdeen and Peterhead granite but also marble and enameled slate.[40]

In 1866 a series of three articles appeared in the *Scotsman* newspaper detailing the granite industry in the north-east. The third of these described the developments and improvements in polishing carried out by Macdonald. This led to an extraordinary anonymous letter castigating the paper for 'puffing up' Macdonald, Field & Co. and Messrs John Fraser & Son, while ignoring other equally worthy granite companies especially: the John Street Granite Works of James Wright & Sons, which it said was established in 1850; the King Street Granite Works of William Keith junior, established in 1856; Robertson & Hunter's Granite Works in Wellington Road; and Westland & Florence's Works on the Spital. The writer goes on to say that Macdonald didn't even discover the process of polishing, citing the Coline Allan advertisement mentioned above. Was this a case of professional jealousy or was there a flaw in the Macdonald story? It's difficult to be sure especially as the author of the letter didn't give his name. His letter does, though, show some of the other yards that were already in operation.[41]

Once the yards were able to polish granite the whole field of funerary work opened up to them, with crosses, vases, urns, pedestals as well as even larger funerary monuments. For all of the nineteenth century it was a luxury product, as pointed out by William Boddie at the annual dinner of the Aberdeen Master Mason's Association in 1880 'it was only when a man had a surplus that he wanted a monument.'[42] This was something the workers used as an argument in their wage negotiations. In 1893 they asked for an increase only to be told that the employers couldn't afford it because the McKinley Tarifff in America had reduced their profits. The men's answer was that 'the people who wanted monuments were the capitalist class and a small percentage added to the cost of the production would not deter them.'[43]

Drinking fountains and troughs were another popular use of granite with occasions such as Queen Victoria's jubilee bringing orders for fountains from all over the country. Even as early as 1858 there were eighteen fountains waiting at Macdonald's yard to be sent out to various locations.[44] Granite was much more durable than other stone, such as marble, for outdoor use, and this made it attractive. Polished and other granite pieces could also be exported and this became a huge growth area for the granite yards, for a time. North America, France, Russia, South America as well as colonies such as Australia, New Zealand and South Africa, were all areas where north-east polished granite was sent in the latter years of the nineteenth century. The export of finished granite products, especially to America, is examined in more detail in Chapter 7.

Polishing in Peterhead

The first granite polishing yard in the Peterhead areas was established by John McGlashan, a local quarrymaster, in 1861, south of the town at Invernettie, where the Glenugie Distillery was later built. He soon moved to Millbank near Boddam and despite McGlashan himself moving to New Zealand in 1871, probably because his quarry business went bankrupt, the polishing firm continued as the Peterhead Granite Polishing Company taking a fifty-seven-year lease on the site at Millbank from George Lendrum of Stirlingbrae. [45]According to Tom Donnelly[46] McGlashan's creditors formed a new firm and paid off McGlashan's debts. This firm became Heslop & Wilson. Donnelly lists the creditors as Thomas and William Heslop, leather merchants in Peterhead; George C. McGlashan, a merchant in Peterhead; George McCrae, a stonemason from Stirling Village; George Rettie, a crofter from Stirlinghill; Robert Ritchie, a crofter/shoemaker from Stirlinghill; and Betty Marcus also from Stirlinghill.

William Heslop's obituary says that he initially went into his father's leather business but then became a successful fish curer. He then bought McGlashan & Co. brewers, a business he carried on at the same time as the granite business. Heslop's obituary describes him as a brewer rather than a granite merchant and, in fact, says that he only took an active part in the business for three or four years. He also served for fourteen years as a councillor in Peterhead from 1874-88.[47] It seems more than likely that Andrew Wilson really ran the company, though in the early years one of the partners, George McCrae, was manager before he moved to the Great North of Scotland Granite Company. Wilson was the one who gave a very detailed talk on the granite industry to the Buchan Field Club in 1892 and he obviously had a detailed knowledge of the granite industry. As well as the granite polishing works the company owned and ran a number of quarries on the Buchan area including Rora, Bog, and Longhaven.

In 1868 a private company, with Alexander Stuart as the senior partner, began polishing at premises near the railway station in Peterhead. This company was taken over by the Great North of Scotland Granite Company Limited in 1871. The company introduced a considerable amount of polishing machinery. According to James Findlay the company shareholders were mainly resident in

Andrew Wilson of Heslop & Wilson, and his wife.

Edinburgh but employed William Stuart, Alexander's nephew, as its first manager. He was followed by Councillor William Morton. Findlay says that they employed seventy men in Peterhead and thirty at their quarry at Blackhills.[48]

Among the monuments made from the red Peterhead granite Diack lists the Strathcona Mausoleum in London, the tomb of Richard Cobden, MP, the pedestal of Sir Francis Drake's statue at Plymouth, the pedestal of Wellington's statue in front of Buckingham Palace. One impressive monument sent to America in 1876 by Heslop & Wilson was the Lick Monument, which is detailed in Chapter 8.

Granite Monuments in Public Places

Wealthy Victorians perhaps saw it as their duty to spend part of their wealth on great public works. This was an era when many of our great parks were established – in Aberdeen the Victoria and Duthie Parks for example. Within these parks and in public spaces in town centres they were keen to commemorate the heroes of the age – leading politicians, generals, leaders of empire, as well as more local people and events. This provided a great source of work for the granite yards. In the Victoria Park representatives of the granite trade erected a fountain displaying fourteen different types of granite (see Chapter 8). In the Duthie Park there are numerous magnificent granite monuments. The re-located McGrigor obelisk has already been mentioned. There are also two granite memorials to the Gordon Highlanders; the lovely little Temperance Fountain of pink/gray/white granite, once known as the Blue Ribbon Fountain because it was funded by more than 16,000 people each giving 1 penny for a blue ribbon to commemorate the Blue Ribbon Army Temperance Parade; the Taylor Well commemorating a local merchant; and the magnificent Duthie Fountain, from Macdonald's own yard, of red Peterhead granite with four carved swans out of whose beaks water ran at the opening of the park, as it does again today. The granite statute of Hygeia is particularly noteworthy. It is set on top of a Corinthian Column in Kemnay granite with four lions in Corrennie granite at the base and commemorates Miss Duthie, donor of the park. It was designed by John Cassidy of Manchester and sculpted by Arthur Taylor at his yard in Jute Street, the first use of pneumatic hammers to sculpt granite, as detailed in Chapter 4.

The Tillycorthie Fountain, as it is now known, stands in Hazlehead Park. Originally it was located in the New Market building in Market Street, Aberdeen. It was manufactured in polished red Peterhead granite in 1883 by John Fraser & Sons at North Broadford. It was said to have been an exact replacement of an earlier fountain that was destroyed by the great fire at the market the previous year. The original was probably manufactured by Macdonald & Leslie who were involved in the building of Market Street. Two large circular pedestals, also of polished Peterhead granite, were erected at the top of the basement stair in the market. They carried iron gas lamps, and one of them stands today near the entrance to the cafeteria at the Duthie Park.[49] At some point the fountain was moved to Tillycorthie House near Udny, built in 1912 by James Rollo Duncan, a local man who made his fortune in the tin mines of Bolivia. The fountain was certainly there in 1933 when a photograph of it appeared in the *Press & Journal*.[50] The University of Aberdeen bought the Tillycorthie estate in 1953 and at a later date, possibly 1978, the granite fountain was returned to Aberdeen and sited at Hazlehead.

Case Study: Alford Fountain

Duthie Park is quite exceptional in the number of granite monuments it houses, but granite monuments can be found all over the north-east. The one illustrated here is from Alford. It is a memorial fountain to Robert Farquharson of Haughton and is positioned in front of the Haughton Arms Hotel. It was designed by Alexander Hogg, a road surveyor in Alford, and made by the Royal Granite Works of James Wright & Sons. Wright had quarries at Peterhead and at Sylavethie near Alford and three types of granite were used in this fountain. From the *Aberdeen Journal* we learn that:

the basins in the north, south and east sides are of finely axed Sylavethy. The delivery urn between them is of polished Peterhead. The four columns with bases and capitals are of Sylavethy with shafts of polished Peterhead. On top of these is a massive block of Sylavethy, cut with richly-moulded arches, forming a groin arch above the centre urn; immediately above this is the cornice, richly moulded, the frieze of polished Peterhead. From the top of the cornice the structure diminishes towards the finial in a spirelet form, from the sloping sides of which are constructed the inscription panels. These are encased in polished Peterhead columns. The panels are of polished Corennie with a ball of polished Peterhead on top.[51]

The use of different granites to obtain a colour contrast was common, both in monuments and buildings, though the range of colours available in the north-east was quite limited. This monument is a fine example of north-east workmanship, the type of monument people will pass every day without giving a thought to the work that went into creating it.

Granite Sculpture and Granite Statutes

Even in the Granite City today there are very few granite portrait statues. For a sculptor granite was difficult to work in a studio situation, it was also difficult for the artist to really express themselves in this most unyielding of materials. In the few granite statutes that do exist it is usually the case that the sculptor designed the statue and the granite yard executed it, with the sculptor possibly adding a few final touches. Granite was more commonly used for the pedestals of statues, the latter made in bronze and other materials. At the high point of the granite industry in the last decade of the nineteenth century there was considerable debate in the press and elsewhere on the merits or otherwise of using granite in formal sculpture. The debate was led by the eminent sculptor Pittendrigh Macgillivray, born in Port Elphinstone near Inverurie, and responsible for the statue in bronze of Lord Byron outside Aberdeen Grammar School on Skene Street.

The Duke of Gordon's Statue: the first granite statue since Ancient Egypt?

Writing to *The Times* much later in 1935 G.M. Fraser said that there were only three granite statues in the UK, two of them being in Aberdeen and one at Greenwich. The one at Greenwich was of William IV by the sculptor Samuel Nixon. The two in Aberdeen were the statue to George Gordon, 5th Duke of Gordon, once at the Castlegate now in Golden Square, and the statue of Priest Gordon by Alexander Brodie, once in St Peter's School in Constitution Street, now on the King Street entrance to St Peters School, Dunbar Street, Old Aberdeen. In a subsequent letter Fraser admitted that he had forgotten another Aberdeen granite statue, the massive one to King Edward VII by Alfred Drury, erected in 1914 at the corner of Union Street and Union Terrace (and difficult to miss!).[52] The first two of these – King William and the Duke of Gordon, vied with each other as to which was the first to be erected. The *Bon Accord Repository* published in 1842 stated that the statue of the Duke, then under completion, was:

> The first attempt that has been made in Europe of making a statue in granite, and good judges
> have pronounced it the most proper material for colossal statutes. Its appearance, we are persuaded,

will convince the public that Aberdeenshire granite is capable of being turned to more useful and ornamental purposes than it has been hitherto.[53]

The King was placed on his pedestal in December 1844 and the Duke in April the same year, but in fact the Duke of Gordon's statute was actually finished in 1842, and can therefore claim to be the first granite statue in the country. The delay in erecting it was due to the debate over the choice of site, a wooden replica was made and tried out in various locations before they decided on the Castlegate.

At the time of the unveiling of the Duke of Gordon's statue, James Giles, the renowned painter, claimed that it was the first granite statue in 2,000 years (since Ancient Egypt). The *Aberdeen Journal* had earlier commented that it was the first statue to be executed in granite in modern times: 'the singular instance of the triumph of genius and art over difficulties which, since the days of the Ptolemies, have been deemed unsurmountable.'[54] Whether or not that was true is very difficult to verify, but it was certainly the first granite statue in Britain. No one seems to know whose idea it was to carve the statue in granite, something that would be really interesting to know. The Committee of Nobleman and Gentlemen convened to raise funds for the statue comprised – the Earl of Aberdeen, the Duke of Richmond, the Marquis of Huntly, Charles Fraser, and R.D.A. Horne-Elphinstone. On 13 July 1839 this committee entered into a contract with the artist Thomas Campbell of Edinburgh and London to erect a granite statue of the Duke 10ft high on a 10ft pedestal. Campbell was to be paid 2,000 guineas in stages, with 500 of those guineas being for the granite. It is not clear if that was simply for the granite itself or for any of the work that was mostly done in the granite yard. Certainly the balance of 1,500 would be a huge payment for the amount of work Campbell actually did![55]

The statue was actually carved by Macdonald & Leslie's yard from a block of Dancing Cairns granite of around 17–20 tons, the red pedestal was from their quarry at Stirlinghill. The block for the statue was carried on a large waggon pulled by ten horses assisted by about 100 men, the waggon subsequently finding a home in Macdonald's yard, though too large for their normal work. Robert Fergusson who, as we have seen above, along with the young Adam Mitchell, helped with the pedestal for the statue, dispelled some of the myths regarding the statue in a letter to the *Journal* in 1895. These related to the statute being carved somewhere near Castle Street and the sculptor and two carvers refreshing and toasting themselves 'unduly'. According to Fergusson a wood and brick tile-covered shed was built at the Aberdeen Granite Works in Constitution Street to house the statue. He names the two carvers as Alexander Chalmers and James Mann, and when he joined as a young apprentice in March 1841, one of them had already done the forehead and nose, the other the two hands resting on the sword. The shed was later used as a polishing shed and was known as the 'Duke's House'. The work took three years and, according to Fergusson, Campbell didn't come to Aberdeen until the work was completed. He then 'went through the performance of taking a chisel and doing a few scrapings, to bring out the artistic effect, as he said'.[56] The *Aberdeen Journal* was a little more flattering to the sculptor: 'Mr. Campbell has just paid a visit to the city, for the purpose of giving this most successful achievement of his talents and skill those finishing touches which no hand save that of the artist can effectively impart.'[57]

The importance of the unveiling of the statue was realised in far away London where *The Times* printed a paragraph from the *Aberdeen Herald* dealing with the occasion. At the same time the *Aberdeen Journal*, in praising the quality of the work, predicted that granite would supersede bronze and other materials to perpetuate the memory of the 'great and the brave'.[58] This never really happened, though some people were convinced of the qualities of granite for statuary work, particularly its ability to last outside. Robert Fergusson once offered to make a granite facsimile of Brodie's marble statue of Queen Victoria in Aberdeen. The latter, of course, was taken into the Town House to protect it from the elements after only twenty years outside. It was Fergusson himself who took down the statue which he found all cracked. He had to bind the cracks with brass clamps, later disguised with plaster of Paris.

J.M. Bulloch was one local figure who joined in the debate over granite statuary in the late nineteenth and early twentieth centuries. Bulloch was a prolific writer, journalist, historian, graduate of Aberdeen University, later given an honorary doctorate for his work on the history of the University. Writing about the Duke's statue in 1904, he lamented that fact that although James Giles, writing sixty years before, hoped that it might ultimately lead to valuable results, 'the results of this splendid beginning are, to say the least of it, extremely disappointing. A new heaven and a new earth have certainly not dawned for the city in point of beautifying itself with statuary.' He also commented that not a single history of the city dwelled in any way on the importance of this first granite statue. He said that even the sculptor's entry in the Dictionary of National Biography fails to mention that he ever carved a granite statue.[59]

G.M. Fraser was presumably using a very narrow definition of granite statue when he said there were only three or four in the UK. The recumbent figure on Sir Charles Napier's tomb at Portsmouth, mentioned earlier, was certainly a statue, and by the time Fraser was writing in 1935 there were granite figures sculpted as war memorials throughout Aberdeenshire, including the lion on the Aberdeen War Memorial. Presumably he did not count these as granite statues because he was talking about portrait statutes, for the same reason he would not have included the statue of Hygeia in the Duthie Park.

The debate in which Pittendrigh Macgillivray became involved in the 1890s had been prompted by the *Aberdeen Journal*'s arguing that a proposed monument to the eminent biologist Thomas Henry Huxley should be made of Aberdeen granite.[60] Huxley had been Rector of Aberdeen University for three years and so the *Journal* felt entitled to an opinion. Macgillivray acknowledged that the ancient Egyptians had used granite for their statutes for the reason that it was available, but he saw the artistic qualities of these statues being based on mass and simplicity. Sculptors of his day were trained to create clay models and then work in marble or bronze.[61] He was talking about figurative sculpture and he didn't think sculptors could adequately portray people or create a sufficiently 'artistic' piece using granite. For him expression and thought could not be produced in granite nor could you convey love or kindness or tenderness in granite. He would not have seen a design created by a sculptor and then passed to a granite craftsman to carve, as true art. He didn't completely dismiss the possibilities of art being produced in granite and his solution for the future was to set up classes for granite sculptors, with lectures on Egyptian and early Greek sculpture by eminent experts such as the archeologist Flinders Petrie, and award prizes annually for the best models created in granite.[62] In fact Macgillivray did subsequently recommend that a statue be made in granite, the one of the Goddess Hygeia mentioned earlier. He was also not above furnishing designs for granite monuments to be carved by granite masons, as with one he did for the Necropolis in Glasgow in 1899 to commemorate a Glasgow shipowner, carved at Macdonald's yard that year.

As we have seen, J. M. Bulloch was another who promoted the use of granite for statuary work. At a dinner in London in 1906 at the time when a statue of Lord Byron was being proposed, Bulloch said that for many years he had urged Aberdonians to make its statues of its own material. He had been told that fine modelling was impossible in granite but his reply was that they needed to create a technique to suit the material. In his opinion, 'all the tariff reform in the world would never do for granite what a proper appreciation of its sculptural possibilites could do.' The well-known sculptor Albert Toft spoke at the same meeting and he supported Bulloch's views. For him granite shouldn't be used for small figures, but rather where figures of heroic proportions were required. He also thought that bronze should be used with granite, in panels and accessories for example, to lighten and warm up the granite.[63] In fact Toft himself sometimes use fairly elaborate granite pedestals for some of his bronze statues, one example being the Boer War memorial in Cannon Hill Park, Birmingham.

Colonel Innes of Learney was another who spoke in favour of Byron's statue being made of granite. In a speech in 1909 at the presentation of prizes to students in original modelling (whose number included potential granite cutters) at Gray's School of Art, he highlighted how recent advances in steel and in pneumatic tools meant there had been considerable advances in granite sculpture (by which he no doubt meant granite carving as opposed to artistic sculpture). Granite, he felt, could now be carved as easily as marble, yet there was still only one granite statue in the city. He claimed to remember as a child seeing the Duke of Gordon's statue being carved and spoke about the great difficulty in executing the carving, something that would be relatively easy at the time he was speaking. He proposed erecting a granite statue of Byron in front of Marischal College, near to the spot where Byron and his mother had once lodged.[64] As noted earlier, though, the statue of Byron was finally made in bronze not granite, and granite was never used extensively for statuary, other than for war memorials. Bulloch himself would return to his theme many years later, as we shall see below.

Henry Bain Smith (or Bainsmith as he took to calling himself) was one who bridged the gap between granite worker and artist. He had completed an apprenticeship with Macdonald, Field & Co., before his artistic abilities took him to the classes at the Mechanics' Institution and the pre-Gray's school of art. Most of his work was in marble and bronze, including the statue of Robert Burns in Aberdeen which he completed in 1892, the year before his death at the age of 36. He did, however, do some pieces in granite, such as a medallion portrait of James Adam, journalist, which is in Nellfield Cemetery.

King Edward VII's Statue

In the mid 1890s a fund was established to erect a granite statue of former Lord Provost Sir Alexander Anderson. This came to nothing – a great pity, as Aberdonians have all but forgotten this most controversial provost and his many achievements. However, in the early twentieth century a decision was made to erect a staute of King Edward VII. For this statue a huge stone from Kemnay No. 1 Quarry was required. There had been some debate as to whether or not the statue should be made in granite or in some other material, but granite was decided upon. Retired granite merchant and ex-town councillor William Boddie was adamant that the statue could be carved in granite. He recommended Kemnay stone as being the nearest of the north-east stones to marble, if they could get a suitable piece – 'a block with a bed of the granite the right way'. In his opinion it had to be done in Aberdeen:

> to suggest that a work of that kind could be done out of Aberdeen seems to me ridiculous, because we have appliances and men for the purpose that are not anywhere else in the world. Those accustomed to work in marble cannot touch granite at all, because it is so much harder. I have cut in granite innumerable examples of carved work. The models were taken off marble and were said to be even more life-like than marble. Give us a model and we can produce anything in granite to the finest detail.[65]

Initially the plan was to sculpt the statute from two pieces of granite, because it was thought impossible to lift a block large enough. Former north-east granite workers in Barre, Vermont, then offered to supply a large enough stone, guaranteed free of blemishes, and have it shipped across the Atlantic. Apparently monumental sculptor Arthur Taylor, on being told by a Barre man back on a visit to Aberdeen of the huge blocks of stone they were able to get from the quarries in Vermont, had joked that maybe they could send over a stone for the king's statue. The Barre granite workers took him seriously and they even suggested that it was impossible to lift a single block of this size from the depths of Kemnay Quarry. This seems to have stung the pride of the north-east men, one commenting, 'the north-east people will not entertain the proposal at all.'[66] The size of the block was variously given as being between 17 and 23 tons.

The operation itself, in December 1911, was a huge undertaking, supervised by James Argo, foreman at No.1, with John Annand, chief engineer, in charge of the machinery. No new machinery was needed but the steel ropes were strengthened and thoroughly tested. The crane was also strengthened with an additional wire stay rope, the crane having a jib 90ft long overhanging the quarry. The stone had to be raised 300ft from the quarry floor and it took twelve minutes before it was level with the top of the quarry, extra time being needed because the decision was taken to provide double power working through a pinion, not driven directly from the shaft. The quarry floor itself was cleared of workers, most of them remaining at the top to watch the operation. When the block reached the top they had decided that rather than put extra strain on the jib by turning it round mechanically, they would use manual labour and a stout rope to pull the stone and the jib to the side. A large number of quarry workers had willingly lent a hand for the job and the instruction

Detail of Edward VII's statue, Aberdeen.

was 'tak' her canny noo, boys, tak' her canny,' until it was manoeuvered on to land. Most of the population of Kemnay came out to watch. After some preparatory work it was reduced to 15 tons and conveyed to Aberdeen by rail. However, there was no four-wheeled bogie waggon in the area strong enough to carry the stone so one had to be brought from the south. Any bridges on the route into Aberdeen had to be checked and strengthened. The last leg of the journey from the railway to the works was by traction engine.[67]

Designed by Alfred Drury, the statue was largely carved by James Philip of Arthur Taylor's yard from a model made by Drury. This wasn't the only work Taylor did for Drury, another example being the massive 17ft-high pedestal in fifty pieces for Drury's bronze statue of Queen Victoria sent out to Wellington in New Zealand. This pedestal was also done in Kemnay granite. By September 1912 the king's statue was almost finished and Drury turned up to 'give the finishing touches himself'. Drury said that it was a particularly fine piece of granite, possibly as fine as could be found, free from any flaw or crack. The main debate now was where would it be sited? Outside Marischal College was popular since the latter had been opened by the King and the two granite edifices would complement each other. Golden Square was another suggestion as was near to the statue of William Wallace. The final location at the corner of Union Street and Union Terrace was opposed by some since it meant that the statue of Prince Albert had to be relocated and this was seen as an insult to the Royal Family.

James Philip: Artist in Granite?

As well as the statue of King Edward, James Philip also carved the war memorial lion in Aberdeen, designed by Gray's School of Art graduate William Macmillan. Philip wasn't always given the credit he deserved for work such as this lion. Well-known artist and art teacher Charles Hemingway wrote in 1934 about the qualities of this lion as compared to less noble beasts of which he said 'London is a den of them.' He went on to say 'Here is a lion, carved with due regard to the nature of the stone, a monument of supreme dignity, expressive and restrained, most fitting tribute. This is the work of

James Philip carving the lion on Aberdeen's War Memorial, possibly using a pointing machine to take measurements from Macmillan's model. (Aberdeen Art Gallery and Museums Collection)

Part of the monument to Edith Cavell, central London, carved by James Philip.

master craftsmen. The sculptor of the lion is a native of Aberdeen, Mr William Macmillian, a past master of his craft and a rare artist.'[68] No mention of James Philip. Other examples of his work in Aberdeen can be seen in the Peace Statue in the Duthie Park's Winter Gardens and the Alexander Cooper Fountain in Hazlehead Park.

Philip was perhaps the finest exponent of granite carving in any of the Aberdeen yards. Born in Woodside he grew up in Bucksburn. He served his apprenticeship with Arthur Taylor, initially walking the four miles from Bucksburn to Jute Street carrying his breakfast and dinner with him. His working day began at six in the morning and he spent his whole working life in Taylor's yard. On occasion his skills were sought for difficult jobs elsewhere in Scotland and in England. Among work he did in England was the granite work for the memorial to British nurse Edith Cavell, shot by the Germans in Brussels in 1915. The monument is sited in St Martin's Place, near Trafalgar Square in London, the granite itself being Cornish not from a north-east quarry. Part of the memorial comprises a British Lion tramping over the snake of German militarism and Philip said he carved it in a 'quarry hole at Cornwall.' He also carved eight of the twelve figures on the Titanic Memorial in Liverpool, the work being done in a sculptors yard in Manchester. Philip himself considered the statue of the soldier on the Inverurie War Memorial to be his finest work, a superbly detailed figure in pink Hill o' Fare granite on a base of Rubislaw granite.[69]

William Hamilton Buchan

Hamilton Buchan, was one local sculptor who did a considerable amount of work with the granite industry in the early years of the twentieth century. Buchan studied at Gray's School of Art where he won a prize in 1894. He subsequently taught modeling at Gray's, initially as a pupil teacher, then part-time, while at the same time carrying on his own studio in Union Row. William McMillan, who designed the Aberdeen War Memorial lion as well as the British War Medal, was his apprentice. In 1902 Buchan designed and cast a model of Aberdeen's Bon Accord Coat of arms in ten pieces. This was then carved in Kemnay granite, 8ft by 7ft, by masons from the main contractor, Leslie Smith.[70] It was placed high up on the new Electricity Works in Millburn Street where it can still be seen. At the same time he was also modelling a figure of a Cape Mounted Rifleman atop a column with four lions at the base. This monument was also carved at Arthur Taylor's yard and sent to Kokstad in what is now the KwaZulu Province of South Africa, the resulting monument bearing similarities to the statue of Hygeia in the Duthie Park (also by Taylor). The following year he designed and made a model of another statue for South Africa, this time for a Cape Mounted Policeman which stands on top of four columns in Kimberley. This statue was done in Kemnay granite by Alexander Macdonald's yard. In 1908 Buchan made a bust in stucco of granite merchant William Boddie. The bust was then carved in Kemnay granite by James Milne jun. of Robert Milne's yard at Provost Blaikie's Quay, and presented to Boddie at a banquet in the County Hotel. Boddie took the occasion to extol the virtues of granite for sculpture work and stated that he thought this bust was the first granite one ever done in the city.[71]

Royal Coat of Arms on old Post Office, Crown Street, Aberdeen.

Among other work carried out by Buchan was modelling for the decorative plasterwork for the interior of His Majesty's Theatre, and modelling the decorative work for the exterior of the Masonic Temple in Crown Street, this work being carved in granite at the yard of Edgar Gauld in Gilcomston Terrace, the *Aberdeen Journal* commented that he occupied a leading place in the city for this kind of work.[72] The most impressive piece Buchan was connected with was probably the Scottish version of the Royal Coat of Arms in finely-axed Kemnay granite, intended for the new Post Office building in Crown Street. Though little noticed today, at the time this piece of granite sculpture, and in fact, the whole Crown Street frontage, was considered to be some of the finest work that the city had produced. The panel was designed by architect of the building, W. W. Robertson, of H.M. Office of Works in Edinburgh (though carried out by his successor, W. T. Oldrieve whose name is usually associated with the building). Buchan again made an intricate model of the heraldic panel. In fact Buchan made models for all the sculpted work for the building although it had originally been intended to use an Edinburgh sculptor for the work. The *Journal* doesn't indicate who actually carved the coat of arms but the contractors for the building work were Peter Bisset & Sons, though it is possible that this particular part of the work may have been sub-contracted to one of the monumental yards.[73] Buchan went on to be the manager of the Douglas Granite Company, a Glasgow Company who had a short-lived presence in Aberdeen in the years before the First World War.

Artist or Craftsman

Who then is the artist? Is it the man who designs the figure, usually making a maquette in some other material, or the man who actually carves the statue from the granite block? Robert Cruickshank, founder of the Albyn Granite Works, was described as a sculptor in his obituary, rather than as a granite merchant, presumably that is how he saw himself. I think we can guess which side of this argument Pittendrigh Macgillivray would come down on. Macgillivray's comments on granite sculpting were made just at the time that pneumatic tools were being introduced to the granite industry. These would change the dynamic of granite carving, both in terms of what was possible, but also, perhaps, by who could do the work, though both statues mentioned above, done after the introduction of these tools, were carved by James Philip not by the artist who designed them. Philip possibly used a pointing machime to take measurements from the artists's maquette, rather than directly carving them, but who could deny that Philip was an artist as well as a master craftsman, and that surely is the way that the greatest of Victorians, William Morris, would have viewed him.

This issue of granite statues arose again at the time of Arthur Taylor's death in 1930. In the *Bon Accord and Northern Pictorial* of 5 April 1930, there appeared a notice of Taylor's death entitled *The Right Spirit of Granite Sculpture*. This article wrongly credited Taylor with the work on the statue of Edward VII and is full of praise for the statue and the work of Taylor and the sculptor Drury. It suggested that the latter had made allowances for the nature of the material by sketching broader surfaces than he would have if working in bronze. It finds the resulting statue to be 'gratifying to the champions of granite statuary'. The statue had 'dignity and humanity, and shows a remarkable advance in the manipulative possibilities of granite compared with the Duke of Gordon's statue' (of some seventy years before). These comments were like a red rag to a bull for Dr J.M. Bulloch. He fired off a letter severely critical of the comments.[74] The previous year an article had appeared in the same publication also critical of granite sculpture, using the same language and exactly the same examples as Bulloch's. The earlier article was in the by-name of *Olim Civis*, which may be translated as something like old-time or long-standing citizen. I'm fairly sure that both articles were by Bulloch, and therefore I will summarise both of them as one. Bulloch said that the great granite architect, Archibald Simpson, did not try to make granite do the work of freestone. He also said that Drury may have been a fine sculptor but knew nothing of granite otherwise he wouldn't have created a statue in which every detail of real life, 'almost to the motto on the buttons, was faithfully copied by the pneumatic tool. The statue of King Edward is simply a marble statue in granite. It is an outrage to make a statue in granite as if it were in marble.' He almost condemns pneumatic machinery because it 'can torture granite into any shape it pleases.' In both articles he praises the broad, simple lines of McMillan's lion on the war memorial at Cowdray Hall (again not mentioning James Philip). His criticism, though, extends to Victorian lettering on memorials and headstones:

Much Victorian lettering makes a walk through our cemeteries a nightmare. Tortured, finnicking alphabets were used almost to the day when Dr Kelly came on the scene. Our country kirkyards are full of beautiful stones and dignified lettering. But we jettisoned them in the name of fashion.

Our monumental masons should have aimed at becoming the greatest artists in granite in the world, as it is our memorials to the dead have been an eyesore to the living.

Taylor himself does escape criticism:

Your accounts of Mr Taylor seems to indicate that either he did not understand the right spirit of granite or that your contributor does not begin to grasp the Gift of Granite, and that Aberdeen monumental masons are still wallowing among weeping willows, broken guns and shafts, anchors and other realistic objects which should go the way of wax flowers or aspidistras in the empty grate of best parlour. That sort of thing will never make Aberdeen the Granite City it ought to be.[75]

This is wonderful stuff and shows the passions that art (and granite) can arouse. I wonder how Bulloch viewed the way that granite was treated in the wedding cake architecture of Marischal College?

Bulloch, as we have seen, did praise the lion at the War Memorial and he also thought that the lettering on the fire station on King Street was to be recommended. The architect William Kelly is undoubtedly Bulloch's saviour and inspiration, mentioned in both articles. There is no doubt that Kelly did design many dignified memorials with beautiful lettering. He also designed some wonderful buildings, often understated, such as St Ninian's Church on Mid Stocket Road in Aberdeen. Kelly understood granite in a way that harked back to Smith and Simpson. Aberdeen's monumental masons would probably have said they were just meeting the demand and that it was not their job to become true artists and lead demand. In many ways it is a matter of taste and fashion and both of those can change with time.

6

THE LIVES OF
THE GRANITE MEN

An old verse, the hard life depicted being applicable to all granite workers, runs:

> The stonecutter's hand is rough and scarred
> The man's back is stooped and bowed
> His brow close bent above the stone
> With lines of strenuous toil is ploughed
> Small ease his honest years have known
> For labour claims him as their own.

Little or no account of life in the various areas of the granite industry survives earlier than the mid-nineteenth century. Towards the end of that century there are a few examples of men remembering their early days as apprentices where many started very young, and this in an industry that was very physical. Young boys often began as nippers, both in the quarries and in the granite yards. Among their jobs would be to deliver and collect tools from masons and settmakers and take them to the blacksmiths for sharpening. A description of Macdonald's granite yard from *The Builder* in 1877 says that they were assured that the masons' chisels became dull after only a few minutes work and had to be taken to the workshop for re-grinding. After this had been done a few times the chisels became too thick at the end and had to be taken to the blacksmith for more regular re-setting.[1] Plenty of work for these boys and also for general labourers, and they used a wheelbarrow to ferry the tools about. John McLaren describes it as a hard job for a young lad, pushing the barrow around the yard or quarry in all weathers.[2] Up to the middle of the nineteenth century these boys could be as young as seven, and ten was common in the second half of the century and the early years of the twentieth century.

Giving evidence to the Royal Commission on Mines and Quarries in 1911 Professor Matthew Hay, Chief Medical Officer for Aberdeen, commented on the working age of men in the monumental yards:

Peter Innes at Kemnay Quarry, aged 18. He started at the quarry aged 14. Thanks to his son Brian now living in North Carolina, USA.

Stone-cutting as practised in the monumental yards is a distinctly skilled form of work, which has to be done with great care and fineness and also wants a good deal of hard work and activity. The result is that when a man gets to 50 years of age he is getting almost past his best, and when he gets to 55 if he falls out of employment it is very difficult to get back again, and by the time he reaches 60 some excuse is apt to be found for getting rid of him, so that he drifts into common labour, and you do not find so many old men remaining in stone-cutting.[3]

The same might well have been true in the quarries although in both areas the introduction of machinery would have helped with the physical side of the work. Despite this physical nature of the work there were many instances of men still working until quite late in life. In 1953 William Henderson was the oldest employee at Kemnay Quarry. He was then aged 76, having started at the quarry when he was ten years old and between 1903 and 1906 he had gone to America three times.[4] William Spence wrote about two long serving members of staff at Rubislaw Quarry. Robert Stewart was a driller at the quarry for sixty years, starting at the age of 13 when the quarry was 250ft deep. He retired in 1950 when it was 430ft. In 1948 William Coutts was the oldest quarryman at Rubislaw, having worked there for fifty-eight years. He retired at the age of 76, still able to climb the vertical 98ft-high Blondin pylon, oil can in hand, to lubricate the wheels.[5] Examples of settmakers, in particular, can be found working to an advanced age, which perhaps reflects the nature of their work (see below).

As Hay said, some aspects of granite work were highly skilled. In the previous chapter we saw the work of James Philip and how his skill meant that he could be sent to other parts of the country for special commissions. Letterers could also he highly prized. In 1938 Andrew Mutch of Fyfe's told the *Bon Accord* that his best carver was working in Ayrshire doing working on a lettering commission for a 'well known peer. If he does one letter a day, he's doing well, for the work needs a great deal of concentration and patience.'[6]

Quarriers and Quarry Masons

In the days before the use of powered tools the quarry cutters needed to be big strong men. John Ritchie says that in the mid-nineteenth century cutting picks weighed from 16 to 20lb.[7] Initially these were iron tools, with steel tips, much heavier than they were by the end of the century.

The quarry masons themselves had a reputation as rough men. Ritchie tells a story that he had heard from John Fyfe himself. Driving home from Inverurie one day he came upon a lady with a basket of provisions. Fyfe offered her a lift in his gig and as they passed Kemnay quarries she exclaimed, 'Oh there's that Kemnay quarries. That's a man Fyfe he has hauled a' the orra folk i' the face o' God's earth in aboot. Kemnay was a dacent place afore that drunken quarriers.'

Once she had finished, Fyfe said, 'Oh don't be so hard on the quarriers, mistress; I'm a quarrier myself.'

'Guid preserve me,' she said, 'let me oot, and far did you steal the horse and the gig.'[8]

Quarrymen at Rubislaw before the First World War. Second from the left is Sandy Mackie with his cousin next to him, Sandy was the grandfather of Alistair whose verse appeared at the beginning of this book.

Quarry masons were also big, powerful men, splendid workmen, says Ritchie, but he does concede that a few of them liked a drink. He wrote that they often visited the markets in places such as Tarland and Alford, and got the place to themselves![9]

According to Brian Innes, quarrymen did develop the muscles used for their work, but hand drillers, in particular, developed great upper body strength. Some of these drillers were subsequently employed at the Inverurie Locomotive Work, cutting rivets on the boilers of steam engines. They found this work relatively easy and were sometimes told by the union representative to slow down because other workers might be expected to work at the same speed. Brian also said that constantly using the same muscles could eventually give problems, in the same way as modern repetitive strain injury. Tendonitis and atrophying of muscles made it hard for them to work at all, with older men being known to lift their 'haimmer airm' with the other, to allow it to bring the hammer down on the drill.[10]

When Professor Matthew Hay gave evidence to the Royal Commission on Mines and Quarries in 1911, he noted that quarry workers were sensitive to the weather, going home in wet weather. According to Hay, in the previous month or two at Rubislaw around a quarter of the quarrymen's time had been lost in this way. He stated that a fair number of the quarrymen were unmarried and didn't mind losing work. In the quarries outside Aberdeen he said this was even more common because many of the country quarrymen also had a croft and could spend their time off working there.[11]

Carters

Originally the granite blocks were transported to the surface by litters or barrows. Litters were also used to move stone from place to place, at least until road surfaces were good enough to permit wheeled vehicles, hence building stones were known as litter stones. In many of the early quarries local farmers would hire out their carts to transport granite, as we have seen at Torry. An advertisement in 1820 for the let of the lands of Greenburn describes the turnpike roads passing through the lands with Dancing Cairns and other quarries situated there, and 'constant employment for horses and carts may be relied upon.' In March 1826 there was an advertisement for carters at the reopened Dyce Quarry. They were also told that they would find constant employment, carrying stone to the shipping place on the Aberdeenshire Canal or transporting the stone directly into Aberdeen. At the quarry there was a good stable capable of holding four horses and a lodging house for men.[12] The parish minister at Nigg, writing about the quarries at Cove in 1793, noted that the heavy work involved in transporting granite led to the introduction of a better breed of horses, though this may have been part of the wider introduction of larger horses to replace oxen for ploughing and other farm work.[13]

As some of the quarries grew in size they began to employ their own fleets of horses and carts, certainly to transport granite blocks to the surface of the quarries. Donnelly credits John Gibb with the replacement of litters with horses and carts to transport granite blocks to the surface of the quarries. Fifty horses were employed at Rubislaw and early photographs of Rubislaw show the track down into the quarry where the carts would travel. Diack says that when he was serving his apprenticeship at the end of the nineteenth century there were still traces of the track, 'up which the junks, half ware and litters were carted by panting horses from the bottom of the dip to the loading bank.'[14]

John Ritchie describes how David Glennie, who ran the Slattie Quarry in the 1860s, had a fleet of the finest horses and it was common for horses to come from the south at £80 or £90 at a time when horses were cheap.[15] This seemed to apply only to horses bringing the stones up from the quarry floor, those taking the carts from the quarry were poorer quality horses.

According to Ritchie the carters who transported the granite from the quarries were a separate class. They were not, of course, working the stone and therefore not subject to the same apprenticeship period. Dressed in white moleskin trouser and sleeved waistcoats, they looked a rough lot, uncouth and not refined in their speech. In the mid-nineteenth century around forty carts travelled three times a day from Slattie.[16] With Tyrebagger, Dancing Cairns, Persley and Clinterty also using the same road, it must have been quite a sight.

To the west of Aberdeen the procession of carters was also a familiar sight, travelling from Rubislaw down the Skene Road to Union Street and beyond. Many of them stopped at Babbie Law's shop at Holburn Junction to slake their thirst with more than just water. Ritchie excuses their fondness for a 'drappie' given that they were out in all weathers. They had affection for their horses despite many of the latter being quite vicious; every other beast had a kicking strap according to John Ritchie.[17]

As the granite blocks grew larger, so did the teams of horses necessary to transport them. In 1840 a team of ten horses pulled the carriage with the stone for the Duke of Gordon's statue from

Dancing Cairns to Macdonald & Leslie's yard in Constitution Street. A similar sized stone, used for the sarcophagus for Prince Albert and Queen Victoria at Frogmore, required twelve Clydesdales to pull it from Cairngall to Macdonald's yard.

Settmakers and Crib-makars

One of the oldest trades in the granite industry were the settmakers, hardy men, out in all weathers. Settmakers worked near the edge of the quarry hole. They had to provide their own tools as well as their portable shelter known as a skathie. Though open at one side the skathie, shaped almost like a rowing boat turned upright, provided some protection from the elements, though it didn't really

Illustration of settmakers skathies from the *Illustrated London News*, 28 March 1857. Almost exactly the same style of skathies were being used in the 1930s. (© Illustrated London News Ltd/Mary Evans Library)

provide a seat. The skathie had a long history; drawings of them appear in the *Illustrated London News* for March 1857. These early ones are almost identical to those seen in photographs nearly eighty years later. This early illustration also shows them being turned open side down for use in wet weather, although it would have been very difficult to work in them when they were in this position. Photographs usually show the settmaker sitting on the ground with his body covered by the skathie, legs spread out, working the stones between his legs. If the settmakers changed quarries they had to take it with them, not an easy thing to do, given their size and awkward shape.

Settmakers started young, in common with other masons. In 1934 George Ritchie Thomson of Bankhead Road, Bucksburn, was the first Scotsman to receive the Institute of Quarrying's Gold Medal. At the age of 80 he was still working as a settmaker, having been at work on the morning of his presentation. Virtually all his working life had been with the firm of A. & F. Manuelle. He began as a 'nipper' at the Sclattie Quarries around the year 1865, when he was aged ten. He had to serve a seven-year apprenticeship with his father before he could call himself a journeyman, 'at that time every settmaker had a boy learning'. According to Thomson a settmaker made 120 setts a day and it was calculated that he had therefore made 2,629,800 setts in the course of his life![18]

Thomas Murray from Woodside started even younger. He died in 1933 aged 77 and had been a quarry worker for seventy years, having begun as a nipper at the age of just 7.[19]

The Old Time Mason who wrote in the *Quarry Manager's Journal* in 1930 described the work of the kerb-maker in the earlier period:

> The quarry masons who specialized in crib-making were experts at the job. With blocking hammer, puncheon and mall and chisel, and an incidental dab of the pick, they could turn out four to five feet lengths of 12 x 8 kerb with a facility that left the ordinary dressers for the builders rubbing their eyes in astonishment. The rates of pay were quite good and in the halcyon days of crib-making the quarry mason earned very good wages.

By 1930, when he was writing, he described the dying days of the kerb-making part of the industry with Tillyfourie deserted and Clintery and Tyrebagger 'silent, apart from an occasional settmaker knappin' stones on the pinnan hill.'[20]

Settmakers were paid on piece rates, so much per ton. A settmaker recorded for a radio programme in the 1930s described their work and tools at that time:

> The haimmer – them that have been to America sometimes ca't the buster. Used for braken the bigger stanes down to the size of a sett – in a roch sort of wye of course. They use small wedges called bull wedges. They make two small holes with a chisel, we ca the point. They're joined by a line marked along the steen wi' this flat-edged chisel we ca' the tracer. Now the bull wedges are put into the holes wi' a thin scale o' iron at the sides of them, and a good hard dunt or twa wi the haimmer is a ye need. A bit o' granite will split easier some wyes than others – there's the bed, the ca', and the rin o'the steen depending on the wye the steen was lying in the quarry. We go to reeling next – this oblong hammer wi' the straight and sharp edges is a reel. It's used for trimming a block. We used to serve a four year apprenticeship, its three now.'[21]

As with most granite workers, the key for the settmaker was to know the run of the stone, in effect the way the grain ran, whether splitting a large block into manageable sections, or shaping the sett itself.

Russians and The Rooshan

There are several versions of the story of the settmaker who went from Kemnay to Odessa in Russia. In one, recounted by John McLaren, James Bissett went to Odessa to show locals how to make setts. The company who took him there went bust and the poor man had to make his own way home accompanied by his wife and small son, the latter having been born in Odessa. He had a fiddle with him and he played for money all the way back to Istanbul where he caught a ship to Marseilles and then through France and across the Channel to England and back to Kemnay.[22]

In another version, told in Sandy Argo's history of Fyfes, Bissett took a copy of Burns with him as well as his fiddle and he was deported by the Tsarist authorities for his democratic views. Argo dates the story to the 1860s.

The story was recorded by John Mutch, Managing Director of John Fyfe Limited, and many years ago an old man was pointed out to him as the 'Rooshan', the settmaker's son born in Odessa. The story is undoubtedly true because the 1881 Census records James Bissett, settmaker, living at Paradise Cottages, Kemnay. He had been born in Chapel of Garioch in 1835. With him at Paradise Cottages he had his wife Margaret or Maggie, and three children two of whom, Margaret and James, were born in Russia, but firmly declared in the census to be British subjects. Margaret was 14 and James 10 at the time. The third child, Isabella, was 7 and had been born in Kemnay. We can therefore work out that James must have gone to Odessa around 1866/67 and been back in Kemnay by 1874.

John Adan, General Secretary of the Settmaker's Union, was another who went to the south of Russia, probably around the same time, employed by an English firm for four years. That was not the end of Aberdeenshire settmakers going to Russia. Around 1897 Aberdeenshire quarry workers, led by a Woodside man called Hadden, went to Russia to instruct local workers in the art of sett making. Odessa is on the Black Sea but these workers were much further north and, along with their Russian apprentices, they paved the streets of St Petersburg.[23]

Monumental and Building Masons

The great American Supreme Court judge, Oliver Wendell Holmes, once said, 'I always take my hat off when I stop to speak to a stonecutter. Why? You ask me. Because I know that his is the only labour which is likely to endure. A score of centuries had not effaced the marks of the Greek or Roman's chisel.'[24]

Aeneas Anderson, born in 1832, looked back from 1895 to when he was an apprentice with Macdonald & Leslie when they were the only yard in the city. At that time a journeyman's wages were 22s per week. There was no artificial light in the yard and in winter the working week was from eight in the morning until four in the afternoon. During his apprenticeship they employed about 100 people and for eighteen months almost all of them were working on small columns for a large public building in Liverpool. This would probably have been St George's Hall, built in the 1840s and opened in 1854, which had numerous polished granite columns although they are not all there today.[25] This gives some idea of the scale of the work in terms of time and manpower that would later have been done by machinery. Alexander Ingram, speaking in Glasgow in 1927, recalled the early granite polishers of sixty years earlier when he had been just in time to see the last of the Aberdeen masons who came to work wearing their silk hats.[26]

In his memoirs John Morgan described the old-time masons he worked with when he was first apprenticed to his uncle, Adam Mitchell. His first job was on the Grammar School in Skene Street in 1862, and he had a high opinion of these older masons: 'During all the time I have been connected with the building trade, I do not remember a set of steadier, or better working tradesmen than were employed on this building.' He went on to describe them as 'elderly men, several wearing tall hats and swallow-tailed coats with bright metal buttons, clean white trousers, and long aprons'.[27] The trousers may well have been the white moleskin trousers that William Grant recalled the masons wearing when he started in the granite trade twenty years later in 1882. Morgan went on to say that 'some had been in business on their own account but had failed, and were content, as they had begun, by earning their daily bread by the toil of their hands, and the sweat of their brows.' The lively life on the building site can be seen in his next comment on the younger workers which also shows that there was intellectual discussion as well as banter:

> The hewers, were a younger and more lively, if also a more commonplace set, and at meal hours there was often a considerable amount of fun and frolic, sometimes bordering on riot and desecration. All sorts of topics, grave and gay, sacred and secular, were discussed in the freest, and most outspoken manner, and discussion on religious questions were as free and common as any other.[28]

Around the year 1890 Charles Macdonald built a large wooden building with slated roof to hold 120 men in conditions where they were protected from the elements but also had sufficient air circulating. At that time a fifty-one-hour working week was the norm for masons, nine hours Monday to Friday and six on Saturday. Stone polishers worked a fifty-six-hour week. Macdonald reduced the mason's hours by two on Saturdays while still paying his men for fifty-one hours. This did not go down well with his fellow employers and he was expelled from their association for a time (see Chapter 10). Macdonald's motives seem to have been philanthropic and his obituary credits him with 'advanced labour views.'

Building masons were often out of work during the winter months, resuming on 1 March. Hence the triumphant comment of the builder's spouse – 'the morn's the first o' March, an my man's a mason,' meaning that money would be coming into the house again. This well-documented saying was actually recounted to me at the end of a talk I gave on the granite industry to a group of senior citizens. The lady who recounted it was in her early 90s but she clearly remembered her mother repeating it to her, probably in the late 1920s or early 1930s.

Building masons on Queen's Road. Building blocks were usually shaped on site, attempts by quarry owners to carry out this work at the quarries could lead to industrial action. (Aberdeen Art Gallery and Museums Collection)

John McLaren records that his father was brought up on a croft between Dunecht and Lyne of Skene, I think it may have been Nether Corskie. He walked 12 miles to his lodgings in Aberdeen on Sunday evenings. When he finished at 1 o'clock on Saturday he walked back to the country.[29] In these rural areas many villages had their local stone mason. In Lyne of Skene, for example, there was Sandy Scott who lived at the crossroads in the village in the nineteenth century. In his younger days he is said to have walked into Aberdeen every day for his work. This scarcely seems credible given that it was 12 miles but I have been assured by someone who lives in the village that it was true. Sandy's handiwork was to be seen all over the parish of Skene in buildings such the mission hall at the Lyne and the spire of the Free Church. Rural masons such as Sandy would also build the many miles of dry stone dykes that we still see in our countryside, the ones around Dunecht being of hammer-blocked stone funded by the wealth of Lord Cowdray, the stone coming from his quarry at Craigenlow.

William Boddie, in an address to the granite trade in 1908, recalled that fifty years before, when wages were 23s 9d a week and there was no Saturday half-day:

The masons were quite content to have to walk to Cults or the Oldmill Reformatory (Woodend Hospital) and be at their work at 6 o'clock – no travelling time allowed. If they got a pair of white moleskin trousers to go down town on a Saturday night they thought themselves braw.[30]

A Granite Polisher in the Twentieth Century:
Robert Taylor Remembers

Robert Taylor was born in Kintore Place, Aberdeen, in 1921. He attended Skene Square School, then Rosemount School:

> Coming from a family with seven children, I had no option but to find work. I delivered milk in the morning before going to school. Jobs were hard to get. Then I met somebody who said I would get a get a job from George Kemp, he runs a granite yard at the back of the kirk. My mother went to that Baptist Church at Gilcomston and it's just at the back of that church that the granite yard was. Oh aye he says I'll give you a job. I don't know what the wage was, no more than 10 shillings a week. I started as a labourer (at the age of 14), cleaning up, tidying up, helping this one and that one. You didn't really have an education but you ended up very educated by the time you finished because you learned a lot through monuments. You learned more from monuments than you learned from the people. It was hard, hard life, you were always working late, you grabbed every half penny that you could make to help feed the family.

Robert was called up to the RAF in the Second World War. Following war service he returned to Aberdeen and found many of the granite yards closing down but Robertson's were one company that continued to prosper and eventually they bought over Kemp's in 1966:

> Sandy Robertson wanted me to take charge of all the hand polishing at Seaforth Road. Over 95 per cent of the granite for monumental work and shop fronts came from other countries – Sweden, Norway etc.
>
> In the yard water was splashing about all over the place. The boys fed these swinging saws, a straight blade going back and fore with wheels driving it. A single blade would cut about an inch an hour unless it was a soft granite such as emerald pearl, widely used for shop fronts on Union Street. Steel blades with steel grit as an abrasive. The water was to keep it cool and it turned to mud – mud, mud, mud all the time. It was the same in the polishing, great big steel wheels – a hell of a weight. We wore wooden soled clogs with steel rims, chapped on. We wore sacks round our legs for the splashing mud. There were boxes all over the yard which were filled with the slurry and lorries took them away to empty.

When asked where they were emptied Robert laughed and said he didn't really know, but he had a good idea and suggested there were areas up around Mastrick where the slurry might have been dumped, there being no houses there at the time.

Regarding accidents, he said:

> There were always accidents. I caught my arm in a machine once, the arm was like a figure S, broken in four places. It was handy, we were right next to the infirmary [Woolmanhill]. It was a good enough life, though not a great life. I was taking home money and every one else was in the

Robert Taylor polishing seven slabs at once at Robertsons' Granite Yard in 1975. (Used by kind permission of D.C. Thomson & Co. Ltd)

same boat. We finished at 12 o'clock on a Saturday and extra hours during the week. By the time I left diamond tipped saws cut a foot an hour. It changed from a foul, orra job to one where I could go dressed to work, I was just watching the machines.[31]

Many of Robert's comments about the nature of work in the yards are echoed in statements made by national union figures to a meeting with the employers after the 1955 strike comparing the conditions in the building sector with the granite yards:

The building industry had travelling time and fares and bonuses. The lack of welfare facilities was against the recruitment of labour on the following grounds – men often had to work under wet conditions; there were no proper facilities for drying clothes. The yards were untidy and little or no attempt was made to keep clear passageways. Dust extraction plant was not adopted universally. While heating units might be provided there was rarely anything to put in them. There were inadequate messing facilities i.e. no tables or forms for the men to use while eating their mid-day lunch. Few facilities for the washing of hands and the lavatories were primitive. There was a high incidence of silicosis and no guaranteed week as applied in certain instances in the building industry.[32]

Apprenticeships in the 1950s: Alec Mackie and Fred Cargill

By the 1950s it was still possible to serve an apprenticeship in the old way, but only just. In the year he retired in St Louis, Missouri, in the year 2000, Alec Mackie remembered back to his apprenticeship in Aberdeen. He had left school at the age of 16 and his mother decided his career for him:

I wanted to be an artist, but my mom had different ideas. She took me down to the unemployment office where the guy says he is looking for a monumental stonecutter. As I wondered what that was, my mother pipes up, that sounds good. Where does he go?'

He was given a six-month trial, 'to see if you had anything in you.' He then served the normal five-year apprenticeship 'under the eye of G. M. Stalker, an old-timer who didn't believe in using the latest machines.' (this was presumably the son of the founder since George M. Stalker died in 1936) 'You had to learn the old way. You had to cut it by hand. Sometimes you went home with broken fingers and bashed-up hands. You've got to miss a few times to make you concentrate harder.' His comment, as he carved a big block of granite with a 3lb hammer and a chisel, thousands of miles from the city of his birth, was, 'You don't try to beat into it. Let the hammer and the chisel do the work themselves. You're just guiding the instrument.'[33]

Alec Mackie's comments are echoed by Fred Cargill who began his apprenticeship in a builder's yard around the same time:

My father had a building business with Jimmy Wyness at Greenbank Road. They had known each other as boys, in building and quarrying. At the age of 16 my father dressed the stones for the balustrade of the Rowett Institute building at Bucksburn (sandstone from Bervie Quarry) I served my time with Jimmy Wyness. At that time the building business in Aberdeen was doing everything to survive. I left school c. 1954 and worked on the building of Kincorth, the last granite scheme. A lot of lobbying went on to have it built of granite. Stone came in big chunks from Rubislaw Quarry. John Rust, a relation of the owners of Rubislaw, had a fleet of trucks and went round all the building sites that were still using granite.

I went in as a labourer, then basic mason work, a five-year apprenticeship. By the time I had finished this type of work was nearly all finished apart from conversions'.

Fred was told by his journeyman mason on his first day that his hand would be like a pound of uncooked mince at the end of the day:

My first job was puncheoning. He said aye laddie you're hand will be like a pun o ra mince by night. Just carry on, you'll seen stop that [i.e. mis-hitting the puncheon!]

This was a time-capsule of the way things had been done in the past. One man carried stones on his back up the ramp to the crane then the crane lifted it up to high bits.

The big block first split by Davy Fiddes (the driller) who had worked making setts on the quarries along the cliff from Cove well before the war, piece-work. Davy spoke to the stone all the time. When you watched Davy drilling the holes by hand it was almost as if the stone was responding to him. Then the blocks went to the blocker who had a colossal hammer. He didn't lift it high. He was invaluable. He cracked the hammer down and broke the stone very straight. The better the blocker the less work the next man. The blocker got a higher rate of pay. The blocker didn't lift the hammer high, no movement in his arms. He used to bend down with his backside sticking out. We used to say it wasn't Jocky who cut the stone, it was his arse!

At this stage the block wasn't quite good enough to be a stone and the next man had a thing called a bull-set. A highly skilled man, a hauder-onerer, because the angle of the bull-set was absolutely critical to cut the granite straight down. It was a two man job, the bull-set and the striker. The better job they did the less work for the mason or dresser with the puncheon to create the face of the stone. The man using the puncheon was the only one given a shelter in winter. Once the labourer and the crane had taken the stone up, the final man built the house with two stones, an inside stone and an outside one. They were all masons but known for their particular skills. The mason might have taken a turn building but not the blocker, the driller would have been wasted up there. Domestic work had always been done like this. When you walk round Aberdeen you can see every man's characteristic marks on the face of the stone. Drove marks. Same pattern and angle.

When the masons came from the granite yards they were completely handless as we called it. They had never done any construction work. Technically they were all masons, all in the same union.[34]

Interestingly at the time Professor Matthew Hay gave his evidence to the Royal Commission in 1911 the blocker was actually classed as a labourer at the quarries but the job was the same. Hay said he would 'give a certain amount of shape to some of the larger stones after they leave the quarry so as to meet the requirements of customers.'[35]

Blacksmiths, Toolsmiths and Other Workers

Both granite yards and quarries employed blacksmiths and toolsmiths whose main job was to sharpen the mason's tools. As we have seen above in the early days this was a continuous process. Most quarries and the larger yards had their own smithy. As John McLaren points out[36] smaller yards in Aberdeen might contract with self employed blacksmiths to collect and repair or sharpen their tools. Blacksmiths could also be useful in carrying out repairs to machinery. According to Bill Mackie in the early twentieth century his grandfather, a driller at Rubislaw Quarry, had between 2s and 2s 6d a fortnight taken from his wages to pay for their tools to be repaired or sharpened.[37]

As late as the mid 1950s Fred Cargill remembers the blacksmith pushing his handcart up to Kincorth where they were building the housing estate:

Lamont the blacksmith came with his handcart with big wheels, from Ashgrove Lane. He had a bag of sharps and took away your blanks, every few days. He was a slightly built wee chap and he pushed this big barrow. He had a squeaky voice. He used to come on to the site and say 'well boys how are the tools the day'. We used to say just absolute shite, too hard, too brittle. He would say, okay, I'll let them know. Next day we would say too soft, just mushrooming. We would never say they were good. The tools didn't stand up to much, especially the puncheon, thumped with the 3 ½ pound hammer. The forge had rows and rows of puncheons being tempered. He took away their blunt tools and brought back sharpened ones he had collected a few days before. Tungsten was coming in at that time. It was too hard, it just burst. It is better now.[38]

Blacksmith's shop at Kemnay Quarry.

As is shown by the paragraph on the Kemnay community below, the quarries might also have specialist engine and crane drivers. Finally there would be a pool of general labourers. In both the quarries and the yards they might be involved in clearing different kinds of waste and helping to move granite blocks.

Accommodation

Many of the quarries provided some kind of housing for their workers, with rent deducted from wages, and whole communities grew up round the quarries. A lodging house for men was mentioned at Dyce Quarry as early as 1826.[39] An advertisement for the lease of the quarries at Cove in 1869 noted that there were labourers cottages 'beside and in the neighbourhood of the quarries which are chiefly tenanted by the quarrymen.'[40]

Shortly after opening his quarry at Kemnay John Fyfe built several two-storey houses for his workmen, recorded as being sufficient to accommodate from 40–50 families.[41] In 1896 he built a further eight or ten houses at Kemnay. The tenement blocks on Paradise Hill were officially called Paradise Cottages, but were more commonly known as 'the Ra'. The other block was known as the 'the Siding'. Brian Innes, now living in North Carolina, but whose father was a settmaker at Kemnay, had memories of the houses:

> Of the three blocks of tenements at the quarry, one was simply called 'The Siding' as it was adjacent to the rail siding. The other two tenements were always known as 'The Ra'. Many families lived there. In their time the tenements were of a relatively high standard, but that was before the advent of indoor bathrooms. Each block was serviced by lavvies, which consisted of a large granite building over a pit. The building had a corrugated-iron roof and a bench seat with the shapes of two posteriors cut in it. One was big, the other was small, the choice was yours. Some quarriers who worked on the hills adjacent to the lavvies enjoyed the sport of waiting till an occupant was in and settled, then throw a rock on the metal roof. The noise and shock would occasionally drive the occupant outside, even in a state of partial undress, to be greeted by the cheers of the stone throwers.[42]

By October 1953 the *Evening Express* carried the headline 'Walls of Paradise will tumble down'.[43] Paradise Siding and Paradise Cottages, as the article referred to them, had been condemned by Aberdeen County Council. There were twenty-one three-roomed homes, but with dilapidated wash-houses and outside water taps, they failed to meet council sanitation standards and Andrew Mutch, Managing Director of Fyfe's, said that it would be too costly to attempt modernisation. Retired settmaker James Reid lived in one of the properties and he remembered the days when the roads around teemed with quarrymen going to the quarry; by then the 180 settmakers of sixty years earlier being reduced to just three. In the old days families of ten or more shared two rooms. However, it was to be more than ten years before the Ra was demolished in 1966–67, and the Siding even later, in 1973, though all the remaining families had been rehoused in the 1960s.[44]

Other quarries also provided some accommodations for their workers. Mowlem Cottages which survive near Tillyfourie Quarry testify to the English company that worked the quarry for much of the nineteenth century. Across the road at Corrennie a few quarry workers cottages also survive today. In Aberdeen three blocks of tenement flats were built around 1889 on the west side of what became Ord Street and these are shown on the second OS map. They were intended for quarry workers at Rubislaw Quarry; the bridge they used to cross the Denburn is still there. There were many other cottages around the Queen's Road area for quarry workers at Rubislaw. Some of those working at the quarries at Cairncry made the long walk to the quarry from Aberdeen, giving its name to Long Walk Road in Mastrick. George Hall the builder also built houses for the workers at his quarry at Persley in around 1899. Quite a number of quarry workers, especially settmakers, lived in the Woodside area. From there, when the work was available, they commuted to quarries as far away as Kemnay and Tillyfourie.

Granite yards also built accommodation for their workers, tenements in Jute Street and the surrounding area for example. Robert Gibb of the Excelsior Yard bought Ladymill Cottage (No. 490 King Street) beside the LadyMill on King Street (later the Bobbin Mill) for himself. A little further along he built Ladymill House for his workers (Nos 496–498 King Street).[45]

For working accommodation we have already seen that at quarries the settmakers had their skathie. Both at the quarries and in the granite yards sheds of one kind or another were usually provided. By-law VII, agreed between the Master Masons' Association and the Operatives Union in 1880, stated that 'sufficient shed accommodation be provided to hewers where practicable'.[46] In 1889 one of the agreements reached with the Polisher's Union was that all hand work be done under cover.[47] The sheds in the larger yards and for stonecutters at the quarries were broadly similar and they can be seen in early photographs of quarries and granite yards. This description comes from an investigation into phthisis (tuberculosis) among granite workers carried out in 1876 by Dr R. Beveridge from Aberdeen Infirmary:

The mason works in long, narrow sheds, completely open on one side; near this open side, he places the stone, and works with his face towards the light and air, and stooping over his work. He is, therefore, practically in the open air, the shed serving simply to protect him from wet; the dust is almost entirely above and behind him; while the muscular exertion necessary to wield his heavy tools is such as to keep him physically warm to resist variations of external temperature.[48]

Judging by the photographs these sheds would have been wooden but certainly in the larger granite yards they were later built of stone. In these larger yards they could be quite long buildings as this description shows. It followed a fire at James Wright's yard in John Street and the building had two floors:

The shed is a stone and lime erection, with tile roof, separated from the remaining portion of the works by a stone wall. It is about 40 or 50 yards in length, and about 15 yards wide, and is used on the ground floor for polishing purposes, and on the attic floor for the storing of shavings and other packing material.[49]

A few years before this in 1891 Charles Macdonald had been the first in Aberdeen to build completely enclosed accommodation for his workers, something he drew praise for in his obituary. Macdonald's building was built of wood with a slated roof and ample air space; it housed 120 stonecutters and afforded them 'complete shelter in all kinds of weather'.[50] Of course, in the light of later views on lung disease, Macdonald may not have been doing his workers a favour.

A Granite Community: Kemnay in 1871

Kemnay was just a typical rural village until John Fyfe opened his quarry there in 1858. We can get some idea from the 1871 Census of the numbers the quarry employed. We have seen above that from early on Fyfe had built accommodation for some of his workers but the men from the quarry and their families lived all over Kemnay parish.

At Quarry Cottages there were 24 men and their families, and at Paradise Siding there were 17 properties with 79 people in total. George Gellie was the Quarry Manager and at the time of the Census he was living with his family at Gellie's Cottage, which he himself had built. James Harvey was the Quarry Overseer. In addition there were 2 foremen quarriers, 19 masons, 15 journeymen masons, 2 apprentice masons (or prentice as the Census called them), 6 stone cutters, 53 stone dressers plus 1 apprentice, 28 quarriers/quarrymen plus 1 apprentice, 2 causeymen, 24 labourers, 1 hammerman, 1 engine fitter, 1 steam cran worker, 4 blacksmiths, 2 engine drivers, 1 hammer sharpener, 1 millwright, and 1 nipper. Over at Leshangie there was 1 quarrier, 7 stone cutters, 4 causey stone dressers, and 3 causeymakers. One might have expected more apprentices but this amounts to around 180 men/boys and most of them had families as well.

The range of trades is also interesting with several specialist workers mainly involved with the machinery of the quarry. To some extent the census taker would just record what they were told by the inhabitants of the property. So, for example, at Leschangie there were causey stone dressers and causeymakers, the same thing. In fact the old term causeymen had disappeared by the time of the 1881 Census and settmaker was used for the first time. A few men worked small crofts as well as having their quarry job, usually crofts of just four or five acres. This was a common feature with other rural masons but perhaps here the rural mason/crofter had taken up work at the quarry. Some workers, such as settmakers, who did piece work, could work their croft when trade was slack. As one would expect, the men came from all over the north-east, with a few from outside the area. This huge influx of people in a relatively short period must have radically transformed the area.

Education and Training

As we have seen already, many granite workers began their working life as young boys. This was not their actual apprenticeship which usually began at a later age, especially once both sides of the industry became organised. Settmakers might be slightly different since their apprentices were actually employed by the settmakers themselves and could start younger, especially if a son was following his father.

Robert Fergusson described his apprenticeship with Alexander Macdonald in the 1840s as being four years, three as a dresser and one as a builder.[51] The 1880 By-laws agreed between the men and their employers, quoted in Chapter 12, specified a minimum apprenticeship of four years. By 1909 the apprenticeship for those in the building sector was five years, i.e. three to the cutting and two to the building; they must not be aged less than 17 years nor over 25. In the monumental sector if an apprentice began before he was 17 then he served five years, if over 17 then it was four years. Four years was also the norm in the polishing sector at this time, though apprenticeships themselves for polishers were introduced at a much later date than for stonecutters and building masons.

As well as on-the-job apprentice training, many granite workers in the city attended more formal classes. By the end of the nineteenth century a debate began as to how these could be improved. This debate involved the recently established Gray's School of Art and the sculptor Pittendrigh Macgillivray.

Long before Gray's was established in 1885, granite workers attended classes at its predecessor, the Mechanics Institution. Aeneas Anderson recalled how he had spent three years learning architectural drawing at the Mechanics Institution. This was probably in the 1850s and his employer, Macdonald & Leslie paid his fees, the classes being in the evening.[52] Adam Mitchell, the noted builder, was another Macdonald apprentice who attended classes at the Mechanics Institution and attributed his later success to those classes. In November 1863 Alexander Macdonald paid the fees of 30 of his apprentices to attend classes at the Mechanics Institution's Art School.[53] Despite some disparaging comments about his workforce, John Morgan took pride in the success of many of his apprentices. He stated that his firm had taken on average four apprentices every year and claimed that:

> With slight exception, our apprentices have turned out to be capable and efficient tradesmen, content to remain such, but have done their best to improve their position. Several have attained honourable positions as employers on their own account, both at home and abroad, and one of them is at present a prominent member of Aberdeen Town Council, while another is Clerk of Works on the Nile irrigation works in Egypt. We have always done our best for our boys, to enable them to learn their trade, and sending them to evening classes during the winter months.[54]

The granite workers also engaged in self-help with a Mutual Improvement Association being formed for the granite trade in 1890, George Younie being its secretary.

In 1896 sculptor Pittendreigh Macgillivray met with members of the Aberdeen Granite Association with a view to not only to establishing better ways of training granite apprentices but also to extend the artistic use of art in granite work and the reverse, granite for artistic work. His view was that to achieve the AGA's aim as regards the latter, 'there must be established an efficient system of instruction, combining art and technical training, including designing and modelling and the reproduction of models with the quality and style of sculptured work.' His idea was for a small school for granite workers with two rooms, one for modelling in clay, the other for reproducing models in granite. The latter could include copying items of Egyptian sculpture for which models could be bought.[55]

In 1896 the Aberdeen Granite Association voted that if a statutory scheme was established to provide technical instruction for granite workers they would give £25 annually towards the scheme. The President and Secretary wrote to Macgillivray to ask him to recommend someone to teach statuary and the art of modelling. They also contacted fellow granite man John Morgan who represented the Town Council on the Board of Governors for Robert Gordon's Technical College, Gray's School of Art being part of that institution. The Technical College were keen to expand into new areas at this time and agreed to provide the free use of a modelling room and the ground for building a shed. As with other pupils of the College, granite pupils would give an undertaking to sit the usual examinations of the National Science and Art Department.[56] The Governors did point out, though, that £25 wouldn't go far since it would need a salary of around £100–150 a year to employ a good teacher of modelling. Fees would provide a further £10 and the Granite Association hoped that the College might apply to the Town Council for support.[57]

The class did get under way in 1897, two nights a week for two hours each night, with workmen and apprentices attending. Rather than being training for every apprentice this was intended as an experiment to give selected workers more opportunity and training to study ornamental stone-cutting. The applicants had therefore to show some ability and entry to the class was by way of competition, hence only twelve attended the initial class. By July 1898 the first prizes and certificates were awarded.[58]

The Art School Prospectus for 1899–1900 lists granite man George F. Ruddiman as teacher of granite cutting with fees for the students of 5s per session. According to the *Aberdeen Journal* that same year, modelling and granite cutting classes at Gray's School of Art were being well attended. The *Journal* felt that the large amount of architectural work being carried out by the yards meant that it was essential that apprentices had at least a rudimentary knowledge of architectural ornament and the principles of design.[59] In 1905, when the sculpture gallery extension was added to the Art Gallery, the value of the exhibits on display was highlighted as being of great importance for granite workers and apprentices.[60]

Classes came to cover drawing of ornament and lettering, modelling and carving, workshop drawing, and architectural drawing.[61] John McLaren recounts how in the 1930s draughtsmen and apprentice masons both attended evening classes where they were taught basic drawing and modelling, if the model was good enough they could make a plaster cast from it. This would probably have been at the Trades College in George Street where the classes continued after the Second World War. After a few years McLaren then attended more advanced courses at Gray's School of Art for both freehand and architectural drawing.[62] Lettercutters, in particular, were sent to the classes at Gray's.

In later years, after the Second World War, evening classes were replaced by day-release classes. The classes were overseen by the Joint Apprenticeship Committee formed by the Granite Association and the Amalgamated Union of Building Trades Workers (AUBTW). In 1949 they consisted of two years at the Day School as stone cutters, with letter cutters going to Gray's for a further year provided they had attained a reasonable standard of workmanship. McLaren saw day release as generally a good thing as it gave the boys regular instruction in various aspects of the trade. The one drawback was that during their on-the-job training the apprentices would spend months learning the various hand tools, while at the classes they quickly moved on to using pneumatic tools. He gave the example of when the classes moved from George Street to the new Technical College in the Gallowgate where they had a very up-to-date workshop with dust extraction equipment and a circular diamond saw. After this experience the apprentices were reluctant to go back to learning the basics in the yards.

By 1966 Gray's School of Art were no longer able to provide facilities for the training of masons, presumably because of their move to the new building out of the city centre at Garthdee. The classes would be wholly provided by the Technical College, which had been created at the new building on the Gallowgate two years before. At this time the representatives of the granite industry wanted a curriculum composed of drawing for carving and ornamental work, lettering and free hand, carving in relief and three dimensions. They also wanted the college to provide training in granite as opposed to sandstone, which had been used at Gray's. By 1973 the classes were under threat because of declining number of apprenticeships. At this point they were given a reprieve. Day-release classes finally ceased in 1976 by which time there were only seventeen apprentices in the whole industry.[63]

THE GRANITE INDUSTRY 1850–1914: THE GOLDEN AGE?

Introduction

The eighteenth century had been a period when the use of granite for paving had been the main force in driving the embryo granite industry, with building in granite also playing a part towards the end of the century. In the first half of the nineteenth century there was a growth in the quarrying industry culminating in John Fyfe opening up the Kemnay Quarry in 1858. The second half of the nineteenth century really saw the huge growth in the number of granite yards, particularly in Aberdeen. In the monumental industry this period saw granite monuments being sent all over the world. Polished granite would also become popular for building fronts and this involved sending finished granite all over the country, some even being sent abroad. Within the city itself there was further expansion of the city's boundaries and the building of prestigious buildings in the centre with equally prestigious housing to the west of the city in areas such as Rubislaw Den and Queen's Road. This undoubtedly was a period of great expansion in the industry but it was by no means a continuous expansion. At various times there were fluctuations in the local and national economy which affected the industry; there were also concerns over tariffs in America and elsewhere, and concerns over the supply of sufficient granite from local quarries. By the end of this period the high point had already been reached and the industry was already in decline, although not many realised this at the time.

The growth of the industry had been rapid. In listing the occupations carried on by the inhabitants of the town the *Bon Accord Repository*, published in 1842, gives the figure of six stone cutters (masons) and six stone merchants. Unfortunately the *Repository* didn't differentiate between building and monumental masons, but at that early date there wouldn't necessarily have been the difference between the two that existed later. The actual numbers were echoed at the Aberdeen Master Mason's annual dinner in February 1878, when several speakers commented that thirty years before there were only eight master masons in Aberdeen, and now thirty were sitting round the table.[1] Similarly thirty years before the Master's dinner Macdonald & Leslie had only recently developed mechanical granite polishing which had previously been done by hand. By 1878 there were thirty granite yards, and a further eight years later, in 1884, the *Free Press* reported that there were sixty or seventy firms purely of sculptors and polishers employing around 1,400 men and boys.[2] By the end of the century there were even more, and steam power was widespread.

John Morgan listed seven mason contractors when he entered service with his uncle in 1862. These were John Fraser & Sons, Low & Chalmers, Ross & Mitchell, George Donaldson, Bisset & Grant, Alexander Wishart, and his uncle Adam Mitchell. By the time he wrote his memoirs in the 1890s there were forty-five.[3] There had been a similar growth in quarrying. Thirty years before 1878 there was no John Fyfe and no Kemnay Quarry with all the technological innovations that came from it. A few years before the above mentioned dinner James Beattie's survey of Rubislaw Quarry had shown that there was 120 years of granite to be extracted at current rates of extraction. The future looked assured.

The progress of the industry was not one of uniform growth. There were certainly periods of depression, more so in the monumental and polishing sector than the building side. In the mid to late 1870s the depressed state of the industry led to successful attempts to reduce the operative's wages. At the annual dinner of the Aberdeen Master Mason's Association in February 1879, the Chairman, James Hunter, commented, 'the state of trade was such as they had never experienced anything like it, and the change that had taken place within the last three or four years with regard to men and employers was very great indeed.'[4] The following year things were no better although at that dinner Vice-Chairman, James H. Bisset, suggested that the building trade had not suffered: 'it was a curious thing that amid all the depression of the past few years the building trade had no reason to complain of lack of work. There had been more work going on in the last year or two than there had ever been.'[5]

The last two decades of the century saw the formation of another employer's organisation, with the Aberdeen Granite Association joining the existing Master Masons' Association. This signified the distinction that came to exist between building masons and the monumental stonecutters as monumental and polished work grew substantially. This did not exist to the same extent in the 1840s and '50s. Larger monumental yards were still involved in the more ornate architectural work including polished building frontages and the very largest yards, as with larger quarriers, might also be involved in large building and civil engineering contracts. For the operatives, although there had been a union earlier in the century, its position had been precarious, but these two decades saw its position strengthened and other unions or branches were formed in the various sectors of the industry. Granite merchants became men of real substance in the city in this period, endowing major developments such as the Art Gallery, becoming directors of companies unrelated to granite, getting elected to the Town Council and becoming Baillies, with two of them, Sir James Taggart and James R. Rust, becoming Lord Provost in the early years of the twentieth century.

This was also the period when English companies became established in the area, notably A. & F. Manuelle and John Mowlem or Mowlem, Burt & Co. In fact Charles Manuelle first appeared as a stone merchant as early as the 1836–37 Aberdeen Directory, becoming M. Manuelle in 1846. Mowlem, Burt & Freeman followed, setting up offices at Blaikie's Quay by the time of the 1858/59 Post Office Directory. These companies owned or leased several quarries in the area as detailed in the chapter on the quarries. They continued to be involved in the quarrying industry for the rest of the century.

The main entrepreneurs in the industry were involved in more than one aspect of the industry. At the start of this period John Gibb had shown the way by being a civil engineer carrying out major construction projects such as dock works, while investing in quarrying his own granite from his own quarries. This continued in the second half of the nineteenth century with builders, contractors, and monumental masons all running quarries. Similarly John Fyfe was just one example of a quarrier who opened his own granite yard in Aberdeen and acted as a contractor for numerous building projects. James Leith from Rayne was another example of this. He had begun as a drystane dyker from the age of 15. He then moved into quarrying in a small way to supply his own stone for dyking and subsequently became involved in railway work. In the mid 1870s he bought the Cairncry Estate, including the Cairncry Quarry, and also leased the Persley Quarry. He became one of Aberdeen's major granite contractors, working on projects such as sewer and waterworks, the Riverside Esplanade and the archway at the north end of the Wellington Suspension Bridge.

Building Within the Granite City

The second half of the nineteenth century saw a continued growth in the city. There were peaks and troughs, usually reflecting the local and national economy, but generally this period saw numerous prestigious buildings appearing in the city centre. As well as buildings a substantial amount of granite was used in the building of the various tunnels, embankments etc., when the railway was taken through the valley of the Denburn from 1865 to 1867. The new Joint Station was also built from granite. As an example of this period of growth in the 1860s John Morgan stated that during that decade his uncle employed over 400 men, in addition to a number of sub-contractors. For several years in succession they did work to the value of £30,000 annually.[6]

Referring to Rubislaw Quarry Aberdeen masons and quarry workers said that 'the half o' Aiberdeen has come oot o' that hole' and some have even put the figure as high as three quarters of Aberdeen's buildings being built of Rubislaw granite. This may well be true in terms of the quantity needed for building the houses of the Granite City. However, the majority of really prestigious buildings, or at the very least their fronts, in this period were built from Kemnay granite. This began with the Municipal Buildings, which included the Town House and Court House, in the 1860s, and continued in the 1890s and early 1900s with the Central Library, His Majesty's Theatre, the Fire Station on King Street, the Salvation Army Citadel in the Castlegate, and culminated in the most stunning of them all, the new Marischal College.

The Municipal Buildings and Court House was a major construction project, probably the largest granite building in the city until the new Marischal College thirty years later. Further west the city continued to creep towards Rubislaw Quarry. In 1870 there was virtually nothing built west of Queen's Cross. East of the Cross, Albyn Place had taken a number of years to develop but by 1870 was filled with elegant villas. The baronial styled Rubislaw Terrace had also taken years to get off the ground with the west end of it (Queen's Terrace) eventually being built much later and in a much plainer style. Once Queen's Cross had been reached Queen's Road began to be built up, including the magnificent Queen's Cross Church, another building that used Kemnay granite. The huge houses of Rubislaw Den followed as did the finest granite house in the city, Rubislaw House at No. 50 Queen's Road, built in 1887–88 for the greatest of the master masons, John Morgan. Nearer the city centre Rosemount Viaduct was built from 1885–89 mainly using white granite from Kemnay, with some blue from Manuelle's Dyce Quarry and inlays of pink Corrennie. The building of the Viaduct helped open up the Rosemount area for further development with several streets of large tenements as well as churches and other buildings. Similarly the building of Victoria Bridge over the River Dee in 1881 led to a spate of building across the water at Torry.

The Town House and Building in Granite

We have already seen in Chapter 3 that the idea of Aberdeen as the Granite City had developed among Aberdonians. The feeling now was that buildings in Aberdeen should only be built of granite. There is a widespread story concerning the material to be used in the building of the new Municipal Buildings and Court House in the late 1860s. It is said that the Edinburgh architects for the project, Peddie & Kinnear, had specified freestone for the building because they felt that adequate supplies of granite were not available. The suggestion 'evoked vigorous protests from patriotic citizens', according to Diack.[7] John Fyfe is supposed to have stepped in to guarantee adequate supplies of Kemnay granite to carry out the building work. At a meeting in Glasgow in August 1900 with representatives of the Settmakers Union, Fyfe himself told the story to illustrate to the workers the danger in restrictive practices in the industry which he claimed had almost destroyed the industry forty years before:

> I myself opened a quarry and could not get a man to work it. Fortunately there came free trade and the consequence was that it encouraged me to open up new quarries. You only have to go to Union Street and find two churches built of freestone because no granite could be got and the Town House was also specified to be built of freestone, but it so happened owing to this freedom that I was able to open the quarry and I went to considerable expense in putting up steam cranes and I was able to go to the Town Council and say that I would supply them with granite.[8]

The two churches he mentioned are Langstane, which is built of sandstone, and Gilcomston, which is part granite, part sandstone. I suspect that cost may have had more to do with the choice of material for these, rather than availability of granite. The problem with the story of the building of the Town House in freestone is that it does not appear in the records of the time. It is not mentioned in the Council Register. Neither the *Free Press* nor the *Aberdeen Journal* have anything on it, one would have expected letters of outrage and editorial comment, as happened with other building projects such as the Torry Bridge. Nor do historians or architectural writers at the time have any mention of it. Perhaps it is apocryphal, or at the very least that Fyfe exaggerated his claims. Certainly the building of the Town House in Kemnay granite would have been good publicity for his quarry at Kemnay, which had only recently opened, and the Town House was the first major building in the city to be built from his Kemnay stone. Peddie & Kinnear were chosen after a competion and it is

South face of Aberdeen Town House.

true that an early elevation by Peddie & Kinnear survives that appears to show a sandstone buildng and sandstone was used for interior stonework. It may have been that their first submissions were done in sandstone because, coming from Edinburgh, that is what they were used to, but it seems to have been changed to granite with no fuss. The one agency which may have raised the issue was the Government. Because it involved the court and prison, the Government was paying part of the cost and they were unhappy that it was costing more than a similar provision for Dundee. However, their own architect, Robert Matheson of Her Majesty's Board of Works, completely supported the use of granite. His report stated:

> The principal elevation is proposed to be exectuted of Aberdeen granite, of which material all the other buildings in the Street [Union Street] are built. The style adopted is of a severe Gothic or Elizabethan character free from any elaborated ornament or detail, very effective, and from its magnitude would be a marked and important public edifice.

He went on to say:

> The expense of building in Aberdeen is considerably greater than at Dundee, the difference in a
> large measure being occasioned by the use of granite, and even if freestone be adopted, the carriage
> is so considerable that it would not in my opinion be expedient to depart from the use of granite.[9]

There are, though, several examples of where the use of a material other than granite did enagage
the attention of the prominent citizens of the town. During the discussions over the proposed
bridge to Torry in 1877, James Tulloch, a prominent shipowner, stated that when it was proposed
to build the new Post Office (at the bottom of Market Street) in freestone, Fyfe had come forward
and offered any sum of money to the Government to change its mind and use granite.[10] Later, when
the Government was building a replacement Post Office in Crown Street at the beginning of the
twentieth century, they were reminded that it should be built of granite. Similarly letters of protest
appeared in the press when it was suggested that the Greyfriars Church end of the new Marischal
College frontage be built of sandstone, made worse by the fact that it was to be built that way with
ratepayers' money!

There are one or two other stories relating to citizens' outrage at the building of landmark buildings in sandstone. George Washington Wilson's son, Charles, recorded that in 1874 his father had
objected to sandstone being used to build Rubislaw Church, diagonally opposite his own house
at Queen's Cross. Wilson offered to pay the difference if granite was used but it was too late, the
contracts had already been exchanged.[11] Another story is that in order to prevent another sandstone
building going up on the corner of Fountainhall Road, just opposite his house, Wilson bought the
land and had a double villa built there, probably by the architect of his own house, J.R. Mackenzie.
This latter property he then rented out.

The Torry Bridge Saga

Although it has been difficult to find evidence of public outcry caused by the possibility of the
Town House being built from sandstone, the material used in building a new bridge across to Torry
certainly did arouse strong feelings among the population. Such were the feelings raised that the
issue filled the press, particularly in May and June of 1877.

A bridge capable of carrying traffic across to Torry had been discussed for many years and the
ferry boat disaster in 1876 heightened the need for a bridge. The following year the Council spent a
considerable time discussing a bridge and how it could be funded. By the end of April word had got
out that plans had 'been drawn up for various types of bridge'. The *Journal* commented that these
were 'locked up in the Town House, and only seen by favour,' and that 'the proposed bridge is, we
understand, one of those cheap and useful structures with which we are familiar at railway stations'.
There were also plans of a composite bridge composed of metal arches on stone piers, described as
'tasteful'. Finally the *Journal* said that they had 'seen the plan of a granite bridge, at the same cost as
the composite bridge, plain but handsome enough in the drawing'.[12]

Right from the outset the Dean of Guild had stated that it should be a bridge worthy of the city, and he implied that he meant a granite bridge. However, the Master of Works, John Willet, along with architect Arthur Clyne, and Blaikie Brothers, iron founders and engineers, supported and had drawn up plans for an iron girder bridge on granite piers, the piers above the water line being Aberdeen granite with columns of Peterhead granite. Tenders were invited to build the bridge. A model and plans of the proposed bridge were displayed in the Town and County Building on 14 May 1877. Derided as the 'iron brander bridge, unworthy of the granite city', in one letter to the *Aberdeen Journal*[13] it was initially the favourite of many on the Council because it was the cheaper option. The brander bridge was even derided in a parody of a nursery rhyme.[14]

The same evening as the plans were unveiled, a group of 'influential gentlemen' called a meeting of concerned citizens in the Douglas Hotel, their aim, expressed at the meeting, being to oppose the iron bridge in favour of a granite bridge. John Forbes White, miller and art lover, spoke against the model of the iron bridge, which he sarcastically described as a 'prettily constructed toy.' But White said it could never be a handsome bridge and if they couldn't have a good bridge over the Dee then he thought they would rather not have a bridge at all. If they compared it with (granite) Union Bridge, they would appreciate the meanness of the iron bridge. White demanded that the Council should build a bridge worthy of the city and of the site. He proposed that they call for a granite bridge to be built and he was seconded by George Reid, the artist. Even before this meeting had been called one of the attendees, James Tulloch, had got John Fyfe involved and Fyfe had characteristically declared, 'I'll build you a bridge, and I guarantee that it will be built in a satisfactory way right off.' Fyfe even gave a cost for the granite bridge, something that was not available as yet for the iron bridge. Among others of the great and good who attended the meeting and were part of the committee to take the motion forward there were future provosts Peter Esslemont and William Henderson of Devanha, as well as William Alexander of the *Free Press*, architect Duncan Macmillan, Thomas Gill, President of the Trades Council, John Miller of Sandilands, and John Webster of Edgehill.[15]

Before the month of May was over a large drawing of a granite bridge was added to other illustrations of proposed bridges on display in the Town and County Hall and a petition supporting that bridge, signed by 2,136 people, was handed to the Town Clerk. The views of one writer to the *Free Press* echoed the opinion of many:

> The stone bridge would, I believe, give general satisfaction. True, it would cost a few thousand pounds more, but ought that to be an insurmountable obstacle. I think not. There has been much miserable wriggling and niggling over this matter. The Town Council has all along shown a disposition to shrink the work, and, now that it must be undertaken, they seem anxious to compel us to accept the shabbiest plan submitted to them. But I am mistaken if public feeling does not impel them to further action, if that is possible. It would be a pity if Aberdeen, present and future, should have to suffer from the narrow-mindedness of a few who happen unfortunately to be in power at this juncture.[16]

A special meeting of the Council was called and they overturned their decision of barely a month before and postponed for a month acceptance of any tenders for the bridge.[17] The momentum was now with the granite bridge, though there was a set back when John Willet, still backing the iron bridge, argued that changes to the approach to the site necessary for a granite bridge added significantly to Fyfe's estimate making it £3,700 higher than the iron bridge. The Council then called in an independent engineer from Edinburgh, Edward Blyth, who reported back in favour of a granite bridge, for which he submitted a design, at a cost not much greater than the iron bridge had been. The latter he described as the ugliest bridge he had ever seen!

The bridge was of course built of granite, with concrete piers faced in granite. Much of the exposed work was of pick-dressed ashlar or hammer-blocked ashlar. The contractor and supplier of the granite was John Fyfe. Named the Victoria Bridge, it contained 11,200 tons of granite from Kemnay and Tom's Forest, and it was officially opened by Provost Esslemont on 2 July 1881. At the opening ceremony James Matthews, architect and future Lord Provost, commented that Fyfe had come forward:

> At a time when the town was drifting into a design of perhaps doubtful propriety, and offered to erect a granite bridge at such a cost as made their respected friends the Town Council pause and consider whether they could not meet the almost unanimous wishes of the citizens by entering into this contract.[18]

The National View of the Granite City

How then did the world beyond Aberdeen view a city built from this one basic material and when did Aberdeen become known as 'The Granite City'?

Scottish judge Lord Henry Cockburn, who had a strong interest in architectural conservation, did not have a high opinion of Archibald Simpson's Marischal College, or indeed of many other buildings in the city. When he visited Aberdeen in 1839 he commented:

> They boast much of their new Marischal College. But confined amidst paltry buildings, its position is bad, it has no architecture, and its erection implies the destruction of the old building, which sets all that they would do utterly at defiance. They should all be squashed, and only King's College kept.[19]

Of course he was not necessarily commenting on the use of granite here, but on the style (or lack of it) of the buildings.

The *Bon Accord Repository* of 1842 commented that Aberdeen had been called the 'marble city of the north' (not the granite city), on account of the nature and look of its granite buildings. The following year an advertisement for a moving panorama of the city on display at the Mechanics' Instution referred to it as displaying 'this Granite City'.[20] In 1844 various local and national newspaper carried an account of Queen Victoria's visit to Scotland and recorded the hope among the citizens of Aberdeen that she would visit their 'granite city'.[21] The same year, the *Bradford Observer* carried a story from the *Spectator* in London referring to the possible extension of railways in

Scotland. This article specifically called Aberdeen 'the granite city'.[22] Though not conclusive it may well have been in the 1840s that Aberdeen began to be known as the Granite City and certainly by 1847 it was being called that in newspapers from London northwards.

Harriet Beecher Stowe visited Aberdeen in 1853 and wrote one of the earliest comments on the appearance of its granite buildings: 'the town of Aberdeen is a very fine one, and owes much of its beauty to the light-colored granite of which most of the houses are built.'[23]

In the 1860s and 1870s Aberdeen and its granite began to feature more in the national press, perhaps following on from the British Association visit to the city in 1859 during which, as noted in Chapter 3, they had been given a lecture on granite by Alexander Gibb. Even before that the *Illustrated London News* in 1857 had featured the granite industry with sketches of quarry blasting, of Rubislaw Quarry and of the quarrymen or settmaker's distinctive huts. It also said that because the city was mainly built of stone from the Rubislaw Quarry it was called the Granite City[24]. The *News* revisited the granite industry five years later and the professional architectural and building press began to take more of an interest in the buildings of the city itself. Often these accounts were reprinted in the *Aberdeen Journal*. Several of these accounts report on how the granite looked in the moonlight:

> The pure colour, especially in the moonlight, gives the building all the appearance of marble.
> *The Architect*, 1872, specifically referring to Archibald Simpson's North of Scotland Bank at the corner of King Street and Castle Street.[25]

> The city presents a still finer and more poetic effect on a calm clear moonlight night, which gives it a pale silvery appearance, perhaps somewhat cold, but extremely chaste-like and beautiful.
> *Building News*, 1866[26]

> By moonlight the coup d'oeil is singularly surprising and romantic.
> *The Builder*, 1865[27]

We can imagine that the effect of moonlight in the era before electric lighting was more pronounced.

The Builder was intrigued by older buildings such as the Wallace Tower, George Jamesone's House in Schoolhill and Mar's Castle in the Gallowgate. It also commented on the vestiges of an ancient tower, originally belonging to the Knight's Templar and apparently still visible in Bothwell Court. These buildings they rightly felt were 'worthy of more study than local antiquaries appear to have bestowed on them.' Late eighteenth century buildings had very little of architectural interest to *The Builder* apart from the house in the Broad Street where Byron had spent part of his childhood. More recent buildings were found to be more worthy of praise, in fact 'these are the most remarkable things of their kind it is possible to conceive.' The writer imagined standing in the Castlegate, described by locals as 'the glory, the pride, and the apple of the eye of Aberdeen', and looking west up Union Street, where 'we have before us a vista such as no other city in the empire could furnish.' That must have gone down well with readers of the *Aberdeen Journal*. He went on 'it is an architectural feature without compeer. A double line of handsome public buildings and houses, all built of a greyish white, and glistening granite.' This, of course, was just before the building of the

Town House, with some older buildings, soon to be swept away, still standing around the old Town House on Union Street and in Narrow Wynd and Huxter Row. The granite-built Union Bridge is praised with the view from it compared to that from North Bridge in Edinburgh. The writer says, 'it is easy to understand why Aberdeen should be called par emphasis The Granite City.' The only criticism the writer makes of all this granite is the lack of colour, with the eye being drawn at Union Bridge to Simpson's red brick-clad spire of the Triple Kirks. He suggested more widespread use of other colours of granite. Finally he praised Simpson's Marischal College, as good a piece of construction and design as he had seen in the North. This view, by an architectural writer, contrasts with that of Lord Cockburn who said of the building that 'it had no architecture.' Both Cockburn and the writer of this article agreed that the entrance from Broad Street, through an archway in a line of more humble buildings, did it no favours. *The Builder* also thought that 'the effect of the beautiful buildings is destroyed by a clumsy and pretentious granite obelisk.' Thank goodness that, as we have already seen, that obelisk is now in the Duthie Park where its massive form can be seen to much better advantage.

The following year the *Building News* wrote that most people outside Aberdeen, and particularly south of the border, were remarkably ignorant of Aberdeen, even as to its location. They had certainly heard of Aberdeen granite, Aberdeen clippers, Aberdeen hose, Aberdeen hats and haddocks, and Aberdeenshire cattle, but they knew virtually nothing of the city itself. Their knowledge of Aberdeen granite was mainly confined to the granite used to pave their streets and build their harbours, and perhaps some of their buildings. The *News* went on to describe the qualities of granite as used in Aberdeen:

> The appearance of this city is unlike any other we have seen, and this is due to the nature of the material of which it is built. The famous granite buildings give it a distinctiveness and an originality peculiarly its own. Bon Accord has been richly blessed with stone which for durability and beauty may vie with marble. By no great stretch of the imagination the visitor imagines that the fronts of the houses are studded with tiny jewels. It is the bright warm sun, reflecting ten thousand particles of mica in its rays, making them sparkle and change colour like diamonds.

We have seen in Chapter 2 that *The Architect* was full of praise for the granite work on Archibald Simpson's North of Scotland (later Clydesdale) Bank.. It also praised newer buildings such as the Grammar School, Trades Hall on Union Street (Trinity Hall), and the new Town House, the latter of axed Kemnay granite. The author described how for plainer buildings hammer-blocked or rustic work was used, with the corners dressed. As with other writers the main criticism was the lack of colour, one way of partly getting round this was by using different finishes on the granite margins as described. This could be further enhanced by using different granites in a building. The article described how the finely dressed white granite of Kemnay was contrasted with hammer-blocked blue granite from Sylavethie. The result had the effect of 'making a very artistic combination of colour, and doing away, to a great extent, with the greyness complained of in our Aberdeen street architecture'. Rubislaw granite was increasingly used in place of Sylavethie, mainly on the grounds of cost and availability, not as striking but still pleasing. The article detailed some buildings by the architect James Souttar, which showed this contrasting use of granites, including the Imperial Hotel (now the Carmelite), Crown Terrace Baptist Church, Belmont Congregational Church, and the old Fraserburgh Academy.

The impact Aberdeen's granite buildings had on a visiting American journalist can be seen in a letter he sent home to his newspaper, the *Danbury News*, in 1875, and reprinted in the *Aberdeen Journal*:

> I didn't expect to find Aberdeen granite in Aberdeen. Never having seen but two or three monuments of the beautiful material, I was somewhat stunned to see a large city built almost entirely of it. But this fact I did not discover until I was told by one of the manufacturers, as the buildings are of the undressed stuff [I think he means unpolished], and, in that condition, it looks very much like other granite.[28]

J.J. Stevenson, the Glasgow-born London architect, gave a paper on Aberdeen granite architecture to the Social Science Congress in 1877. He suggested that because granite was the finest material with which to build, there was in Aberdeen an attitude that it was impossible to build bad buildings in granite. He disagreed with this (as many of us know architects can build badly in any material!), claiming that while it was the finest of materials it was also the most intractable and the most difficult to use correctly. Stevenson actually preferred the warmer colours of field gathered granite, such as was used in St Machar Cathedral, to what he saw as the cold white buildings of Union Street. These older stones were from the surface and had weathered and softened in a way that those 'cut from the solid rock deep in the quarry' probably never would. While praising Archibald Simpson's use of the classical (mainly Greek) style in his granite buildings, and seeing granite as ideally suited to that style, he nevertheless thought the style never looked quite happy in this climate. It reminded him of a 'Hindoo shivering in his white dress in the streets on a sleety day,' and I think we can all sympathise with that image. In contrast to other writers he did not think that the new Town House and Simpson's Marischal College worked well, the workmanship being too good for the design. Stevenson preferred the wider joints and softer look of the older buildings such as St Machar. Again, in contrast to the previous writer, Stevenson did not like the use of contrasting granites, citing an example of a row of houses built from dark Tillyfourie granite with the dressings round the windows and corbie-stepped gables of the lighter Kemnay. Because the surface area was small it was reduced to a mere stripe by the contrasting dressings. Working in London, Stevenson would have been aware of the beginning of the trend towards the use of polished granite for building fronts. This was another use of granite of which he did not approve, one that was even more difficult to get right. 'Apt to look too fine for its place', was his comment. The polished surface showing dirt easily and it needed cleaning as often as windows. Its use in pillars detracted from the look of solidity by turning them into reflective mirrors. Even polished headstones did not escape Stevenson's criticism:

> It lends itself too easily to the modern love of display, and its brilliancy is apt to strike harshly among the moss-grown tombs and the quiet of country churchyards, but if rightly used it is capable of producing magnificent effects in architecture, as in rounded forms and great broad masses of polished wall surfaces.[29]

So there we have a few different opinions on Aberdeen and its granite architecture, written in the middle of the great granite-building century. I wonder what these writers would have made of the wedding cake architecture that was to come with the building of the new Marischal College at the end of the century.

The Export of Finished Granite Products Particularly to North America

From the middle of the nineteenth century onwards the geographical spread of a yard's orders came to be considerable. James Wright's order book from 1869 already demonstrates this. Towards the end of the century the *Granite Chips* column reported in 1898 that Taggart's yard was working on orders from the following places – Bristol, Wick, London, Berwick, Auchterless, Llandysull, Kirkcaldy, Larbert, Banchory, Monquhitter, Slains, Clatt, Strichen, Arbroath, Cheshire, York, Melrose, Glenbucket, Edinburgh, Alloa, Flint, Glenlivet, Tillycoultry, Kingussie, Cape Town (two monuments), and Barbados. This did not include orders within Aberdeen itself and was purely for work in Rubislaw granite, they also had many orders for other granites. Taggart's at this time was by no means one of the largest yards. However, it was the trade with America in particular that made many of the yards.[30]

Although most writers on granite state that exports of granite monuments to America began after the end of the American Civil War in 1865,[31] we have seen in Chapter 5 that Harriet Beecher Stowe, on her visit to Aberdeen in 1853, commented in a letter that there were many specimens of Aberdeen granite in America and that she herself was shown a funeral monument in Macdonald & Leslie's yard destined for New York. This trade almost certainly arose because their work was seen at the Great Exhibition two years earlier in 1851. Moreover a description of Macdonald's yard in 1856 states that even at this early date polished Aberdeenshire granite was being exported to Russia, India, the Crimea, Australia and China as well as America.[32] As regards the latter, however, it would certainly have been the case that the trade increased after the Civil War; shipping conditions would probably have meant that there was little in the way of granite exports during the war. The drive for industrialisation to meet the war effort created prosperity in the northern states and this continued after the war. The vast casualties suffered during the war would also have created demand for funerary monuments. America would become by far the biggest export market for the Aberdeen granite yards. In 1869, just four years after the end of the war, James Wright & Sons order book shows an order of twenty-one monuments for James Sharkey of New York (see below).

One American journalist on a visit to Aberdeen in 1875 describes the impact of a granite monument from Aberdeen on his home town many years before. In describing Aberdeen he wrote:

> Its name is familiar to every American who takes an interest in graveyards. I remember the first stone from its workshops which was erected in the Danbury cemetery. It was two years before it had a fellow, and in that time was frequently visited by everybody, as its polished shaft attracted attention from all directions in the grounds. We call it Aberdeen marble.[33]

He goes on to say that there is no material as beautiful as polished Aberdeen granite. In his visit to Macdonald's yard he was shown the polishing process and he stated that half the work of the granite polishers was for America and that nearly every piece he saw being polished at Macdonald's 'was for enterprising Americans who have been dead only a few years'.

At some point architectural pieces such as turned granite columns were also exported. One early example was for the German Hebrew Congregation of Rodeph Shalom in Philadelphia, the foundation stone of which was laid in 1869, some seven years before the first World's Fair to be held in America took place in Philadelphia in 1876. On either side of the main entrance of this Moorish influenced building were four columns of 'highly wrought and polished Aberdeen granite.'[34] These columns were probably supplied by either Macdonald's or Wright's and, although described as being of Aberdeen granite, they may well have been red Peterhead stone given the reds and browns used in the rest of the building. The specification for these would have been placed sometime before the laying of the foundation stone, especially given the time it took to manufacture such columns at the time. Unfortunately the building was demolished in the 1920s and replaced by a larger building.

Overseas trade became hugely important for the Aberdeen granite yards, especially the larger ones. In the 1880s demand from America was generally high despite a 20 per cent tariff. In 1884 the *Free Press* reported that orders came in from America during the winter when conditions in many of the granite areas of America were severe. The Americans also realised that they could have work carried out at a reduced price from the Aberdeen yards in winter because in winter the yards here received fewer orders from elsewhere. The reason given by the *Free Press* for the high demand from America was that wages were lower in Aberdeen, the workmanship and material were better, and the machinery used was more advanced. Much of this would change by the next decade, especially regarding machinery and workmanship.[35]

By 1893 the Granite Association Minute Books recorded that 'the greatest number of orders comes from America but the trade with that country is mainly conducted by wholesale dealers who have agents in Aberdeen.'[36]

An example of how overseas work compared to domestic work can seen with Bower & Florence in 1894. That year they reported that the value of their work was £13,000 comprising:

Home work £7,000
America £3,000
Australia £1,500
Cape of Good Hope and China £800
Europe £700[37]

How typical this particular year was for Bower & Florence it is difficult to say. If anything, though, the amount of trade with America might be on the low side since throughout the industry generally it was actually a year of low orders from America due to uncertainty over tariff proposals which were not settled until September. US Congressman William McKinley had increased the tariff on granite imports from 20 per cent to 40 per cent in 1890. At the end of 1893 and into 1894 the American dealers had held off placing orders because they expected a tariff reduction. There were also money problems in the US and their own industry was quiet that year. For the first nine months of 1893 the value of American trade was £69,000. For the same period in 1894 it was £44,700, a fall of almost a third. The Wilson-Gorman Tariff subsequently reduced the rate to 30 per cent in 1894.[38] In a normal year, then, the figures given above for Bower & Florence might have shown that the American market was even more important.

By 1900 a notable symbolic highlight was reached when Macdonald's exported a granite monument back to the land where it all began, Egypt. The monument, 16ft in height, was to be erected in Alexandria to commemorate the Khedive Nubar Pasha, famous Egyptian statesman and first Prime Minister of the country, who had died in Paris the previous year. Created from red granite from Stirlinghill, it was in the form of an Egyptian temple. A massive base supported two columns with lotus flowers carved at the base and capitals. The columns and back wall supported a large entablature with a decorated cornice and sloping roof. Most of the granite was polished and in Alexandria a marble statute of the Khedive was inserted on a pedestal in the back wall of the monument. The *Aberdeen Journal* reported that the workmanship was of the highest order and would add to Macdonald's reputation.[39]

The American Connection: Aberdeen's Export of Granite Expertise

The American market was very important for north-east granite yards but it was not just finished granite products that were exported to America. The expertise of the Aberdeenshire granite men was also a sought after commodity in North America, as has been well documented by Dr Marjory Harper of Aberdeen University.

Sir George Adam Smith, Principal of the University of Aberdeen, originally came to Aberdeen in 1881 as the first minister of the newly built Queen's Cross Church. At the jubilee of the church in 1931 he remembered that not long after he took up his charge about 20 families left the area and emigrated to the granite quarries of Vermont. That was quite an unusual occurrence at that time; it was much more common for only the men to go, sometimes for a few months, sometimes for a few years.

Councillor and granite merchant William Boddie said that he was one of the first to go to America in 1869. He credits Aberdonians with introducing granite cutting to America, though in fact there were workers from others areas in Britain involved as well as former marble workers from Italy. Boddie, though, particularly credited his fellow countrymen with developing granite statuary at Westerly, Rhode Island. In fact he stated that 'that class of work was introduced by an Aberdonian called McHardy who, after returning to the city, executed a lot of allegorical figures at the Crown Granite Works.'[40] At Dix Island, Maine, one of the great boarding houses for granite workers, eventually demolished in 1896, was known as the 'Aberdeen' house.[41]

Numbers going to America could be substantial. For example the *Granite Chips* column in April 1896, recorded one group of twenty-six stonecutters leaving for America with more to follow.[42]

This group would only have been a small part of the exodus which could reach 250 in any one year and this exodus helped the Aberdeen industry build up connections for trading with North America and, as we will see in the next section, a number of the returning workers used the capital they had acquired in America to set up there own yards when they came back to Aberdeen. In 1886 a large number of men were being sought by one of the American agents, George Berry. As described by Marjory Harper,[43] he wanted to recruit around 150 men cutting stone for the new State Capital in Austin, Texas and he was offering good money for the job. Berry eventually left Aberdeen with eighty-five men but what he hadn't told them was that they would be working on a construction job that had been boycotted by the American Granite Cutters' Union because of the use of convict labour. The Union also wanted Berry and his employer, Gus Wilke, prosecuted for illegally bringing in foreign contract labour. The union tried to intercept the Aberdeen men when they landed in New York and a number did leave the group to find less controversial work. Others continued on to Texas and they sent varying accounts about their working conditions back to Aberdeen. Following the completion of the contract the Union tried to have the Aberdeen men blacklisted from other work elsewhere in America. Wilke did eventual admit in court that he had illegally imported foreign contract labour but the incident does not seem to have harmed long term relations between the Union and Aberdeen workers, the former lending the latter support in some of their own industrial disputes back home in Aberdeen.

Robert Hall, the builder, was involved in recruiting the men to go to Austin, or at least he spoke up for the move having himself worked for four years in South Carolina. Hall chaired one of the recruitment meetings held in the Northern Friendly Society's Hall in April 1886.[44] In 1887 he was presented with a silver cup, sent over from a Gus Wilke or Wilkie of Austin who he had never met, to thank him for his assistance. The cup went on display at an ironmongers in Gilcomston Steps, near Hall's premises in Gilcomston Land.[45]

Some north-east granite men stayed in America and began businesses there. Among the most successful were the Booth Brothers of New York. William Booth was a settmaker who worked at Kemnay just before he left for America.

In the city of Barre, Vermont, and the surrounding area alone there are numerous instances of men from the north-east establishing successful businesses. One of the greatest success stories was that of William Barclay. Born in Fraserburgh he started his working life as a farm servant before serving his apprenticeship to a mason and builder in New Pitsligo. He then crossed and recrossed the Atlantic several times – to Montreal in Canada, to Quincy in Massachusetts – before settling permanently in the other granite city of Barre in 1886. There he established a business, initially with William S. Littlejohn. Then, when Littlejohn retired in 1890, Barclay's brother Andrew joined him and the company became Barclay Brothers, one of the largest granite companies in America. William Barclay was a pillar of the community in Barre, serving three terms as Mayor, as well as being President of the Granite Manufacturers' Association and of the Burns Club. William was succeeded in the business by his two sons, William Jr., and Douglas, both of whom had been born in Aberdeen. Others from the north-east involved in Barre were Adie & Milne, James Adie being from New Aberdour and James S. Milne from Aberdeen; the Young Brothers from Fyvie; the Smith Brothers from Aberdeen; Charles W. McMillan from Aberdeen; Rust & Brew, established by William

James Macdonald's headstone for a young girl in Barre, Vermont, 1890s.

Brown who had served his time with William Hunter in Aberdeen, it later became Rust & Brew with Rust having come to Barre from Aberdeen at the age of just 16, and Brew having served his apprenticeship with the Froghall Granite Works of Charles Macdonald. And there were many more in this one region alone.

James Macdonald was another north-east granite worker who spent some time in Barre in the 1890s. Macdonald lodged with a family in Barre and the first time he went there their young daughter, Margaret, was ill. When he returned the following year Margaret had died and according to Macdonald's family he carved this statue for the girl's grave. It is sited in the Hope Cememtery in Barre, which is full of impressive craved granite memorials and tomb-stones. Macdonald was so taken by the little girl that he gave his daughter the middle name Margaret. Following his return from America Macdonald went on to become foreman at Fyfe's yard in Aberdeen, eventually becoming manager. He worked on Lord Cowdrey's coat of arms for the hall and estate offices at Dunecht, and His Majesty's Theatre and can been seen in Chapter 8 alongside the heraldic placque destined for the bridge over the Thames at Kew.

Other nationalities were also involved in the granite industry in the north-eastern states of America, notably Italians, many of whom had worked in the marble industry in Italy. A survey carried out in 1919 as to the origins of the granite cutters in Barre stated that 557 were of Italian origin, 181 Scottish and 87 Spanish. This probably indicates that Scottish granite workers were mainly seasonal and transitory whereas the Italian tended to settle permanently.[46]

A Mr Harvey, a settmaker interviewed for a radio programme in the 1930s, described his experi-ences in America before the First World War:

> In America it was either a boom or naething. We were paid by the coont, here it is by weight. Of course there was nae work in the winter time, we came back here in the winter. I was in Wisconsin, makin' blocks for Chicago. Then down south in Virginia, Carolina and Georgia. We worked in tents or open canvas shelters, but of course none of the labourin' work was done by whites.[47]

Even by the later 1950s you can find examples of granite men emigrating from Aberdeen to North America. Alec Mackie, quoted at length in Chapter 6, was one such. He had served his apprenticeship with the firm of G. M. Stalker c.1953–58 and ended in St Louis, Missouri. When he retired in 2000 he was virtually the last traditional mason in the area. One of the most prestigious pieces he carved was the stone seal of the United States for the American Embassy in Riyadh, Saudi Arabia.

It wasn't just as granite workers that north-east men made their mark. James Duncan from Aberdeen was national secretary of the American Granitecutters' Union and editor of their journal at the end of the nineteenth century.

Proliferation of Granite Yards

John Fyfe used to say that when he entered the business the whole of the granite industry in Aberdeen consisted of three journeymen masons and a dog. By the end of the century there were a huge number of granite yards in the city, many of them substantial businesses employing hundreds of men, others on a much smaller scale.

Following Alexander Macdonald, some of those who set up businesses on their own were men who had served their apprenticeship with him, Robert D. Cruickshank of the Albyn Granite Works, for example. Some yards were established by men who had gone to America to work and returned with sufficient capital to start their own business. Charles Macdonald came from a granite family and emigrated to America. One of his brothers stayed there but Charles came back around 1877 and set up a small yard in Gerrard Street. He subsequently moved to Nelson Street before establishing the Froghall Granite Works in Jute Street, employing 150 men.

Robert Gibb was another who, after serving his apprenticeship with William Keith, spent eighteen months in America before returning and setting up for himself in 1875 in Nelson Street, just himself and a boy initially. He subsequently moved to King Street, eventually moving to larger premises and becoming known as the Excelsior Granite Works who employed 108 hands in 1895.[48] The wife of William Edwards of the Nelson Granite Works surprised him on his return by having saved enough of the money he had sent back to enable him to set up in business on his own. Numerous other examples of men who began their own businesses after returning from America can be found in Appendix 1.

At the 1880 annual dinner of the Aberdeen Master Masons' Association, George Henderson commented on the depressed state of the monumental and polishing sector by saying that he 'accounted for the falling off in the polishing trade by its having been overdone in its prosperity by the inducement it held out for people to go into it.' At the same dinner William Boddie disagreed with this assessment saying, to applause and laughter, that 'hitherto it had been a monopoly; now it was a healthy trade'[49] Were they still laughing into the 1880s when the *Aberdeen Journal* bemoaned the fact that there had been an increase in the number of yards and that the resulting competition was unhealthy for the industry? According to the *Journal*, the more recent yards had been established by working men using their savings and setting up on a co-operative basis. These yards were worked by the men themselves with apprentices and the older established yards were being undercut or had to tender for work at rates that were barely profitable. These newer yards were also working overtime and employing too many apprentices in relation to journeymen.[50] Was it unfair,

Masons at James Forbes's Ernan Granite Work in the 1880s. Compare this with the illustration on page 78 showing pneumatic tools at Taggart's yard some twenty years later. (Aberdeen Art Gallery and Museums Collection)

or was this simply the *Journal* acting as the mouthpiece of the larger employers? In any case the various groups involved in the industry met and agreed more uniform working practices, and also agreed to limit the proportion of apprentices. The formation of the Aberdeen Granite Association at the end of 1887 also led to an attempt by the larger yards to control the number of smaller yards. As early as their inaugural dinner the following April, James Littlejohn said that one of the chief aims of the Association was to stop the downward trend in prices which he said would ruin them. He gave the main cause of this as being the increasing numbers of polishing yards which he thought should be discouraged. William Stewart of Stewart & Co. echoed this in his speech, given to applause, in which he stated that:

At present they were running wild with the extension of new firms, of which there were seven or eight every year. Hitherto the firms had been composed of workmen from the ranks – foremen and superior workmen, and men with a little capital. But now with the cheap polishing and other facilities, men could enter the trade with no capital at all. This he deprecated, and he held that if a man commenced with a little capital and experience the field was open still.[51]

As reported by the *Journal* the AGA met with their journeymen masons to try to come to an agreement to limit the number of apprentices in the industry as well as standardise working hours, something the men and their fledgling unions supported.[52] As we will see in Chapter 10, another way in which the Association would try to limit the number of smaller businesses entering the trade was to control the trade by making membership of the Association a necessity and then gradually increasing their membership fees.

Even earlier in 1884 the *Daily Free Press* was taking a similar line as the *Aberdeen Journal* when it gave a lengthy statement on the state of the industry at the end of that year. The *Free Press* gave the total number of firms of sculptors and polishers as between sixty and seventy, employing around 1,400 men and boys. In addition there were a considerable number of blacksmiths and mechanics, as well as quarriers and carters. The growth in the number of firms up to that point had been very rapid. According to the *Free Press*, twenty years before there had been only three firms and of the total at that point in 1884 about fifty had started in the last fifteen years. In order to get work these small yards were producing monuments at low prices which actually increased demand 'especially as regards the less moneyed classes of the community'.[53] Perhaps feeling the competition, in 1885 John Fraser & Son's advertisement in the Post Office Directory stated, 'as there is an increasing demand for a cheap class of granite gravemarks, headstones, and monuments, they have been able to make arrangements to supply the same from forty-five shillings.'

But the smaller yards were also attracting workers, especially younger ones, from the larger yards to do overtime after their normal working day was finished. The complaints of overworking from the larger yards seem to have had the support of the Trades Council:

> There is, however, a great danger in the case of boys of overworking the system before it is equal to the strain, and if the lads in the work they give to one employer use the tools with which they have been provided by another their conduct is clearly incorrect, while as regards both apprentices and journeymen it is obvious that when they prolong their labours far into the night or early morning they cannot be able to give to those who employ them during the daytime the service which they are entitled to expect. It is not surprising, therefore, that firms who have discovered that the energies of their employees were thus being dissipated should have made firm protest and dismissed the men whom they found to be taking advantage of them.

The *Free Press* view was that the larger firms had invested heavily in machinery and premises and were now suffering from the undercutting of these smaller firms.[54]

As noted earlier the growth in the number of yards was not continuous. In 1895 the *Aberdeen Journal* reported that over-competition for American business had led to six yards closing down, though the total number of yards in the city still grew. Even a large, long established yard such as Alexander Macdonald's could go into liquidation as it did in the early years of the next century.

We can get a good picture of a large granite yard at the turn of the nineteenth century from the description of James Knowles's new yard on Ashgrove Road which was reckoned to be one of the best equipped in the city at the time. The main building was 336ft x 40ft. Inside there was a travelling crane, a polishing carriage, three vertical polishers and two Jenny Linds, all of these made by the engineering firm of John A. Sangster in St Clair Street. In addition there were four stone saws, two polishing pendulums, a stone turning lathe and four polishing lathes all made by the well known local engineering firm of John M. Henderson of King Street. Outside there was a 5-ton derrick, a 3-ton hand crane and a 2-ton hand crane. All the machinery was driven by a condensing engine and in the engine room there was a powerful air compressor for the new pneumatic tools and this had been supplied by Clayton of Brooklyn, New York.[55] It had electric lighting throughout, with fifty incandescent lamps and six arc lamps, the first yard in the city to install electrc lighting. At the switching on ceremony several of the local granite merchants were in attendance including Alex Wilson, President of the AGA, Arthur Taylor, Archibald A. Brown, William Morgan, Robert Cruickshamk and representaives from Charles Macdonalds and Alexander Macdonalds.[56] (See also the description of Alexander Wilson's new yard in Balmoral Road in Appendix 1.)

It was only the larger yards that had their own machinery on any scale. In 1895 the *Aberdeen Journal* reported that, including half a dozen show yards, there were eighty monumental granite yards in the city. Of these, thirty-four had polishing machinery –mainly driven by steam, with a few using gas. Twenty-nine of the thirty-four had power saws, and nine had machinery for stone turning. There were also two works for the manufacture of chilled shot, which was used in the sawing and polishing. As the *Journal* said, monumental yards varied from a man and a boy to the largest which employed 200 hands. Altogether the 80 yards employed 2,500 people.[57]

The larger yards were more diverse in the work they did. To some extent this helped protect them from the cyclical nature of much of the industry. For example, when there were problems with exports to America and uncertainty over the issue of tariffs on imports into America, the trade with America all but dried up in some years. 1894 was a particularly bad year for trade with America. This could have a significant impact on smaller yards, whose work was mainly monumental. During the 1890s polished granite fronts began to be popular for shops, banks, offices, hotels and restaurants etc. Larger works might hope to make up the slack with this kind of architectural work.

The Fashion for Polished Granite Frontages

As well as monumental work, the larger yards were also involved in architectural work, carrying out much of the decorative work in more elaborate buildings. In the late nineteenth century, polished granite panels became popular for shop and office fronts as well as hotels and restaurants. Large-scale polished granite fronts were exported to the rest of the country and even overseas. For these buildings granite was only used for the prestigious part at ground-floor level, less expensive stone being used above that level. In 1894, for example, among some of the work being carried out in London by John Whitehead & Son was a polished red and grey granite frontage for the North British and Mercantile Marine Insurance Offices. The total frontage was 63ft long, 16ft high, of polished granite. At the same time among other frontages they were working on was a polished grey granite one for the Commercial Union Assurance Company Offices in London – a building on three frontages 60ft, 60ft and 50ft in length respectively, with the granite up to a height of 20ft and granite interspersed with the stone work above that; a red and grey polished front for the

Polished granite columns by William Keith at the former Colonial Institute, Northumberland Avenue, London.

Detail of doorway of Union Bank of Australia, Cornhill, London.

Guardian Assurance Offices; new post offices in Liverpool and Nottingham; the Clydesdale Bank in Lombard Street, the Capital and Counties Bank in Piccadily, the North British and Mercantile Marine Offices in Threadneedle Street, and the Guardian Fire & Life Insurance Company's Offices in Lombard Street, all in London.[58]

In 1893 Alexander Macdonald's were said to be working on polished red granite columns for a Roman Catholic Cathedral in Melbourne, Australia. This was possibly St Mary Star of the Sea, actually a parish church rather than a cathedral, which does have polished red colonettes described as being of Aberdeen granite, i.e. probably Peterhead. It also has red columns of Swedish granite which were worked in Aberdeen. At the same time Macdonald's were also working on granite columns for the Halifax and Huddersfield Banking Company in Elland, each at 18ft long and weighing 8 tons, the largest columns ever turned in Aberdeen.[59] In 1894 Macdonald's had finished or were finishing a basement in five courses for a bank in Glasgow; thirty-four polished red granite columns each 10ft long for a building in London; polished red and grey granite piers for a large block of buildings in St Paul's Churchyard, London; and an extension of the Buenos Aires branch of the London and River Plate Bank. For the latter they had some years before supplied several thousand pounds worth of polished granite.[60] The following year the 75ft-long frontage was actually set up in their yard for the architect to inspect. Also in 1895 Macdonald's sent off the first part of a consignment of large, beautifully polished Peterhead granite columns for the Opera Comique in Paris. These six columns drew a crowd as each made its way to the quay transported by six two-horse wagons.[61] James Wright's at the Royal Granite Works were also doing a large job in London in 1894. This was a polished granite front for the new offices of the Union Bank of Australia in Cornhill, London, in light grey granite. It was one of the largest jobs of its kind in any of the Aberdeen yards up to that point. By December that year they had been working on it for thirteen months, with a few months erection time in London to follow. The granite work was for the first storey but comprised 150 tons of material, and was 60ft in length and 24ft high. As well as the central doorway with a deeply moulded architrave, there were six panelled pilasters, each over 2ft thick and with Ionic capitals, framing the doorway and four windows. A cornice and ornate freeze ran the whole length of the building. The *Aberdeen Journal* commented, 'The general effect is massive and elegant, and, in the opinion of experts, the workmanship displayed is among the finest ever produced by granite sculptors'.[62] This, of course, was just before the introduction of pneumatic tools for carving granite. Fortunately the building is still standing.

In the work of these three yards we can see the possible size and value of these contracts. John Fyfe was another who found work all over Britain and, in February 1896, he was entertained to a dinner in the Council Chamber of the Holborn Restaurant in London, by merchants and tenants of the Brixton area. In the late 1880s Fyfe had built Electric Avenue in Brixton, notable for its iron and glass canopies in front of the shops, and by the fact that it is thought to have been the first shopping street in the country to be lit by electricity.[63] The electricity was actually the work of Fyfe's younger brother, John Leslie Fyfe, whose Fyfe-Main Electric Lighting and Construction Company exhibited at Crystal Palace in 1882. The street was later immortalised in a chart topping song by Eddy Grant, based on the Brixton riots of 1981.

Location and Layout of the Yards

The greatest concentration of yards was in the east end of the city. In the 1930s John McLaren describes the 48 yards then in existence as being mainly located in the King Street, Pittodrie, King's Crescent, Jute Street and Froghall area.[64] Eight yards were in the area bounded by King's Crescent, Jute Street and Froghall, with five in the Holland Street/Fraser Road area and three in lower Ashgrove Road and Back Hilton Road. A few others were situated outside this area in Great Western Road, the Hardgate and Torry. Macdonald's yard had been in Constitution Street. It has been suggested that this area drew granite yards because of proximity to the canal. I'm not sure that this is really convincing. Macdonald's yard had been established in the 1830s by which time the canal had been in operation for some thirty years but how much granite traffic actually came by canal at that time? Certainly granite from Rubislaw and from the Peterhead yards would not have been transported by canal. I'm not sure that the quarries to the north of the town around Cairncry would have used the canal, though Dyce, Sclattie and Persley did use it and Dancing Cairns may

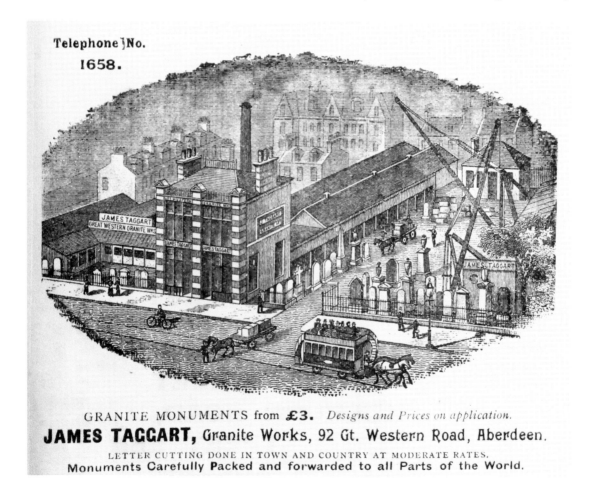

Advertisement for James Taggart's yard, 1899 from Aberdeen Street Directory.

have to some extent. I think it more likely that proximity to the harbour was more important, with Peterhead granite arriving by sea and granite for London and elsewhere being sent by sea before the coming of the railways. Both English companies, Mowlem and Manuelle, when they set up in the town, did so at the quays. It may have been that the available land nearest the harbour was along the King Street corridor.

From the late 1880s to the time Henry Hamilton was writing, around the time of the Second World War, the layout of many yards, especially smaller ones, changed little. Hamilton describes this as being arranged in a square with sawing processes and machines at one side, a polishing mill on another, and the stonecutters and polishers on a third side, all of them within the radius of a centrally positioned derrick crane which could move stone from one area to another.[65] Granite yard advertisements and surviving photographs give us an idea of how this looked. Increasing the size of the yard meant additional investment in stone moving machinery. Larger yards could have movable overhead cranes and even rails connecting different parts of the yard. John McLaren's diagram of Bower & Florence's yard from the 1920s shows seven or eight overhead cranes as well as the bogies and rails connecting the north and south yards.[66]

Granite Imports

Importation of granite into Aberdeen possibly began in the year 1880. William S. Grant recalled that in the summer of 1882 Heslop, Wilson & Co. of Peterhead, via Aberdeen granite merchants J. & J. Ogg, imported around 200 tons of a German grey granite into Boddam Harbour. Grant said that this proved to be a failure because after polishing it developed yellow stains.[67] However, by 1884 the *Free Press* reported that:

> On account of the limited supply of granite in the neighbourhood and the drawbacks that attend the work of quarrying it, local granite merchants have begun to draw upon other places for mate-rial, and an experiment has been made in importing granite from Germany and Sweden.[68]

This move undoubtedly had the potential to divide the granite industry. The imports were mainly for the monumental industry with the growing demand for new colours, especially from North America, being given as the main reason. Swedish green granite was initially the most popular. As noted by the *Free Press* there were also concerns over the ability of the native quarries to supply sufficient amounts of blocks of the quality and size that the industry needed. As the use of foreign granite extended there were also issues of cost as the Scandinavian granite was often nearer the surface, without a layer of tirr. These quarries were also near the coast for easier transportation. This really became an issue when Scandinavian countries began to develop their own stone-cutting industries and were able to transport even relatively low cost items such as setts directly to cities along the east coast of Britain. In 1884 the *Free Press* was already commenting that Swedish granite had decreased in price in the few years since importing began. Initially it was 15s per cubic foot, then it reduced to 9s, and then to 5s by 1884.

The growth in granite imports over the next two or three decades can be seen in figures produced by the Aberdeen Granite Association in 1916. The figures were compiled from the Harbour Board Accounts.[69]

1892: 7,680 tons
1897: 13,824 tons
1901: 20,607 tons
1908: 27,390 tons
1911: 30,386 tons
1913: 22,496 tons

Norway followed Sweden, and there was also granite from various areas of Germany as well as India and elsewhere, with Bower & Florence introducing an Oriental red granite of exquisite colour in 1894. Thereafter the imports were not restricted to coloured stone. Very early on some in the industry were quite critical of these imports and the effect they would have on the local industry. The *Aberdeen Weekly Journal*, in 1888, wrote that although at first glance imported stone from Germany and Sweden might look like the local stone, closer inspection showed the differences in grain and colour. Generally the imported stone was already tooled and squared, unlike the rough stone from local quarries, and although this might mean a small saving the *Journal* was concerned about the effect on the reputation of the Aberdeen product if they used this imported material.[70] In 1894 the Granite Chips column in the *Evening Express* commented:

> Foreign granite may have the effect of damaging the reputation of Aberdeen granite, as doubtless many who get their orders executed in Aberdeen do not take the trouble to enquire as to where the granite comes from, but take it for granted that it is a home production, and naturally get disappointed when the granite loses its brightness and shows signs of decay. The stones that come from Sweden, although all classed as granite, include specimens which are deficient either in quartz or mica, and in some cases lime takes the place of felspar. Some of these stones look beautiful when newly finished, but soon fade and lose their brilliant appearance.[71]

The sensitivity of this issue of importing granite to the Granite City can perhaps be seen in the fact that the granite yards often used local names for the imported granite. For example there was Victoria Grey, Balmoral Red, Froghall Grey, Glencoe and Bon-Accord Black. Charles Macdonald Ltd at the Froghall Granite Works were one of the pioneers in importing granite, especially from Norway and Sweden. In 1896, for example, they did the granite work for a bank in Leeds, 70ft long by 30ft high, in Froghall Grey contrasted with dark Labrador. The interior granite work was in Swedish red granite.[72] Not all the examples given above were coloured and the Granite Chips column in 1895 was clear what the reason was for importing grey granite in addition to coloured stone:

> It looks like carrying coals to Newcastle to bring foreign grey granite to Aberdeen, but the competition was brought on by the output of our native quarries not being equal to the demand.

The supplies could not be depended on, and the granite master had to look elsewhere. The number of foreign reds used is also considerable.[73]

The column goes on to admit that one quarry where there was difficulty in getting adequate supplies of grey granite was Rubislaw. While understanding and even supporting the importation of foreign granite to Aberdeen the very same column saw no contradiction in being critical of the Council for accepting a tender to build the Beach Bathing Station from brick even after a local mason had given them a similar tender for a granite building.

By 1903 the *Evening Gazette* commented that if it was not for imported granite the industry in Aberdeen would go to the wall. It gave the estimate of £50,000 of foreign granite imported that year and quoted an un-named member of the granite trade as saying that two-thirds of granite manufactured in the city came from abroad, a quite staggering figure if true.[74] By the 1930s, 80 per cent of the granite used in the monumental yards came from abroad.[75]

Already in the years before the First World War there was a cry for protection of the home granite industry and this would continue right into the period after the Second World War. However, as the *People's Journal* wryly commented in 1905:

The cry just now is beware of Sweden and several of the most ardent Protectionists among the Aberdeen granite merchants have been the readiest to avail themselves of the free importation of the foreign raw material. Hundreds of tons of Swedish granite are lying at the yard of the Aberdeen Granite Supply Association – a body that comprises the majority of stone-cutting employers of labour.

Unlike the comment quoted above from the *Evening Express*, the *People's Journal* was in no doubt of the qualities of Swedish stone:

Aberdeenshire granite is possibly the best stone in the world, but it does not have the variety of texture and grain that can be found in the Swedish quarries, and the monumentalists would be unwilling for a mere political whim to sacrifice the beautiful 'Emerald pearls' which, to many eyes, are incomparably the richest of the polishing stones that can be procured.[76]

The Aberdeen Granite Case

Passing off foreign granite as Aberdeen granite was one of the issues in what was known in the press as the Aberdeen Granite Case. In January 1914 Frederick Wright, of the old established firm of James Wright & Sons, brought an action at the High Court in London in front of the Official Referee against Bringes & Goodwin, manufacturers of paint crushing machinery, for an outstanding payment of £36 for granite rollers. Bringes & Goodwin argued that they had been supplied with rollers made from Swedish granite that were not suitable for the purpose, they having ordered Aberdeen granite rollers. Their counter-claim was for £200 for loss of goodwill and £300 for loss of profit. Wright argued that he had supplied a Swedish granite known as 'dressing grey' because it was fine grained and in his opinion more suitable for the purpose. He had always endeavoured to select the granite most suitable for the defenders' purpose. He also said that Bringes & Goodwin had been sent samples and that they should therefore have known what they were getting as it was easily distinguishable from Aberdeen grey (Rubislaw), the latter being darker and coarse grained, and there being no such things as fine grained grey Aberdeen granite. Wright had actually dealt with the defenders for thirty or forty years, the disputed transaction having taken place in 1905. Despite stating that the Swedish stone had been tested and found to withstand a pressure of 22,000lb to the square inch as opposed to almost 14,00lb for Rubislaw, Wright lost the case, perhaps partly because he had described the granite supplied as No.16 which was an Aberdeenshire granite, rather than the Swedish stone that was actually supplied. Wright also erred in stating that the cost of both Swedish and Aberdeen granites was the same once they had been made into rollers. He then had to admit by letter that in fact the Swedish rollers cost 10 per cent more. The Referee stated that the defenders were entitled to refuse payment, or at least set the sum off against the cost of the defective rollers. However, loss of goodwill and profit had not been proven and he only awarded Bringes & Goodwin £51 8s 4d plus costs.

Granite Supply Association

As we have seen many of the granite yards were quite small businesses and it must have been difficult for the smaller yards to access supplies of imported granite. Various types of merchants were initially involved in importing granite, particularly coal merchants. In 1897, under the auspices of the Aberdeen Granite Association, a joint stock company was established to carry on the business of importing granite. It was known as the Granite Supply Association and was originally based in Palmerston Road, but in 1901 they moved to 105 Urquhart Road, opposite the City Hospital and much nearer to the majority of the granite yards. Also in 1901 the directors appointed John Stuart Sutherland, who had worked for one of the coal merchants, as manager of the business. The same year Sutherland applied to the AGA to become members of that association. The Supply Association subsequently resigned from the AGA in 1913 during the price dispute within the AGA.[77] The Supply Association wanted the freedom to trade with anyone, not just members of the AGA.

John Sutherland was manager for forty-five years, was appointed to the board in 1917, and was subsequently chairman of directors for a long period, retiring as manager in 1946. When he died in 1951 he had been involved with the Association for fifty years. His son, also John S. Sutherland, succeeded him as manager.[78]

The Association also supplied other material for use by the trade, such as emery, timber, and putty powder. They became agents for the Carborundum Company of Manchester and John Sutherland senior was also Chairman of Mowat's Grit Company.

Their yard at Urquhart Road was originally 2 acres, gradually growing to 5.5 acres over a period of twenty years. In 1920 they bought the land on which the yard stood from the Incorporated Trades of Aberdeen. As with the granite yards the Association yard had its own granite-moving equipment – seven cranes, originally hand-operated, later converted to steam and then, around 1920, to electricity. In 1926, owing to the effects of the General Strike, they bought their own 3-ton motor lorry. In 1928 the office building situated opposite the gates of the city hospital was built, to the designs of John McLennan of Jenkins and Marr, architects. During the years of the Second World War the yard was mainly used for handling and storing heavy goods needed by the government for the war effort.

At the time Henry Hamilton was writing he was of the opinion that the Association had been a very useful organisation when it was broadly representative of the granite industry but of late it tended to become a highly concentrated monopoly able to dominate and control the import of granite (and of Rubislaw granite) because of its ability to make bulk purchases and keep large stocks in its depot. It then refused to supply any firms that did not buy all their granite through the Association.[79]

As with other organisations in the industry, the Supply Association was involved in campaigns to maintain or restart the importation of granite during and after both world wars. It would not always have been in agreement with some of the other areas of the industry, particularly the quarry owners.

In 1958 the Directors were Alexander Wilson, Alfred Wright, John S. Sutherland, Alexander Gibb and Robert Crofts. In the mid 1960s John Sutherland junior retired from the company and was succeeded by his son Alistair, who had been associated with the company since 1951. The company survived until around 1993 when it was taken over by John Fyfe Ltd. and moved to Westhill. Alistair Sutherland left shortly after and set up his own business selling abrasives from the Carborundum Company of Manchester.

Setts and Settmaking

We have seen already that the Scots term for a sett was cassie, with the man making it a causey-man, deriving from the word causeway. These words were beginning to die out in the granite trade in the second half of the nineteenth century as indicated by its use in the 1871 and 1881 Census for Kemnay (see Chapter 6). Cassie, though, is still used by north-east folk today. According to Diack the view in the granite trade is that the word sett came from the workman setting or hand setting the shaped stone into the roadway. This would date it to the late eighteenth or early nineteenth centuries.[80]

Knight describes the setts supplied to London for pavements at the time he was writing in 1832, though he didn't use the term sett. There were Common Sixes – 10in x 6in and 6in deep. Half-sovereigns were the same length and width but were 7in deep. *Sovereigns* 10in x 8in and 7–8in in depth.[81] In the days of horse drawn transport 3in x 4in setts were often used on inclines to help the horses to get a grip. In 1866 the *Building News* said that the common sizes of paving setts were know as common fours and three by fives. Kerbstones were better made, dressed smooth on top and the side facing the channel, with the back being simply hammered. They were generally 12in in width and 8in in depth.[82] In 1912 John Fyfe jun. said that 5in stones were for a cheap job such as side streets, 6in for principal streets.

Most quarries provided some work for settmakers but Tillyfourie was particularly noted as centre of the sett and crib or kerb stone trade. In 1900 around 400 men were employed as settmakers in Aberdeenshire. Their vulnerability to the fluctuations of demand meant that working in America was an attractive option for some. At the end of the nineteenth century and in the early twentieth century there was high demand for setts in America, and a significant number of north-east sett-makers left for America.

Signs of decline in the use of setts to surface roads was already in evidence in 1898 when the *Aberdeen Journal* reported that in that year 28,665 square yards of the city's roads had been tar mac-adamed. This was an increase of 5,885 on the previous year. Ordinary macadam was replaced with tar in Berryden and Belmont Roads, but at Woolmanhill and part of St Andrew Street granite setts were replaced to lessen noise around the Royal Infirmary. This was reversed the following year. In the city in 1898 1,635 tons of setts were laid and 28,655 square yards of road tar macadamed. In 1899 there were 11,079 tons setts compared with 9,926 square yards of tarmacadam.[83]

There were, then, great fluctuations in the amount of setts being used according to the amount of road work being done. In 1903 41,000 tons of setts were used in Aberdeen, the high water mark for setts.[84] The boom in demand for setts around this time was due to the introduction of electric trams in Aberdeen and other cities, with tramlines being laid or relaid.

Exports of setts rose throughout the last decade of the nineteenth century:

1892/93: 17,436 tons
1896/97: 31.403 tons
1898/99: 38,984 tons[85]

There was considerable debate over the merits of different forms of road surfaces in the latter years of the nineteenth century. Advocates of granite argued that although initial costs were undoubtedly higher for setts as compared with tar they lasted longer, needed less maintenance and were easier to lift to lay or access services below with less noise than was involved in lifting a tarred road. This continued into the 1920s as granite setts came under even more pressure. The introduction of motor vehicles initially made granite setts unpopular because of the noise, then pneumatic tyres replaced solid ones and the noise was reduced somewhat. Diack described the three types of finishes during the era of the motor car: 'The standard or reeled setts, the heads of which are roughly finished with the reel; a better quality finished with puncheoned surface; and nidged setts representing the best class of finish.'[86] The *Evening Express* in 1926 quoted Osmond Cattlin of Lambeth giving a lecture on road paving to the Institute of Municipal and County Engineers: 'London streets are paved with gold where the engineers use Aberdeen granite setts,' according to Cattlin. In 1921 the Albert Embankment had been laid with 132 tons of granite setts 4in x 6in on a 9in concrete base. Although Swedish and Norwegian setts were ostensibly cheaper initially, over a period of time the maintenance costs for Aberdeen granite setts was significantly less.[87]

At a conference of municipal and county engineers held in Brighton in 1896 one paper, read by C. H. Cooper, gave it as his opinion that:

A load of sets from granite merchant James Leith, at Ferryhill, *c*.1905. The engine is from James Barrack of Skene.

the stone that stands best is Aberdeen granite, but owing to the reduced price that Norway granite is delivered in the London market, little Aberdeen granite is now used. Newry and Cornish granites are used but neither are well dressed, and so far as the author has seen, both are coarse grained.[88]

However, the sett making industry was another that had to face competition from foreign imports, notably Norwegian and Swedish. The anonymous author of the article on the passing of the sett and kerb makers remembered that in the 1890s he heard John Adan, Secretary of the Settmakers' Union, attacking foreign imports and trying to get the support of the Aberdeen Trades Council to safeguard the local industry. The author went on to say that the main advantage enjoyed by Norwegian kerbs and setts was not lower wages but rather rock that was easier to quarry because the stone was on rocky hillsides with no need to blast down deep into the ground, with less investment needed in machinery for lifting the stone. Also Norwegian stone was softer and therefore easier to work. This, of course, meant it didn't last as long and became slippery with wear but local authorities have never been ones to think long term. Transport costs were relatively low, Norwegian quarries being near the sea, and the stone could be taken directly to ports such as London and Newcastle.[89]

Settmaking survived until the Second World War with Diack optimistically writing that wartime had brought a renewed interest in using setts for road surfaces. He described how in the 1930s Princess Street in Edinburgh was paved with finely nidged setts supplied by John Fyfe, 5in in width and 4in deep and 6in to 10in in length. Diack quotes the engineer responsible for this work,

William Macartney, saying that these sett-paved streets will last from thirty to fifty years.[90] Diack thought they would last even longer with a report by the Aberdeen City Engineer in 1937 showing that some streets then carrying fairly heavy traffic had been laid out in the 1870s and 1880s. A visitor to Edinburgh today will find that it has retained far more granite setts than Aberdeen where they have largely been tarred over.

Granite Waste and Adamant Paving

Towards the end of the nineteenth century there was a considerable growth in the use of granite waste for rubble, chips, granite dust and road material. In 1898 the *Aberdeen Journal* reported that granite crushing machines were now found all over the county. The *Journal* also reported that 14,616 tons of this type of material was exported that year, an increase of 3,399 tons on the previous year. Kemnay's crushers were turning out 150 tons a day. Adamant pavements were another recent use for granite waste. The *Journal* reported that the export of this was 2,898 tons in 1897/98, an increase of 1,058 tons on the previous year. As the *Journal* commented, this use of waste had several advantages. As well as providing income from a waste material, it also reduced the cost of removing that waste and freed up the space it had occupied. Moreover there might be profitable amounts of granite underneath older piles of waste. The *Journal* gave the example of McAdam & Sons reopening an old quarry at Auchmill. Whereas it wouldn't have been profitable to clear the huge pyramid of waste just to see if there was good stone underneath it, clearing it for use as chips etc, had led to the reopening of the quarry to exploit the stone thus uncovered.[91]

In the 1890s Manuelle's Dancing Cairns Quarry became a major centre for the production of Adamant Paving. W.B. Wight of Manuelle's became the local manager of the Patent Adamant Stone Company; Manuelle's being the local agents of the company, which also had premises in Greenwich, London. The manufacture of these paving slabs involved mixing crushed granite with Portland Cement and water, and it made use of the waste material left over from granite quarrying. In September 1891 Wight invited a group of councillors, architects, businessmen and granite merchants, as well as the chairman of the company, to a demonstration of the new, improved powerful machinery used in the process. The inventor of the process, Mr A. McLean, was also noted as being present.[92] Fielding & Platt of Gloucester manufactured the crushing machine. Examples of these paving slabs, often labelled Aberdeen Adamant, can still be found in Aberdeen, London and elsewhere. The Adamant Works used up waste from Sclattie Quarry. In 1906 the Aberdeen Association of Civil Engineers visited Sclattie and Dancing Cairns quarries as well as the Adamant Works. The latter was steam driven with the crushing machinery reducing the granite to a fine granulary state. The crushed granite and cement were automatically mixed and then powerful hydraulic presses compressed the mixture.[93]

John Fyfe's at the Beginning of the Twentieth Century

In 1903 Robert Arthur Theatres Limited, who ran Her Majesty's Theatre (which later became The Tivoli), asked the Town Magistrates for an extension of one year on their licence, the reason being that there was a delay in building the much anticipated new theatre on Rosemount Viaduct. Partly this was due to legal matters relating to the charter for the new theatre, but another reason was that John Fyfe could not supply the granite required. The reasons Fyfe gave were that he had other orders in hand and that the quarries at Kemnay were in an 'inferior' condition. I imagine that it must have been difficult for Fyfe to admit this, given his attitude relating to other developments we have already discussed in this chapter. Regarding the theatre the Council had gone further than specifying that it should be of granite, they wanted it built of Kemnay granite to match the two buildings west of it – the South United Free Church and Aberdeen Public Library. The theatre company tried to see if Persley or Rubislaw stone could be used as a substitute, but Persley couldn't supply enough stone and Rubislaw was rejected because it didn't match the other buildings. Fyfe was approached again and stated that he could supply enough stone if it could be the same as that used in the Art Gallery some twenty years before (presumably he meant the mixture of Kemnay and Corrennie as used in the Gallery, which might given us an interesting building). Issues of over-crowding at the old theatre meant that the magistrates only granted a two-month extension of the licence for that theatre and they urged the company to build the new theatre within the agreed three-year period once Fyfe could supply the granite.[94]

Fyfe's did indeed have a lot of work on his plate at this time, and his workforce as well as his quarries must have been working flat out. As noted in Chapter 3, Kemnay Quarry was operating day and night using electric lighting. Among other contracts they were, of course, supplying Kemnay stone for the massive building at Marischal College. Outwith Aberdeen two huge projects, using stone from Kemnay, Corrennie and Tom's Forest, were the bridge over the Thames at Kew and the first floor of the Royal Insurance Company's head office in Liverpool (see Chapter 8).

Fyfe did eventually state that he could begin a supply of granite from Kemnay for a year, beginning on 12 April 1904, and the frontage of the theatre was built from Kemnay stone, the sides being either Tillyfourie or Tom's Forest.

The Industry on the Eve of the First World War

At the end of 1898 the *Aberdeen Journal* reported that there were 1,000 men employed in the building sector and 950 in the monumental, an increase of fifty in each sector over the previous year. In addition there were around 650 apprentices.[95] The following year this had increased to 1,200 building masons and 1,000 monumental with about 750 apprentices.[96] However, as we have already seen, the industry faced a number of threats. There were tariff issues in America and the substantial growth of America's own granite industry; there was also the issue of imported granite from Europe to be followed by imports of finished products; in road surfaces granite setts faced competition from other materials. Although the Institution of Mechanical Engineers reported in 1907 that Rubislaw and Kemnay were the largest granite quarries in Britain, each with a depth of over 300ft,[97] many of the other prominent quarries in the north-east were either past their best or couldn't supply the quality of stone needed to compete with foreign imports and a significant number of quarries had already closed by the outbreak of war.

Most of these points were made in the *Aberdeen Journal* when it reviewed the industry at the end of 1912.[98] It reported the continuing decline in quarry output, expected to be the lowest for twenty years, with many quarries filling with water, not because the rock was exhausted but because the price obtained for the stone was too small to make a profit. The quarry holes at Cairncry and Persley were being considered for dumping the city's rubbish. The *Journal* reported that the building industry was suffering a period of depression that particularly hit Rubislaw, and although there was demand for polishing stones from Rubislaw such a substantial quarry could not quarry for them alone, it needed to find a market for smaller stones. Although there was demand for setts from outwith Aberdeen, the trade had been hit by the recent industrial dispute.

The war, when it came, would also bring serious problems to the industry as will be seen in Chapter 13.

SOME CASE STUDIES FROM THE GOLDEN AGE

The Granite Globe

In 1877 a cube of grey granite weighing nearly 3 tons was transported from Mowlem & Co.'s quarry at Persley to Councillor James Hunter's yard at King Street in Aberdeen. Over the next year that block was fashioned into a perfect polished sphere. On the surface of the sphere the outline of the continents were cut, edged in gold to highlight them, and with the rivers coloured in blue, the seas white. Major features such as large lakes and inland seas were also coloured in gold. The resulting globe weighed 1.75 tons and on it was fixed a brass arc, running from pole to pole, which could be turned to any meridian. The globe was constructed for George Burt, John Mowlem's nephew and partner, and was intended for Purbeck House, a house he had built for himself in Swanage, Dorset. It was exhibited for a week at Hunter's yard and the *Aberdeen Journal* urged its reader to go and view this magnificent work of granite art.[1] Burt must have had a passion for globes because when he subsequently built a folly known as Durlston Castle on his estate there, he had an even larger globe made. This one was constructed in 1887 from Portland stone at the company's yard in Greenwich, and it weighed 40 tons. Known as the Great Globe, it is still there, a tourist attraction at the Council-owned estate. Around the year 1919 Edwin Burt, grandson of George, sold Purbeck House and moved the original granite globe to his house overlooking the Beaulieu River in Hampshire. The globe is still there.

James Wright & Sons Order Book 1869–72

This rare order book survived in the care of Wright's descendant, the late Michael O'Connor, who ran the company and was twice President of the Granite Association in the 1970s. It gives a wonderful view into the work carried on by the second oldest granite yard in Aberdeen in a decade when the monumental industry really took off. It contains nearly 400 pages of orders for polished obelisks, gravestones, columns, fireplaces etc. with each monument or piece described and drawn in precise detail, with measurements for every part. A few monuments were made in marble but

The granite globe at Purbeck House, Swanage. (Courtesy of Swanage Museum)

the vast majority are granite, coloured to reflect whether the granite was grey or red. The quarry that the granite came from is listed, including from Wright's own quarries. Rubislaw and Alford were used a lot, the latter undoubtedly being their own quarry at Syllavethie. Occasionally Dyce, Kemnay or Sclattie appears. A few orders were also received from John Beaton, the clerk of works at Balmoral, with headstones and one polished pedestal in granite from Balmoral itself.

For the many red monuments in the book no quarry name is given but it would almost certainly be their own quarry at Stirlinghill that supplied the reds. Also listed are the dates when each piece was supplied and the month when it was ordered, giving us an idea as to how long it took to make each piece. The cost of each piece is also give.

The first three pages of the order book contain a substantial order from James Sharkey, Marble and Granite Merchant of Brooklyn, New York. Sharkey's order is for twenty-one ornaments in total, including three of some of them, with most being highly polished. The total cost of the order is £918. The most impressive monument in terms of size and cost is an obelisk in Peterhead granite, 22ft 6½in high, costing £212 5s (approx £20,000 in today's values). The overall order is dated February 1869, and the monument was finished on 23 November that year. Further orders from Sharkey also appear in the order book. A surviving order book from one of the American companies that Wrights dealt with, William Pitbladdo and his son Thomas's Marble & Granite Works in Brooklyn, shows that 'Scotch Peterhead' granite was highly sought after and consequently cost more.

Other companies in America that Wright's were supplying included J.G. Batterson, Hartford, Connecticut, builder and owner of the New England Granite Works; Joseph J. Spurr of Newark, New Jersey, Joseph having arrived in America a few years before in 1864; Passmore & Meeker, Newark, New Jersey; David S. Arnott, Brooklyn, whose entry in the directories at the time advertised *Monuments of Scotch and American Granite Always on Hand*; John Wilson, Marble Works, Brooklyn; James Hall, Brooklyn; Alexander Edwards, Brooklyn, Morgan & Anderson, Brooklyn, founded by James Morgan from Fife; John Shaw, Greenwood, Brooklyn; Fisher & Bird, Steam Marble Works, New York; William S. See, New York; George Brown & Co., Newark, New Jersey; Passmore & Meeker, Newark, New Jersey; J.M. Andrus, Marble & Granite Works, Aurora, Illinois, whose letterhead at the time announced that they were importers of red and gray granite direct from Scotland; M. Muldoon & Co., of Louisville, Kentucky who are still in business; Alfred White of Cincinnati, Ohio; Charles Rule, Cincinnati, Ohio; J.H. Bristor, Steubenville, Ohio; J.M. Martin, Cleveland, Ohio; L.M. Jones, Ravenna, Ohio; Wellinghoff & Co., Hamilton, Ohio; Dodds & Caskey, Xenia, Ohio; F.B. & E.W. Palmer, Terre Haute, Indiana; Park & McLintock, St Louis, Missouri; B.W. Williams, Barre, New York; J.A. Carrol, Wheeling, West Virginia; Peter Bechtel, Philadelphia; William Gray, Philadelphia; Van Gunden & Young, Philadelphia; Edwin Greble. Philadephia Marble Works, Chestnut Street (sometimes wrongly written as Edward Greeble in the order book); Edwin L. Gowan, Gowen Marble Works, Chicago; Thomas Joyce, Louisville, Kentucky.

The company in America would normally have added the lettering on the monuments, there are only about a dozen examples of Wrights doing the lettering before dispatch of the order. One of the most prestigious was a monument ordered by Muldoon & Co., of Louisville, Kentucky. It was for James Guthrie, of Scottish descent, a US Senator from Kentucky and Secretary of the Treasury under President Franklin Pierce. Guthrie died in March 1869 and an order was placed with Wrights in October that year. The monument is a colossal obelisk, 29½ft high, in highly polished Rubislaw granite, made in two pieces. It took just over a year to manufacture and including lettering it cost £453 13s, making it the most expensive single item in the order book. It stands at the Cave Hill Cemetery in Louisville.

In addition to monuments, Wright's also supplied granite columns such as the twelve polished red columns supplied to Wm. Armstrong, Architect, Lombard Street, Philadelphia. Orders for American companies went by rail to Glasgow and then were shipped from there. Orders within the U.K. normally went by rail, with a few going by ship.

Within the UK the order book shows monuments, columns etc., being sent all over the country including as far south as Dorset, as far north as Orkney, and across the Irish Sea to Belfast. One of the main dealers who Wrights supplied was A. Nicholson a stone dealer based at Mark Lane in London. As well as funerary monuments Nicholson also placed orders for pilaster and columns. One important order for Nicholsons came in January 1879 and was for seventeen polished red columns in Peterhead granite for the Home and Colonial Office, as it was then known. Each column was in three pieces, totaling a height of 9ft 9in, and the order took around nine months to complete. The following year a further thirty-eight columns were ordered with that order being worth £493 (around £49,000 in today's money). Wright's also supplied an order for seventeen polished red columns for A. & F. Manuelles to be sent to their London premises. A similar order for ten red columns went to Robert Dennett of Nottingham. Although at this date there were no orders for the polished granite building fronts which would become more common in jst a few years, there is one order for six pilasters for a shop front. This order is also for Nicholsons, but unfortunately it doesn't give the address of the shop.

The Lick Monument

One of the finest monuments produced by Heslop & Wilson, of the Peterhead Granite Polishing Company at Millbank, was for the Lick Monument at Fredericksburg, Pennsylvania, inscribed as being erected in 1876, though it wasn't actually finished until 1877. It was erected by James Lick from Fredericksburg who had gone to California and become a millionaire, said to have been the wealthiest man in California at the time of his death in 1876. The monument commemorated various members of his family, especially his grandfather who had fought against the British in the War of Independence a hundred years earlier. The monument used red granite from their Blackhill Quarry. At the time it was described as:

> The basement, which is in three courses, one splayed and two moulded, is fifteen feet square. The corners are in buttress form, and so constructed as to form pedestals for four large statues. In front the word 'Lick' is carved in large raised letters. Upon this basement rests the die course, consisting of four pilasters and four paneled jambs, on which the inscriptions are cut. The size of each panel is 6ft 5in by 3ft 8in. The die-course is surmounted by a handsome cornice-course, above which is a corbel-course, followed by a niche-course with four niches, in which are to be placed full-sized statues, four pilasters and four polished columns, the latter having boldly cut Corinthian capitals. Above this is a niche-cover-course, with a piece of magnificent carved work, followed by a course consisting of two large stones, diagonally jointed, with four raised shields, on one of which is the name 'Valley Forge' in raised letters. Above this is the top cornice-course, and the whole is sur-mounted by a large stone at the corners of which are four boldly-carved and polished leaves, and which is to form a pedestal for a marble statue of Liberty. This stone is 2ft 6in square. The height of the whole is 29ft 9in. but the statue to be placed on top will add about 10ft to the height. The weight of the granite, exclusive of the statues, is 95 tons, and will cost about £1,500.[2]

This description gives some idea of the size and intricacy of the work that could be carried out at a yard at this time. This was a huge and expensive piece sent across to Amcrica. Moreover, the yard that supplied it had not been established for very long but they were already capable of winning a substantial order such as this one from the other side of the Atlantic.

The Victoria Park Granite Fountain

In 1878 John Morgan, on behalf of the Aberdeen Master Masons' Association and as proposed at their annual dinner in February 1878, offered to gift a granite fountain to the City, which they hoped would be sited somewhere visible below Union Terrace. The fountain was to exemplify the finest material and the finest work that they could produce.[3] For various reasons the Union Terrace location didn't happen, leading to some slightly sarcastic comments in the press, and it was finally agreed two years later to erect it in the Victoria Park.[4] Further delays occurred as the water spouts weren't big enough nor was the basin sufficient to catch the water in windy weather! Moreover the 'generous' master masons were not going to cover the cost of erecting the fountain or of the base and surrounding platform on which to mount it! The Masons' Association said that when it was designed they did not know where it was to be sited and consequently had not designed a base. There was a certain amount of argument in the Council regarding the extra cost that would therefore fall on them. At a subsequent ward election meeting, one irate ratepayer asked why ratepayers' money should be given to what was a master masons' advertisement! Eventually it was agreed to proceed and the Council began to erect it at the very end of 1880, though it wasn't finished until the following May. The Council-funded outer basin was 45ft in diameter and the Council-funded base rose from the centre of it. Finally there was the fountain itself, hexagonal and 15ft in diameter with a polished granite cup at each corner, not all of which survives today. From the centre rises a pedestal supporting two further basins. The fountain itself, designed by Morgan's associate and friend, the architect John Bridgeford Pirie, is a fine example of the granite art of the time, a fitting memorial to the granite industry. It is made from pink and grey granite with the initials or monograms of the contributing firms carved around it, hence the comment on it being an advertisement for the granite industry. It represented the work of most of the master masons in the city and was assembled at James Hunter's yard. The *Aberdeen Journal* commented that 'many may take exception to the appearance of the monograms, and in one of two cases the full names, of the donors carved on the various stones, but that is a comparatively small defect in view of the general excellence of the structure.' John Fyfe was highlighted as having provided some of the most expensive and artistic parts of the fountain.[5]

Part of Victoria Park granite fountain showing the names of George & Robert Hall, builders, and the monogram of J. & J. Ogg.

The Kruger Monument

Another example of a huge monumental piece that was sent abroad was the base for the monument for Paul Kruger's statue in Pretoria. This was potentially a controversial monument because it was intended to commemorate the abortive Jameson Raid on Kruger's Transvaal Republic by Leander Jameson and other British adventurers. The work was carried out in 1898 by Bower & Florence in some secrecy. Curiously at around the same time Jameson himself arrived at Dinnet on a fishing holiday! Inevitably word of this giant monument leaked out and was reported in the *Aberdeen Journal*. The work was in Peterhead Granite, partly executed at their quarry at Cruden, and finished at their works in the Spital. The work was described as weighing about 300 tons, 55ft from side to side at the lower part of the base, and as being probably the largest monument ever manufactured in the city, so huge that it couldn't be erected at the Spital works. The description in the *Granite Chips* column of the *Journal* in 1898 was as follows:

> Above the upper portion of the basement is a large polished dado, which is followed by a huge die, worked into octagonal shape. Then comes a richly moulded and polished cornice, which is followed by a polished plinth, and surmounted by an elaborately moulded frieze, on which rests a finely polished stone that is to form the base of the statue of President Kruger. The monument rises to a height of 36 feet.[6]

Crathie Church

Crathie Church is the church used by members of the Royal Family when they are holidaying at Balmoral and Birkhall. It was designed by the noted Aberdeen architect A. Marshall Mackenzie and built by Pringle & Slessor, also of Aberdeen. The building itself was built from rock-faced light grey granite from the Inver Quarry on the Invercauld Estate. Inside the church, though, is a testimony to the granite industry in Scotland. The baptismal font has a basin of Kemnay granite with a stem of Rubislaw. The pulpit contains no less than fifteen kinds of Scottish granite. The base and cornices are of finely dressed Inver granite. Five sides are respectively of Dalmore, Rubislaw, Ben Cruachan, Dyce and Sylavethie. As well as fine axed margins there are polished centre portions with, at each angle, a cluster of polished columns of three different granites, with moulded bases and capitals. Both the font and pulpit were made by Alexander Macdonald & Co., to designs by the architect.[7]

The Saltoun Arms

In the middle of the nineteenth century finely polished granite columns had been the preserve of prestigious buildings such as the British Museum and St George's Hall in Liverpool, and as we saw in Chapter 5 even the museum couldn't afford the number of columns they had originally wanted. These photographs show that by the end of the nineteenth century even a fairly small,

Polished granite columns at the corner entrance to the Saltoun Arms.

Detail of granite work at the Saltoun Arms.

quite humble bar was capable of some beautiful granite work, using granite from different quarries. The Saltoun Arms stands at the corner of Frederick Street and Wales Street. It was rebuilt in 1896 for R.L. Mearns, by the architects Brown & Watt. The piers on the sides of the building are of rock-faced or slightly rustic granite from Whithead's Dyce Quarry, and they support a moulded lintel course running round the building. The architects have made good use of the corner site by making the entrance there and it is flanked by two Doric-style columns in polished Rubislaw granite. The columns were polished at Macdonald & Co.'s yard just along the road in Constitution Street. The columns support a corner corbel constructed of a series of brackets of finely dressed Persley granite. Three different granites used in this wonderful little building.[8]

The Royal Insurance Company Headquarters, Liverpool

In 1902 the Liverpool building had been under construction for five years. Huge blocks for this project and the bridge at Kew were being sent by rail and sea at around the same time. Built around a steel frame the Royal Insurance building was the largest granite building contract ever undertaken in Britain, outside of Aberdeen. Over 2,000 tons of granite had been used, with individual blocks being between 9 and 11 tons each when delivered from the quarry to Fyfe's yard in Aberdeen. The basement and first floor were in granite, 40ft high in all, with 27ft above pavement level, the upper floors being of Welsh freestone. The main frontage was 220ft long, all the granite in the building was fine axed, with a granite staircase leading to the entrance and polished granite in the entrance hall. The doorway was 11ft wide with an arch of rusticated stones supported by two columns on each side, the columns built in two courses with rounded and square projecting stones, the base stones of these arches being the ones that weighed 11 tons when brought from the quarry. The elaborately moulded cornice over the arch was formed of five stones, weighing in total over 40 tons, and projecting 6ft over the building line. The *Aberdeen Journal* of 31 January 1902 carried illustrations of the highly decorated keystone for the entrance arch, a seven-ton stone, and the inner arch beyond the vestibule. The *Journal* commented that the stones for the main doorway and other special parts of the building had been completed in a very short time, these stones having been in the quarry only a few months before.

The Bridge over the River Thames at Kew

The bridge at Kew was opened by the King and Queen in May 1903, the bridge initially being named the Edward VII Bridge in his honour. The main contractors for the bridge were Easton Gibb & Son, the company whose predecessors had operated the Rubislaw Quarry for most of the nineteenth century. As such they would have known John Fyfe well. Although Wikipedia states that the granite used was from Cornwall, accounts at the time state that it was nearly all Aberdeenshire granite, the parapet and arches being from Kemnay Quarry. The granite blocks were prepared at the quarries and the *Aberdeen Journal* at the time noted that the workmanship was such that 'when the

Wall of field gathered stone.

Top of Marischal Street showing buildings built from Loanhead granite. On extreme right the granite changed to better quality Rubislaw.

Plaques from four of the granite columns in Aberdeen Art Gallery.

Reconstructed manual Scotch derrick crane at Ballater, originally used at the Cambus O'May Quarry.

Part of statue of Hygeia, Duthie Park, Aberdeen.

Eighteen-foot column of polished Cairngall granite, St George's Hall, Liverpool.

Clockwise from left: Tillycorthie Fountain, Hazlehead Park, Aberdeen; Memorial to the Great Exhibition, outside Royal Albert Hall; Alford Fountain.

Clockwise from top left: Duke of Gordon's statue, Golden Square, Aberdeen; Detail from Duke of Gordon's statue; Locally known as 'The Tartan Kirkie', St Mary's Episcopal Church was built from 1862–64. It was built in Rubislaw, Tyrebagger, and Kemnay granite as well two kinds of sandstone. Polished red Peterhead granite is also used in some of the detail outside and in. It sustained bomb damaged in the Second World War; West face of Aberdeen Town House.

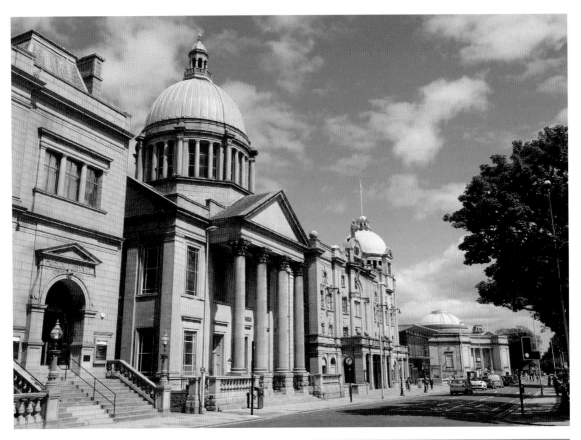

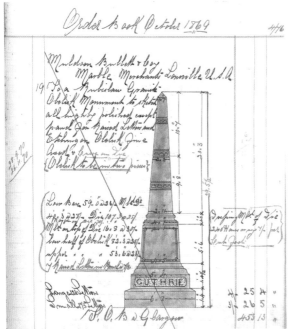

Clockwise from top: Central Library, St. Marks, His Majesty's Theatre, and Aberdeen War Memorial, all largely Kemnay granite; Guthrie Monument, Louisville, Kentucky; The Guthrie Monument from James Wright & Sons order book, October 1869.

Clockwise from left: The Lick Monument, Fredericksburg, Pennsylvania; Pulpit at Crathie Kirk; Order dated February 1872 for 38 polished granite columns in Peterhead granite, each in three pieces. Supplied to the Home and Colonial Offices (Foreign Office) in Whitehall by James Wright & Sons.

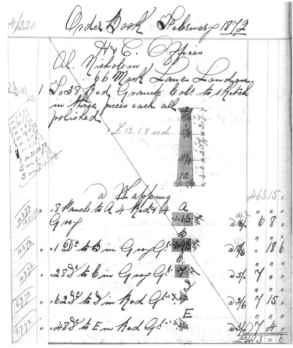

Clockwise from top: Granite columns in Aberdeen Art Gallery; Granite shards reaching for the sky on the unusual memorial stone for granite merchant Henry Hutcheon in Springbank Cemetery, Aberdeen; Old explosive store, Stirlinghill, Peterhead.

+ IN MEMORIAM +
HENRY HUTCHEON J.P.
GRANITE MERCHANT
ABERDEEN
DIED OCTOBER 3, 1934
AGED 67 YEARS.
ALSO HIS WIFE
MARY JANE ADAMS
DIED JANUARY 11, 1951
AGED 80 YEARS.

Heraldic panel in John Fyfe's yard in Aberdeen, James Macdonald on the right.

The panel on the bridge over the Thames at Kew.

blocks were relaid over the steel centres they fitted so perfectly that they met over the keystone cor-rect to within a quarter of an inch.'⁹ As well as supplying the stone for the bridge itself, Fyfe's yard in Aberdeen also supplied four heraldic or pseudo-heraldic panels, in Kemnay granite, for the bridge. The one illustrated was 7ft across, the head being Father Thames.'¹⁰ On the right of the photograph is James Macdonald , Fyfe's foreman in Aberdeen. The Aberdeen connection went further with engineers John M. Henderson of King Street supplying a blondin to help demolish the old bridge and erect the new one. Many of the masons who worked on the bridge were also from Aberdeen, a London correspondent of the *Aberdeen Journal* commented that 'the unmistakable accent lends novelty to the historic spot where the bridge crosses the Thames.'¹¹ Easton Gibb's foreman on the job was also an Aberdeen man, a Mr Riach, who was fatally injured in a crane accident. He was succeeded by William Legge, another Aberdonian.

The Granite Columns in the Art Gallery

On 27 March 1902 a public meeting was held regarding a proposed sculpture gallery for the Art Gallery in Aberdeen. The Aberdeen Granite Association was represented by its secretary James Jeffrey, and the Operatives Union by George Younie. The following July, John Morgan approached the AGA asking them if members would be willing to supply twelve granite columns for the gallery. This they agreed to do and there are in fact 28 columns with duplicates, four each from Kemnay and Rubislaw for example.

The columns and bases were supplied as follows:

Rough stones provided by:

John Fyfe (Kemnay, Corrennie and Tillyfourie
Henry Hutcheon (Hill O' Fare)
Fred Wright, Royal Granite Works (Peterhead)
John Littlejohn (Craigton)
William Kennedy (Peterhead)
A. & F. Manuelle (Sclattie)
Heslop, Wilson & Co. (Rora)
Rubislaw Granite Co. (Rubislaw)
Granite Supply Association (Royal Blue, Emerald Pearl. Both Swedish)

The columns were polished by:

Charles Macdonald Ltd, Froghall Granite Works
Stewart & Co., Bon-accord Granite Works
Garden & Co., Victoria Granite Works

R.D. Cruickshank & Co., Albyn Granite Works
James Pope, Torry Granite Works
Edward Hutcheon, Cemetery Granite Works
A.Macdonald & Co., Aberdeen Granite Works
A.A. Brown, St Nicholas Granite Works
Baillie Martin, Great North Granite Works, Peterhead
Arthur Taylor, Jute Street
William Boddie, St Clair Street
James Rae, Crown Granite Works

The column bases were polished by:

James Mitchell, Holland Street
George Kemp & Co., Gilcomston Park
James Chalmers, Empire Granite Works
William Morgan, Portland Street
Robert Lawrence, University Granite Works
Kittybrewster Granite Works
W. Edwards & Son, Nelson Granite Works
Henderson & Webster, Affleck Street
George Stalker, Jute Street
Simpson Brothers, Cotton Street
Baillie Robert Simpson, North British Granite Works[12]

A DREAM CARVED IN GRANITE: JOHN MORGAN THE MASTER MASON AND THE BUILDING OF A GRANITE ICON

John Gibb in the first half of the nineteenth century, followed by John Fyfe in the second half of the century, were the two great quarrymen of the granite industry, commercial and technological innovators who created what became the two super quarries of Rubislaw and Kemnay. Alexander Macdonald was almost single-handedly responsible for the whole granite polishing and monumental industry that grew up in the second half of the nineteenth century. For granite buildings Alexander Rainnie built several of Archibald Simpson's granite buildings including his Marischal College, but perhaps the greatest master mason was John Morgan, responsible for so many of the buildings built in the second half of the nineteenth century culminating in the supreme granite icon of the new Marischal College.

John Morgan was a man of great contrasts. He came from a humble, even poor background, had little formal education, but he became literate to a very high level, largely through his own efforts. Described in his obituary as quiet, self-contained and almost retiring, he nevertheless entered local politics and in that role could be tough and irascible, to the point where he was almost pig-headed, especially with other building contractors. Despite his humble start in life and beginning work as an ordinary mason, as an employer he showed no sympathy for his workers when they engaged in disputes with him and there was a quite nasty, vindictive side to his character in his views on the working man.

Morgan was born at Craigton Farm on the estate of Craighall in the parish of Kennethmont in 1844, eldest of seven children. The farm was situated just north of the village of Kennethmont on the road that runs across from the Leithhall towards Rhynie, the railway line running along the north-east edge of the farm. The farm had originally been of around 40 acres and was called Beggardykes, testimony to the poor quality of the land. Morgan described it as 'high, exposed and cold. Harvests late, crops light and poor. Rough, stony in higher parts, stiff and sour on the lower reaches.'[1] Through the efforts of his father and grandfather, in reclaiming land from moorland, the farm had doubled in size by the time he left, a new house had been built and the name changed. Morgan himself had to work on the farm from the age of 10, threshing fodder for the cattle with an antiquated flail. He also

John Morgan. (Aberdeen City Libraries)

attended the village school, sitting alongside the sons of ministers and gentlemen farmers. The education wasn't free, though Morgan commented that 'I pay more for the education of one of my daughters during a single term than my father paid for the education of the whole family all the time they were at school.'[2] He seems to have enjoyed school and his main teacher was Frederick August Wilson, brother of the famous Aberdeen photographer George Washington Wilson, Frederick encouraging the young Morgan's taste for drawing and a love of art that would be very important in his later life.

Despite the basic education he received at the village school he was largely self-educated, and educated to a considerable standard. In 1865 he was a founder member of the Aberdeen Senate, a debating society, and, in 1877, he joined the Aberdeen Philosophical Society. As part of his education, in 1887, Morgan went on the 'Grand Tour', visiting the major cities and sights in Italy. Towards the end of his life, in 1901, he visited Egypt and the Sudan, describing it in his memoirs as the 'longest and most enjoyable holiday I have ever had'. Morgan built up a substantial library of 4,500 volumes, described at the time as being 'as choice and valuable a one as is owned by any individual in Aberdeen'.[3] This included works by the men who influenced his ideas most, Carlyle, Ruskin and Tennyson. His library contained most of Carlyle's writings but it was John Ruskin, art critic and social theorist, who was his main inspiration. He had over 450 works by and about Ruskin, in his own words the finest collection in Scotland. Many of the volumes were rare, privately printed items, including some from the Pre-Raphaelite Brotherhood who Ruskin championed. Morgan corresponded with Ruskin and became a companion of Ruskin's philanthropic Guild of St George, which at the time had only fifteen members. Late in life he developed a fascination for the work of Edward Fitzgerald, collecting 115 separate editions of *The Rubaiyat of Omar Khayyam*.

Apprenticed to Adam Mitchell

Morgan moved to Aberdeen in 1862 and was apprenticed to Adam Mitchell, his mother's youngest brother. Mitchell had also come from a humble background in Kennethmont, though his father had been one of the largest farmers in the area before a failed litigation against the laird ruined him. The reduced circumstances of the family meant that Mitchell was fee'd to a local farmer from an early age.

Around the age of 18 he obtained an apprenticeship with Macdonald & Leslie, as we have seen earlier. One of the major jobs he worked on as a young apprentice was at Dunrobin Castle. Mitchell attended classes at the Mechanics' Institution for several years, even after completing his apprenticeship, and shortly after completing that apprenticeship he set up by himself in a small way. Among the major contracts that Mitchell subsequently carried out were the building of Aberdeen Grammar School, Corse House, Glenmuick House and the Palace Hotel on Union Bridge (later demolished). The Grammar School contract was one of his first, won against competition from more established firms such as John Fraser & Sons, George Donaldson and Gavin Low.[4] The largest contract carried out by Mitchell was the building of the Joint Station and the railway north through the Denburn Valley, built from 1865-67. As well as the station building this involved blasting though granite and building a series of tunnels, bridges and retaining walls. A few years after the completion of this project, in 1871, Mitchell was elected to Aberdeen Town Council, later becoming a magistrate and Master of Shore Works.

We have already seen that Morgan's first introduction to working in granite was at the building of the Grammar School in 1862, the same year that he joined his uncle. Very quickly Mitchell decided that his young nephew would be more useful in the office and Morgan was involved in drawing up the plans and specifications for the Denburn Valley Railway. As his uncle became more involved in politics and his estate at Heathcote, Morgan became his partner and was effectively running the business by the time of Mitchell's death in January 1877. Thereafter he ran the business with the trustees on behalf of himself and Mitchell's family. Mitchell's oldest daughter married the Rev. William Grundy, headmaster of King's Grammar School at Warwick. According to Morgan, Grundy fancied himself as a man of business and found fault with Morgan's running of the building firm. Grundy died shortly after and Morgan was able to get legal advice to show the trustees that he had acted competently. However, he said that 'the incident soured relations with his cousin to who he felt disgust at the ingratitude for all he had done. I was glad when the expiry of the partnership arrived and the dissolution was effected on 13 January 1893.'[5]

During Morgan's management of the company he built many of the buildings that we are familiar with in Aberdeen, particularly in the West End of the city. In the centre of Aberdeen these included Canada House on Union Street and one of Alexander Marshall Mackenzie's finest buildings, the Head Office of the Northern Assurance Company at the corner Union Street and Union Terrace (known locally as the Monkey House), the pair also built a similar building for the Isle of Man Banking Company at Douglas on the Isle of Man. Morgan also built the Grand Hotel on Union Terrace (later the Caledonian). Elsewhere in the city he built Kittybrewster School and a number of churches including Queen's Cross, Carden Place United Free Church and St Ninian's Church on Midstocket Road. Around 150 houses were built by Morgan in Aberdeen, including at Thomson Street, Belvidere Street and Crescent, Argyll Place, Hamilton Place, Queen's Road and Rubislaw Den South and North; outside Aberdeen there was Blackhall Castle, Kincardine Castle and Craigmyle House (later demolished). One of his closest friends was the architect John Bridgeford Pirie. Together they built Pirie's magnificent Queen's Cross Free Church in 1881 and houses in Argyll Place already mentioned. They also built Pirie's very distinctive houses on the north side of Hamilton Place, details from which were copied by other local architects including such a notable architect as A. Marshall Mackenzie.

Morgan had mixed views on the granite that he fashioned so well, and on some of Aberdeen's granite architects. Although he was of the opinion that most of Aberdeen's buildings by its leading architects showed fine taste, to him there were glaring exceptions 'flaring monstrosities, enough to damn forever the reputation of a whole street.' Streets and terraces in the suburbs he saw as being 'full of pretence and vulgarity where architecture, taste, and skill are alike absent'. On the material itself he wrote:

> It is the fashion to belaud Aberdeen for its white and clean appearance. Its white and grey granite when well dressed, have a fine sparkle in the sunshine, and when there is wind enough to clear away the smoke, and light is full upon the spires, and they look as though they were built of white marble. But there is another side to the picture, in some lights, and under other conditions the granite looks cold, hard, repellent and colourless.[6]

The House that Morgan Built

In June 1871 Morgan married Matilda Murray. They lived in various addresses including 'over the shop' in Charlotte Street, before moving, in 1874, to a house he built at No. 57 Thomson Street, overlooking the Victoria Park. By 1886 he was ready to build a grander house and he knocked down the old country house of the Skenes of Rubislaw on Queen's Road and built a new Rubislaw House. Morgan said that he wanted to keep the old house and remodel it but that the City of Aberdeen Land Association, which was developing parts of the old Rubislaw Estate 'had resolved to straighten Queen's Road which brought the old house too near the street and beyond the Town Council's building line'. The old house was built for Arthur Forbes in 1675 but with vestiges of an even older building. It came into the possession of the Skenes in 1687; their town house (Provost Skene's) still stands in what remains of the Guestrow. Morgan did incorporate the steps of the old house in his conservatory and built the dated lintel with initials AF (Arthur Forbes) into the outside kitchen entrance to his new house.

The new Rubislaw House, Number 50 Queen's Road, was designed by his friend Pirie. The extent to which they viewed this house as a personal statement and pinnacle of their domestic work together is clear in Morgan's comment in his memoirs that 'both Mr Pirie and myself put so much of ourselves into the details and arrangements of this work.'[7] Hence he included the monograms of both men on one of the buttresses at the front of the house.

It is a building that has divided opinion in Aberdeen's architectural community. Fenton Wyness called it 'an essay in bizarre gothic' and it has also been described as 'rogue gothic', terms that are self explanatory, if not particularly complimentary. I have heard it described as being like an apprentice piece, showing every detail or trick the architect and builder were capable of, and also that it used pieces that Morgan already had in his granite yard. There may be truth in this as it would certainly have been a showcase for their work, some of the details in No.50 had already appeared in work the pair had done in Hamilton Place (opposite the Whitehall Bowling Club), and in Queen's Cross Church. There are more ecclesiastical details than you would normally find

Detail of No. 50 Queen's Road, also showing the plaque to John Morgan.

in a domestic building, for example the use of the quatrefoil motif, inlaid with pink granite (was it left over from the building of Queen's Cross Church or a statement of Morgan and Pirie's Ruskinian views?). Alongside the Gothic there are elements of early or proto-art nouveau. The building was given Category A status when it was listed in 1967, a grading opposed by the City Planning Department on the grounds that they thought it wasn't worthy of that status. The listing has certainly helped to keep it as a home rather than being turned into an office, casino, hotel or worse, as has happened to so many houses in Queen's Road and Albyn Place. My own opinion is that even after more than a century it is still a stunning building and that if you had to pick one stand-out house to represent mid- to late nineteenth-century granite house-building in Aberdeen then surely this would be the one. I would even argue that it is the finest granite house in Aberdeen, time and changing fashions have not altered its impact especially on those who see it up close for the first time.

Morgan included the image of his new house on his library bookplates together with the message adapted from the Bible – 'Except the Lord do build the house, the builders work is vain'. The library was on the first floor and we can imagine Morgan in his Egyptian robe and fez sitting in his library by the huge fireplace with its elaborate plasterwork, with his literary heroes – Scott, Homer, Shakespeare, Carlyle, Dante and others depicted in its stained glass windows. Elsewhere in the house there are stained-glass windows reflecting the influence of the Pre-Raphaelites. At the top of the stairs on the first floor are three windows representing respectively 'Faith, Hope and Charity'. Elsewhere are the Greek Muses, goddesses of art and science. On his death in 1907 the *Free Press* commented 'not only did Mr Morgan possess books but he also read them.'[8] Many of the rarest items in his library subsequently went to London for sale but a substantial part of the library was sold at Milne's auction rooms in North Silver Street, the sale continuing over four consecutive evenings.

Morgan the employer

Morgan is described in his obituary as a quiet unassuming, almost retiring man, though 'genial, courteous and a delightful companion and raconteur'. There was certainly a tough, steely side to his character, though. He followed his uncle by entering the Town Council, holding various posts including Treasurer and represented the Council on the Governors of Robert Gordon's College. He was a director of a number of companies including the granite business of A. Macdonald and Co, the Seaton Brick and Tile Company and the Aberdeen District Suburban Tramways Company. As an employer, and also Secretary then President of the Master Mason's Association, he was involved in several workmen's strikes. During the masons' strike of 1868 the then Lord Provost, Alexander Nicol, sent for him to look for a compromise with the workmen as the dispute had gone on for several weeks. Morgan knew that the workmen and their families were suffering and that the strike was on its last legs and he told the Provost that the granite masters were in no mood to 'surrender'. He commented, slightly smugly, that the Provost 'acquiesced rather sulkily as I thought and before the week was ended matters had righted themselves by the men's return to work on the old terms and conditions'.[9] He took a hard line, especially coming from someone who was just 24 years old at this time and who just a few years before had worked alongside some of these men. A similar approach was taken in the joiners' strike at the end of the century. He also compares the farm workers of his youth with his own workers:

> what a contrast between then and now, when I pay careless and indifferent workmen about as much per hour as I received for a whole day, and I am not sure but the ten pence per day farm workers of that time were as good members of the common-wealth, and as happy in their way as the not over contended but snobbish artisans of today.[10]

There is a certain romantic, nostalgic view here for the older workmen of a bygone day, as there was in his memories of the old-time masons he first worked with at the building of the Grammar School. Perhaps this romantic view of the past helped him justify the harsh treatment he meted out to his workers, who were, in reality, merely trying to achieve a living wage for a very hard working life.

Marischal College

Wedged in behind the huge Town house, in an expensive and attractive mid-Victorian baronial style, I saw a cluster of silver-white pinnacles. As I turned down a lane towards them, the frontage broadened out. Oh! Bigger than any cathedral, tower on tower, forests of pinnacles, a group of palatial buildings rivalled only by the Houses of Parliament at Westminster. This was the famous Marischal College. Imagine the Victorian tower with a spire on top, and all that well-grouped architecture below of lesser towers. And lines of pinnacles executed in the hardest white Kemnay granite and looking out over the grey-green North Sea and you have some idea of the first impression this gigantic building creates. It rises on top of a simple Gothic one designed by Simpson in

1840. But all these spires and towers and pinnacles are the work of this century and were designed by Alexander Marshall Mackenzie. You have to see them to believe them.

John Betjeman[11]

Marischal College is reputedly the second-largest granite building in the world, second only to El Escorial, Philip II of Spain's palace in the hills outside Madrid. It is also the second largest Perpendicular Gothic building in Britain after the Palace of Westminster. Legend has it that it was Adolf Hitler's favourite building in Britain and that he spared it from the bombing during the Second World War because he hoped to make it his headquarters after the war!

The building is much loved by Aberdonians, though it is not without its critics both from within the city and outside. It has been called a 'granite wedding cake' and 'sugar translated into stone'. Since its establishment in 1593 by the Earl Marischal on the site of the Franciscan (or Grey Friars) Friary on the Braidgait, Marischal College had occupied various buildings. Originally it used the old friary buildings, with these being restored and extended by William Adam in the late 1730s. These were replaced in the nineteenth century by Archibald Simpson's new Tudor Gothic building, the foundation stone of which was laid in 1837 and the building finished in 1841. Simpson's building formed three sides of the quadrangle and was screened from Broad Street by a line of buildings, mostly dating from the late eighteenth century, with entry to the college being through an archway. Indeed when one of these buildings, the Water House, was built in 1766 the residents of the Broad Street area successfully petitioned the Council to have a clock installed in the Water House because they could no longer get the time from the College clock! Simpson had produced a proposal to remove the Broad Street buildings and create a façade on Broad Street to match his building but this didn't happen until the new Marischal was built at the end of the Century

Marischal merged with King's College in the 1860s to become the University of Aberdeen but the Marischal buildings continued to be part of the University's teaching accommodation. By the late 1880s it was in need of expansion, particularly for the medical school. Right from the start the University Extension Scheme, as it became known, attracted controversy. The Council initially supported the idea and was keen to see the slums of Longacre swept away to provide the buildings on the south side of the site. They were also keen to provide a frontage on Broad Street by removing the buildings on Broad Street and widening that street. As well as the Water House this would include a late seventeenth-century turreted building and the building where Lord Byron and his mother lodged when he attended the old Grammar School on Schoolhill.

The first part of the work was the extension of the south wing, which necessitated knocking down some of the houses in Longacre. This began in 1889 and was finished by 1890. When the main proposals for the rest of the development came before the University Court in 1891 there was a counter proposal from some on the Town Council for the University to vacate the site and build a new building at Rosemount. Baillie Rust reported on behalf of a committee which was against spending a lot of money on the existing site, especially on a new Greyfriars Church, and on buying and knocking down other old buildings on Broad Street. They also queried that it would actually widen Broad Street, only part of the Gallowgate would actually be widened. There was also a proposal from some in the university to move everything to Old Aberdeen. These issues were soon overcome; the majority on the University Court being adamant that the Broad Street site should be the one that was developed and the Town Council voted £10,000 to the scheme from the Common Good Fund. The other problem concerned Greyfriars Church, virtually the only pre-Reformation church in Aberdeen, and one of the oldest buildings in the city. It was built between 1518 and 1532, and was the work of Alexander Galloway, parson of Kinkell, at the instigation of Bishop Gavin Dunbar. Though known as the 'College Kirk' it belonged to the town not the university, and its future continued to be a problem right up to the beginning of the twentieth century.

Matthews & Mackenzie was the architect's practice chosen to develop the site, with Alexander Marshall Mackenzie the lead architect. His partner James Matthews, a former Lord Provost, was then coming to the end of his active career. Over the next ten years Mackenzie drew up several plans for the site, including several variations of the now familiar frontage. From the beginning the plans included demolishing Greyfriars, despite objections in 1891 from the Aberdeen Ecclesiological Society.[12] Demolition of the church was stated in the relevant Act of Parliament of 1893 and, some argued, it was on this basis that much of the funding for the building was raised. The Town Council was to fund a new church for the congregation with the university providing the site. Retaining the old church was then actively proposed by the Lord Rector of the university, the Marquis of Huntly, in a speech made to the University Court in November 1897. The principal of the university, Sir William Geddes, spoke against the retention at the same meeting. In fact the issue caused Principal Geddes to resign from the Sites and Plans Committee. He subsequently withdrew his resignation and remarkably did a complete volte-face by writing a pamphlet in support of retaining the church, suspicion being that Huntly's powers of persuasion had been at work. Marshall Mackenzie's plans included rehousing the Greyfriars congregation in a new church at the south side of the site with a substantial tower at the south-west corner, fronting on Broad Street. To balance this there was to be another tower at the north-west corner.

Mackenzie proceeded to draw up plans retaining the old church, for use solely by the University, but with the more modern end taken down, a new bay added and the beautiful seven windows facing Broad Street filled with tracery. One of his plans included a thin screen on Broad Street in front of the old church, echoes of Archibald Simpson's earlier plan. As late as February 1898, Mackenzie wrote an open letter to Lord Huntly stating that he had repeatedly advised retaining old Greyfriars for artistic as well as antiquarian and historic reason. He thought its dark freestone would provide a 'refreshing contrast with Marischal', and that the slight deviation from the symmetrical position of the south tower would be a distinct gain.[13] In that same issue of the *Aberdeen Journal* there was a letter to the Town Council and the University Court supporting retention of the old church. This was signed by local and national figures including Mackenzie himself, Sir George Reid, and architects Robert Lorimer, William Kelly, A.H.L. Mackinnon, J. Ross Macmillan, James Souttar, George Watt and Robert Gordon Wilson. In 1898 an anonymous donor had offered £10,000 to the scheme if the Council would hand over Greyfriars to the University to be retained and restored. The donor was later revealed to be C.W. Mitchell, son of the main donor to the overall project, the late Charles Mitchell, and that retention was in line with his father's wishes.[14] A number of letters to the press pointed out that the original Act of Parliament had specifically stated that the old church was to be demolished. When Sir Hugh Gilzean Reid wrote in support of the church he was dismissed by one letter to the *Journal* as an interfering antiquarian busybody from the south. This anonymous graduate of the College wrote that it was a greater piece of vandalism to disfigure Marischal College than to clear away the 'auld clay biggin.' Granite merchant Councillor William Boddie was another who had little time for the old kirk, describing it as 'an old clay building' which he had examined and a 'plainer building in freestone he never looked on'. To keep it, he declared, 'in front of such a magnificent granite building such as Marischal College would be a disgrace to the city of Aberdeen.'[15] Boddie couldn't understand the attitude of the Lord Provost and made it clear he would vote against retention but in 1898 the Council voted by 15 to 13 to adopt a report of the Finance Committee, accepting Mitchell's offer and retaining the church. Less than a year later, in January 1899 and under new Lord Provost Fleming, the council completely reversed its position and voted to demolish Greyfriars.

Within the quadrangle Simpson's original buildings were to be retained but substantially added to and a new graduation hall included at the east end of the site. Simpson's existing graduation hall was to become a picture gallery/anteroom for the new hall. The most notable feature was the huge addition to Simpson's tower, the ensuing tower ending up at 260ft. To carry the extra weight the thickness of the walls of the old tower was increased, the foundations strengthened, and a central brick support built. The tower and the graduation hall were to be named after one of the major

Window tracery of the Mitchell Tower showing the brick core.

donors to the project, Charles Mitchell, an Aberdeen-born engineer who had attended classes at Marischal College before going on to be a major force in the development of shipbuilding on the River Tyne in Newcastle. Rather than there being a tender for the whole project, it was tendered in stages over the decade. This was probably due to funding having to be raised from different sources as the project progressed, and the ever-changing plans also reflected this. John Morgan won the tender for the building of the graduation hall in June 1893, and in September for the extension of the tower. The north wing and its accompanying tower were the only major parts of the building for which the tender was not won by Morgan. It went to another notable Aberdeen mason, Edgar Gauld, who began by demolishing buildings on Broad Street opposite Upperkirkgate. Why Gauld won the contract for this part is unclear but since the funding was being raised bit by bit, and the building was being built in the same gradual way, the University obviously could only tender for each part as they raised the funds and Gauld may simply have tendered lower than Morgan for that part of the building.

By August 1894 the Mitchell Tower had been raised to 116ft, about half its total height, and a start had been made to the graduation hall. Morgan finished the Mitchell Tower in July 1895. At the time he had forty stonecutters dressing the mullions and tracery of the window facing West North Street, the window being 30ft high and 30ft broad with about 120 divisions. One challenging episode followed in October 1895. This involved placing the bell into the tower. The bell weighed 1.67 tons and the only opening able to take it was through the opening where the clock was to go. Measurements had shown that the bell would fit but with only 6in to spare. It was moved by slow degrees by lever power rollers and by one o'clock it had been brought to the bottom of the slide. A steam engine was to raise it but they had to wait until the pressure of 60 lbs had been reached. The engine was supposedly capable of lifting 2 tons but had only previously lifted one. The steel cable had been tested to 3 tons. When it was almost at the opening the bell caught on one of the projecting timbers causing it to swing to one side. The stays of the upper portion of the lift had been removed to make way for the bell, and part of the lift itself had been cut away. With the lip of the bell resting on wooden stays the brake below lost its grip for a moment and the weight of the bell broke the stays into splinters and the bell swung out with a jerk. Thankfully the cable held and the workmen waiting inside the tower were able to attach strong tackle to the top of the bell and a rope round the middle and gradually pull it in through the opening. By four o'clock it was finally in place.[16]

In a letter to his friend James Tulloch in March 1895, Charles Mitchell expressed his concern at the slow progress in building the Mitchell Tower and its accompanying Mitchell Hall.[17] Above all he was concerned that it must be ready to be opened in October 'during the term of our friend the Lord Provost'. This was Sir David Stewart of Banchory whose term of office would finish at the end of October. In September there was still concern as to whether or not the building would be ready and Tulloch sent the earlier letter from Mitchell to the Aberdeen Journal which reprinted it on 17 September. As we have seen the tower was largely finished in July and the rest of the building did meet the October deadline. Unfortunately Mitchell himself died in August and did not see the opening. The beauty of the Mitchell Hall is well known, especially the heraldic window described by heraldic expert Gordon Casely as 'one of the gems of heraldic artistry in Scotland.'[18]

The Mitchell Tower cannot be ignored by anyone, soaring as it does to 260ft above the skyline of a city full of magnificent lofty spires.

In a book on granite we should look at the inside stone-work of the hall where, in the midst of this vast building of Kemnay granite, we find some pink stone from Corrennie. It is worth quoting the description given by the *Aberdeen Journal* in 17 September 1895:

> The walls of pink Corrennie granite set in gilded pointing, and the result is singularly effective. The blocks of stone, with their soft warmth of colour, seem to be encased in bands of gold (the jointing or pointing). The shafts of the circular columns are highly polished, and the rounded surfaces glance prettily in the light, in striking contrast to the dull-polished or sand-rubbed groundwork of the flat walls. The mouldings at the windows and arches are fine-axe dressed, producing still another shade of colour in the masonry. One result of the general treatment of the granite is to produce an air of warmth probably never before attained in an interior of naked stone.

Praise for this stage of the building came from across the Atlantic when a representative from Barnum & Bailey's Circus, writing on his impressions of Scotland in the *Glasgow Herald*, said:

> I think there are more handsome spires of entirely different patterns in Aberdeen than I have ever seen grouped together in so small a space anywhere. The Mitchell Tower of Marischal College could not be surpassed anywhere for gracefulness of outline and delicate beauty. It is a marvel how granite can be made to appear so frail. It appears almost like a creation of fairyland.

This comment came before the Broad Street frontage was even begun.[19]

The Finished Building

The opening of the Mitchell Hall and the building of the Mitchell Tower were by no means the end of it. With the issue of the demolition of old Greyfriars Church resolved there was still the frontage on Broad Street to be built. As late as 1901 Mackenzie was still producing variations on his plan for the frontage before he finally settled on the 400ft long one familiar to generations of Aberdonians. On 3 May 1903 the University accepted the tender from John Morgan for the Broad Street frontage and work began the following month.

According to the *Free Press* the Broad Street frontage used the finest close picked Kemnay granite, all the stones specially selected with only the best quality used. The late John Fyfe had taken a deep personal interest in the whole operation which had given continuous employment to a large number of men at the Kemnay quarry. The *Free Press* also praised the work of John Morgan and his men:

> the contract for the mason work was the most important on the whole undertaking representing as it did over £20,000 [this figure being for the west frontage only]. Mr John Morgan has carried

out the work to the entire satisfaction of all concerned, and when congratulations are being so widely extended he well deserves special indebtedness. It is no secret that on the contract and the character of the work which had to be done Mr Morgan was a considerable financial loser. But he has displayed admirable public spirit, and has the satisfaction that his name will be honourably and inseparably associated with the great building which the King will open.[20]

This comment about the financial loss echoes an urban myth in Aberdeen that Morgan was bankrupted because after his tender was accepted the university said they wanted finished granite on both sides of the building. Morgan was too proud to go back and ask for more money. There does not seem to be any truth in this story, though the above comment shows that he did in fact make a loss. Radical Socialist James Leathem later wrote that it was suggested that Morgan lost money because of the detail work done on stone for higher parts of the building that could have done in less detail without any detriment to the overall appearance of the building.[21] In any case Morgan was to die the year after the official opening of his masterpiece.

In a ceremony on 7 December 1905, James Tulloch, former councillor and supporter of the University Extension Scheme, as well as a friend of the late Charles Mitchell, placed the final finial of the south turret over the entrance archway of Marischal College. The towers on either side of the entrance were 108ft high and Tulloch was accompanied up the steps by John Morgan and George Reid, the clerk of works. Above the entrance archway were coats of arms cut in the Kemnay granite. The *Aberdeen Journal* spoke about the mason work of the entrance gable being panelled instead of plain which greatly enhanced the effect produced, noted that there was an ornamental cornice above the coats of arms, and declared the moulded rybats and decorative rosettes 'a piece of the most beautiful ornamentation ever executed in a granite building.'[22] At the request of the university, Broad Street from the Gallowgate to Queen Street was paved with wooden sets to lessen the noise for staff and students.

Remarkably, perhaps, only one man is known to have died during the fifteen years of building work on Marischal College. This came during the building of the Mitchell Tower, when a young apprentice carpenter named William Reith, just 20 years of age, was passing from one side of the scaffolding to another to help a fellow workman. Instead of using the gangways he climbed over the stays supporting the pulley beams, the stay gave way and he fell 80ft on to the concrete landing marking the junction between the old and new parts of the tower. Although he landed feet first, his head had come into contact with the scaffolding on the inside of the tower. Despite almost immediate attention from doctors and professors teaching classes in the college, he died soon after.

The completed building was officially opened in September 1906 by King Edward VII and Queen Alexandra, perhaps the most glittering occasion in Aberdeen's recent history. At the time the *Aberdeen Journal* wrote that while many of the buildings elsewhere in the centre of Aberdeen were profusely decorated with bunting, foliage etc.: 'Marischal College was left exposed in all its naked loveliness. It's myriad gold-tipped, delicately carved spires and pinnacles and beautiful lines sparkled in the rays of a brilliant sun, and the whole magical tracery beneath was lighted up in a manner which was most bewitching and entrancing.'[23]

Marischal College at the time of its opening in 1906.

The uniqueness of the treatment of granite in the building of Marischal College was expressed in the *Free Press* when, in praising the architect, it commented:

> Many men entitled to speak with authority have frankly confessed that never before had they fully realised the beauty of form and line which could be obtained by the use of granite. The contrast between the masses of restrained and dignified masonry which forms the lower part of the wall, and the sparkling dance of pinnacles and fretted crests, one above the other, each striving as it were to reach the top first and rejoicing in the struggle. It will never lose its charms. The surpassing and stately grandeur, the artistic brilliance and splendour seen either in mass or detail will abide.[24]

From London the *Daily Telegraph* said that it surpassed in beauty The Escorial in Spain, and that:

> there is about the building an expression of lightness and cheerfulness, combined with stern sever-
> ity, which harmonises well with the sparkle of the granite, and its hard and everlasting nature. This
> sympathy between the design and the material is the secret of the success of this remarkable build-
> ing, which impresses all who see it as a harmonious and beautiful piece of architecture.[25]

One slight criticism came from *The Times* correspondent, who wrote:

> The only drawback is that the quadrangle is not large enough for the buildings that enclose it. The
> original proportions (i.e. of the Archibald Simpson building) are lost, and the quadrangle looks
> cramped. But taken as a whole, Marischal College is truly remarkable; it would be remarkable merely
> as a pile of granite buildings; but as a homogenous group of scientific workrooms it surpasses any-
> thing of the kind that I have seen elsewhere, and I know the best in America and Germany.[26]

At the opening ceremony Lord Provost Lyon was knighted and there had been some thought that
Marshall Mackenzie would receive the same honour. It was not to be. But what about the master
mason, John Morgan. He often seems the forgotten man in all
of this, absent from the platform party and its role of honour,
though the *Free Press* did carry a half column about him as
part of its coverage of the opening event. Marshall Mackenzie
may have had the vision but it was Morgan and his masons
who turned it into the 'dream carved in granite' (see below).

Buildings later seen as iconic and which come to be seen as
a symbol of a city, are often harshly dealt with at the time of
their construction. Examples of this are the Eiffel Tower and
the later Pompidou Centre in Paris. This was not the case with
Marischal College; it impressed people right from the start.
In August 1906 Henry B. Blunt from Wakefield submitted a
poem to the *Aberdeen Journal*. Though not the best of poetry
it does capture the essence of the building, its architecture and
its construction. The first verse ran:

A dream carved in granite, a picture in stone
Marischal College appeals to the eye
For its beauty of structure its rivals hath none
And can all in the kingdom defy

Finial on Marischal College.

Another verse goes:

> On that tall, graceful column the Mitchell Tower gaze
> As its tracery skyward doth rise
> Of the two thoughts that strike you, the first one is praise
> And the other you feel is surprise[27]

Blunt must have had Aberdeen connections or been familiar with the site because he went on to talk about the removal of Greyfriars and also of the obelisk in the quadrangle. He praised the new entrance, the old one 'deemed a disgrace'. This feeling of surprise recalls John Betjeman's description quoted earlier and it is something we don't really get today. Once the Guestrow and the area on the west side of Broad Street had been demolished, as well as the south side of Upperkirkgate, Marischal became visible from a distance. In a later defence of his father's work his son, A.G.R. Mackenzie, himself an architect, commented:

> It should be remembered the building was designed to be seen in a narrow street. Now that Broad Street is being widened it is not being shown to advantage. But when the City Square is completed and there are trees in the centre it will once again be in its proper environment.[28]

This view perhaps echoes the cathedral in many older European cities where you wander along narrow streets, turn a corner and there is the magnificent, soaring building you have been looking for. It is also something that has been forgotten in the arguments over the new city square in Broad Street.

Aberdonians over the years have been quick to defend their iconic building against any criticism. Fashions can change in architecture and in 1937 I.C. Hannah, MP for Bilston had the temerity to describe it as a 'gingerbread nightmare' and a 'beastly eyesore'. Lord Provost Watt was quick to describe his comments as ridiculous, and Marshall Mackenzie's son wrote:

> My father's design was a new treatment of granite, and one feature of it was that it showed the sparkle of the granite to great advantage. It is true that since then fashions have changed and that now the fashion in architecture is towards the plain and functional, but nobody knows if this will be a passing fancy or not.

He then made the comments quoted in the previous paragraph.[29]

The Largest Granite Building?

In the years since it was built Aberdonians have been wont to proudly proclaim that Marischal College was the largest granite building in the world. In more recent years informed comment has finally persuaded them that it is the second largest granite building, though the eminent *Architects' Journal* was still making the claim that it was the largest in 1975.[30] This controversy, though, arose at the time of its building and its place behind the Escorial Palace near Madrid was stated in the *Aberdeen Journal* of 18 July 1904, so the matter should have been put to bed then. As early as 1892 Principal Geddes, spoke about the proposed building at a meeting in St Andrew's Square in Edinburgh. Even with the plans then under consideration, and they would be considerably enlarged over the next ten years, he said that it would be the largest granite building in the British Empire. By April 1897 an editorial in the *Aberdeen Journal* modestly stated that when finished it would be the largest granite building in the United Kingdom (not necessarily much to boast about in that). Then in October 1906 Harry Hems, an English ecclesiastical sculptor and Gothic aficionado, wrote to the *Aberdeen Journal* proclaiming that he had received a postcard from Aberdeen of Marischal College on which some one had written 'the largest granite building in the world'. Hems took exception to this and, using figures obtained from *The Builder* for the size of Marischal, he proceeded to claim there were larger granite buildings in America. In particular he cited the new Pennsylvania State Capitol, built of light grey granite from the quarries of Vermont. According to Hems this building was 520ft long, with a width varying between 212 and 254ft, a height of 100ft at the top of the balustrades reaching 272ft at the top of the dome. It had cost the amazing sum of £2,600,000![31] This prompted Marshall Mackenzie to reply. He claimed Hems's figures were for the Broad Street frontage only, one side of the quadrangle. When the rest of the quad was taken into consideration Marischal was larger than the Pennsylvania building. According to Mackenzie the statement about Marischal being the largest granite building in the world did not come from Aberdeen, rather it first appeared in London newspapers. In any case, he said, as Marischal College cannot be seen as a whole the question of its size was not of interest to architects. However, it has to be said that at the time of the official opening in 1906 the *Aberdeen Free Press* was calling it 'the largest and most imposing granite building in the world.'[32] One London newspaper did get its facts correct. The *Aberdeen Journal* for 14 September 1906, quoted the *Daily Telegraph* as saying that Marischal College was the second largest granite building in the world, next to the Escorial. So even at the time this fact was known and there was no excuse for later Aberdonians getting it wrong.

Postscript

In the years after the Second World War Aberdeen University gradually moved teaching and research from Marischal College to Old Aberdeen and Foresterhill. Marischal Museum still remained but it became imperative to find another use for the building to stop further deterioration of the fabric of the building, inside and out. A hotel chain was interested but nothing came of that. Eventually, in 2006, Aberdeen City Council having taken the decision to demolish St Nicholas House, just opposite Marischal, agreed a lease on the College itself to accommodate various council functions and staff. The lease was to be for 175 years, with the university retaining the Mitchell Tower and Hall, as well as the rooms formerly occupied by the museum. The Church of Scotland still owned the Greyfriars Church end of the building.

The cleaning of the outer stonework of Marischal College was not initially part of the Council's massive renovation and rebuilding project, but by the time the work started in 2009 this had been included in the budget for the project. Sir Robert Macalpine was the main contractor, with Laing Traditional Masonry and Glasgow-based LaserClean involved in the cleaning and restoration of the masonry. The cleaning used a technique that involved firing an abrasive material at the stone. The work also used the last of the granite stockpiled at Kemnay Quarry. By December 2010 the gleaming frontage was finely revealed as the scaffolding began to be taken down.

THE ABERDEEN GRANITE ASSOCIATION AND ITS EFFORTS TO CONTROL THE GRANITE INDUSTRY

The Aberdeen Granite Association (AGA) was to become the main employers' association for much of the granite industry, especially the granite yards. It didn't encompass the builders who had their own organization, the Aberdeen Master Mason's Association, and, although partly initiated by quarriers and with its first president a representative of quarriers, the latter already had their own organization and didn't play a leading role in the AGA.

At the outset the idea that it would exercise some kind of monopoly control over the industry was resented by many potential members. However, that is what it soon tried to do, with varying degrees of success, and that would bring it into conflict with some of its own members. The range in the size of the members of the organisation was considerable, from large quarriers such as John Fyfe and national companies such as Manuelle's, to large granite yards with perhaps 200 workers, down to very small yards, some no more than one man, an apprentice and a boy. This created problems because their interests and outlook were often not shared, with many smaller yards unwilling to be dictated to by the larger ones. Even within the larger yards there were disagreements and, at one point, these would threaten to tear the organisation apart. In a toast at the inaugural dinner in 1888 William Stewart of Stewart & Co. declared 'the difficulty they would experience would be in keeping the rules and regulations. The trade had come to a crisis, and he supposed it was necessity that had driven them into each others arms.'[1] Necessity then, rather than comradeship, his words would prove to be prophetic.

The inaugural meeting of the AGA was held on 23 December 1887, with John Fyfe in the chair. The formation of a society was proposed by George Leslie Jamieson of the Crown Granite Works and seconded by Charles Macdonald. At a show of hands for support, barely half responded. Macdonald and William Boddie then outlined what the aims of the society would be – regulating the price of polishing, overtime and apprentices. It needed the issue of the price of polishing to be dropped before there was unanimous response in favour of an association, an indication that many in the room were against price fixing, though that is what would later be attempted. William B. Wight of A. & F. Manuelle was appointed the first President and membership was to be open to all local granite manufacturers and quarry owners. The objects of the Association were suitably vague, the main ones being 'the general improvement and elevation of the granite interests, the mutual benefits of manufacturers and consumers, and the promotion of a friendly feeling amongst its members'.[2] By March of the following year fifty-six firms had become members. This did not include the doyen of the yards, Alexander Macdonald's, though they did join along with nine others in the next few months. The Secretary was instructed to write to firms in Peterhead, Aboyne, Banchory and Blackburn with a view to getting them to join the Association, the President and Vice-president being tasked with seeing other local firms who had not joined. By 1893 there were eighty-seven members employing 1,600 stonecutters (masons) and 400 polishers as well as other trades such as firemen, blacksmiths, labourers etc.

From the beginning the Association covered a wide range of activities. The less contentious of these included negotiating with railway and shipping companies over the rates they charged for transporting granite, and the maintenance of a blacklist of companies, particularly those in England, who were late in paying their bills (this list being known as the Private and Confidential List). Members were urged not to trade with those on the blacklist and they were prohibited from giving out the names on the list, the maintenance of this list being a somewhat sensitive issue to say the least.

By 1892 the Rules of the Association had already expanded to include an entry fee of £10 with an annual membership of 5 shillings; agreements with the masons and polishers union over working hours and apprenticeships as detailed in Chapter 12; that members should use local granite if possible and if using foreign granite market it as such; members should charge non-members who were eligible for membership 25 per cent more than members. In 1891 a circular had been sent to all quarriers and polishers asking them to enforce Rule XIV regarding the charges for non-members and also requesting that no one get stones until they had become a member of the Association.[3] In May 1892 the Rubislaw Granite Quarrying Company was called to account for selling granite outside Aberdeen while demand in the city was not satisfied.[4] There was some hypocrisy in this since the granite yards were the ones who had instigated the import of granite from overseas. Rubislaw replied that their policy was always to meet the needs of the local trade first.

In 1891 one of the largest yards in the city, Charles Macdonald's, had its membership taken away because they intended to slightly reduce the men's working hours from fifty-one hours to forty-nine, by reducing the hours worked on Saturdays, thus breaking Rule XII of the Association which laid down the length of the working week.[5] (Arthur Taylor actually resigned his membership at the same time over the issue of the polishers' request for a nine-hour day.) (See Chapter 12/) Macdonald remained excluded from membership for just over a year. In the words of his obituary, 'Mr. Macdonald suffered somewhat at the hands of his professional brethren in the city.'[6] He reapplied for admission in June the following year. His men were mainly polishers on piece work and he was willing for them to work the recognised fifty-one hours for six months of the year during winter. He was readmitted in July 1892, though Macdonald himself died in October the same year aged just 43.

The above two examples show that very soon after it was formed the AGA was already aiming to control and monopolise the granite industry in Aberdeen and the north-east and was willing to challenge the largest of its members.

An issue that came up between members was the poaching of staff from other members by offering higher wages, known as 'buying men'. Obviously this would be more common when an employer was under pressure because he had secured plenty of work and labour was scarce. It could also occur after a strike when labour might be in short supply because men had gone elsewhere or left the industry. Following the 1913 strike over wages there was an agreement not to employ men from other firms for three months after the strike. However, there were quite a number of instances of just that taking place. For example, James Hutcheon complained that James Wright & Son had employed one of his men. Wright's were told they should not have employed him. James Coutts also complained that George Stott had taken his grinder, Stott replying that McKay & Son had taken his grinder. McKay said he thought the agreement only applied to stonecutters, an indication that the rules or agreements were sometimes misunderstood.[7] The agreement was even applied to non-members of the Association, as when the Aberdeen Turning Company (ATC) complained that Robert Lawrence had taken one of their men. Lawrence argued that as the ATC were not members of the Association (though several members of the ATC were, in fact, directors of the Association) he was entitled to employ the man. The AGA Directors disagreed and Lawrence had to send the man back.[8]

It was difficult to police the poaching of staff, it relied on individual firms making a complaint and then the Association Directors would hear both sides of the argument. There was always the danger of it becoming a free for all. In March 1914, having just lost a man to Boddie's yard, Henry Hutcheon complained, 'If this policy of buying men is to pass unchallenged, then we are out just to buy men.'[9]

Control of the Industry: The Case of Stephen Crichton

We have seen in Chapter 8 that in the late 1880s the *Aberdeen Journal* voiced the view that there too many small yards with little or no capital undercutting the larger yards, this view being echoed by a speaker at the inaugural dinner of the AGA. The latter sought to control and monopolise the trade, mainly for the benefit of larger yards. As early as 1888 the Association came to an agreement with the trade unions to regulate the number of apprentices compared to the number of journeymen as a way of limiting competition from smaller yards.[10] Other methods used to achieve a monopoly were to try to restrict the supply of granite to non-members; to deter members from trading with non-members; and to increase the entrance fee to put membership out of reach of smaller businesses. The fee was steadily increased to £50, then at the end of 1904 to £100. The following year Stephen Crichton of Magdala Place, Aberdeen, brought an action against all the Directors of the AGA alleging conspiracy to boycott him and destroy his business, and of acting outwith their own by-laws. He stated that the recent increase in the fee was aimed at him and a few other stonecutters who had just started up their businesses. He claimed that he only did work for members of the Association and therefore was not in competition with members. He also accused his own brother of getting the AGA to act out of malice towards him.

Crichton usually carved monuments, especially urns, for other traders and then had them polished by a yard which had the necessary equipment. He worked from a small shed with only a boy to help him. In 1902 this was reported to the AGA. At the time he said he couldn't afford to join the Association but undertook not to buy any stones and do nothing but urn-cutting. This didn't satisfy the AGA, and in October 1904 they had his premises watch by private detectives, the results being inconclusive. The following year they laid a trap for him by sending someone who claimed he was not a member of the Association, with an order for a monument. Crichton did the work and sent it to Association member George Kemp to have it polished. On 29 March 1905, Kemp was fined for this indiscretion, and two days later the Secretary of the Association sent members a circular headed 'Irregular Traders' reminding them of an earlier circular of 8 April 1903 that informed them of Crichton's activities.

The AGA denied that the increase in fees was aimed at Crichton; they said that he had been invited to join when the fee was only £50 and that any action they had taken against him was within the aims and objects of the Association, including protecting their members. A minority of Directors thought it was harsh to take action against Crichton, one being Councillor Nicholas Reilly who gave evidence in court to that effect. Reilly also said that he had been a member since the entrance fee was £5, that now it was £100 there were no benefits in being a member, he simply was forced to be a member in order to get granite from the quarry owners, and then at a 15 per cent discount. This was a view repeated by another granite merchant, James Knowles. Their views would subsequently lead to a dispute that almost tore the Association apart.

Poor Crichton lost his case and the subsequent appeal. The sheriff accepting that there was no malice on the part of the AGA; that they acted within their stated aims and objectives; that a majority of the Directors thought that they were not being harsh in their actions towards Crichton; that their object was to secure control of the trade with a monopoly which enhanced their profits and that these were legal objectives.[11]

Agreement with the National Association of Master Monumental Masons and Sculptors: 1909

This organisation was more prominent in England but there were a number of Aberdeen Monumental Masters who were members. In addition AGA members traded with members of this Association in the rest of the country. As part of their desire to control the granite trade the AGA came to an agreement with them in April 1909 with the following regulations to control the trade between members of the two associations:

1.   Firms in the AGA will not supply memorials to anyone who does not either
     a. Carry some stock of memorials or
     b. Employ at least one practical mason or
     c. Is himself a practical mason
2.   Retail trade is to be continued by the firms in the AGA but not personal canvassing for same. The price to private persons shall be at least 15 % over the price to retail trade
3.   System known as 'Sale or Return' to be discontinued

4.   Memorials are not to be sold by firms in AGA or bought by firms in the National Association from wholesale marble merchants who have offices in Scotland

5.   This agreement is to apply only to deliveries of goods in any place in England and Wales[12]

The AGA in Crisis

The Crichton case showed the lengths the AGA would go to control the industry, a control resented by a sizeable minority of the Association. There is certainly an element of the Association making an example of a very small enterprise, though as we have seen they were prepared to take on larger yards. The whole issue of control over the industry was to boil over in a dispute in 1912, which almost led to a rival organisation being set up.

From as early as 1890 the AGA had produced a price list for monumental work as a guideline. This subsequently became a recommended price, and then on 25 October 1910 a fixed price list for work intended for North America was introduced, with a minimum price list for work within the UK being passed on 9 January 1911.[13] The North American list came about as a result of increasing competition for that work, with yards often reducing the standard of the work to cut costs. This led to complaints by agents for American companies. The yards response was that they would improve the standard provided they were paid adequately, hence a fixed price was introduced with a margin of 2.5 per cent. The AGA introduced inspectors to police the scheme and an annual levy to pay the inspectors as well as other costs of the association, the levy being 6s 8d for every £100 of business a yard transacted. Members agreed that the inspectors could see details of all their contracts. Yards could be fined for not adhering to the price list, with a fine of £5 for a first offence, £20 for a second and rising for subsequent offences. Even as early as May 1910, Crofts & Flett were charged with infringing the price list and were fined £5 as a first offence.[14] Anyone trying to evade detection was to be expelled. Very quickly quite a number of yards saw this as interference in their businesses and it also led to accusations of under-cutting. As was pointed out at the time, if there was very little flexibility in the pricing of contracts and thirty firms went after one contract, then the twenty-nine unsuccessful yards were likely to accuse the successful bidder of under-pricing. This is just what started to happen.

In August 1911 James Pope was charged with infringing the price list and required to appear before the Directors, followed by Peter Henry, Whinhill Road, the following month. Pope denied the charge but was found guilty and fined £5. The issue didn't end there, though, and in November 1911 there were thirty signatories to a motion calling for the price list to be abolished, some of these signatories being founder members of the AGA.[15] They were led by James Pope and included major names in the industry such as James Knowles, William Taggart, and Cruickshank & Co. At the meeting to debate the matter James Pope proposed abolishing the price list and William Stewart moved that it be confirmed. Stewart's motion won, but only by thirty-six votes to thirty. Part of Stewart's motion was that a special committee be set up to examine how the price list could best be applied. The committee had ten members – five appointed by the Directors and five nominated by the meeting. The latter included James Pope.

In 1912 James Hadden of the Imperial Granite Works, Back Hilton Road, was accused of under-cutting the price list. The directors suspected 27 other members of under-cutting but didn't have sufficient proof to charge them. Hadden was told to pay a £5 fine but he refused, and within a week had received notice of his expulsion, the first member to be threatened with expulsion over the issue. Hadden had been asked to produce his day book, cash book and bank book but felt that the Association had no right to see his bank book. He was also accused of showing false contracts to the inspectors. At the same time James Mitchell of Holland Street refused to pay his levy to the inspectors because he said he didn't receive value for it. It was suggested to the Directors that a number of other members were also threatening to take a similar stand. The Directors' hard-line response was to expel Mitchell. They further called on the Granite Cutter's Union to withdraw their men from the two yards.[16]

Hadden didn't take it lying down. He threatened legal action for £1,000 against the Association. As well as protesting his innocence he said that he had shown the inspector his contracts in confidence and now the names of his clients had been disclosed. In a letter to the men's union his solicitor claimed that the Association's actions, as well as being high-handed and tyrannical, were also illegal. In a letter to the *Aberdeen Journal* the solicitor also said there were thirty-five members of the Association who had protested against the treatment of Hadden and Mitchell. Hadden himself said:

Art Deco style headstone for James Hadden, granite merchant, and his family.

All the charges you make are wild random shots, and I am astonished that a board of businessmen, under the tuition of a legal gentlemen (the Secretary), should indulge in this, perhaps amusing, but silly practice. Other members received months to pay a fine. I have been singled out and fined without the slightest scrap of evidence. The trade now realize the autocratic power invested in the directorate and are thoroughly alarmed.'[17]

Mitchell told the *Journal* that he did not intend to take action against the Association unless they asked the Union to get their members to leave his yard, if that happened he would 'seek protection from the law'.

The issue of the Union involvement shows the nature of the agreements that had been introduced over time between them and the AGA. Association members would not employ men who were non-union members and the Association now asked the Union to withdraw their men from yards that were not members of the Association. The Union was undecided, the majority building and district branches cautioning against taking action. The Union did decide that if the men were called out they would demand that the Association pay the wages of the men affected. Hadden and Mitchell sent a letter to Joseph Fraser of the Union asking him to keep the Union out of the dispute. Their letter was signed by thirty-five granite merchants, including James Taggart, James Wright & Sons, James Knowles and James Pope. It quoted the agreement between the Union and the Association pointing out that the agreement was intended 'to prevent incompetent and inefficient masters and men coming into the granite business,' and had no bearing on any dispute amongst members of the Association.[18] In December 1912 a meeting of the AGA agreed, by a majority of five, to ask the Union to call out their men and if not the agreements between the two bodies were to be broken off. Some Directors even urged that they threaten the Union with a lock-out if it did not support the Association. At a further meeting the divisions within the Association, as well as the pressure monumental firms were under from their competitors, was brought out over the degree of coercion that should be applied to the Union. Some members wanted an immediate lock-out, some wanted to give the Union more time to consider the issue, and some led by James Taggart wanted no action taken at all. The vote was in favour of giving the Union a further week to decide. Perhaps if the Union had known of the divisions within the Association they might have stuck to their initial decision but a week after the Union had voted not to call out the men they quickly gave in to the pressure and changed their decision. Both Hadden and Mitchell thought their men wouldn't stop work with Mitchell's view being that the Union wasn't as strong as it seemed and that he could easily fill any vacancies. He commented 'the fun is only beginning now'.[19]

At the same time as all this was happening a meeting of AGA members was held in the Imperial Hotel in September, with seventy of the eighty-four members turning up. The Chairman, Henry Hutcheon, called for a vote of confidence in the Directors and there was heated debate over whether or not the Directors could vote on their own motion. During that debate there was, in the words of the *Aberdeen Daily Journal*, 'some straight talking'.[20] Some of the Directors were themselves accused of undercutting, with the inspectors seen as being ineffective if they could only find proof against one member. The vote was thirty-two to twenty-two in favour of the Directors, with the votes of the ten directors tipping the balance.

However, the dissenters didn't go away and thirty-five were refusing to pay the levy and allow inspectors into their yards. Further than that, in October, at least twenty-seven of them agreed to form a new association, though how serious they were is not clear. On 13 November Frederick Singer put a motion to the Association calling for the abandonment of the price lists. This was defeated by thirty-two votes to twenty-seven. In January 1913 Pope and Taggart acted as conciliators by visiting the two expelled yards and put a compromise to them – pay the fine and be re-instated. They both refused this but did agree to pay the levy. The dissenters drew up proposals 'to save the breaking up of the Granite Association whereby Hadden and Mitchell would pay the levy; the thirty-five dissenters would withdraw their objections; the Directors would call a general meeting and recommend abolishing the inspectors and that the compulsory price list be kept purely as a 'basis of calculation'.[21] Pope sent a letter outlining these proposals to the Directors. One official of the Association called these proposals ridiculous and that withdrawing the inspectors would mean they couldn't enforce the price list, but on receipt of the letter the Directors immediately resolved to resign, claiming to have been 'thwarted in carrying out the rules and regulations of the Association by a considerable section of the trade'.[22] They realised that the Association would be crippled if thirty-five members refused the levy and denied the inspectors access to their yards, and they called a meeting of the Association for 14 January. At that meeting Henry Hutcheon resigned as President and the resignation of the Directors was formally announced. A new board was elected, split five and five between the majority party and the dissenters. William Edwards (majority) was elected President over James Taggart (dissenter) by a narrow majority of twenty-four votes to twenty-three. At the first meeting of the new Directors they agreed to recommend dropping the price list and all fines levied on firms breaking the price list were subsequently repaid.

Although those in favour of enforcing the price lists had a majority, those against were a sizeable minority as can be seen by the even split of the new board and the closeness of the vote for a new President. The outgoing board realised that to continue with their hard-line approach would simply weaken the Association. There doesn't seem to be any pattern to the composition of both sides. It certainly wasn't simply a matter of the Directors representing larger yards trying to dictate to smaller ones. The thirty-five dissenters included major businesses such as James Wright & Sons, a long established business which employed over 200 men. The dissenters also included prominent citizens such as Councillors Nicholas Reilly and James Taggart. James Pope seems to have been the main leader of the dissenters and he may have felt that he secured revenge for his earlier fine for breaking the price list. However, he wasn't popular enough to be elected to the new board, coming eleventh in the vote.

Following the dispute the Association did re-affirm that they would not employ operatives who were not members of the Union and the Union agreed that their men would not work for any employer who was not a member of the Association.[23]

A Further Crisis for the Granite Association

The effect of the First World War on the granite industry is detailed in Chapter 13, as are the steps taken by the Aberdeen Granite Manufacturers' Association, as they became in 1920, to combat foreign imports and protect their industry. In 1925 the pressure on the granite yards eventually led to another attempt by the Directors of the Association to enforce a price list in order to prevent undercutting and maintain a reasonable profit for the trade. The following was agreed

- An estimating book of standard patterns to be kept by each member, open to inspection by an outside auditor appointed by the Directors
- If there was any complaint or if the auditor was dissatisfied, a member must submit any further books or correspondence that the auditor may desire
- In the event of any member not adhering to the Price List the Directors will take such steps they consider necessary to withhold supplies of granite[24]

The AGM in May 1925 only approved the Price List by one vote.[25] In August that year James Robertson & Son wrote to the Association criticizing the price list and they said that no agent or inspector would be welcomed by them, and that they preferred to run their business themselves. The Secretary of the Association wrote back pointing out there were heavy penalties for non-compliance and that the price list was a minimum price.[26] The issue came to a head in January 1926 when there were complaints of undercutting against one of the longest established firms, James Wright & Sons. The first complaint related to work quoted for before the by-law was introduced and this was accepted, but a second complaint was investigated and Wright's refused to allow the auditors to inspect their books. They were fined £10 and given three days to pay. Since no reply was received Frederick Wright, as nominated member, was expelled from the Association. Wright appealed but this was dismissed by seventeen votes to eleven.[27] As with the earlier dispute the Association enlisted the help of the trade union to withdraw Union membership from Wright's men. Wright's shop stewards and their workforce agreed to stay with the firm, which meant that they became a non-union firm, and Wright then sued the Association for Breach of Interdict by encouraging their men to break their contracts. Wright lost the case and also the subsequent appeal.[28]

Once again the issue caused great division within the Association and the authority of the Directors was questioned. At a meeting in October 1927 the President, William McKay, proposed that if a member was expelled then 'no member shall in the course of their business as manufacturers, importers, or quarrymasters have any business with them.'[29] Henry Hutcheon proposed an amendment that said the exact opposite. Once again leading figures lined up on different sides. James Stewart and Councillor William G. Edwards spoke in favour of McKay's motion, Sir James Taggart spoke against it, and Hutcheon's amendment was passed by 15 votes to 12. The President resigned, along with fellow Directors Alexander Wilson and James Stewart. Once tempers had cooled, McKay and Stewart were re-elected as Directors the following February, with James R. Rust as the new President. An anonymous letter to the *Press & Journal* in October 1927 commented:

the Directors of the AGMA expelled James Wright & Sons for failing to observe a by-law passed by them enforcing a new scale of charges. Not satisfied with this the Directors yesterday submitted a new by-law to the effect that no member should have any transactions in their business as manufacturers or quarrymasters with any member who had been expelled from the Association. This by-law was rejected by 17 votes to 12 and of the latter more than half were given by Directors themselves. Evidently the tradesmen's unions still have a good deal to learn from the methods adopted by combinations of employers.[30]

It wasn't until November 1931 that Frederick Wright was approached to rejoin the Association, an offer he accepted.

Aberdeen Designs Limited

In September 1936 Mr G.E. Russell approached the President of the Association with a proposal to offer his services as a designer, submitting samples of his design work. Russell had studied at various art schools, had travelled widely on the Continent and he wanted a starting salary of £500. The Association was sufficiently interested that it set up a committee to look into Russell's proposals. The committee reported back that, though they were favourable to Russell's proposals, as an association of employers they had no power to carry on any business. They suggested that the way forward was to establish a limited liability company. The Directors agreed and invited members to join the proposed company. By the end of October Aberdeen Designs Limited was floated with £5,000 in capital raised by selling 5,000 shares at £1 each.[31]

At the time William Diack saw the formation of this design company as being 'testimony to the practical and business-like fashion in which the local manufacturers are tackling the problems of the trade and are endeavouring to grade up the standard of memorials erected in the churchyards and cemeteries of Britain.'[32]

According to John McLaren the aim of the Company was:

To produce up to date memorial designs in a smart brochure format. These could be purchased by the shareholders of the company for distribution to their customers. Aberdeen Designs Ltd was not in fact the success hoped for. The brochures were expensive, the designs few in number and mostly labour intensive and therefore costly to manufacture. The designer had worked for marble and sandstone markets and failed to take into account that granite was a much more difficult material to process. An additional drawback was that members were all circulating and marketing the same designs which added to the domestic competition.[33]

I think it was also the case that, as with other initiatives, some members of the Association saw it as interference and were very much opposed to its activities. In July 1938 ten firms, including James Pope & Son and William McKay & Son, signed a letter objecting to the Book of Designs from

Aberdeen Designs being exhibited as part of the Aberdeen Granite Manufacturers Association's display at the Empire Exhibition in Glasgow.

The Association in the Period after the Second World War

In 1951 the Association agreed to register itself under the Trade Union Acts. A new constitution was drawn up and it reverted back to being called the Aberdeen Granite Association. However, the industry faced the same problems as it had before the war, as will be detailed in Chapter 15. In June 1952 there was yet another attempt to introduce a fixed price list but it was defeated by twenty votes to ten. But just a few months later John M. Gibb of Alfred Gibb & Co. asked 'whether anything could be done in connection with what he would term the "suicidal" price cutting going on meantime'.[34] Once again the Association turned to the idea of a fixed price list with the same outcome as previously. In January 1953 A. F. Taylor of Stewart & Co. reported on the sub-committee he had chaired on the question of a minimum price list. Taylor said:

> prices from the Aberdeen granite merchants were so erratic it was causing retailers in England to withhold placing orders in Aberdeen, hoping for further reductions in prices. Also it is important to produce high grade memorials, well polished. If shoddy work goes out so as to cut costs, you will have opened the door wide for the foreign made material.[35]

Although there was a narrow majority in favour of a fixed price list it did not achieve the two thirds majority necessary. As in previous disputes this led to the resignation of the President, William R. H. Gibb, as well as James McLeod of A. A. Brown Ltd and James Rust of Charles Macdonald Ltd.

The feeling among the remaining Directors towards the membership can perhaps be judged by Vice-President Alexander R. Robertson calling an emergency meeting with the following on the agenda – prices and price-cutting; sabotaging of meetings; criticism of sending representatives to vote without adding anything to discussions; criticism of Constitution which had been duly passed; criticism of negotiation with the Union; leakage of information to Union and retailers; lack of appreciation of the work of the British Stone Federation.[36] These were a summary of the reasons given by the three Directors for their resignation which was not solely due to the decision taken at the price list meeting. Obviously things had been building up for some time. At the emergency meeting a number of members were of the opinion that the three Directors were justified in the views they had expressed in their letter of resignation with one member stating that this kind of thing had been going on for many, many years (perhaps even more years than he realised!). However the meeting agreed that Robertson would lead a delegation that would meet with the three Directors, express the membership's appreciation of everything they had done for the Association and ask them to re-consider in the light of the difficult position their resignation would leave the Association. The members present further agreed that the Association 'will in future use every endeavour to co-operate in the smooth working of the Association, but reserving the right of constructive criticism'.[37] All three Directors duly returned to their posts at the AGM in April 1953.

The next twenty to thirty years saw a steady decline in the number of members in the Granite Association, reflecting the decline in the industry. The pressure on the industry was such that, only a year after the previous effort, in 1954, another attempt was made by the Directors to introduce a minimum price list. This attempt was voted down, and again the Directors resigned. Subsequently some of them were re-elected to the new board, a board reduced in number from ten to eight, with Andrew Mutch as the new President.

Despite the decline in membership and in the industry generally, the Association was still trying to exercise some control over the industry. In May 1965 Charles Macdonald's were fined 100 guineas for paying overtime rates without permission from the Association. In 1974 the President himself, W.J. Mackay, was criticised for increasing his men's minimum earnings from £34 per week to £36. This caused considerable upset in the trade as men in other yards then wanted the 'Mackay £2'. Mackay said he had done nothing wrong. At the Association meeting where this issue was discussed the minutes concluded with the sarcastic comment 'the meeting closed with a small vote of thanks to the chair!'[38]

1971 saw the last of the Aberdeen Granite Association annual dances, by 1973 the number of members was just 11 and by 1977 this had become just 7. The Association struggled on but by 1983 it had become just A.R. Roberston as President and John Mutch of Fyfe's as Secretary, though Fyfe's operated two manufacturing units and (with Charles Macdonald Ltd) three trading names. The two agreed that the Association be wound up with effect from 31 December 1983.

In an interview carried out with the late Michael O'Connor, owner of James Wright & Sons and twice President of the AGA in the 1970s, he commented, 'There was a lot of infighting. It was a terribly inward-looking lot.' There can be no doubt that his comments are accurate and that the infighting had gone on for many years, if not from the beginning of the Association. The Association did manage to influence and control some aspects of the industry. Its relations with the trade unions and its attempts to combat imported granite and halt the decline in the industry will be dealt with in other chapters. Where it continually came into conflict with a sizeable section of its members was when it tried to interfere with the freedom of these members to run their businesses, particularly on the regulation of prices. However, this independent attitude among members of the Association was also a major contributory factor in the overall decline of the Aberdeen granite industry, leading to an unwillingness to co-operate or consider merging businesses to form larger, more efficient units.

HEALTH, SAFETY AND DISEASE IN THE GRANITE INDUSTRY

Accidents, Explosions and Rock Falls at the Quarries

Every aspect of granite working had the potential to be hazardous, but perhaps the most dangerous were the quarries because these involved the combination of explosives and the movement of large rocks. Several very early examples exist of fatalities in the quarrying industry, even at a time before they really started to blast down into the rock. Several of these early examples involve gunpowder exploding prematurely. One of the earliest recorded was in 1768 when a man named Elmslie was preparing to blow up a stone at Cove Quarry when the train unexpectedly caught fire and the explosion injured his head and face. He died a few days later in the infirmary.[1] The following year quarrier James Whyte fractured his skull when the gunpowder he was using caught fire and blew the rammer, used for packing the explosive into the borehole, into his face.[2] William Ross, a quarrier at Rubislaw was crushed to death in 1780.[3] In 1796 George Mellon, quarrier at Dancing Cairns, had his right leg shattered when a spark ignited the charge he was preparing. He bled for more than two hours before he was brought to the infirmary where he later died. His death led Doctor Livingston from the infirmary to issue instructions to quarries as to how to apply a type of tourniquet – 'eight or ten folds of linen rag, hard bound up, should be placed on the inside of the thigh, secured with a piece of linen, and two strong garters should be twisted with a small roller of wood round the whole, and secured with a firm knot.'[4]

In 1831 William Bickford invented the safety fuse for use in Cornish mines and Jeffrey credits this with reducing some of the risks involved in blasting in the quarries. He commented that in his time some were old enough to remember quarrymen with sightless eyes and disfigurements.[5]

There could even be risks to passers-by near the quarries. In an oft-quoted incident a man was killed on the Skene Turnpike by a piece of stone from Rubislaw Quarry.[6] This seems to have led the magistrate to decree that blasting be restricted to certain times and a warning flag to be displayed when it was about to happen, something that continued into the twentieth century when housewives in the area of Rubislaw Quarry were given warning of a blast so that they could take in their washing or risk having it covered in dust.

Warnings were also given to other quarry workers to clear the area when an explosion was imminent. For example in the 1880s at New Pitsligo Quarry a horn was sounded when a blast was about to take place. In 1884 James Alexander, a quarrier with more than twenty years' experience, had been laying the charge when it went off and blew away half of his face, as well as severely burning his right arm. Incredibly Alexander had been smoking his pipe as he was about to light the fuse and it was thought that a spark from his pipe had ignited the powder.[7]

Prior to the introduction of electricity to fire the charge any kind of spark could set off the powder. In 1869 at the Duffus Quarry at Stirlinghill, operated by Macdonald, Field & Co., one man was killed instantly and another suffered severe injuries after being blown 16 yards. They had completed a bore of 13ft, packed in the powder and then added a quantity of gravel that they were ramming down. It was thought that the friction between the iron rod and the gravel caused a spark, which ignited the powder.[8]

Accidents such as these continued throughout the nineteenth century but for nearly all of that time there are no real figures available to allow us to quantify the number of accidents at the quarries and compare them with other industries. One area that was controlled was the storage of explosives. Quarries were required to have a licence to store explosives and the premises in which they were stored were inspected e.g. in September 1876 the *Aberdeen Journal* reported two licences were granted because the storage buildings had tiled roofs, two were refused because the buildings had turf roofs.[9] The stone-built explosive stores have survived at a number of quarries such as Hill O'Fare and Stirlinghill.

It was not unknown for injured men to sue for compensation and a number of cases appeared at court in the last two decades of the nineteenth century, following on from the Employers' Liability Act of 1880. In 1886 George Moir from Woodside brought a claim for £200 compensation against James Leith, the quarrymaster of Cairncry Quarry. Moir, along with William McLean and foreman George Deans, were a boring squad, responsible for manually drilling the hole with a jumper to take the charge for blasting. After their dinner break Moir was about to get into position to hold the jumper while Deans and McLean took turns in striking it. Moir alleged that Deans brought down his hammer before he was ready, hitting Moir's right hand such that he had been unable to work since. The case rested on the evidence of the two men, McLean claimed that he had been looking the other way when the accident happened! Moir lost the case.[10]

Leith was involved in another action in 1893, this time as a result of an accident at his Persley Quarry. Mrs. Mary Gray, then living in Ontario, brought an action for £1,000 for the loss of her husband. He had been operating a steam crane at the quarry in December 1892. The crane was positioned at the edge of the quarry to lift stone from the quarry floor to the bank. When it swung round to deposit the stone the platform on which the operator stood was then above the quarry. On this occasion the foundations of the crane gave way and the crane and Mr Gray fell down into the quarry where he was killed instantly. Mrs. Gray alleged that the crane was inadequately anchored to the bank and that the jib was of unusual length and not strong enough to bear the load. Leith denied this and said that the rule when operating these cranes was for the jib not to be lower than a 45-degree angle. The crane had a capacity of 10 tons and the stone lifted on this occasion was only 5 tons. Leith further argued that Gray had been negligent because once the stone was on the bank he had moved it again, putting it on top of some other stones. This was not only unnecessary but it required him to lower the jib below 45 degrees. The load had slipped off these other stones, dragging the jib down and subsequently the whole crane. The sheriff found that no one was to blame for the crane giving way; it had simply been an accident for which no one was responsible.[11]

Some cases were successful, however. In 1890 John McKenzie, a quarry worker from Paradise Cottage, Kemnay, successfully brought an action against John Fyfe and his quarry overseer Alexander Moir. McKenzie's son, also John, was working as a settmaker near a large tier of ashlar stones when the latter gave way and killed the young man. McKenzie senior contended that Moir had not built the pile of stones correctly, placing smaller ones at the base rather than the larger ones. The day before the accident a heavy chain from a derrick crane had struck the pile of stones and had given it a shake. This had been brought to Moir's attention but he neglected to properly examine the stones. Fyfe contended that a sudden change in the weather (i.e. frost) had been responsible for dislodging the stones and also that since it was accepted that Moir was a competent foreman then Fyfe had no liability, though he did offer three years wages as a settlement based on a weekly wage of 6s 6d (McKenzie was claiming £300). Fyfe lost the case and the appeal, and was held jointly responsible with Moir for the damages, which, at £65 plus costs, were considerably less than McKenzie had claimed.[12]

The passing of the Quarries Act in 1894 brought the appointment of a Quarry Inspectorate, prior to that only quarries with steam machinery came under the Factory Inspectorate. This also meant that more accurate records were kept of accidents, with the first report for 1895 recording two fatalities in the quarries in Aberdeenshire, one at Tom's Forest and one at Corrennie. From these figures Donnelly includes a table of fatal accidents between the years 1895 and 1914.[13] Giving evidence to the Royal Commission on Mines and Quarries in 1912, John Malcolm Fyfe said that at Kemnay there had been 131 accidents of all kinds in the last ten years. He thought that figure was very low and that the number of accidents was diminishing, no doubt helped by the introduction of inspectors.[14]

Accidents did continue, however, as at Kemnay in 1929 when two men from a team of twelve clearing a ledge halfway up the quarry were swept over the ledge by a rockfall. Despite wearing safety ropes one man, William Tough, fell 250ft to his death after his rope snapped. The other man, Andrew Robb, was fortunate that his rope held and despite falling 30ft and with debris raining down on him, he was able to gain a foothold on the face of the quarry and he was subsequently hauled to safety by his workmates.[15] Six years later at Corrennie two local men from Tillyfourie were killed following a blast and while preparing for a second blast. The foreman had gone down to mark a large stone for cutting while the other man went on to the ledge above the quarry. The ledge gave way carrying him down into the quarry and partly burying the foreman.[16]

Building Masons and the Granite Yards

The growth of the granite yards from the 1850s onwards brought new hazards to the granite workers. An early example of a fatality came in James Wright's John Street Marble and Granite Works in 1853. When a young man was placing a block (in this case of marble) into the cutting machine it fell on him causing internal injuries from which he later died.[17]

John McLaren describes the danger to the eyes of granite workers in the yards. Sharp grit or broken fragments of shot were a problem but could often be removed with care. A greater hazard was 'fires', fiery fragments of steel splintered off when striking steel tools with steel hammers. This required proper medical treatment.[18] John Morgan described how early in his apprenticeship one of his eyes was badly cut by a bit of steel from a tool. He commented that it was removed by Doctor Wolfe and he made a full recovery.[19] Not so lucky was Aberdeen's best-known local historian, G.M. Fraser. He started his working life as a mason in the yards but had to give it up when he lost an eye. He subsequently went into journalism before becoming City Librarian in 1899. Motivated by these hazards granite yards made financial contributions to eye treatment centres. In August 1905, for example, the Aberdeen Ophthalmic Institution received donations from workers and employers at James Taggart's, Macdonald's, Simpson Brothers, the Wellington Granite Works of John Robb, James Hadden's Imperial Granite Works, the Ernan Granite Works of James Forbes,

It wasn't just your own actions that could lead to eye damage. A letter to the *Operative Mason's Journal* in 1910 criticised the practice, which still existed in some yards, of 'double berths' with two rows of men in a shed. This increased the danger of eye injuries and the letter further stated that, in the last year or two, six out of 1,000 stonecutters suffered serious eye injuries.[20]

The introduction of machinery brought other hazards. The *Aberdeen Journal* in 1871 describes an accident involving machinery at Ogg's granite polishing works at Clayhills. A young lad called Alexander Gordon was replacing a belt on the drum of a polishing machine when his clothes got caught in the revolving shaft. He was then dragged round and crushed between the shaft and the roof of the building. He died a few days later.[21] A similar fatality was recorded in 1868 when a wright working at at McGlashan's works at Peterhead also caught his clothes in the shaft of a machine.[22]

Other dangers described by John McLaren include men's bonnets catching fire if they got too close to gas lights, with one polisher's facial hair catching fire when he got too close to a form of early lighting known as a 'bubbly lamp' – a teapot-shaped vessel with a wick using paraffin and oil as fuel.[23]

Even into the 1930s granite yards were still dangerous places. John McLaren describes how young saw boys whose job was to feed the abrasive that helped saws cut through granite slabs, worked in close proximity to only partly guarded machinery. With the disregard of danger that young boys have, they added to it by swinging over and under the saws.

The growth of the trade unions in the granite industry gave the workers a more powerful voice in fighting for increased safety in the workplace. There was also more legislation including the Workmen's Compensation Acts of 1897, which came into operation two years later. These replaced the Employers' Liability Act and meant that injured workers no longer needed to sue the employer. These acts led the Aberdeen Granite Association to recommend that its members take out insurance to cover themselves. One effect of the Compensation Acts was that quarry owners forbade the men from riding in trolleys and waggons, especially on inclines. Workers were also told to take more notice of the regulations regarding blasting operations and older workers were especially urged to avoid taking risks otherwise they would be suspended, which didn't go down well with 'old-timers'.[24]

Safety Equipment

With the introduction of safety legislation both employers and unions encouraged the introduction of safety equipment. There was often reluctance on the part of the men to use this equipment, mainly because it was uncomfortable and difficult to work with, especially in the early years. In 1903 Heslop & Wilson suggested to the AGA that pressure be put on workers in quarries to wear goggles.[25] Settmakers were also vulnerable to eye injuries but the goggles available at the time were difficult to wear while working. In his evidence to the Royal Commission in 1910, James Slevin, General Secretary of the Settmakers Union, when asked if he was in favour of goggles stated, 'if the goggles could be of a sufficiently good nature. If I saw one that did not prevent a man doing his best at work, I should use it, but I have not seen one yet.'[26] These early goggles did not have glass in them, rather it was gauze. The same applied to wool respirators meant for use by those involved in crushing granite which, Slevin said, induced a choking sensation in the men using them. John Fordyce, President of the Kemnay branch, also spoke against the goggles: 'I have tried goggles myself of the wire netting and wire netting with glass in the centre, and I found them very disagreeable in the respect that in the warm weather they cause a sweating sensation about the eyes.' He went on to say that they were becoming more common among stonecutters, but that once you started to wear them you had to continue because the eye lost the faculty of defending itself.[27]

Early in 1939 Fyfe's sent a letter to the AGA quoting a letter they had received from the Inspector of Factories stating that there was a requirement under the new act to provide goggles or effective screen for all workers employed in breaking or dressing stone. This was referring to the Factories Act 1937.[28] However, into the 1950s safety equipment was still difficult to wear as detailed in the next section.

Silicosis and the Public Perception of the Dangers in Granite Working

An article on Alexander Macdonald from the *Press & Journal* in June 1929 has this to say about the healthiness of granite work:

> Some years ago a prejudice got abroad that the granite trade was an unhealthy one, and that it affected the lungs. This fallacy has been gradually exploded, and the statistics show that lung trouble is distinctly decreasing in the trade, one medical authority in Aberdeen attributing this to better conditions in the home – more open windows, and outdoor life. The granite trade today is indeed a pleasant and interesting calling, and, with a new lease of life ahead, opens up an avenue for the absorbing of young men who perhaps experience difficulty in cutting out for themselves a career.[29]

This perception of the unhealthiness of granite work was widespread and had certainly not been exploded by the 1920s; in fact well into the 1950s it continued to be given as one reason why young men were reluctant to enter the trade. The connection between granite dust and what became known as silicosis was something that the granite employers vehemently denied for many years. The initial objection the workers had to the introduction of the surface cutting machine or dunter from 1901 onwards was regarding who should operate it (see Chapter 12). However, once its use became more widespread they also objected to it on the grounds of the dust it created and men did refuse to operate it for that reason. It was eventually agreed that it should be screened off from men doing other stone cutting work, though the implementation of that agreement was not universal or quick.[30] When an article appeared in the press in 1918 alleging that granite work was unhealthy and liable to cause tuberculosis the Granite Association claimed that a scientific enquiry was needed to refute any complaints.[31] There had, though, already been two medical reports or studies in the city relating to silicosis.

Dr R. Beveridge of Aberdeen Royal Infirmary carried out a study in the 1870s, which he wrote up in the *British Medical Journal* in 1877. At this point silicosis had not been identified as a separate disease, rather Beveridge referred to phthisis or tuberculosis. With the limited data he had available Beveridge made a study of two ten-year periods: 1839–48 and 1859–68. He then covered the period from 1869–75. In his study he compared the rate of phthisis amongst masons with that of the wider population of the town, especially factory workers. Beveridge concluded that although the rate of phthisis among masons had doubled in the previous thirty years, it had increased by considerably more among the rest of the working class in Aberdeen. This seems to have puzzled Beveridge who expected the fine granite dust to have caused as much lung problems as other kinds of dust created for other workers in factories. His answer was that because the masons worked in open sheds, facing towards the light and air, they were practically working in the open air. He was also told that the work of the mason had not changed in the past thirty years; the polishing part being done by machinery after the mason had completed his work. Since this was the case any increase in phthisis among the masons must have another cause. The cause he came up with related to the type of men entering the industry. According to Beveridge the lure of high wages in America had drained the best workers from Aberdeen, these workers being 'stout, robust, healthy lads from the country.' In their place had come 'a class of young lads inferior in physical strength, weaker town bred lads, unable to resist the exposure necessary to keep the work from being positively injurious'.[32]

In June 1906 the union representing workers in the monumental industry held a meeting with their employers on the subject of dust generally. They reported that three quarters of the deaths in their branch were due to lung trouble. They raised the general issue of shed accommodation, with some sheds being over-crowded, and also wanted surface cutting machines (later known as dunters) to be moved outside and the practice of blowing dust off the stone and off men's clothing to be stopped.[33] Although the employer's agreed to these requests they were slow to implement them as in 1912 Matthew Hay, the Medical Officer for the city, said that pneumatic tubes were still being used to blow off dust despite there being a rule against the practice. He requested that steps should be taken to enforce the practice.[34]

The next major study of the incidence of phthisis in granite workers came with the evidence given by Professor Matthew Hay to the Royal Commission on Metalliferous Mines and Quarries in 1911. As well as being a professor at Aberdeen University, Hay had been the Medical Officer of

Health for the City of Aberdeen since 1888. Presumably, then, he was aware of the earlier work done by Beveridge. Hay's evidence was meant to relate to quarries, as indeed was the remit of the Commission. However, he went on to talk about workers in the granite yards and the Commission, in fact, chose to extend its remit to include the yards. As medical officer of the city Hay's study of granite workers really related to the quarries in the city, at that time limited to Rubislaw, Cairncry which was on its last legs, and a smaller one recently opened which he called Weir's Quarry.

Hay concluded that workers in the quarrying side of the industry were not susceptible to phthisis, with rates similar to other occupations in the city, because most of their work was done outside. However, for stonecutters and masons in the building and monumental sector his conclusions were very different. He studied death rates among these workers over a ten-year period, 1900-09. He included in his study those that he said were locally called 'wallers' i.e. men in the building trade who simply placed the stone together with lime and were not exposed to any dust. Nevertheless he concluded that the death rate from phthisis, including pulmonary and tubercular phthisis, was 5.7 per thousand, almost exactly three time the rate among the adult male population in Aberdeen.[35] He went on to state that in his ten-year study 316 masons and stonecutters over the age of 21 had died from all causes, and of those 99 died had died from phthisis, just under a third. The average age of death for masons and stonecutters was 51, for joiners it was 60 and for engineers and blacksmiths it was 55.

There were certainly flaws in Hay's survey which he was well aware of. For example he pointed out, as we have already seen, that the physical nature of much of the work in the monumental yards was such that men often left the industry from the age of 50 onwards, many becoming labourers. When these men died their occupation might be registered as labourer rather than masons or stonecutters and therefore they would not be included in his figures, thus causing a reduction in the average age of death of masons. Again while analysing deaths from phthisis since the introduction of pneumatic tools he produced a table of total deaths in three separate periods – 1895–99, 1900–04, 1904–09. However, these figures were affected by the considerable downturn in the building industry in the third period resulting in far fewer masons being employed in building in that period.

Nevertheless Hay was convinced that the introduction of pneumatic tools and closed sheds had increased the danger of phthisis among granite workers. His evidence led to headlines in the press such as 'The Dust Danger'. In 1913 the *Aberdeen Journal* reported on an International Medical Congress attended by Hay and other Aberdeen medical men. Figures were quoted from the Operatives' Union which stated that among building workers, working mainly outdoors, there was a median death age between 55 and 56 and 25 per cent of deaths were due to pulmonary tuberculosis, 13.8 per cent due to other respiratory diseases. Among monumental workers the median age at death was between 45 and 46, with 38 per cent due to pulmonary tuberculosis and 16.3 per cent to other respiratory diseases.[36] Hay was also of the opinion that what he called 'constitutional susceptibility' played a part in workers developing phthisis. Therefore young men entering the trade should be medically examined and their family medical history also looked into.

In 1913 the Granite Association Minutes recorded that in a lecture to the Red Cross, Dr Edgar L. Collis, HM Medical Inspector of Factories, said that what made granite workers more susceptible to phthisis than workers in flint or sandstone was the presence of silica in granite.[37] In December

1913 the *Aberdeen Journal*, in reporting on a health exhibition in the Music Hall, carried the headline 'Expert's Indictment'. This referred to Collis's paper in which he described how granite dust affected the lungs of the workers, and he quoted Hay's work. Collis went on to say that 'he felt confident that the City of Aberdeen would not rest until the accusation was wiped off the slate of harbouring an industry of such infamous notoriety'. At an evening session Collis displayed examples of respirators and urged those present, mainly granite employers and workers, to give them a trial.[38]

These reports and headlines helped cement the image of the granite yards as unhealthy places and the Granite Association developed a defensiveness in the face of these views. They continued to deny that the work was unhealthy and blamed this erroneous image, as they saw it, for poor recruitment into the industry, rather than poor working conditions, long hours and low rates of pay. Hence their claim, quoted above, that a scientific enquiry was needed to refute these claims.

Hay's work was influential and large parts of it, along with his tables of statistics, were quoted, along with the findings of Collis, in a major American report *The problem of dust phthisis in the granite-stone industry*, authored by Frederick L. Hoffman for the U.S. Department of Labor in 1922. This was despite Hoffman describing Hay's report as 'practically inaccessible and rarely referred to in the literature of tuberculosis or industrial hygiene.'

The 1918 article in the press mentioned earlier came from the *Aberdeen Journal*. It referred to a Bill going through Parliament to set up mutual insurance schemes for miners' phthisis. This may have been the Workmen's Compensation (Silicosis) Act 1918. The article suggested that the granite trade would be very interested in this legislation and described phthisis as 'the scourge of the industry' which had killed 13 members of the workers' union the previous year. According to the article, all bar one were in the prime of life. Following on from Hay's report, blame was put on the closed sheds and pneumatic tools, although suction devices had been introduced where dunters were used. Although the article didn't give any figures it 'confidently' stated that a majority of men left the industry while still in their 40s because of fears of the effects of dust.[39]

In 1925 the union itself organised a lecture on how to limit the effects of phthisis. The lecture, attended by representatives of the employers, was given by Dr Banks, the TB medical officer for Aberdeen. Banks's message was that workers needed as much fresh air as possible, both at home and at work, with the move back from closed sheds to open ones being a positive step. He also supported the introduction of mechanical exhaust ventilation, while recognizing that these were expensive to install and maintain. At this stage respirators were still cumbersome and inefficient, the only one he could recommend was one called a 'nasal filter' which was made up of a light frame fitting over the nostrils and holding fine meshed gauze.[40]

The 1918 Act seems to have been applied to freestone in the first instance, but in the late 1920s the government tried to extend it to other areas such as mining, slate quarrying, and granite. These industries fought to keep themselves out of the scheme and the granite industry was represented in the discussion by James Stewart, President of the Granite Association. Stewart argued that it was up to the government to prove that there was silicosis in the granite industry, and he cited the evidence of various eminent medical men to the contrary. Stewart's views seemed to be accepted by Sir Malcolm Delevingne, Permanent Under-Secretary at the Home Office.[41] Granite was therefore excluded from the Various Industries (Silicosis) Scheme 1928. However, the following year the Secretary of State instigated an enquiry into the occurrence of the disease in granite workers, the report being published in the autumn of 1930. The enquiry was carried out by E.L. Middleton, HM Medical Officer of Factories. Of 139 building masons examined, 25 showed signs of silicosis and among crushers it was 8 out of 109. In the monumental sector 9 out of 29 X-rayed showed signs of the disease and all of the 9 had been in the industry quite a number of years. In fact the oldest case had worked in the yards for forty-eight years – for eighteen of those with hand chisels and for thirty years with the pneumatic dunter, all of this being in open sheds. The shortest time worked in the industry was twenty-eight years, with nineteen continuous years on the dunter, and twenty-six in total using pneumatic tools. No polishers showed signs of silicosis, although only seven were tested. The outcome of this report led to those engaged in dressing stone for building, civil engineering, and monumental work being included in the scheme, but not settmakers. It was to take effect from 1 February 1931. It led to the Directors of the Granite Association looking for insurance for their workers, but, since the insurers would insist on the men being examined, there was the threat that men found to have symptoms of silicosis would be dismissed, otherwise the employer would have to bear the risk.[42] By June 1931 the *Press & Journal* reported that the first case under the compensation scheme had already been settled whereby a widow of a recently deceased granite worker was paid £300 compensation when his death was diagnosed as being from pulmonary tuberculosis and silicosis.[43]

In 1945 the Minutes of the Granite Association recorded that deaths from silicosis were less frequent than was generally supposed and that most of those who died from the disease had worked in America where, they said, conditions were inferior to conditions in Aberdeen.[44] This latter comment goes back to what had been thought earlier in the century when the huge enclosed sheds, often quite crowded, common in America, were viewed as unhealthy. However, the Association's prayers were answered in June 1950 when Dr Alexander Mair of the University of Aberdeen read a paper at a meeting of the Tuberculosis Society of Scotland detailing his two-year study of granite workers. He followed that up with a talk to granite workers held in the Music Hall on 4 August. The paper was published the following year in the *Edinburgh Medical Journal*. Mair had carried out a programme of X-ray examination of over 500 men working in areas of the monumental trade where there was a known risk of exposure to dust. He also examined thirty-three retired stonemasons. His conclusions were:

> That while silicosis exists to a moderate extent, it commences so late in life and appears to progress so slowly that in all probability many stonecutters live to comparative old age and die of other diseases common to this age period without symptoms of a serious respiratory nature ever manifesting themselves as silicosis.

On average, thirty-two years' exposure was needed to produce early stages of the disease. For tuberculosis itself Mair found that the incidence among granite workers was no higher than men elsewhere in the community and he suggested that the 'high number of deaths amongst stonecutters in Aberdeen during the early part of the century and registered as phthisis was actually due to tuberculosis and not to silicosis alone or silicosis complicated by tuberculosis'.[45] In his Music Hall talk, Mair pressed the case for granite workers to be given priority in new housing to alleviate the overcrowding which encouraged the spread of tuberculosis. At the time priority was given to key workers such as policemen and agricultural workers but Mair pointed out that both of those groups spent a lot of their working time outdoors, the healthiest place to be in his opinion.[46]

Mair's work was greeted in the local press with the headlines of 'Silicosis Unmasked', and 'Fear of Disabling Silicosis Unjustified' and the comment that the unpopularity of the industry was therefore 'due to ignorance of the true facts and confusion among the workers themselves between silicosis and tuberculosis'.[47] The workers themselves were not convinced, and their Union continued to request a forty-hour week on the grounds that the industry was unhealthy and caused silicosis.[48] Nor was the public convinced, and the granite trade continued to be unpopular. In fact, early in 1953 the *Evening Express* ran a story that said that the granite industry was the most unpopular trade among young men. In the previous year out of 1,200 boys interviewed by the Youth Employment Department only three had entered the granite trade, and even those three didn't last long.[49] During the 1955 strike, David Craig and Alexander Kilgour of the AUBTW painted a grim picture of work in the granite yards. They were quoted in the press stating that:

> the terrible scourge of silicosis hangs over the industry – a veritable Sword of Damocles. That the hard, soul-destroying, arduous work and the terrible conditions, coupled with the evil history and the unprogressive prospects for the future are some of the things that keep young folk from giving any consideration to a future linked with the granite industry.[50]

The same year, an Aberdeen motion was tabled at the annual conference of the AUBTW, expressing concern at the levels of silicosis in the granite industry and a union official commented that they had already raised the issue with the government. John McLaren's opinion on Mair's conclusions, written many years later in his memoirs, was 'that by careful selection of young lads with a good health record, free from tuberculosis or bronchial complaints and medically examined prior to acceptance as apprentices, there would not be undue risk of their succumbing to silicosis'.[51]

Dust Extractors and Respirators

During the 1955 strike there were several letters in the press relating to conditions in the granite yards. One worker wrote that the workers were 'forced to work in sheds where you can hardly see one end from the other through the clouds of dust'. In his opinion this could be avoided by the introduction of dust extractors, the Granite Association having refused the union request to have them installed in all the yards. In fact only one yard had installed the extractors. Respirators were said to be uncomfortable to wear, as they had been earlier in the century, making it difficult to breathe if you had to wear them for hours on end.[52] In his memoirs John McLaren wrote:

dust filtering masks were clumsy and uncomfortable. And both the A.U.B.T.W. and H.M. Factory Inspectorate pressed for introduction of dust extraction equipment. This was more easily asked for than accomplished. The dust collecting head had to be sufficiently flexible to adjust to varying heights and angles to collect the dangerous fine dust. It should not hamper the mason's freedom of working or reduce his vision of his working area. Also it had to be robust enough to withstand abrasive effect of granite dust.[53]

Eventually a design was approved in 1963.

Nationally an emergency meeting was held in London on the 30 October 1956, to discuss 'Dust Suppression in Granite Works'. As well as various government departments, there were representatives from a number of employer's organisations including two from the Aberdeen Granite Association. There was, however, no union representation. Sir George Barnett, Chief Inspector of Factories, chaired the meeting. He expressed concern at the number of silicosis and pneumoconiosis cases among stone masons, though it was accepted that the risk to granite workers was less than for those working in sandstone and gritstone. His inspectors reported that little had been done to suppress dust in granite yards. Research had shown that wetting the stone was of little value and that natural ventilation in partly open sheds could not be relied on. He also accepted that respirators could not be worn for long periods. Two options had been found to be practical in the stone industry: 'the provision of an exhaust hood at the end of a flexible duct which the mason could adjust to the point at which he was working' and 'an exhaust hood or duct surrounding and attached to the tool'. A.R. Robertson, one of the Aberdeen representatives, did raise the results of Dr Mair's research. He also stated that workers coming into the industry in Aberdeen were medically examined and X-rayed with further X-rays at regular intervals. Younger workers were more willing to use respirators and Robertson mentioned one of his workers had shown him a 'Martindale' respirator, which was used in some mines and was reasonably comfortable to wear. According to Robertson, masons in Aberdeen on finishing work often blew dust from their clothes using compressed air, causing clouds of dust. As we have already seen, this practice was supposed to have been outlawed before the First World War. The Factory Inspectorate took the view that Mair's research still showed that silicosis was a hazard in the granite trade and that 'any free silica in the air was dangerous'. They seem to have been concerned that there might be civil claims for damages due to silicosis, something that had recently happened in the foundry industry.[54]

The Factory Inspectorate continued to press for the installation of dust extractors and the employers continued to drag their heels. In 1962 they met with the Granite Association to give them technical advice and by this time a pilot scheme had been introduced at Stewart & Co.'s yard. For the Association, J.R.H. Hogg stated that it would require most yards to invest between £2,000 and £3,000. The Inspectorate replied that provided yards made a start with the installation they would be agreeable to the process being spread over three years. The following year the Aberdeen inspectors had approved a prototype extraction plant with the Granite Association reporting that 134 units would be needed in total, fifty-five of them in the next twelve months.[55] The dust extractors were designed and built by A.D. Cameron of Aberdeen Engineering Design, and by 1965

President of the Granite Association J.R. Ruddiman reported that the installation carried out at Robertson's yard in the Hardgate had been completed. However, it was found to be ineffective with inadequate suction, lack of mobility and the discharge to the outside atmosphere was liable to pollute that atmosphere.[56] Cameron made some adjustments and at long last it was reported in May 1965 that the extractors were now satisfactory.

A further study of Aberdeen granite workers was carried out in 1973 and, although its methodology didn't allow exact comparison with Mair's earlier survey, its findings were broadly similar. No major change could be detected in granite workers over the previous twenty years and 'evidence of pneumoconiosis was not observed on workers exposed for less than twenty years.'[57]

Today the last remaining granite yard in Aberdeen, Robertson's, has a contract with a medical supply company to examine their work force weekly, not just for the effects of dust, but also for hearing problems and repetitive strain problems. Of course so much of their granite is supplied from India and China ready finished that dust itself would not really be a problem for the current workforce.

LABOUR RELATIONS AND UNIONISATION IN THE GRANITE INDUSTRIES

In this chapter I make no apologies for concentrating on the various disputes in the different trades within the granite industry in the second half of the nineteenth century. These disputes were fundamental to the issue of whether or not there would be active unionization in the industry. Later disputes were often concerned with specific issues relating to wage rates and working hours, though the issue of the nature of the craft was also important especially as mechanization was gradually introduced throughout the twentieth century.

The Seven Incorporated Trades, dating from late Medieval times and including wrights, coopers, hammermen and bakers, still exists in some form today in Aberdeen. The masons are no longer one of these incorporated trades now but they were at one time. Munro finds mention of a 'luge' for the masons as early as the late fifteenth century, the masons then working on St Nicholas Church being bound together by some common bond with the term 'masownys of the luge' used. Various rules and regulations governed the activities of the trade as with other incorporated trades. According to Munro and Miller, the masons, together with the wrights and coopers, obtained a Seal of Cause on 5 August 1527 (Ebenezer Bain gives the date as 1532). This was awarded by the Magistrates of Aberdeen to bodies of craftsmen and allowed them certain privileges including the right to organise into a society. Rather than form a body with the wrights and coopers, the masons formed their own society, elected their own deacon, established by-laws and gathered funds. The Council Register has very few mentions of the deacon of the masons and very few masons were admitted as burgesses, but this was probably because there would not have been many masons in the town at this time since most of the buildings were wooden. However, in May 1554, various trades brought a complaint against the smiths and hammermen for not keeping their proper place in one of the religious pageants held in the town in pre-Reformation times.

One of those bringing the complaint was 'William Jamesoune, dekyne of the masons'. William was the grandfather of the artist George Jamesone, sometimes known as the Scottish Van Dyke. George's father, Andrew, was also a mason, and William and Andrew were responsible for building some of the earliest stone houses in the town including what became known as Provost Ross's House in the Shiprow (now the Maritime Museum) and Jamesone's own house in Schoolhill, demolished in the 1880s. William was admitted as a burgess in 1541 and he may have built the first stone house ever built in the burgh in 1535, Menzies of Pitfodels Lodgings in the Castlegate. Both William and Andrew served as master of the town's works, responsible for public buildings built of stone as well as the town's stone bridges.

Bain records that free or 'speculative' masonry was introduced into Aberdeen in the mid-seventeenth century, but that it wasn't until about 1670 that a lodge was formed associated with the Mason's Craft Society. However, a convincing case is made by Munro and Miller for a much earlier introduction of this non-operative masonry. Records of Lodge of Aberdeen No. 1 do indeed commence in 1670, but of the forty-nine master masons and eleven apprentices listed at that date only ten were operative masons. The others ranged from noblemen, ministers, merchants, surgeons as well as various types of tradesmen. The fact that the lodge records list these diverse men as members would indicate that it had been in existence for some time and that these important people found benefit in being members. Moreover it lists three of the members as masters of the lodge, indicating that at least two of them had been masters before 1670.[1] The traditions of the lodge state that a house was acquired for the lodge on the west side of the Gallowgate on or near the site later occupied by St Paul's Chapel and that their records were destroyed in a fire possibly during the Civil War in the 1640s. The tradition that the lodge existed for up to 100 years before 1670 may well be true but it is certainly true that gradually the freemasonry lodge became the more important part of the mason's society, incorporating many non-masons, and largely for this reason the masons are not part of the Incorporated Trades today.[2]

However, freemasonry, as was the case with the incorporated trades, never fulfilled the role of a trade union. Initially the function of the incorporated trades was to protect the trade and had the masons continued as an incorporated trade then that organisation would have represented the master masons, the employers, not the journeymen masons. Union organisation for the latter would have to wait until the middle of the nineteenth century.

Both the employers and the workers in the granite industry had their associations in the second half of the nineteenth century. The diverse nature of the work along with the geographical separation of the workforce meant that no one organisation encompassed either group. Eventually the quarry owners, master masons, master polishers and granite manufacturers each had their own association. Similarly the operative masons and stonecutters, the operative polishers, the settmakers and the quarrymen all developed their organisations. With the growth of the monumental sector in the second half of the nineteenth century the stone masons split into two sectors of their union – one for building masons and one for monumental stonecutters. Some of the men working in the industry also belonged to organisations outwith those specifically for granite workers, such as blacksmiths and tool sharpeners, and firemen.

Granite was an industry in which most of the yards were established by men who had served their apprenticeship as masons. Most of those who became employers would have been union members themselves at one time, some even holding office in one of the unions. George Younie, for example, was first permanent secretary of the Operative Masons' Society, a post he held for four or five years. He then formed a business with William D. Coutts and became a prominent member of the employer's organisation, the Aberdeen Granite Association. Because he had served in both camps Younie is said to have helped create a good relationship between the employers and their workforce. John Soper, President of the Central Council of the Settmakers' Union in the 1890s, was another who crossed over from worker to employer. Soper came from Cove where he was first apprenticed as a settmaker. He later moved to Woodside, spent some time in America before working for Manuelle's at Slattie Quarry. He was also, at times, a quarry master in his own right. The fact that many yard owners came up through the ranks, as it were, may be one reason why workers could be very loyal to their employer and there are several instances of a workforce siding with their employer, even opting to leave the union, when their employer was faced with disciplinary action from the AGA and the union. This happened, for example, in the 1926 Price List Dispute detailed in Chapter 10.

Early Unionisation

In 1877 *The Architect* magazine wrote:

> about a dozen years ago when the big strike took place, an arrangement helped on by a pretty vigorous trade union, was made that 6 pence per hour should be recognized as the standard wage. Although the union has not only long ceased to exercise the slightest influence on rate of pay, but has itself practically passed out of existence, 6 pence per hour has since continued the standard.[3]

This apparent obituary for the union was somewhat premature as the last two decades of the century would not only see the regrowth of the masons' union but also the formation of the other granite industry unions mentioned above. The masons were the first to organise and theirs was essentially a craft union, composed of skilled artisans, and they were very protective of their status, just as the medieval trade society had been protective of its position in a religious pageant. This led to disputes, for example, when mechanisation led to employers attempting to have unskilled men working machines in a process previously done by the hand of a mason or polisher.

According to Diack the United Operative Masons' Association of Scotland was formed in 1831, with an Aberdeen branch being formed some three years later. It folded about a year later, but a second union was formed in 1836 and Diack quotes from the minute book of this union to show that members of the previous union were given free admission to the new one.[4] In 1837 the far sighted United Operative Masons tried to establish a reading room in the city 'for the benefit of the working classes generally, on the ground principally that they would be more profitably employed there, than in idly perambulating the streets, or drinking in spirit shops, after the labours of the day have ceased'.[5] Although Provost Milne supported the scheme it seems that lack of funds prevented any progress being made. Diack records an early dispute in 1842 when the employers tried to reduce the men's wages. The men were out on strike for a month but eventually had to accept the reduction.[6] Around the same time the Aberdeen men broke away from the national body, unable to afford their contribution to strikes taking place elsewhere in the country, those strikers already earning more than their Aberdeen counterparts. In July and August 1845 there was a further dispute when the masons struck for higher wages. The masons seem to have chosen a good time to strike, as the *Aberdeen Journal* commented: 'they have chosen a fitting time to gain their objective, from the extent of building at hand, or projected'. The *Journal* went on to advise them not to be unreasonable in their demands 'as building is not so brisk everywhere as it happens to be in Aberdeen; as hands are abundant, and not difficult to be had.'[7] The threat was there, then, to bring in men from outside the area at a time when unions were weak or non-existent. The strike lasted around two weeks and the implication of the report in the *Journal* was that the men had some success, with the employers agreeing to pay them £1 1*s* a week in summer and 15*s* in winter. It was further agreed that a meeting would be held in February each year to set the wages for the coming season.[8]

At this time the working week for masons was around sixty hours, with Saturday a full working day. In 1850 the union secretary, William Brebner, wrote to the Master Masons' Secretary saying that he had heard that there was proposal to reduce the working hours on a Saturday to eight rather than the normal ten. Appealing to the religious side of the employers, Brebner suggested that this would mean that the men would use the time in recreation rather than carrying this on during the Sabbath. Eventually it was agreed to stop work at three o'clock on Saturday. Initially the time was to be made up earlier in the week but by 1854 work stopped at two on a Saturday and the working week was reduced to fifty-seven hours. This change on a Saturday was particularly welcome by men working on rural jobs, such as those then working at Balmoral, who had a long journey home after work. Alexander Macdonald was one who objected claiming that this Saturday half-day 'crippled his business and sometimes prevented him from completing his orders in time'. By 1872 the week had been further reduced to 51 hours, nine during the week and six on Saturday).[9]

As with many unions in other industries the growth and later strength of the granite unions was forged in a series of disputes some of which we will look at in more detail below.

The 1868 Strike

The major strike of 1868 involved both monumental and building masons, it was only later that the two sectors became separate branches of the same union, with separate wage rates. As was the case with the 1842 strike, this one was in response to the employers trying to reduce wages from 5½*d* an hour to 5*d*. Initially 336 men went on strike, with 200 still working. The strike lasted ten weeks before going to arbitration and over the period some men left to work elsewhere and some went back to work. The employers claimed that a depression in the industry meant that the men's wages had to be reduced. However, one mason wrote to the *Free Press* pointing out that the staged increase from 5*d* to 5½*d* pence two years earlier was the first increase in twelve years and that there was no depression in the industry since there were only seven unemployed masons in the city out of a workforce of 600. This letter also suggests that the some of the employers 'were determined to stamp us out' i.e. to destroy the union.[10] Another letter from a mason not involved in the strike claimed 'the contest is not hinged on the bawbee now. It is whether there is to be combination [unionisation] or not. The difficulty [regarding arbitration] is that the men desire to make it a question of wages, the masters, of course, desire to include more than that.'[11] There is certainly evidence that this was the case.

The arbiter's report states that nineteen masters had men on strike and twenty-two did not. However, the nineteen employed 464 men with the twenty-two employing just 134. It was, then, the larger employers who had men on strike. The smaller employers were not affected because they continued to pay the old rate. The arbiter pointed out these nineteen masters:

> Have continued to pay the old rate to 255 men, while 206 men, forming the Masons' Union are unemployed. The masters, while the strike had continued have been voluntarily paying 5½ pence per hour to a large portion of the workmen, and yet contend for 5 pence per hour hereafter. [12]

Another letter to the press pointed out that masters still paying the 5½d were still doing reasonable business and quoted an estimate given by an employer who was paying 5½d, which was less than one from an employer paying 5¼d. Moreover, a third of the masons employed in the city at the time were actually working on the new Municipal Buildings or Town House and that contract had been agreed eighteen months before the attempt to reduce the men's wages, 'yet the contractor for those buildings is foremost amongst those employers who wish to reduce the men's wages under the plea of scarcity of work'. [13]

The case of the Town House shows the solidarity that existed amongst masons not directly involved in the dispute, and that the union already had some say in the way that the building trade was conducted. The stones for the Town House came from Kemnay Quarry and at the time the union ensured that buildings stones were dressed on site, not at the quarries. Because Fyfe's trade with England was in a period of slackness he tried to get his stone cutters at Kemnay to dress the stones for the Town House. His men refused to do this and instead they came out on strike in support their fellow workers. [14]

The masters tried to influence the situation in the dispute by suggesting that there was intimidation from the union and they promised to protect from victimisation any workmen who returned to work. This was ridiculed by the mason quoted above in the *Free Press*:

> The masters are willing to give them their protection – a noble resolve. Protection from what? Is the law so lax in Aberdeen that these men would not be protected independently of them, or do they intend to make the public believe that the Operative Masons of Aberdeen are coming out with revolvers and bowie knives. Since 1836, when our Society was formed, we ask them, has there been any act or resolution made or attempted to be carried out but what was in accordance with reason and justice?' [15] Another letter commented 'some of our employers have been hiring men in from the country by false representations. This, if it came from a workman, would be called mean. Some of them have been threatening some of their men with future persecution if they did not comply with their demands. This, if it came from a workman, would be called intimidation. [16]

Eventually representatives from both sides met and an agreement was reached. Prominent granite merchants Adam Mitchell, William Keith junior, and Robert Ferguson (of Macdonald, Field & Co.) represented the employers. Alexander Kidd, John Farquharson and George Rae represented the men. They agreed that the men would return to work without interfering with the foremen and other workmen who had continued working; to go to arbitration on the wages issue; that all future disputes would be referred to a committee drawn from both sides, with arbitration if necessary. As we have seen, the arbiter, advocate John Duncan, gave a very detailed summary of the dispute and was reasonably fair to both sides, pointing out, for example, some of the inconsistencies in the employers' case. In the end the question of wage rates was a compromise with the arbiter stating that with a rate of 5¼d per hour, 'justice will be done to both parties'. The Union itself does seem to have be somewhat weakened by the strike with the arbiter reporting that at the commencement of the dispute 337 men were on strike, but by the end there were only 200 men on the union roll with upwards of 100 having left Aberdeenshire for work elsewhere.[17] However, the *Free Press* did report that at a meeting towards the end of the dispute between 300 and 400 men turned up.[18]

One positive outcome of the dispute from the point of view of the wider union movement was that it led to the formation of the Aberdeen Trades Council. An earlier attempt in 1846 to form what was called a 'Committee of Sympathy' had been initiated following a strike by the Aberdeen joiners. The masons' union had been in the forefront of the committee to support the joiners. Although this committee ceased after a few years the idea had been planted and at the end of the 1868 masons' strike the joiners revived the idea in support of the masons, this time with more success. As recorded by William Carnie, the above named masons' delegate, Alexander Kidd, was appointed first President of the Aberdeen Trades Council at the election the following year in the Town's School in Little Belmont Street.[19]

George Rae is an interesting man, obviously politically active. He worked for Adam Mitchell and Mitchell's nephew, John Morgan, wrote about remembering the hustings being erected in Castle Street in front of the Duke of Gordon's statue when William Dingwall Fordyce of Brucklay defeated Sir James Elphinstone of Logie Elphinstone to be elected to Parliament to represent Aberdeenshire. This was in 1866 and Morgan remembered that two of the speakers were Alexander Pirie of Waterton and George Rae, one of his uncle's masons.[20] That same year Rae was a Director, probably elected, of the Aberdeen Co-operative Building Society (Ltd). In 1864 a meeting of working men was held in the Mechanic's Institution Hall with a view to presenting an address to Giuseppe Garibaldi, the Italian nationalist and revolutionary. George Rae was the man asked to propose the address. He spoke of their support for Garibaldi because he was also a working man who had drawn 'the sword to cleave the shackles of honest toil'. In a stirring speech, delivered to cheers, he went on to say 'we understand why you should be ready to fight wherever those who would enrich the world by the sweat of their brow are down trodden and disabled by inveterate tyrannies. The principles that actuate you belong not merely to patriotism, but to humanity.'[21] It really is impressive stuff from a humble mason. Even if others may also have had a hand in writing it, it was Rae who was asked to deliver it. One wonders how it went down with Morgan given his feelings towards the strikers during the 1868 strike.

At around the time of the strike the Operative Masons seem to have formed their own building company known as the Aberdeen Operative Masons' Building Company Ltd. The first ordinary meeting of shareholders held in the United Presbyterian Hall in St Paul Street on 28 October 1868. Although the company seems to have been short lived among the building they are known to have built are Tarland Parish Church, opened in 1870, and Dyce Parish Church, opened in 1872 but later demolished.[22]

The 1877 Strike

By 1877 the building and monumental masons were making separate wages claims and this dispute began with the building masons' demand for an increase in wages from 7½d an hour to 8d. On 9 January 1873 there had been a meeting held in the United Presbyterian Hall in St Paul Street which dissolved the Aberdeen Operative Masons' Society. It was replaced almost immediately by an Aberdeen lodge of the Scotland-wide United Operative Masons' Association, the latter having been formed in Glasgow in 1852.[23] At the time of the dispute it had around 450 members out of 600 masons in Aberdeen. The change does not seem to have been noticed by the employers, or they chose to ignore it, because when the men submitted their wage demand the employers ignored it and instead queried who this body was that they were being asked to deal with.[24] Leading builder John Morgan was Secretary of the Master Masons' Association at the time and he duly wrote to his counterpart, Alexander Johnston, of the United Operative Masons of Scotland:

> they [the employers] have had no previous negotiations of a nature such as indicated in your letter with the association you represent (having hitherto managed all matters affecting the relations between them and their workmen through the Aberdeen Operative Masons' Society), and as they are not aware of how far your society is representative of the views of their employees, they resolved to decline entering into the merits of your proposals till they received some enlighten-ment on the above point.[25]

This response was ridiculed by Johnston who pointed out that the dissolution of the Masons' Society in 1872/73 had been widely advertised in the press and that the employers had already had negotiations with the new body in 1875. Morgan then went on to query whether or not the wage claim was on behalf of all operatives, union and non-union, to which Johnston replied that it was on behalf of both. The issue of recognition of the new Operative Masons' Association was impor-tant because Morgan claimed that the men had not given three months notice of their demand as had been agreed in the agreement drawn up after the 1868 strike. The union side stated that as the 1868 agreement had been with the Aberdeen Society, agreements entered into by any society terminate on its extinction.[26]

This exchange set the tone for what was to be a bitter dispute, described a few years later as 'a dispute which for bitterness had scarcely ever been equalled in this quarter'.[27] On Saturday 26 May 1877, over 400 men met in a lengthy meeting held in the Mechanics' Institution Hall in Market Street. At the meeting they were informed that the Masters had turned down the demand and had threatened to lock-out union members in polishing yards, despite these yards not being involved in the dispute, if the men carried out their threat to strike from 1 June.[28] This would affect around 600 men in total, with 450 being members of the union. Once again the Masters were intent on weakening the union by forcing union members in polishing yards to give up union membership. Certainly the conservative *Aberdeen Journal* seemed to accept that the aim was to crush the union and that this would mean a long struggle.[29] The union itself paid its members 12s a week strike pay: 'this sum we fear will be quite inadequate to eke out anything like a comfortable existence' was the comment of the *Aberdeen Journal*.[30] The Masters refused the request of non-union men in the polishing yards to allow union members in those yards to return to work, some of the former subsequently coming out in support of their union colleagues. The employers even set up a committee to look into the possibility of recruiting workers from overseas.[31]

Provost Alexander Nicol was asked to be a mediator, a move welcomed by the press, but despite his efforts the dispute continued throughout June with some men again leaving the City to look for work elsewhere. By the end of the month there were 157 names on the strike roll.

Initially the men had rejected arbitration because they felt that it would inevitably lead to a compromise of a ¼d increase, but as the strike dragged on they moved to accept it. John Morgan took a hard line in this dispute. In his memoirs he commented on Nicol and the dispute:

> During the masons strike in 1877 he sent for me to confer with him as to some suggested compromise with the workmen. The dispute had gone on for many weeks, the workmen and their families were suffering, and the Provost's own business in the brick and tile line (the Seaton Brick & Tile Works) was as good as shut up, owing to the total stoppage of building operations. I knew by this time that the strike was on its last legs, and on the eve of a general collapse. I told the Provost so, and intimated that the Masters were not in the temper to entertain any surrender. He acquiesced rather sulkily as I thought and before the week was ended matters had righted themselves by the men's return on the old terms and conditions.[32]

As well as returning at the old rates the men also accepted arbitration in future disputes, three months notice before any future dispute should take place, and that whatever the result of arbitration in the current dispute it would not take effect until three months after the return to work. The dispute had lasted almost eleven weeks and there seems little doubt that this was a defeat for the operatives, although the Union was still able to offer to pay £1 to those who wanted to continue the strike.[33] The weakened position of the men and their union led to two reductions of wages, each of a halfpenny an hour, during 1878, three months' notice duly being given on each occasion. Wages were now 6d an hour[34] and would even go down to 5½d. In fact they wouldn't return to 7d an hour until 1898.

In January 1878 the General Secretary of the United Operative Masons' Association, Matthew Allan, and other representatives from Glasgow attended a reunion of the Masons' Society in the ballroom of the Music Hall for which more than 250 tickets had been sold. In describing its activities he said it was more of a friendly than a trade society. This can be seen in its expenditure for 1876. At that point it had 113 branches with 12,000 members. It had spent just over £35,000 on benevolent purposes such as sick allowances, accident provision and funeral allowances, as compared to £19,365 on strikes and other trade issues. It had around £17,000 in the bank. All of this was achieved on a levy of 3d a week. Towards the end of 1878 the Association suffered a severe set back when it lost a large part of its funds in the City of Glasgow Bank collapse.[35]

1880 By-laws

Despite the defeat of 1878, the Union did not go out of existence and in 1880 it agreed a series of by-laws with the Master Masons. These included:

- The working day will be nine hours (Saturday excepted) within the hours of 6 a.m. – 5 p.m. Monday to Friday, and to 1 p.m. on a Saturday. (This working week of 51 hours had been agreed eight years earlier)
- Wages 6 pence per hour with builders having the option of paying their outside men an extra ½ p per hour
- An apprenticeship period of not less than 4 years
- Both sides will endeavour to abolish sub-contracting and piece work except quarry wrought materials for exportation.
  Sufficient shed accommodation be provided for hewers where practicable.
- All disputes be referred to a committee of 4 masters and 4 operatives. If unable to agree the dispute will go to arbitration.[36]

According to Raymond Postgate[37] the perilous state of the national union, with falling membership and funds, caused the Aberdeen Lodge to fold around 1887, only for a new union to be formed a year later. This was in October 1888 when a mass meeting was held in the Northern Friendly

Operative Masons' Union 1888. (Aberdeen Art Gallery and Museums Collection)

Society's Hall to hear a report by a committee established earlier to draw up a set of rules as a basis for the formation of a society. The name of the new society was to be The Aberdeen Operative Masons and Stonecutters' Society, and the primary object was to be 'the protection of their trade and the advancement of their interests in society'.[38] By December a sub-committee of the Aberdeen Master Masons' Association and the newly formed Aberdeen Granite Association (AGA) met with the new operatives' society to agree the by-laws listed later in this chapter.

By 1894 the Operatives' Union had increased dramatically with nearly 1,900 members – 'an unprecedently large membership for a local trades union' according to the *Free Press*.[39] On a visit to Aberdeen in 1894 Keir Hardie unfurled the new banner of the Aberdeen Operative Masons' and Stonecutters' Society.[40] With the growth in the monumental side of the granite industry, and the formation of the AGA as a separate association for monumental employers, in 1896 the Operatives' Union was divided into a monumental branch and a building branch.[41]

Aberdeen Master Masons' Association

This was the main organisation for the employers in the building industry, though it also represented the quarriers, and the monumental and polishing employers until the establishment of the Aberdeen Granite Association. It was formed around 1861 when, according to John Fyfe, there were only nine or ten building firms in the city.[42] By the annual dinner of 1884 there were seventy members on the role, although Secretary John Morgan commented that only twenty-six had paid their subscription![43] In 1903 it was renamed the Aberdeen Master Masons' Incorporation Limited.

In 1879, for his services as Secretary, Morgan was presented with a carved antique oak cabinet which he treasured because according to him they were:

> generally a queer lot, intensely jealous of one another, but their close association together for trade purposes, and mutual help, has done much to break down and remove many of the old barriers of mistrust and isolation , and in this respect through their association they have of late years more than once proved an object lesson to several of the other allied trades.[44]

Morgan was actually Secretary from 1875 to 1894, and thereafter was its President for several years. As detailed in Chapter 10, this fractiousness among the members of the Master's Association was also prevalent in the separate Granite Association when it was formed.

There was also a separate Quarry Masters' Association, although quarry owners such as John Fyfe tended to belong to the Master Masons and the Granite Association as well.

Polishers' Union

In 1888 a mass meeting of granite polishers, held in the Northern Friendly Society Hall in George Street, agreed to form the Aberdeen & District Granite Polishers' Protective Union. The motion that was unanimously carried at the meeting declared that 'the step we are taking has been too long delayed, for an organisation was the only means which they could adopt for the redress of their grievances and protecting their interests against further or future encroachment'. Thomas Cormack was elected the first President.[45] In the granite yards the training for polishers was less than for stone cutters or masons, there was no apprenticeship, and their wages were lower (4*d* an hour in 1889). Within a year membership of the union was 265, although some initial members had already left and quite a number of polishers had not joined, claiming it had done nothing for its members.[46] By 1890 numbers had reached 312 out of 350 polishers in the city.

As we have seen above the masons achieved a nine-hour working day in 1880. In 1891 the polishers were still working a ten-hour day in most yards and in June that year they requested the employers to agree to a nine-hour day. This was turned down by the Granite Association.[47] In February 1892 they submitted the request again, citing the unhealthy nature of polishing; that ten hours was too long a day; that many yards were already working a nine-hour day; that this would make them the same as the stonecutters; and that the last hour after the stonecutters had gone home was less productive.[48] Polishers were also expected to work long periods of overtime, including mealtimes with little or no overtime payment, and with little or no notice.[49] The men agreed to ban overtime in a bid to have their hours made the same as others in the industry. Polishers in Archibald A. Brown's yard walked out after one of their colleagues was dismissed for refusing to work ten hours.[50] Men in some other yards joined them and there were also dismissals at Robert Gibb's yard.[51] The men's threat of strike action was countered by a lock-out by AGA members. On 16 February, notices went up in various yards discharging all union members.[52] Following a meeting of the Conciliation Board established by the Chamber of Commerce, the employers agreed to withdraw the lock-out if the men withdrew the strike order subsequent to a meeting of the two sides, but, crucially, they only agreed to take back as many men as there were places for. This was unacceptable to the union who required that all the men be taken back.

This was a particularly bitter dispute with accusations coming from both sides and the union belief that the aim of the AGA was to destroy them; hence union members were being laid off. The weakness of the union position was spelled out to the men by their President, Robert Fraser, at a mass meeting held in Greyfriar's Hall on 13 February. He told them that they would have to consider the position of the union as regards its funds. He also admitted that their industry was carried on by unskilled labour, though there was a great amount of skill in their work. They had to recognise the possibility that the masters would employ other unskilled workers to fill their places, something that did happen in a limited way despite the efforts of the union members to prevent it.

It was at this time that the widely respected Charles Macdonald was expelled from the Granite Association for reducing the working hours in his yard (see Chapter 10). Arthur Taylor, another prominent figure, actually resigned from the AGA 'rather than adhere to the high-handed policy of locking-out my polishers, having had no grievance with them on the present occasion'.[53] By the middle of February there were only three yards where polishing was being done by union members – Charles Macdonald's, Arthur Taylor's, and Macdonald & Co., who between them were employing around 100 polishers on a nine-hour day. Following their meeting on 17 February almost 300 men marched in support to Taylors's yard, then to Charles Macdonald's one and finally to Town

Councillor Robert Simpson's yard, he being another AGA member who was also sympathetic to the polishers, and who was certainly in favour of a nine-hour day. Simpson had been absent through illness at the original meeting of the AGA that voted to lock-out the men. One of the problems at the AGA, as far as the union were concerned, was that only a minority of AGA members actually employed polishers, around a third. The union wanted discussion with the AGA to be confined to those members with polishers and polishing equipment. Simpson agreed with this and he also maintained that:

> those parties in the trade who worked overtime, and made a persistent practice of working over-time, were asking the whole strength of the Association to support them in doing so. He strongly objected to the practice of working overtime and the whole dispute had been caused by three firms – Robert Gibb's Excelsior Works, A. Brown's St Nicholas Granite Works, and Cruickshank & Co.'s Albyn Granite Works. He considered the men were perfectly entitled to refuse to work more than ten hours a day when so many people were unemployed.[54]

The dispute even led to heated exchanges at the Aberdeen Trades Council when the polishers' representative accused a foreman mason of doing polishers work, the mason's union saying it had no power to stop him doing it. On the other hand when three apprentice masons refused to do polishing work they were ordered to do so by their union. At their first quarterly meeting after the end of the polishers' strike the Operative Masons defended their stance during the strike saying that their actions did not justify the anger directed at them and that they would not let anyone from outside their society interfere in its management. This lingering resentment might explain why in 1893 the *Evening Express* printed a disclaimer from John Shand, late Secretary of the Polishers' Union, pointing out that it had described a certain William Buyers as a stonepolisher, when in fact he was a stonecutter![55]

Finally, on 29 February, the men went back to work, pending further discussions between the two sides. The previous Saturday they had marched in procession from the Oddfellows Hall in Crooked Lane. Their route took them via St Andrew Street, George Street, Hutcheon Street, Causewayend, Nelson Street, King Street, Marischal Street, the Quay, Guild Street, Bridge Street, Union Street, Belmont Street and back to the hall. They thus passed the main areas where the granite yards were located. They carried flags and banners, one bearing the representation of a tombstone inscribed 'Sacred to the Memory of the Ten Hour Day. Trades Council Sculptors.'[56]

Eventually virtually all the men who had been locked-out were taken back and the employers made some concessions on overtime rates. However, the employers did not budge on the issue of a nine-hour day and therefore the result can be seen as a defeat for the union.

The dispute greatly damaged the union; in fact it seems to have folded for a period of three years. A meeting was held in the Trades Hall in 1896, led by the Trades Council, aimed at reviving the polishers' union. John Keir, President of the Trades Council, declared the necessity for the union was shown by the fact that polishers were still working ten hours a day while the others sectors in the granite trade were only working nine. Everyone in the crowded hall signed up for the revived union.[57] The name of the union became the Aberdeen Granite Polishers and Workers' Union.

However, it seems to have struggled in the years ahead and during the 1913 strike (see below) one of their aims was to have a union recognised for them.

John McLaren says that polishers were paid one penny the hour under the rate for masons and he quotes a minute of a directors' meeting in 1940, which gives the following rates of pay:

Granite cutters, turners and scabblers	1s 7½d per hour
Polishers	1s 6½d per hour
Sawmen (leading sawmen)	1s 4½d per hour
Toolsmiths	1s 7½d per hour

McLaren believed that this dated from the days when polishers were not apprenticed. The differential was maintained even after an apprenticeship was introduced for polishers. At times this created a friction between polishers and masons but the latter were in the majority and jealously guarded their differential. It wasn't until 1969 that equal pay between the two was agreed.[58]

Settmakers' Union

The Settmakers' Union was formed in Woodside, Aberdeen in the 1880s. It began with settmakers in Sclattie, Dyce, Persley and Dancing Cairns, with Rubislaw joining later. A second branch was formed at Kemnay and this encompassed the other Donside Quarries as well as Cove and Kincardineshire. It also included quarry workers and spread to the rest of Scotland, becoming the Scottish Settmakers' Union. At a meeting held in Edinburgh in 1890, with Aberdeen's John Adan in the chair, it merged with the National Union of Quarrymen of England, becoming the Amalgamated Union of Stone and Quarry Workers. By 1895 it had 31 branches including a new one in Belfast.[59] It later became the Amalgamated Union of Quarry Workers and Settmakers. The Edinburgh meeting also resolved that when membership reached 1,500 it would publish its own paper. Its central office remained at Woodside for a number of years.

John Adan was one of the best-known officials of the Union in its early days. Adan was born in Old Aberdeen and served his apprenticeship at Dancing Cairns Quarry, before moving to Tillyfourie. Adan spent four years working for an English firm in the south of Russia and twice went to America before settling in Kemnay. He then moved into Aberdeen and around 1894 was appointed General Secretary of the Union and editor of their publication *Settmakers and Stoneworkers's Journal*. During his time the Union added eleven branches and nearly 1,000 members.

The location of the headquarters was decided annually by a vote of the members. At the end of 1905 the membership voted to move the headquarters to Glasgow. At this point John Adan stood down as General Secretary. It later moved to Leicestershire. By 1933 it had 10,000 members nationwide in over sixty branches. In January 1934 it became a section of the National Union of General and Municipal Workers.[60]

In 1912 the settmakers were involved in one of the longest ever disputes in the north-east granite industry. The dispute was over the price per ton of different sizes of setts. It lasted around six months, affected 400 men and caused quarries to be closed and other workers laid off. Inevitably it ended in a compromise.[61]

A union for stonecutters at the quarries was formed in 1895 at Kemnay. It aimed to be a national union with branches all over the country, hence its name – The National Quarry Stonecutters Union of Great Britain. Initially at least its headquarters were to be at Kemnay. In July that same year the new union met with representatives of the Operatives' Union with a view to forming a closer relationship between the two and, in fact, the Quarry Stonecutters may have become a branch of the Operatives.[62]

Labour Relations in the Last Two Decades of the Nineteenth Century

The rapid expansion of the granite yards in the second half of the nineteenth century, coupled with the formation of the Aberdeen Granite Association as an employers organisation aiming to control the industry, gave rise to a number of agreements and disputes in the last few years of the nineteenth century. The AGA joined with the Master Masons' Association to negotiate with the operatives' unions. In 1888 draft by-laws regulating the building and stone cutting trades were agreed by the Aberdeen Master Masons' Association, the Aberdeen Granite Association, and the Aberdeen Operative Masons & Stonecutters' Society. Among the by-laws agreed were the following:

I   Working time shall not exceed 9 hours, 6 on a Saturday, all overtime at least time and a quarter.
II   Employers and operatives shall endeavour to abolish sub-contracting and piece work, and the operatives shall not sub-contract themselves or work to those who do so, operatives may work to an employer who contracts from another, provided the latter conform to these bylaws.
III   Employers and operatives shall establish and maintain a standard rate of wages. Employers may pay higher but no more than ¼ of employees below the standard.
IV   Number of apprentices should be considerably less than the number of journeymen. Boys or individuals under 17 shall be bound for a period of 5 years, above 17 for not less than 4 years.
V   Disputes shall be submitted to arbitration.[63]

It was the nature of the industry that the Granite Polishers Protective Union didn't accept these by-laws and agreed their own ones separately. Among their agreements was that all hand work be done under cover and that union members would be fined if found working overtime for another employer.

Initially the employers were unwilling to recognise a closed shop for their workers. In October 1889 Edgar Gauld had a dispute with the Stonecutters' Society, who objected to two men being employed by him who were not members of the Society. He refused to discharge the men or force them to join the Society. The AGA and the Master Masons' resolved that men were at liberty to join the Society or not.[64] They did agree, though, that masters would not take on men who had left the employ of another master without the latter's agreement. They also resolved that foremen should not be members of the Society. Within a few years, however, the employers did agree a closed shop. It was already in existence in 1898 but perhaps not fully implemented since in that year the *Aberdeen Journal* reported that it would henceforth be rigidly enforced by the Master Mason's Association.[65] For the AGA it was included in the 1907 By-laws:

5   Regulation of the trade. None but competent and efficient persons should be engaged therein, either as employers or workmen, and members of the Operatives' Union hereby bind themselves not to work to employers who are not members of the Granite Association, members of said Association likewise binding themselves not to employ operatives who are not members of the Union. Should any employer or employee violate any of these rules the opposite association shall take such steps as may seem most expedient for dealing with such an employer or employee.

6   Definition of Employers. No person shall be recognized as an employer who does not employ at least one member of the Operatives' Union nor will he be allowed to employ an apprentice unless he is employing at least two members of the Operatives' Union.

Clearly both sides saw benefits in this agreement and within a few years the Association called on the Union to call out their men in a dispute within members of the Association. (See Chapter 10) Nevertheless the agreement does highlight the growing strength of the Operatives' Union. An example of the agreement working for the Union came in 1920 when Angus Brothers, non-members of the AGA, were using non-Union men. As Angus, Hardie & Co. they had applied for membership of the AGA in May, and then Alex Angus withdrew their application. A high level delegation, comprising President Stewart, Sir James Taggart, and Messrs Gibb and Hutcheon, was sent from the AGA to the Granite Supply Association to get the latter to stop supplying Angus Brothers with granite. Within a week Angus Brothers had become members of the Association, having presumably agreed to abide by their by-laws.[66]

The 1898 Quarry Labourers' Strike

This dispute began on 13 August and lasted until 22 September. It started at Dancing Cairns, where fifteen labourers claimed they were paid less than similar workers elsewhere and asked for an increase from *4d* to *5d* an hour – a rate the men claimed was being paid at Sclattie. The quarry manager, W.B. Wight of Manuelle's, refused to negotiate with the men's union, the Scottish Quarrymens' Union, stating that he would only deal with the men individually. The dispute then escalated into one of union recognition for this group of workers and other quarry workers came out in support. Settmakers and various other quarry workers were then locked-out, up to a total of 480 men. The exception was the Rubislaw Granite Company which, as a limited liability company, had to consult shareholders in any decision. In fact the nature of the dispute caused Rubislaw to leave the Masters Masons' Association because the latter tried to stop their members from buying granite from Rubislaw. In a letter to the Association, printed in the *Aberdeen Journal*, George Proctor, Secretary of the Rubislaw Company stated:

> Owing to your recent action in connection with the strike at Dancing Cairns, and in view of your passing the following resolution, viz. – 'That it would be an infringement of the rules to take stones from Rubislaw during this dispute' we beg at once to tender our resignation as members of your association.[67]

It seems that the actions of Rubislaw in staying out of the dispute significantly affected the outcome. Then in the middle of September building employers in the city took the decision to lock-out their workers. This was really a cost cutting exercise as the lack of stone meant there was little work for their men. Other trades in the building sector were also in danger of being laid off through lack of work and there was even a danger the effects of the strike would spread to the monumental industry. The Master Masons put pressure on the Quarry Masters to end the dispute and very quickly the Quarry Masters agreed to award the men at Dancing Cairns the same rates as elsewhere and to recognise their union. Once again the strikers had won sympathy in the editorial of the *Aberdeen Journal*,[68] something commented on by the union secretary, A. Mackenzie, at the end of the dispute, when he thanked the *Journal* and the *Evening Express* for their 'fair and reasonable' coverage.[69]

Provision of Tools

One perennial dispute was over the issue of employers providing tools for their workers, and meeting the costs of sharpening the tools. In 1890 the men claimed that they were disadvantaged compared with men who had worked in America. The latter were provided with tools that they were able to bring back with them. The men claimed that no one had a full set of tools and that it was difficult to borrow another man's tools. They further claimed that masters could get tools more cheaply because of bulk purchasing, and that apprentices found it difficult to afford tools. The employers flatly refused to countenance their buying of tools.[70] This issue particularly affected the settmakers and, in 1896, there was a strike lasting four or five weeks over this issue. Settmakers elsewhere in the country had their tools provided and sharpened by their employers but not in the north-east.[71] The settmakers won the support of the editorial in the *Aberdeen Journal*, which commented:

> The expense to the settmaker in supplying his own tools and paying for sharpening is presumably a tangible deduction in proportion to his gross earnings. The trade, moreover, is a monotonous and laborious one, and considering the prosperity of this branch of the granite industry it might have reasonably been expected that the quarry masters would have received the request of the men in a far different spirit from what has been the case.

The *Journal* went on to castigate Aberdeen Town Council, who only employed two or three sett-makers, but refused to meet the cost of supplying their tools despite the minimal cost and the fact that all other Council workmen were supplied with tools as were settmakers employed by councils in Edinburgh, Glasgow and Dundee. The total cost would only be £10 per year and it described the treatment of the settmakers as 'shabby' and posited that it was only possible because the settmakers were so few in number and could be easily replaced.[72] Initially John Fyfe claimed that his men at Kemnay had no sympathy with the strike but he then told them that if the men around Aberdeen went on strike then he would lock-out his men at Kemnay and elsewhere. This indeed happened, leading to a total of 268 men on strike, the union paying them strike pay of 10*s* a week. During the dispute John Fyfe employed settmakers from Leicestershire at his quarries, with a number Aberdeen men moving elsewhere for work. Eventually as many as 100 settmakers left the Woodside/Bucksburn area.

The *Journal* still called the men's demands 'just and reasonable which the quarry owners ought to have conceded' but the owners had adopted a policy of outright hostility, preferring to close the quarries rather than concede what the men asked.[73] Finally as a compromise the quarry owners agreed to provide free sharpening of the tools but not the tools themselves.[74]

In 1909 the by-laws agreed by the Granite Association and the Operatives Union did include a provision to supply all tools for stonecutters in the monumental yards, except for bush hammers, hand hammers, squares, bush chisels and winding blocks. Four years later this was expanded on to specify that each man provide himself with three bush hammers (6, 8 and 10 cut) as well as the other tools already mentioned.

Scabbling and Dunting

Long-serving granite worker Robert Taylor, interviewed during the 1985 granite strike, recalled that at the time of the last major dispute in 1955 the men 'so cherished their reputation they were reluctant to let semi-skilled men do their job'.[75] This attitude was also seen in a much earlier dispute. In August 1892 the Operative Masons were in dispute with Robert Singer over the issue of Singer employing labourers to operate the scabbling machine. This was a machine for turning stone columns and Singer and other members of the AGA contended that scabbling was an operation that didn't require a skilled mason. The Operatives argued that the two operations ran into each other and that gradually these scabblers would acquire the skills of journeymen masons, the implication being that these 'unskilled' workers would gradually do the work of time-served masons. The AGA stood firm and refused to accept the Operatives argument and stated that if any cases arose of scabblers doing the work of masons then they would deal with them. At their AGM in December 1892 the AGA stated that their position was that scabblers were distinct from masons and that their members must not put scabblers to masons' work.[76] In his memoirs John Morgan saw one of the advantages of introducing new machinery as 'keeping in check the arrogant and often unreasoning assumptions and restrictions of labour'. He also said that it would reduce the amount of highly paid skilled labour.[77] Little wonder that the men were wary of the introduction of machinery.

A similar dispute arose in 1903 when Bower & Florence used a non-mason to work a stone surfacing machine, sometimes called the handsurfacer tool, and later known as a dunter. They said that they had put a mason on to the machine but he didn't want to do it because it would effectively de-skill him and he would be unable to do normal mason's work. Moreover the company wanted the work to be done as piecework, as in America, but the masons refused this. The Union argued that in America, where the machine originated, it was worked by masons, the work done by the machine had previously been done by masons and therefore they should continue to do that work using the machine. The AGA argued that since it was not a tool supplied by the masons they couldn't claim the work. It was a machine and could be operated by unskilled labour. Their view was that within six weeks a man off the street could operate it as well as a time-served mason and that in any case it was generating so much extra work that all the masons would be needed for the fine work. The Union disputed this.[78] The issue was not resolved and as the introduction of the new machine spread so the issue came up again, and the men also decided they didn't want to work it on health grounds, because of the dust it generated. In June 1906 the AGA met with the Union to discuss moving the machines outside because of the dust they generated. Blowing the dust with air pipes was not satisfactory and it was agreed the practice should be stopped and that surface cutters should be outside, though often there was in fact nowhere else for them to go.

In 1907 By-law 7 agreed between the Union and the Association for the use of both machines was as follows:

> Scabblers employed in the various yards who have not served a regular apprenticeship to the trade shall be confined exclusively to circular work but under no circumstances shall they be allowed to do any part of squaring work, including jointing. Stonecutters shall operate surfacecutting machines, or any other class of machines that may be introduced to do any part of the stonecutters work.[79]

Presumably these by-laws had been under discussion earlier that year when Garden & Co. at the Victoria Granite Works had been told by the Union that their scabbler could scabble anything he wanted provided he only used the puncheon. Garden & Co. withdrew their man from scabbling except for circular work.

The Granite Association did take action against members who breached this by-law as in 1914 when Bower & Florence were accused of employing a scabbler to do squaring work. The Association agreed with the complaint and wrote to Bower & Florence.

By 1910 there were over twenty surface-cutting machines in the city and, in September, James Wright's men refused to work the machine because of the dust. Initially the AGA took a hard line saying that if the men refused to use the machine then it would call into question the exclusive right of the Operatives to work all pneumatic cutting tools. However, following a meeting with the Union it appeared that members of the Association were not forcing men to work the machine. Likewise the Union was not preventing men working it but could not force them to. General practice seemed to be that the machine was kept in a shed, available for use but that no man was forced to use it.[80]

By March 1913, John Fyfe's proposed that the Association be no longer bound by By-law 7 in so far as it referred to the use of surfacing tools set in frames. This was agreed and the Union informed.[81]

The 1913 Strike in the Monumental Sector

In January 1913 the Operatives' Union wrote to the Granite Association requesting a reduction in the working day to eight hours on week days and four hours on Saturday, coupled with an increase in wages from $7\frac{1}{2}d$ per hour to $9d$, the request later being reduced to $8\frac{1}{2}d$. The Association claimed they had not received the required notice for the wage request but there was also some delay in dealing with the request, partly as a result of the turmoil within the AGA which had resulted in the resignation of the Directors. (See Chapter 10.) The request was, however, rejected out of hand by the employers who offered $\frac{1}{2}d$ increase and no reduction in the working week. The men refused arbitration, stating that the matter had been delayed too long to go to arbitration and in March voted to strike from 1 April, though they did drop the requirement for changes in the working week. For their part the members of the Granite Association agreed 'to stand by one another in the coming struggle,' not to employ any members of the Union until the Association authorised it, and to only employ men at the old rate. They also wrote to the Master Masons' Association asking them not to employ any monumental men, which they agreed to.[82] On the workers side the polishers and turners, as well as other workers including blacksmiths also became involved, the latter requesting to become a branch of the Operatives' Union. The polishers also wanted recognition of a union for them as a branch of the Operatives' Union. The *Journal* reported that when a load of stones was sent from a yard where the polishers were on strike to one where they were still working, the polishers at that yard immediately held a meeting and decided to come out.[83] In all over 1,500 men were on strike, including stonecutters, blacksmiths, polishers, labourers and others. 513 working men were working, more than two-thirds of them apprentices. The Granite Association claimed intimidation and a laxity in police attitudes.

According to the *Aberdeen Journal*, the Union had funds of £12,000, sufficient to pay full strike pay of £1 a week for two months. They also received offers of financial assistance from the Granitecutters Union of America. As with other disputes large numbers left the local industry, quite a number going to America and others to Cornwall and Bute.[84]

Once again a Lord Provost intervened, in this case Adam Maitland. It all got rather petty with the Association saying they would attend a meeting but only if the Union asked for it. The Union wouldn't ask, though they were willing to attend a meeting at the Town House. The Association then refused to attend. To try to divide the strikers the Association offered to pay an increase of $\frac{1}{2}d$ per hour to any man who worked during the strike. The Secretary of the Board of Trade happened to be in Aberdeen and he tried to get both sides to attend a meeting but again the Association insisted that the Union must ask for a meeting. Eventually, on 6 May, the Union did ask for a meeting, at which they said they were willing to settle for $1d$ per hour on all grades, with recognition of the branches formed by the polishers, granitecutters and blacksmiths. This was rejected by the Association.

The strike lasted around eight weeks and ended on 13 May, with the press initially being asked to suppress the story in case it might prejudice the settlement. The editors agreed on the condition that they got a report of the Granite Association General Meeting which agreed to the eventual settlement. In the end the stonecutters and blacksmiths (or toolsmiths) received a ½*d* increase, with the blacksmiths being recognised as part of the Operatives' Union. Shortly after the employer's association for blacksmiths, the Master Toolsmiths' Association, applied to become a branch of the Granite Association, 'and to stand by you in case of trouble provided you establish a rule: 1) prohibiting members who employ toolsmiths in their yards to sharpen tools from other members; 2) members who do not employ toolsmiths to send their tools to any of our shops.'

The polishers received no increase but their union was recognised by the employers and they became a branch of the Operatives' Union almost immediately. They did retain some special by-laws, applicable only to them and agreed with the Granite Association.[85]

1913–55

For a period of over forty years there was no major strike in the granite industry. The struggle for a reduction in the working week went on all this time, as did continual battles over wage rates, but there was no long-term stoppage. During the First World War the shortage of labour prompted more complaints to the AGA by individual members or by the Union alleging breach of the by-laws as employers struggled to maintain a workforce e.g. poaching workers by offering over the accepted wage rates or employing mature men as apprentices. The Union also tried to use the situation to their advantage by claiming an increase in wages. They had some success with the stonecutters and toolsmiths agreeing an increase in 1918, though the polishers rejected this increase. In June 1921 President Stewart of the Granite Association reported that in his four-year term of office wages had increased by 133 per cent and working hours had been reduced from fifty to forty-four hours per week. However, later that same year wages were actually reduced by 3*d* an hour.

From 1 January 1921 the Operative Masons & Graniteworkers Union was incorporated with the Building and Monumental Workers Association of Scotland. In 1942 they would become part of the. The latter would become part of the Union of Construction, Allied Trades and Technicians (UCATT) in 1971.

In 1948 the Union requested a forty-hour week but this was rejected by the Granite Association. The unhealthy nature of the industry was one reason given for the need to reduce the working week. For a time that year the men introduced their own forty-hour week by attending mass meetings in the Belmont Cinema on a Saturday morning. The Granite Association claimed not to object to the forty-hour week, but refused to pay wages for a forty-four-hour week if the men were only working forty hours.[86] The dispute got nowhere.

The 1955 Strike

John McLaren was involved right through the long-running strike of 1955. In his memoirs he said that the dispute arose after several years of trying to get non-craftsmen to operate carborundum circular saws. During negotiations for the 1955/56 wage scale, a small majority of employers voted to tie the increase to the issue of non-craftsmen operating the saws. Union members rejected this, wages and working conditions had always been separate. The final settlement was a wage increase and the saw to be operated by craftsmen.[87]

The introduction of the carborundum saws, as with the dunters at the beginning of the century, was indeed a part of the 1955 strike. The saws had been introduced in a limited way before the Second World War, but it was after the war that a dispute arose. The Union wanted one man per saw and crucially they wanted masons to operate them. The granite trade was proving unpopular and it was difficult to attract apprentices. The employers claimed that they could increase the manpower in the industry by training labourers to do carbo-saw work. The men wanted a *3d* an hour increase, which was the national increase. The employers initially offered *2d* but they were worried about the possibility of a strike, which would lose them orders, and also about the loss of men from the industry. They therefore gave their negotiators the authority to offer 3p but with the condition that labourers be allowed to operate the saws. The men would not agree to this. Joseph Rennie, Secretary of the Scottish granite section of the AUBTW was quoted in the *Press & Journal:* 'the Union regarded this operation as craftsmen's work and a craft union could not give away a prescriptive right which the mason had secured for himself by doing a five-year apprenticeship.'[88] R.B. Williamson, Secretary of the Joint Employers' Committee, comprising the Scottish Monumental Sculptors' Association and the Aberdeen Granite Association, claimed that:

> When the saws first came in before the war an argument arose as to whether they should be operated by craftsmen or trained sawmen. At that time there was a surplus of masons so the employers agreed to allow masons to work them. Now there is a shortage of masons and a great many of the men won't work the saws.[89]

A strike notice was called at the end of April, the strike to begin on 5 May, with the strike also going ahead in Glasgow and Edinburgh. According to the press 800 masons were on strike, though where they got that figure from is unclear since the employers claimed that the number of masons in the monumental yards had gone down from 453 in 1948 to 327 at the time of the strike. Possibly the higher figure included polishers, it certainly didn't include apprentices who did not come out on strike. By the middle of June Edinburgh had agreed a *3d* increase, with trainee operators allowed to operate carbo-saws, but in the event of unemployment the trainees would go first. Glasgow also went back at around the same time, agreeing a *3d* increase and the issue of the saws going to arbitration.

In Aberdeen around 100 masons left the industry, claiming that there was no future in it. The rest of the Aberdeen men held out, finally agreeing to go back on 8 August. The terms of the agreement were that the men would be awarded the national increase of *3d* per hour; with a view to assist in the manpower shortages in the industry there would be no restriction on the intake of apprentices and that apprentices would be given the opportunity of being trained in the use of circular saws in the final year of their apprenticeship; a Joint Committee would be set up to look into the labour requirements of the industry with representation from the employers and the Union. The strike had lasted around thirteen weeks.

Relations After the Strike

Just prior to the strike Andrew Mutch, President of the Granite Association, had declared, 'if we do fight it must be a fight to the finish. There must be no patched up peace.'[90] In the aftermath of the strike a certain amount of bitter feeling seems to have lingered between the two sides. In June 1956, as a result of a petty dispute over the date of a meeting to discuss overtime rates, the Union brought in an overtime ban. The Directors of the Association considered this a breach of the by-laws and wouldn't meet with the men until the ban was lifted, apart from meeting to discuss apprenticeship matters. The Union finally withdrew the overtime ban from 31 January 1960, in the hope that it would lead to better relations with the employers. The absurdity of the situation can be seen in the fact that generally both sides were of the opinion that it was to the benefit of the industry not to work overtime.

The next big issue for the Union side was the length of the working week, with the Union stating that there had been no reduction in the working week since 1920, during which time some other industries had reduced it by up to five hours.[91] The reduction was achieved in stages without recourse to any industrial action. A forty-two-hour week was introduced in November, followed by a forty-hour week one a year later.

The 1985 Strike

The 1985 strike was the last major dispute in the granite industry, by then a much reduced industry. Although it was reported in the press at the time as involving three firms – William McKay & Sons, John Fyfe, and A. & J. Robertson (Granite) Ltd, in fact, as noted in Appendix 1, McKay's had been taken over by Fyfe's two years before the dispute. Their name was retained, however, with their managing director, John Mutch, being widely quoted in the press regarding the strike. On the men's side the main reason for the dispute was the issue of negotiating wages and conditions locally. Until two years earlier they had negotiated with the Aberdeen Granite Association which had now ceased to exist. Around 110 masons, polishers and labourers were involved, with a two-thirds majority in favour of strike action.

The strike began on 21 October and the headline in the *Business Journal* of the *Press & Journal* was 'Aberdeen's men of granite rock solid in fight for their pride'. In the middle of November the situation was exacerbated by Robertson's issuing sacking notices to 50 employees. Glen Grassick, regional organiser of UCATT, said that 'we have been left with no choice but to escalate the strike.' This involved the Union calling on support from the wider trade union movement. The bitterness of the dispute can be seen when, in late November, Robertson's sent a letter to their dismissed workers offering all of them employment on the same terms and conditions as before the strike. The Union side then claimed that Robertson's were claiming that some men had gone back, a point the Union disputed. UCATT organiser Ewen Sinclair claimed 'its dirty tricks to come away with this.' Strike Committee chairman, Bill Elsey, said that no one had crossed the picket line that week and that 'we are convinced that the employers are in a desperate situation and are trying everything to get us to go back to work.' (EE 27 November 1985.) Robertson's policy of not speaking to the press meant that these Union comments were not refuted at the time. However, it seems more likely that it was the men who were in a desperate position and by early December some 23 men had returned to work at Robertson's. Graeme Robertson recalls that 'Andy Verdaille of UCATT in London flew up to Aberdeen to "negotiate" on behalf of the strikers. He told them that they were incorrect in their understanding of plant bargaining and that they should return to work; which they did.' (Personal communication with Graeme Robertson, October 2018.)

Agreement to end the strike came on Friday 13 December 1985 with the workers returning the following Tuesday. Fyfe's and McKay's decided not to recognise the Union at that time, though they did agree to 'continue discussions in the hope of coming to some form of agreement'. (P. & J., 17 December 1985.) All sacked workers were to get their jobs back, although at Robertson's they had to re-apply, and the men were to have a union representative on the national negotiating committee.

Polisher Robert Taylor was one of the few men involved in this dispute and the earlier one in 1955. For the 1955 dispute he maintained that 'the pride of the men had a lot to do with it. In 1955 they so cherished their reputation they were reluctant to let semi-skilled men do their job.' Of the 1985 dispute he said:

> This right to negotiate wages and conditions ourselves has been on the go for 100 years, and why they want to change that now, I don't know. The employers are prepared to honour the rights and wages we have so why not leave the system the way it is? It's sad to see the enmity a strike creates because it hardens attitudes and creates divisions which can remain for the rest of your working life. It would be a shame to see the industry which has been the heart of Aberdeen degenerate or even disintegrate through a simple lack of communication, and I believe the two sides should immediately get round the table and not rise until this things has been settled.

Despite Robert's comments this seems a particularly futile dispute in a declining industry and there does appear to have been a potentially damaging stubbornness on both sides.

THE GRANITE INDUSTRY
1914–1939

The First World War

The First World War had a profound effect on the granite industry with shortages of men granite and work, leading to some yards closing completely. As well as a shortage of imported granite, due to embargoes or blockades, there could even be the loss of an actual order due to enemy action as on 9 March 1915 with the sinking of SS *Princess Victoria* by a German submarine. The *Victoria* was travelling from Aberdeen to Liverpool and the yard of George M. Stalker took a considerable loss from the sinking.[1]

As early as 2 September 1914, at a meeting of the Aberdeen Granite Association, a letter was read from Henry Hutcheon Ltd., stating that nineteen of their men had been called up to join the army. Verbal reports round the table showed that in numerous other yards men had also been called up.[2] By 4 November a note in the margin of the AGA Minute Book recorded:

> there is a scarcity of workmen but that the demand is falling off and it may be that in a month there will be considerable slackness, that a shortage of granite is anticipated in about six months unless communications can be maintained with the Norwegian, Swedish and Russian ports in the Baltic.

At the same date it was reported that 250 out of 1,500 men had joined the army.[3] By May the following year that figure had risen to 600, with forty-four of Hutcheon's men now in the forces.[4] However, a report by the Directors of the AGA in March 1915 reported that there were too many men for the work that was coming.[5] The Directors were mainly referring to the monumental and polishing part of the industry, with tombs and ornamental fronts not in high demand. There was a possible opportunity to pick up work formerly done in Germany for the French market and French architects did contact Aberdeen yards but the prices offered were too low to be considered. Work for America also suffered with financial problems being felt in the United States.

By 1916 the situation had changed with the AGA report now stating that there was a shortage of labour.[6] Although the polishing and monumental trade with America and Canada had collapsed there was work to be had from England, possibly as a result of increasing demand for headstones.

However, supplies of granite were a major problem. The home quarries were affected by losing men to the war and the virtual embargo on building work meant that the quarries were no longer profitable to operate. From the outset of the war freight prices from the Scandinavian countries had increased substantially and imports dropped considerable. Then the Government introduced a ban on imports unless you had a licence from the Board of Trade, something granite importers were unlikely to be granted. In compiling a submission to go to the Board of Trade to plead their case the AGA took figures from the Harbour Board Accounts that showed that in 1913 there had been 22,496 tons of granite imported. By 1915 this figure had dropped to 11,013 tons.[7] The AGA submission also quoted figures from the Operatives Union which stated that there were 2,308 stonecutters and polishers employed by 70 firms. Of these 687 had enlisted and 150 were engaged in munitions work. In addition there were normally around 360 apprentices but the great majority of them had enlisted. These figures did not include labourers and other workers. As well as this submission from the Association the Aberdeen Chamber of Commerce also submitted a report pointing out that with fishing devastated by the partial ban on fishing and the requisition of boats and fishermen for the war effort, Aberdeen's other major industry was granite and the city could ill afford to have it similarly devastated. Moreover there would be loss of exports to neutral countries such as America and Argentina. The Operatives Union and the local MP, George B. Esslemont, also wrote to the Board of Trade. Lord Provost Taggart, while on a visit to London on Town Council business, also met with Sir Guy Granet, controller of import restrictions. All this achieved was that one shipment of 1,500 tons of imported granite from Scandinavia was allowed in, barely enough to keep the yards going for a month. In February 1917 the AGA reported that figures from the Harbour Board showed that for the year ending 30 September 1916 only 5,029 tons of granite had been imported, 5,984 tons less than the previous year. Despite that 6,368 tons of polished granite had been exported, up 86 tons on the previous year.[8]

Lord Provost Taggart did have one success with the Labour Bureau in that the latter would not take stonecutters for munitions works. However, this did not apply to other granite workers such as blacksmiths, tool sharpeners, crane operators and labourers.

Both the building side of the granite industry and the settmakers were also severely affected by the war. There was very little building work done, especially in the first few years of the war. The *Aberdeen Daily Journal* reported in 1915 that building work was at its lowest for at least 50 years.[9] Settmaking was very dependant on work from local authorities who took the decision to carry out only a minimum of work on road improvements. The same report in the *Journal* recorded that in 1914 25,840 tons of granite setts had been exported from the harbour, in 1915 it had dropped to 8,907 tons. This drop in activity for builders and settmakers impacted on the quarries, though their biggest problem was a decline in their workforce. In 1915 Manuelle's closed their Dancing Cairns Quarry, though the majority of the sixty men affected were to be transferred to their other quarries at Sclattie and Dyce. One saving grace for the quarries was that they did get higher prices for stone suitable for monumental work, mainly as a result of the lack of imports from Scandinavia.

One of the issues that arose as a result of the shortage of labour was the employment of women in the granite yards. In February 1916 James Knowles wrote to the AGA stating that he had taken on some women as apprentice polishers.[10] In March the AGA agreed with the Union that wages to women should not be less than other apprentices and that the situation of women in the yards would be reviewed within three months of the war ending. The type of work women were allowed to do and were thought capable of doing also became an issue. In May Stewart & Co. telephoned the Association to ask if women could be allowed to work the Jenny Lind polishing machines. The President replied 'yes but he had considerable doubts as to the ability of women to handle a Jenny Lind'.[11] The Association did want the women to do some of the lighter jobs such as lettering and scrolling but the use of women for these skilled areas was resisted by the Union. In fact the polishers' branch of the Union were willing to accept female labour but the monumental branch were not, a fact that was reported to the Board of Trade under the National Service Scheme.[12]

Among other effects of the war were the introduction of regulations regarding lighting of workplaces with windows skylights and glass doors to be screened. The Union did manage to get the Secretary of State to allow lighting in the yards from 7.30 a.m. to 5.30 p.m. and this became the working day in the winter months. A system was also put in place whereby if the lights had to be extinguished the police would inform ten yards who would then pass the information to others.

According to John McLaren his father's firm, Bower & Florence, saw their workforce of 100 men cut by 75 per cent during the war. At the end of the war his father was released early from service after a request by his partner, Haddon Bower.[13] In March 1917 the AGA recorded that a report had appeared in the newspapers purporting to be the first list of restricted occupations and that it included granite quarrying and granite cutting and polishing.[14] This report may not have been accurate because in the last year of the war the granite industry was still under threat of losing more of its workforce, especially as an order came into force calling up men up to the age of 43. The Director of National Service had given an undertaking to keep a nucleus of men in each non-essential industry so that they could be revived after the war. The Employment Exchange in Aberdeen was instructed to stop enrolling granite cutters and drillers as War Munition Volunteers, War Work Volunteers etc., but it needed Lord Provost Taggart and President James Stewart of the AGA to personally visit the Director of National Service in Edinburgh before it was agreed that granite workers would no longer be called up for military service.[15]

The reality was that the industry was barely surviving during the war years. Several yards closed and others were just ticking over in the hope that by keeping as much of their workforce as possible and their contacts with customers, they would be able to resume relatively normal working as soon as the war was over. The *Free Press* carried a long article at the end of 1917 detailing the perilous position of the industry and commented that 'it would be difficult to find a trade that has been more hardly hit by the war than the granite industry'. As noted by John McLaren, the *Press* stated that most yards were left with just 20 per cent of their pre-war workforce. With letter cutters being especially in short supply, though discharged soldiers were in the process of being taught this particular skill. As well as shortage of labour and material, the *Press* highlighted problems with transport. Faced with their own problems, rail and steamship companies did not look favourably on transporting blocks of granite. Steel for tools and for polishing was either very difficult to get hold of, or prohibitively expensive. The same applied to other materials used by the industry such as emery, putty, wood and carborundum. An unnamed local merchant, noted as being one of the pessimists, declared:

the granite trade of Aberdeen is now engaged in a grim struggle for existence. Always independent and suspicious of each other, each manufacturer is struggling on his own. There has been no
combined effort to protect the interests of this once important industry. The so-called Granite
Association has done practically nothing to help its members, and each is left to sink or swim, and
since 1914 many have gone out of business.

This was not really true since the Association had made efforts on behalf of the industry as we have
already seen. In any case the AGA was not a separate organisation, it was composed and run by its
members who elected its directors. The anonymous source went on, somewhat bitterly:

It is now realised how insignificant this trade can become, dependent as it has been for years for the
supply of its raw material so largely from foreign soil, and which has now been entirely prohibited
for over a year. If the quarrying of Scotch granite had been developed and encouraged and capital
put into local enterprises, instead of into a trust, which in the happy days before the war had the
trade under its thumb, and controlled the importation of raw granite, the position today would
not have been so disastrous.

This refers to the Granite Supply Association's control of the supply of imported granite as well
as of some local granite and echoes some of the comments from Henry Hamilton mentioned
in Chapter 8. The comments may be from someone who suffered withdrawal of supplies by the
Granite Supply Association, which had after all been established by the AGA. It may also be true
that some were regretting putting most of their eggs in the basket of foreign imports rather than
investing in local quarries, easy to be wise after the event and few if any granite yards opposed the
importation of raw granite in pre-war times. A slightly more optimistic granite merchant was also
quoted by the Press. Despite the acknowledged gloom this source commented:

When everything is considered , it is really surprising that the granite trade has been able to
carry on as well as it has done; certainly few men in the trade would have prophesied that after
three years of war so many yards would still be able to keep pegging away. The firm that has the
material and can turn out the work has no difficulty in getting a good figure for their goods. As
a luxury trade, the most that one can look for is marking time, and if this is so, the granite trade
of Aberdeen is to 'warsel' through all right, perhaps all the better for the cleansing time through
which we are passing.[16]

Time, and the progress of the industry through the 1920s, would tell which of these views would
prove correct.

    In common with many other trades and professions many granite workers laid down their
lives for the war effort. Built into a wall near the site of Macdonald's Aberdeen Granite Works in
Constitution Street is a granite plaque. It lists the ten men, aged from 19 to 40, from that one yard,
who died serving in the First World War.

The Situation at the End of the War

By the last year of the war John M. Fyfe and James Stewart of the Granite Association reported to the Special Committee of the Labour Employment Bureau that employment in the granite industry was one third of what it had been before the war. In some quarries it was one fifth, quarrymen generally being younger and fitter as compared with those working in the granite yards, suffered higher rates of enlistment.[17] With foreign imports drastically reduced, stocks of these were virtually at zero. The stocks of home produced granite were also very low and it needed the quarries to begin production before the trade could resume anything like normal levels of production. Quarry workers were given early demobilisation to help the situation but as we will see below the quarries themselves were well past their heyday.

   The Operatives Union reported in 1918 that 600 men were currently employed in the building and monumental sector, compared with the normal 2,000 before the war. Over 100 members of the Union had been killed and a similar number discharged and unable to resume their previous employment. The *Aberdeen Journal* claimed that the granite industry had been the most patriotic trade in the whole country. It also suggested that the strain of managing their businesses through the difficult war years had been responsible for so many employers dying during that period, almost twenty being the figure they gave.[18] These included several major figures in the industry such as William Boddie, Archibald Brown, William Edwards and Nicholas Reilly, three of whom were former Presidents of the Granite Association. Raw material costs had risen substantially, 45 per cent according to the AGA, and the Government Committee on Production had awarded large wage increases to the operatives, a consequence of price rises caused by the war. According to the *Aberdeen Journal* the price of finished monuments was 130 per cent higher than it had been immediately before the war.[19]

Trade with America

The value of exports to America had dropped from £28,015 in 1914 to just £300 in 1918. However, in a talk to the Aberdeen Rotary in 1919, W. F. Pratt of W. C. Townsend, and one of the partners of the British Granite and Marble Company, declared that home demand for monuments was in excess of supply, no doubt because of demand for monuments for some of those killed in the war, and that overseas customers were looking elsewhere. When home demand fell away there would be no overseas customers to fill the gap and that the Aberdeen yards really needed to change their tactics and expand otherwise the industry would have to 'cut its own tombstones'.[20] The Aberdeen yards never did recover the American trade, other than for a brief period after the war. High tariffs to protect the home industry had been an issue since the McKinley tariff legislation in 1890 and in the 1920s they stood at 50 per cent for finished work, with some American legislators, encouraged by the American granite industry, trying to get this doubled. This, along with competition from other European countries, meant that the Aberdeen product in both rough stone and finished goods was too expensive. In 1926 the total value of imported manufactured granite to the

United States was 321,000 dollars. Of this total German monuments alone commanded over half at nearly 165,000 dollars. Finland and Czechoslovakia also had a sizeable share of the market. Rough stone had a much lower duty and many American companies imported stone from continental Europe, especially from Sweden and Finland.[21] The paradox here was that the Aberdeen industry opposed increased tariffs in America but wanted tariffs imposed by the British Government on European granite and monuments.

Figures given in the *Quarry Manager's Journal* in 1930 show the decline in value of Aberdeen's trade with the United States.

1884	£26,269
1889	£59,842
1890	£81,763
1895	£60,777
1897	£36,901
1903	£20,859
1920	£29,830
1923	£18,132
1928	£3,500 [22]

The high point was reached in the year that the McKinley Tariff was introduced. From then on there was gradual decline with the greatest decline being in the 1920s. By 1931 the value had reached £741. The decline at the end of the decade was further exasperated by the general slump in America with John Taggart of William Taggart & Son having to sack half his workforce and put the remainder on to short-time working solely because of the loss of the American trade.[23]

The drop in trade with America was also reflected in the colonies with Australia and New Zealand introducing tariffs to protect their own industry. They began importing rough granite directly from Scandinavia. France, where the tariff before the war had been low enough to have very little impact, introduced such a high rate of tariff that, coupled with the devaluation of the franc, the export of monuments and polished building stone from Aberdeen ceased completely.

The 1920s

Pratt's warnings, although contested by the Aberdeen Granite Association, was a prescient one. As ever with granite the industry went through a succession of highs and lows in this decade. The first year or two after the war saw an upturn in demand from the home market brought about by the demand for monuments and war memorials, but the industry did face various challenges. There were problems in recruiting men to the industry, partly due to the image of the industry and growing concerns regarding the unhealthy nature of the work. Then there were the wage demands from workers in the granite yards at the end of the war. The Union claimed that low wages was one reason for poor recruitment; ordinary labourers in other industries could earn more than journeymen granite workers. Also wages were higher in Glasgow and elsewhere and were also higher in the building sector, something that had been the case for many years. At a meeting held in the Labour Exchange in September 1920, between employers, workers, medical men and members of the Juvenile Advisory Committee, the latter body stated that they had 80 vacancies on their books for granite apprentices that they could not fill. J.R. Cowie, Secretary of the Operatives Union blamed low wages and the unhealthy nature of the industry. He gave figures for the monumental sector showing that at the highpoint for apprentice numbers in 1904 there were 472 apprentices, compared with 63 at present. The decline in journeymen was not nearly so drastic with 892 in 1904 compared with 752 at present. James Stewart, President of the AGA claimed that there was no difficulty getting apprentices, that they were well paid and he put some of the blame for low numbers on restrictions placed on them by the operatives themselves, with Henry Hutcheon also saying that the apprentices were given little encouragement by the journeymen. The employers also argued that the reason for poor recruitment after the war was not low wages but the unwillingness of young men to indenture themselves for the fairly lengthy period of their apprenticeship.[24]

The industry faced competition from abroad for both rough stone and finished monumental and architectural stone. One area of the latter which was reasonably successful during the 1920s was in the provision of polished granite for building fronts. These were still popular with architects but again this trade could very cyclical, depending to a great extent on the well-being of the economy generally. A building boom one year in London could be followed by a slump the following year. The same was true of the building industry in Aberdeen itself. The expected post-war boom in construction didn't happen and building yards were accused of taking on monumental and architectural work to make up the short-fall. Already by 1922 the *Quarry Manager's Journal* was reporting on the growing threat from brick in building.[25] This was being used in house building in areas such as Woodside and Tannfield. In the wider economy there was the General Strike and then the economic crash followed by the Great Depression which didn't help matters.

German and Scandinavian Competition

The early years of the decade saw increased competition from Germany for monumental and architectural stone. In 1921 Aberdeen prices were still 150–175 per cent above pre-war levels and Aberdeen merchants claimed that the low level of the German mark, longer hours worked, and lower wages gave the German manufacturers a considerable price advantage, with their workers paid 6 pence an hour compared with 1s 6d for British workers. The Germans employed agents in many of the larger English towns and also imported their products into England via Ireland. They were undercutting Aberdeen yards by 20 to 25 per cent.[26] The Aberdeen Granite Manufacturers' Association (as the AGA became in 1920) waged a long campaign to have German imports subject to an increased tariff and also for German imports to be marked as such, a move that was opposed by the National Association of Master Monumental Masons.

Part of the industry campaign was to have granite included in the Safeguarding of Industries Act, 1921, designed to protect key British industries after the war. To the great disappointment of the

Aberdeen manufacturers, in 1924 the Government actually reduced the tariff on Germany imports from 26 per cent to 5 per cent. President of the AGAM, James Rust, expressed tremendous surprise that the Government had done this without referring it to the House of Commons.[27] A resolution of protest was sent to the Prime Minister, the Chancellor of the Exchequer, and to local MPs. In 1925 the editorial on the situation in the *Quarry Manager's Journal* finished with the comment'the future does not appear at all rosy for the monumental trade of the Granite City'.[28]

In 1923 the Granite Association agreed to levy their members to raise £2,000 to fund a publicity campaign. This was intended to make customers aware of the advantages of the Aberdeen products, especially the range of colours and the durability of granite as compared to other stones and to marble. They also played the patriotic card by trying to make English towns aware that their war memorials were being supplied by their war-time enemies and this seems to have had some effect for a time. The issue of trademarking home products, although introduced, was not universally viewed as being likely to succeed. One unnamed local trader commented cynically in the press:

> There is nothing to prevent the retailer from sticking the trademark on to his foreign-made produce. The majority of traders, with no great love for Aberdeen, do not care a brass farthing where the work is manufactured if they can sell it a price to beat their neighbour. The proposed trade mark to be fixed to Aberdeen finished Scotch or Scandinavian granite memorials is being treated as a joke throughout the retail trade of the country.[29]

The Merchandise Marks Act, which was eventually passed in 1926, was intended to prevent foreign manufactured goods being sold as of British manufacture. For the granite industry the issue dragged on for most of the decade with James Stewart and W. D. Esslemont, advocate, giving evidence on behalf of the Granite Association to a Board of Trade Committee in 1928. In their evidence they stated that Germany and Czechoslovakia were sending large quantities of monumental and architectural granite into the country and they wanted a duty of 35 per cent for five years. The industry had suffered a great loss of manpower during the war and was 'overstocked with elderly men'. Whereas in 1908 there had been 400 apprentices, now there were only 132, with 18 fewer firms than in 1913.[30]

There was even competition from Europe for relatively low-cost finished materials for road-making stone and road setts. In a letter to the *Press & Journal* in March 1929 H.J. Grace, President of the National Federation of Granite and Roadstone Quarry Owners, stated that the previous year 320,000 tons of broken roadstone had been imported into Britain.[31] In the pages of the *Quarry Manager's Journal* there was some debate as to why Norwegian setts were cheaper than home produced ones. J. R. Jeffrey, long serving Secretary of the Aberdeen Granite Association, had considerable experience of the Scandinavian countries and he was of the opinion that it wasn't due to low wages as was the case with competition from Germany in the monumental trade. Norwegian workers had active trade unions and good working conditions. Rather it seems to be the case that the granite was easier to extract as compared with Scotland. Because of the action of glaciers Scandinavian quarries had no layer of tirr and they were above surface level so there was not the need to invest in expensive lifting machinery or for pumping gear. Uncultivated land was cheap in

Settmakers at Corrennie Quarry, 1920s.

Norway so that rents were cheaper. There was also some suggestion that Norwegian and Swedish quarries were being subsidised. The stone from these quarries had a straight and reliable grain and so was easier to split with Jeffrey estimating that Norwegian settmakers could turn out 20 to 25 per cent more setts than an Aberdeenshire worker. The downside was that Scandinavian setts did not stand up to the same wear as British ones; they chipped easier and would be rejected if supplied by a British quarry owner.[32]

By the end of the decade the granite merchants eventually had some success in their battle against foreign imports when the Merchandise Mark's Committee at last agreed to have imported monuments marked with a stencil to show the country of origin. The merchants had actually wanted an incised mark but the Committee felt that this would be too expensive to remove after sale, and would damage the monuments, making it more difficult to sell them. Almost immediately several English companies were prosecuted, the Liverpool firm of John Stubb & Son being one of the first to be fined in September 1929, following an unannounced visit to their yard by Aberdeen merchant William Forbes, who seems to have passed himself off as a buyer.[33] The following year J. Ashley & Sons of Blackburn were fined for selling a number of headstones with no indication that they were foreign. The action against them had been brought by the Aberdeen Granite Manufacturers' Association.[34] As predicted by the editor of the *Quarry Manager's Journal* the granite trade had failed to have their industry protected by the Safeguarding Act and the marking of granite was seen as second best.

The General Strike 1926

Although granite workers were not involved in the General Strike the strike did have an effect on the industry. Power supplies were greatly reduced and the import and movement of both raw and finished material was affected. This led to most of the yards agreeing to move to part-time working early in May. After some discussion the members of the AGMA agreed to work normally Monday–Wednesday and then close down the rest of the week. As it happened the strike was called off shortly after this agreement was made, though the restrictions continued for another month.

The Sydney Harbour Bridge

Although the Aberdeen granite industry might have been in decline in the post-war period, the expertise of its granite workers was still in demand. In December 1926 the *Press & Journal* reported that earlier that year thirty men had left the city to work on the Sydney Harbour Bridge. The *Journal* noted that letters sent home from the men indicated that they were more than happy with their working conditions – a forty-hour week being worked and the wage that they had signed up to had already been increased by 10 shillings a week. A further four polishers were due to go out in January, the last contingent as the quota agreed with the government, contractors, and union, was complete. The report in the *Journal* came as part of a lengthy article headed 'Granite Revival Delayed', reporting on the depressed state of the industry in the north-east. This helps explain why when a representative of Dorman Long of Middlesborough, the company building the bridge, visited Aberdeen to recruit granite workers, he received almost 250 application forms. Dorman Long had appointed John Gilmore to manage the granite quarry at Moruya, 200 miles south of Sydney. Gilmore was born at Harthill, Kintore, and had worked at Kemnay, Rubislaw, Peterhead, Brechin and Ailsa Craig quarries. He also spent time in North America. The first party of workers from the north-east left Aberdeen in February 1926 with another group following in May. Unlike most of the granite workers who had gone to work in North America, this group took their families with them, and children were born in Australia who later moved backed to Aberdeen with their parents. Gilmore himself took his wife, son and eight daughters on the seven-week voyage. For the north-east men the contract was for three years with the possibility of further work beyond that, though that didn't really happen. In the community known as Granite Town that grew up at the quarry, they were joined by Australian and Italian stone masons.[35]

The granite these men worked on was used for the four impressive 89 metre high pylons, but the pylons are actually constructed from concrete, the granite, 17,000 cubic metres of it, being used to face them. In addition the pylons are an architectural feature, not a structural one, the official bridge website describing them as 'decorative'.[36]

The Quarries in the 1920s and 1930s

At the beginning of the twentieth century there were over a hundred quarries in Aberdeenshire employing around 2,100 men. Already by 1911 this number had almost halved to around 1,100.[37] A number of quarries closed just before the First World War, including Cairncry, Little Clinterty, one quarry at Dyce and Wright's quarries at Peterhead. The inter-war period saw a continuing decline for many of the older quarries with some closing completely, others simply providing crushed material for roads, with Dyce and Sclattie no longer producing quality stone for polished work. The *Aberdeen Journal* reported in 1920 that quarrying was fast dying out in the suburbs of Aberdeen – the employers blaming shortage of labour, the workers blaming lack of a guarantee of steady employment. Quarry workers had gone into the munitions factories during the war, conditions and wages being better. Many had stayed in the factories after the war.[38] The two largest quarries, Rubislaw and Kemnay, continued to grow, to be invested in, and effectively become super-quarries, at least by north-east standards. Each of them had originally been composed of several quarries, but now Rubislaw had become one large hole.

One threat to the quarries came from imported granite from the Scandinavian countries. This was nothing new, of course, but in times of pressure on the quarries it became more of an issue. Here there was a conflict of interest as the quarry owners wanted freight charges reduced and a

Settmakers at Kemnay Quarry 1930s. Their skathie is identical to the one shown earlier from 1857.

heavy duty on imported stone, while the manufacturers wanted the cost of imported granite to be substantially reduced to help them compete with German yards who also imported most of their granite from Scandinavia.

J.G.C.Anderson described the position of the quarries just before the Second World War. Dyce had been abandoned and the rubbish tips of the Tyrebagger quarries were used for roadstone. Clinterty was a moderately sized quarry and was still operating, worked with cranes and a light railway. Tom's Forest was closed, though it would reopen and is still open today. At Kemnay there were still two openings – No. 1 and No. 2, though the south wall of No. 1 had been partly broken into by No. 2. Stone from 1 was slightly finer and better suited to polishing, but 2 was more easily worked. There were four openings at Corrennie, still producing both grey and pink. Tillyfourie was completely abandoned.[39]

Rubislaw was the first quarry in the UK to electrify in the years after the First World War.[40] It was described in 1924 as covering a 20-acre site, with the actual quarry being 7 acres. It was producing 30,000 tons annually, less than a third of the peak output around 1900, and it employed between 80 and 100 men. The greatest depth at that time was 320ft. The giant stone crushing machines on the top of Rubislaw Hill were visible all over the city.[41] Shortly after, in 1929, the Rubislaw Granite Company installed what was thought to be the largest blondin in the UK. It was built by local firm John M. Henderson & Co., had a span of 838ft and was capable of lifting up to 20 tons from the floor of the quarry. This completely eclipsed the quarry's four existing blondins each of which were only able to lift 5 tons. These were mainly used for lifting stone for crushing and for sett making. The new blondin was to be used for larger blocks for monumental work. Not only was it able to lift large blocks, it also greatly reduced the time taken to bring stone up from the bottom of the quarry. According to Henry Hamilton it took one hour and fifteen minutes to lift a large stone from the south-west end of the quarry to the top of the north-east end, a distance of 1,200ft. The 20-ton blondin could do that in five minutes, and that included the return journey for the next load.[42]

By 1934 George Ross, manager of the Rubislaw Granite Company, gave the area at the top of the quarry as 13 acres and a maximum depth of 400ft below the original surface of the ground. (F.S. Anderson, in a talk he gave at the time, said that the depth was 370ft which Ross said was from the edge of the quarry to the bottom of the 'dip'.)[43]

Despite poor trading conditions Manuelle's did keep Slattie Quarry open and invested in completely electrifying the quarry, a process begun in 1920 and finished the following year. Having worked for various granite companies William Grant joined Manuelle's in April 1920. In his invaluable little booklet of memories he remembered that they were already in the process of reorganising their quarries, finally completing the switch from steam power to electricity in 1922–23.[44] Stone-breaking and tar-mining plant were installed at Slattie by the Town Council.[45]

In November 1936 Fyfe's closed down the Tom's Forest Quarry and began dismantling the machinery. At the time it employed about 40 men, most of whom lost their jobs. It would open again later and is still operating today.[46]

In the Peterhead area most of the quarries were relatively small, with numerous quarries in the Blackhill and Stirlinghill areas. None of them went on to consolidate into large quarries as happened with Rubislaw and Kemnay. Most of the Peterhead quarries were closed in the period between the two world wars. William Grant, who began his working life in the Peterhead area, told Diack that in the 50 or 60 years prior to 1940 as many as 23 red and 8 grey granite quarries had closed in this area. By 1940 only the Admiralty Quarry and one of Heslop & Wilson's quarries at Stirlinghill were operational in any real way. Several of the Blackhills quarries closed in the 1920s with some of the Stirlinghill ones closing before the First World War. Power gives the figures of 395 men employed in the granite industry around Peterhead in 1910, this figure falling to ninety-five by 1937.[47] Diack attributes the decline in the Peterhead area as being due to the limited uses that could be made from Peterhead granite. Very little building was done locally and Peterhead granite was not suitable for setts or road stones. Peterhead was mainly used for monumental work and a considerable amount of good building stone was just dumped into the sea.[48] Having only the one main use made it more susceptible to competition from imported granite.

The Granite Yards in the 1930s

The 1920s ended with the trade more optimistic than it had been anytime since the end of the war. Henry Hutcheon of the Aberdeen Granite Works, formerly Alexander Macdonald's, claimed that 1929 had been the busiest year in the company's 100-year history. Demand from architects at home and in the colonies for polished granite fronts for buildings was increasing and the trade had high hopes for the effect of the Merchandise Mark's Act. Norwegian setts were 'pouring into the country' but in Aberdeen 1,800 tons of local setts had been used in improvements to Great Northern Road and 2,000 tons supplied for King Street with a further 6,000 tons on order. Several of the quarries had installed additional plant and, although output and stocks were low, the effect of the marking of granite seemed to have led to a demand for local stone.[49] The industry looked forward to the new decade with a certain amount of optimism.

Much of Hutcheon's optimism was misplaced. In 1931 the *Press & Journal* quoted Board of Trade figures that showed that imports of monumental and architectural granite from Germany alone into the UK had increased by 20 per cent in 1930, and for half of that year the marking of granite had actually been in effect. The figures were 6,546 tons, up from 5,868 tons; the value being £208,031, up from £170,959. The *Journal* calculated that with 80 per cent of the value of manufactured granite being wages, the cost of these imports could have supported 1,100 British workers.[50] The *Journal* commented that this vindicated the view of the Aberdeen merchants that something more needed to be done. A year later, in 1932, the *Quarry Manager's Journal* reported that total imports of manufactured granite had increased by 30 per cent since the order had come into effect.[51] There were even setts being imported from India and in 1933 the *Press & Journal* carried an article by William Diack with the headline 'Watch Russia – she has begun to send tombstones.'[52] This referred to a small order of Russian tombstones that had been landed at Liverpool. Just before that Russia had also exported granite setts to Argentina. Two years before that the Soviet Government had ordered 700 pneumatic drills and other stone working tools from the Consolidated Pneumatic Tool Company (CPT) in Fraserburgh. Although much of this was for use in the home market, Diack warned that here was another possible longer-term threat to the Aberdeen trade.

Masons' shed at the Victoria Granite Works c.1930. (Aberdeen Art Gallery and Museums Collection)

Following the limited effect of the Merchandise Marks Act, in 1932 the industry received a small boost by the introduction of a 10 per cent duty on all imported granite including rough stone, setts, kerbstones, and monumental and architectural granite. This was later increased to 15 per cent and then to 20 per cent on monumental work in 1934. Although the building trade was buoyant in the first half of the decade, by March 1935 representatives of the Granite Association were in London asking for a further increase in the tariff as the monumental trade continued to decline. At that date there were 150 fewer men working in the monumental yards than had been the case the previous March.[53]

The Association visit met with success and the tariff was increased to 30 per cent in 1936. This did have an effect on German imports, seen as being good quality work, but imports of poorer quality work from Finland began to increase followed by material from Czechoslovakia. By 1938 Czechoslovakia was supplying a third of the volume of imported tombstones into Britain.[54] The press in Aberdeen almost welcomed Hitler's annexation of the Sudetenland region of Czechoslovakia in 1938 because it cut off the supply of Czech granite to the UK. This event actually caused a mini-revival in the monumental trade.[55] In 1948 the President of the AGMA, in reviewing the previous thirty years, reported that despite all the efforts made to curb imports of granite manufacturers, these had increased from £23,522 in 1921 to £345,764 in 1938.[56]

At the end of the 1920s the quarries in Norway and Sweden began to get slightly more difficult to work and in 1928 the *Press & Journal* reported the first increase in the price of their granite since the war.[57] This coupled with the duty now imposed meant that foreign stone was actually 20 per cent dearer than home stone but, of course, price had never been the sole reason for importing Scandinavian stone, colour and availability were also factors. The duty on imported raw stone actually harmed the Aberdeen merchants since it increased the cost of their finished product in comparison to that of Germany and Czechoslovakia who didn't have an import tariff.

Polished Granite for Buildings

Granite was still seen as an attractive material for prestigious work and in the later years of the decade an increasing amount of the work done in the monumental yards was for polished building fronts.[58] In fact the *Press & Journal* in 1938 claimed that such was the popularity for polished granite shop fronts that 'Aberdeen has now practically all the shop front work in the country'. Around 50 per cent of the work of the yards at this time was for polished building slabs.[59] Aberdeen firms were involved in the building of the massive St Andrew's House on the Calton Hill, though the building itself was not built from granite. Stewart & Co. supplied polished granite, giving them two years of work, though the granite came from their Creetown quarries, with Charles Macdonald also supplying black granite for decorative facings. However, in this area of polished building fronts the Aberdeen yards were beginning to face competition from foreign sources. In London, Edinburgh and Glasgow 1938 saw large quantities of imported polished slabs for building work. The *Press & Journal* commented, 'it seems only a question of time before they will be introduced in the Granite City itself'.[60]

Figures given for employment in the trade generally at end of 1938, the eve of the Second World War were 600 men in the building sector and 700 in the monumental yards.

Granite for the Royal Infirmary and Council Housing

We have seen in earlier chapters that the idea of Aberdeen as a city of granite buildings grew in the minds of its citizens. There were substantial protests from leading citizens when it was proposed the build an iron girder bridge over to Torry in the 1870s. Similar protests ensued at the beginning of the twentieth century with proposals to build the new Post Office in Crown Street and Greyfriars Church from sandstone rather than granite. In the 1930s similar battles were fought, the main one being over the new infirmary at Foresterhill.

The building of a new infirmary was the result of a huge fund raising exercise by the people of the north-east, raising about £420,000. Plans were drawn up by Kelly and Nicol, architects in Aberdeen, but when these were submitted to the consulting architects in London significant changes were made for operational reasons. This resulted in a huge cost increase for the building and the directors started to look for cost savings. One of these was to change the material of construction to brick. *The Bon Accord and Northern Pictorial* commented that the Infirmary Directors were up against it with local sentiment strongly for granite: 'The feeling was so emphatically in favour of granite that one can imagine it will take more than an ordinary measure of courage for those who have the scheme in hand to go on with the building in brick and steel.'[61] Granite with concrete dressing was to cost £24,897 more than brick; granite with granite dressings £50,877 more. The British Portland Cement Association wrote a letter to the *Press & Journal* making the case for precast concrete with a steel or reinforced concrete frame. Either method, they suggested, would still require large amounts of crushed granite for making the concrete and would employ large amounts of unskilled men. The granite industry could supply dressed granite for facings.[62] However, the granite industry lobbied the directors, stressing the importance of granite in the local economy and the contribution made by granite workers to local hospitals. With leading granite man, James Rust, wearing the Lord Provost's chain, and local quarry owners offering to supply granite at a reasonable cost, the directors came under severe pressure and they gave in. The building would be built of granite with concrete dressings.

In March 1934 Aberdeen Councillor H.H. Ceiron Jones put forward a motion that with the scarcity of granite masons and the need to build around 6,000 new homes in the next five years, he asked the Housing Committee to consider building houses from brick or concrete blocks. Councillor Jones's motion does not seem to have had many supporters in the city and the local correspondent of the *Quarry Manager's Journal* commented:

> Councillor Jones, who is by the way the Unitarian minister of Aberdeen, is a Welshman and is probably not closely in touch with Aberdeen conditions and requirements. Erection of concrete block houses requires masons just as do granite houses. Bricklayers are also as scarce as building masons in Aberdeen. There are ample stores of excellent quality granite in the neighbourhood – sufficient to build another Aberdeen.[63]

In July the same year there were protests from the granite trade at the decision of Aberdeenshire County Council to build brick houses in Forgue, Gartly, Blackburn and Kirkton of Skene. William Diack noted in 1938 that there had appeared in Aberdeen 'a number of brick dwellings and drab concrete structures right in the heart of the Granite City and within easy reach of some of the finest granite quarries in the kingdom'.[64]

The last granite tenement block to be built in Aberdeen was Rosemount Square. It was planned and designed in 1938 by Leo Durnin of the City Architects' Department, but not finished until 1947-48, winning a Saltire Society Award in 1948. The sculpted figures above two of the entrances were designed by T.B. Huxley Jones, Head of Sculpture at Gray's School of Art. They were carved by John McKay of William Taggart's Allenvale Granite Works. There were meant to be three and their cost had been included in the budget, but because it was 1940 and wartime, permission for the expenditure had to be sought from the Department of Health. This was refused but an anonymous donor came forward with funding for two of the sculptures. Kincorth was the last council housing estate to be built from granite in the city. It was planned before the Second World War but not actually built until after it and will be discussed in the final chapter. Following the war the new estates such as Mastrick and Northfield would contain little or no granite.

Rosemount Square.

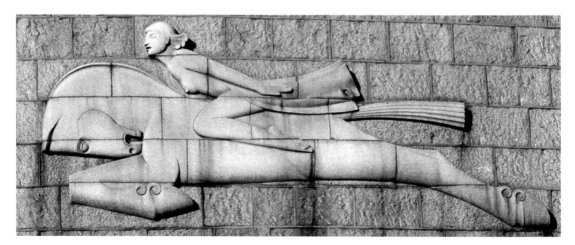

Sculpture on Rosemount Square.

The Empire Exhibition, Glasgow 1938

The granite trade took advantage of the Empire Exhibition to display many of its wares including polished building fronts. The event was not without controversy in the ranks of the Aberdeen Granite Manufacturer's Association. Ten members signed a letter demanding that a book of monument designs from the recently established Aberdeen Designs Limited be withdrawn from the Association's display at the Exhibition. This was agreed to. However, one highlight of the industry's contribution to the event was the huge 14ft-high monolith erected at the site in Bellahouston. This permanent reminder of the event began as a 16-ton block taken from Rubislaw Quarry. It was then dressed by Charles Macdonald's yard in Jute Street and reduced to 12 tons. King George VI unveiled the inscription on the stone on 9 July 1937.

The Future

The booklet produced by Aberdeen Town Council for the Empire Exhibition understandably took an optimistic view on the future of the granite industry. According to it supplies of granite from Aberdeen and the surrounding area were virtually inexhaustible, with Rubislaw the largest quarry in the country, and Kemnay the second largest. The future looked, if not rosy, then certainly assured.

GRANITE IN THE PERIOD OF DECLINE

In the years from 1939 onwards all areas of the granite industry faced significant challenges. In the building industry granite was under threat from other materials, this also impacted on some of the work of the manufacturing yards. The granite yards faced competition from abroad, declining overseas markets, and changing fashions in architectural frontages and monumental work. For the quarries, those that survived also faced competition from abroad as well as a declining market, and a decline in the quality and volume of stone capable of being extracted from them. The virtual ending of the sett making part of quarry work also had an effect on the quarries and on the numbers employed at the quarries. In hindsight it seems inevitable that the industry would shrink to the level it is at with just two significant granite yards in Aberdeenshire and none actually in the city, and a few quarries producing mainly crushed stone and aggregate. But was this in fact inevitable?

Writing immediately after the Second World War, though using mostly pre-war data, Henry Hamilton identified many of the problems which would lead to the decline in the industry. As well as the amount of imports, raw and finished, he identified the large number of firms in the industry, most with small staff numbers and little capital investment in equipment. There was, therefore, little in the way of economies of scale. The industry had not kept up-to-date with changes in machinery, with Germany (pre-war) having made significant advances in polishing machinery. He suggested that low labour costs were therefore not the only cause of large scale imports. He also criticised the manufacturers for not co-operating in marketing as they had in the importation of the raw material. His comment, written well before the 1950s, was prophetic on the decline that would ensue in that and subsequent decades: 'the fact seems to be that manufacturers have so long enjoyed a virtual monopoly of the granite trade in this country that they find it difficult to see anything wrong with their organisation and are reluctant to face up to a situation radically different from a generation ago.'[1]

According to John McLaren there were ninety yards in Aberdeen in 1914 and forty-eight yards in the city when he started in the 1930s. William Grant actually listed ninety-two granite merchants in Aberdeen and Peterhead who had gone out of business in the period from 1882–1948.[2] This sounds a very dramatic decline, though not all of these were business failures. Some may have ceased because the proprietor had died and there was no one to take over the business. The era of

men going to America and returning with sufficient capital to open a small business ended with
the First World War and, in any case, greater capital was needed to finance the growing mechanisation in the industry. According to Henry Hamilton there had been no new yards established in
Aberdeen for many years before the period when he was writing (*c.* 1939). He estimated that in
1939 establishing a medium-sized yard required capital of around £8,000, with even a small yard
requiring around £4,000. Hamilton details what a hypothetical yard investing £8,000 and with
around forty employees would look like:

1 dunter-machine (1 man, sometimes 2)	1 man
5 saw machines	5 men
3 large polishing machines	3 men
4 vertical polishing machines for small stones	4 men
2 electric polishing machines for small stones	2 men
Skilled stonecutters	18 men
Bed-setter, sawman, labourer, foreman, manager and office staff	8 men

(Source: Hamilton p.194)

This gives a total work-force of 41 but there would also be some apprentices as well.

A decline in the number of yards and even in the numbers of the workforce does not necessarily mean
that the industry itself was in decline. Increasing mechanisation would mean fewer men were needed
and that only yards able to finance investment in machinery would survive. For example, one unnamed
firm in 1961 stated that it employed half the men it had in 1939 but had four times the output.[3]

Hamilton gives a table from 1939 showing that the days of the very small yard seemed over:

Below 10 employees	2 firms
11–24 employees	12 firms
25–49 employees	21 firms
50–99 employees	5 firms
100–199 employees	2 firms

(Source: Hamilton, p.192)

The Effects of the Second World War

The onset of the Second World War had a significant impact on some of the granite yards. According
to the AGMA the effects of the war were broadly similar to the First World War: lack of imported
raw materials; reduced output from the home quarries as a result of the labour force being used
for Government work; and shortage of labour generally. Hamilton gives the figure of 1,116 skilled
workers and 119 apprentices in the industry in 1938, falling to 547 workers and 13 apprentices in
1941.[4] He doesn't say so, but I presume he is talking about the granite yards rather than other areas
of the industry. John McLaren describes losing several young men at the very start of the war with

more to follow, including himself. His father, who had been looking forward to stepping back a little, had to keep working, eventually dying in the last year of the war. Older men came out of retirement to help the yard continue. There was also a shortage of supplies of steel for saw blades, tools and machinery. Once again, as had happened in the First World War, there was an increase in firms poaching staff from each other and complaining to the Association. In 1942 Stewart & Co. arbitrarily increased their men's wages because they had already lost men to the war effort and wanted to stop their remaining workers leaving for other employment. The Association deplored this action and said they should have come to them first. David Ruddiman, a Director of the Association, was severely censured for paying his men a 10*s* bonus.[5] Late that year members agreed to help each other out as far as possible on a voluntary basis.

Looking to the future members of the stone industry throughout Britain met in 1941 and agreed to form a federation. The following year W.B. Esslemont of Esslemont & Cameron, Advocates and Notaries, along with James Rust, junior, President of the Aberdeen Granite Manufacturers' Association, helped draw up the draft constitution of the British Stone Federation. This provided a national association for those involved in quarrying and working in natural stone.[6] One of its main aims was to campaign against the importation of manufactured stone.

Chapman & Riley's Report – Granite City: A Plan for Aberdeen

At the request of the Corporation of the City of Aberdeen, in 1952 W. Dobson Chapman and Charles F. Riley published a plan for all aspects of the future of development of the city. Their section on the granite industry echoed some of the comments made by Henry Hamilton and others. They commented on the small scale of granite yards, the largest employing around 100 men and the smallest twelve. The post-war embargo on imports of foreign stone restricted trade, though conversely it helped the industry by giving it a larger share of the home market. They saw a shortage of apprentices coming into the industry as a major problem and the increased use of sandblasting gave less opportunity for skills to be passed on to younger men, thereby affecting the standard of workmanship. In their view, 'the future of the granite industry is uncertain. Because of developments elsewhere it seems that in future the Aberdeen granite manufacturer will have to face a situation in which he no longer has a virtual monopoly as he had 50 years ago.' In a telling comment they said that although there were now far fewer firms than at the end of the nineteenth century, the organisation of the industry was substantially the same:

> It seems reasonable to deduce that a method of organization based on conditions such as those existing at the end of the nineteenth century is not the most efficient for the competitive conditions of today. It would seem that only by concerted action and deliberate economic planning can the granite manufacturers of Aberdeen hope to maintain the prosperity of the industry.[7]

As far as building in granite was concerned, Chapman & Riley repeated the oft stated comment that a visitor arriving in Aberdeen on a sunny day will regard the 'Silver City' as an apt name for the city. However, one arriving on a wet and dark winter's day will find the greyness of the granite and slate somewhat cold and bleak. They saw it as inevitable that building in non-traditional materials, which had begun since the war, would continue despite opposition from some in the city:

> Aberdeen is becoming too large to be built of one material only, and it would be of undoubted benefit if not only the new houses on the outskirts but some of the larger buildings in the centre were to be built of a carefully chosen new material. The relief thus achieved would, in fact, enhance the existing granite, acting as foil to the grey in the same way as do the many trees in the city. There is also scope for a more imaginative use of granite itself, both by resorting to more interesting textures, and by using variegated granites which give a far livelier and warmer face than a single grey granite.[8]

The future of building in granite wasn't all doom and gloom in their opinion, then. It is not really the place of this book to discuss whether or not new materials were carefully chosen for buildings within the city centre. Our concern is whether or not there was any future for building in granite in any shape of form.

The Post-War Period

With the rebuilding of the country after the war there were grounds for some optimism in the industry. John McLaren describes how Bower & Florence, acting with a company in London, won several jobs including for the new head offices of the Bank of England, at that time the largest post-war contract for an Aberdeen yard, though it used Creetown granite. Granite was being used for cladding buildings, even for multi-storey building with new techniques being devised. In 1950 the new University of Aberdeen chemistry building at Old Aberdeen made use of local granite. However, the structure itself was to be of reinforced concrete with the cladding in granite, in different shades of grey, brown and red to harmonise with older buildings around King's College. The quarries which supplied the stone were Raemoir, Corrennie, Sclattie and Monymusk. Work on the building was actually held up by a shortage of stone masons.[9]

Elsewhere granite was still seen as being the material to use in prestigious monuments. In 1950, for example, the architect Ian G. Lindsay was commissioned by the War Department to design a memorial to the 51st Highland Division at St Valery in Normandy. Granite was the material decided upon but they needed a block 24ft high. Alexander Hall & Son, the builders, were given the job of sourcing the stone but it proved almost impossible to find the right stone until Andrew Mutch, Managing Director of Fyfe's, found one at the lesser known quarry of Inver near Balmoral. The stone was then carved by Fyfe's masons and transported to France. At the same time two granite pillars in Kemnay granite were sent to the military cemetery at St Valery. These were part of the north-east's tribute to the people of St Valery and they had to be completed in three weeks from the design by architect G. Angus Mitchell being approved by War Graves Commission. In total there were 314 letters on the pillars and if ordinary cutting methods had been used they would not have been ready in time. Following some experiments the letters were done by sand blasting. Andrew Mutch was also involved in this work as were Hall's who erected the pillars.[10]

The impression given is that the Aberdeen granite yards after the war were antiquated in their machinery and their methods. John McLaren describes how, in 1948, three men involved in the local industry, Frank Cassie of George Cassie & Sons, Engineers, Andrew Mutch of John Fyfe Ltd., and Robert Crofts of Robert Croft & Sons, went on a two-week visit to America to look at their working methods. The size of American production operations, the investment they had made in modern machinery, and the way they marketed their product, all impressed the Aberdeen men who reported all this back to their fellow granite manufacturers in the AGMA.[11] The problems in Aberdeen were the small-scale nature of many of the yards, their locations were not suitable to large-scale expansion and they lacked the financial resources to invest in new buildings and machinery, especially after post-war repairs to buildings and machinery.

In the monumental and quarrying industries granite imports were still a major issue. In October 1950 John M. Gibb reported to the Granite Association on a meeting of the British Stone Federation he had attended on their behalf. One English firm had agreed to buy the whole of the Finnish worked output because Finland had indicated that those who purchased most worked granite would receive most of the rough stone, something Gibb said that would have a very serious effect on the Aberdeen industry. This showed in the figures of imported stone for that year so far. Whereas from Sweden £58,000 of rough stone had been imported and £5,000 of worked granite, for Finland £12,000 of rough and £35,000 of worked had been imported. Again for rough stone cost was a major factor with Norway, for example, supplying stone delivered at 21s per cubic foot, which included 30 per cent duty. Home produced stone cost 40s per cubic foot. Gibb commented that a 100 per cent tariff would be needed to protect the home industry.[12]

James Rust of Charles Macdonald Ltd., and a past president of the British Stone Federation, was Scotland's representative on the Government's Consultative Committee for the Stone Industry. He maintained that what he saw as the mass dumping of foreign worked granite might lead to the closure of many of the city's granite yards. According to Rust, the Second World War had actually saved the local industry from collapse because it shut off foreign imports. Rust told the *Press & Journal* that 'what was needed to save the industry from the serious decline of the inter-war years was Government action to restore confidence in the future. The men must be re-assured that never again will they be put on the scrap heap through preference to foreign labour.'[13]

As well as the threat of imports the monumental sector also suffered a lack of orders because of a general lack of money in the country, the spread of cremations and lawn cemeteries, and the increased use of cheaper materials.[14] As detailed in Chapter 10 this led to what was termed at the time 'suicidal price cutting'.[15] Understandably there was outrage in the granite trade when the superintendent of amenities for Aberdeenshire, actually tried to ban tombstones in favour of small plaques.[16]

Construction in the Immediate Post-War Period and the Building of Kincorth

In the construction sector, the Second World War is often seen as the turning point for granite building in the Granite City. The period after the war was one which saw massive housing projects as people were moved from slum areas in the centre of the city to the large housing estates around its then periphery. The Kincorth estate, planned just before the war and built just after, was the last major council housing development where granite was extensively used. Kincorth became a battleground for the granite industry. As an *Evening Express* editorial commented in 1954 'Kincorth on its rocky hill, was the last stronghold of the granite tradition'.[17]

In 1949 George Watt, Organising Secretary of the AUBTW campaigned to get Kincorth School built of granite. The same year the President of the AGMA met with the President of the Aberdeen Quarry Owners' Association, the Aberdeen Master Masons' Association, and union officials to see if they could bring pressure to bear on local and national government to call for increased use of granite in building. They were fighting a losing battle.

The importance of building in granite was recognised in 1950 by Councillor Frank Magee, convener of the City's Housing Committee, when the committee approved over 150 granite houses at Kincorth. Magee commented that 'by building them of granite it was hoped to maintain the standard of employment in the industry locally and to keep a steady flow of apprentices in the trade'.[18] However, at the same time as Kincorth was being built in granite, other estates such as Mastrick and Garthdee were being built of brick.

The Kincorth Quarry was reopened to provide granite for building at Kincorth, though some also came from Rubislaw. By 1954 half of the 2,430 houses planned for Kincorth had been built but the issue of brick versus granite threatened the rest. Brick houses were around £200 cheaper than granite ones. The Department of Health pressed the Council to build the cheaper brick house but Councillor Robert Lennox took the view that 'Kincorth has been the mainstay of the trade in the post-war years and should granite housebuilding come to an end, the question of employment and prosperity is involved.' Lennox said that if need be they would fight the Department on this issue.[19] A local builder, quoted in the *Evening Express* was of the opinion that before the war the price of a 9in brick wall was the same as a 16in granite one, and you also had to harl the brick. He stated that the reason for the £200 difference after the war was the cost of the material and the rates of pay.[20] The granite trade argued that although the initial cost of granite was higher, mainly a result of the work need to prepare granite for building work, in the long run it worked out cheaper because it required no maintenance. Granite used for house building was termed 'rubble', a byproduct of the cubed stone used for larger building work. If the trade couldn't find a use for this stone it would push up the price of large cube stone. One unnamed manufacturer stated that the cost of using granite could be reduced by reducing the dressing done on the stone, cutting out the puncheon work and using stone direct from the blocking hammer would reduce the work needed by 50 per cent.[21] In an effort to close the price differential in December 1954 it was proposed to build 18 houses using coursed rubble, with the granite not being squared or dressed.[22] Fred Cargill, who served his apprenticeship on the building of Kincorth, remembers this actually happening.

According to Fred, initially the City's Clerk of Works specified that the plug and feather holes had to be puncheoned out, but as the development wore on this requirement was removed and in the later Kincorth houses these holes can be seen.[23] In the end granite house building at Kincorth did come to an end, with those houses built in the late 1950s and into the 1960s being built of other materials. However, the character of the estate is of a largely granite development.

In 1954 the Minister of Works, Sir David Eccles, actually saw a bright future for the Aberdeen granite trade. He spoke in Aberdeen in February that year and stated that he hoped to help the industry by granting licences for the building of large buildings, especially commercial and industrial buildings and shops such as the one agreed for the site of the former Palace Hotel at the corner of Union Street and Bridge Street. This was the C. & A. Modes, again built using granite cladding panels.[24] At around the same time, though, a large government building, Greyfriars House in the Gallowgate, was built of artificial stone. At the annual conference of the Amalgamated Union of Building Trade Workers in 1953, W. Stables, an Aberdeen mason, spoke in favour of a motion urging the Architectural Association to use more natural stone. Stables used the example of Greyfriars House to condemn the government for its growing tendency to use artificial stone rather than granite.[25]

John Fyfe Limited and Kemnay in the Post-War Period

Despite the post-war problems of the granite industry Kemnay was still a major quarry and would remain so for fifty years and more. In the first few years after the war there were several major blasts at the quarry, producing huge amounts of stone.

Even before the war ended plans were laid for a massive blast at Kemnay. In echoes of the blast carried out by John Fyfe in 1878, described in Chapter 3, a tunnel was driven 63ft from the top of the 400ft sheer face of the quarry. The tunnel ran for 36ft into the granite face and then tunnels went off to the right and left, each about 40ft long. This work had taken nine months. Although the tunnels were blasted using ordinary blasting material, the big blast itself used almost two tons of ammonal (ammonium nitrate and aluminium powder) and was carried out by R. Hancock and J. Westwater of Imperial Chemical Industries (I.C.I.). Finally in August 1945 the quarry siren signaled that they were ready for the blast and, as reported in the press at the time, a posse of policemen, led by Inspector Adam from Inverurie, held up all the traffic in the area and the quarry worker gathered 'at the heid o' the hill' across from the quarry to watch the blast. For a brief moment the blast was coloured crimson and orange, before around 25,000 tons of granite, along with a layer of topsoil, was dislodged into the quarry hole. George Ross, manager of Rubislaw Quarry, witnessed the explosion and was one of the first to congratulate Andrew Mutch of Fyfe's.[26]

The following year there was an even bigger blast, using three and a half tons of explosive, dislodging 50,000 tons of granite at Kemnay. This time there was a 43ft tunnel blasted into the face 100ft from the top. This led to a 50ft tunnel to the right and a 30ft one to the left.[27]

Kemnay wasn't finished with big blasts, and in September 1956 one of the biggest ever rocks was produced at the Kemnay Quarry. It was estimated to weigh over 1,000 tons, blasted from the quarry with 200lb of explosive by fireman William Law. James Clark, the foreman, commented, 'Ay,

The huge stone blasted from the face of Kemnay Quarry in September 1956. The men on the stone are Robbie Thomson, Bill Law and James Clark. (Used by kind permission of D.C. Thomson & Co. Ltd)

it's a gey chunk of a' rock. I have been here for forty years and I have seen some big stones in that time but never one as big as that.'

The giant rock was intended to be broken up for use at the C. & A. Modes building mentioned above. It was also used for the widening of the Bridge of Don and at Telephone House in Dundee.[28]

Fyfe's had always been innovators and after the Second World War Andrew Mutch, Managing Director of Fyfe's, installed machines for manufacturing concrete bricks or blocks and coloured facing bricks, using up the vast amounts of granite dust at Kemnay and other quarries.[29] The process was virtually automatic, with the machines mixing the materials, pressing and then ejecting the blocks. The idea was not especially new. As long ago as 1890 something similar had been described in the *Aberdeen Journal*. This seems to have been an American process whereby the stone was crushed and then passed through rollers to produce a fine powder. This could then be moulded to accurate shapes and 'burned and hardened'. The use envisioned at the time was for cornices, friezes, window sills etc., at a tenth of the cost of cutting them from the original stone. It was even claimed that the granite dust could be 'vitrified' to enable it to take on a gloss as fine as polished granite.[30] Eventually one of these products, developed c.1957/58 as a cheap alternative to granite, was a masonry block known as Fyfestone, and it came to be found in walls, buildings etc., all over the country. It is still produced today by Breedon Aggregates, in a variety of colours and finishes.

A modern granite saw at Fyfe Glenrock, Old Meldrum.

In February 1965 Fyfe's became a public company, quoted on the Stock Exchange with a share capital of £400,000. Shortly afterwards they became part of the Aberdeen Construction Group who, by 1968, owned and operated the quarries at Corrennie, Dyce, Kemnay, Rubislaw and Tom's Forest, most of the output from these quarries being crushed for road surfacing, concrete work and exposed aggregate panels. The Aberdeen Construction Group actually began to acquire a number of Aberdeen granite yards such as George Stalker's, Charles Macdonald's, and later William McKay's. However, they were not doing this to sustain and grow the granite side of their business, rather they wanted the ground the yards stood on and, in many cases, they built housing on the sites. In 1987 the granite side of Fyfe's left Seaforth Road and consolidated at Westhill, later becoming known as Fyfe Glenrock. From then on Fyfe's were bought by a succession of mainly aggregate companies: Raine Industries, Evered Holdings, Bardon, Aggregate Industries, and finally, in 2013, Breedon Aggregates. Around that time the quarry at Kemnay was closed for good, though Tom's Forest still operates, as does Corrennie to a limited extent.

In 2006 Fyfe Glenrock moved to custom-built premises at Old Meldrum where they carried out a wide variety of work including architectural and hard landscaping as well as some monumental work. They were already separate from the quarry and part of Pisani PLC, who at the time were the largest supplier of natural stone in the UK. However, in June 2017 Pisani went into administration.

Fortunately Fyfe Glenrock were acquired by a local company, Leiths (Scotland) Ltd, the largest family-owned, independent quarrying and construction materials supplier in Scotland. This takeover ensures that the Fyfe name survives.

Unlike at Rubislaw, there was no major closure announcement at Kemnay. It was much more of a gradual run-down, the quarry going through several years when it was not actively worked but could still produce some stone if required, all the time facing similar problems as Rubislaw with water having to be pumped out. One final hurrah for the quarry, and perhaps for the north-east granite industry, came in 2000 when Kemnay granite was chosen to clad the Scottish Parliament building in Edinburgh, a political rather than economic decision. Fyfe Glenrock did the work, although the quarry at that time was owned by Aggregate Industries. The stone was specially cut from the quarry but such was the quality of stone available that Alan Bruce, then general manager of Fyfe Glenrock, was quoted in the press as stating that:

> In the preparatory work done over the past four or five weeks, more than 10,000 tonnes of material had to be extracted. Out of that 10,000 tonnes, we like to think there will be about 1000 tonnes of dimensional material - large pieces for use in construction or civil engineering - and out of that 1000 tonnes, we will probably only see about 200 tonnes into our workshop, (i.e. for use at the parliament building).[31]

Rubislaw Quarry

Rubislaw quarry, once seen as having almost unlimited amounts of granite, only survived for twenty-five years after the end of the Second World War. There still seemed to be life in the quarry in the 1950s and in 1952 builders William Tawse Limited lowered a 19-ton digger to the quarry floor in on piece, to help move stone around. As early as 1965 it was thought that the quarry might close but in 1967 the Aberdeen Construction Group, which included John Fyfe Ltd, acquired the quarry. John McLaren wrote that around this time his amalgamated company of Bower & Florence and Stewart & Co. were working on a large contract for granite cladding for new offices for the National Westminster Bank in London. It was to be of Rubislaw granite, with the contract in two phases spread over five years. It became obvious to them that Rubislaw was nearing its end, with the large blocks for the cornice almost impossible to obtain. Any delay in the preparation work could mean that they would not be able to provide the necessary granite. McLaren describes it as a close run thing to get the job completed before the quarry closed.[32] At around the same time (early 1970) Fyfe's were working on a Bank of England contract in Manchester. The lack of suitable stone from Rubislaw had delayed the work to such an extent that the architects decided to complete the job using foreign granite, sawn abroad, with Fyfe's being offered the job of finishing the slabs.[33]

The momentous announcement of the end of the quarry came in the *Press & Journal* for 28 April 1970, the front page headline reading: 'Its Rubislaw Quarry's last blast after 200 years'. The news of the quarry's end was shared on the front page with the equally dramatic announcement 'North Sea oil strike – boom day: a new source of raw material opens up as an old and famous one closes.' This referred to a major new oil strike in the Norwegian sector of the North Sea some 200 miles from Aberdeen, and perhaps this news lessened the impact of quarry closure. As we have seen Rubislaw was struggling to fulfill orders and the Aberdeen Construction Group revealed that it had been approaching exhaustion for the previous two years with no worthwhile rock having come out of it in that time. The workforce at the time numbered twenty-six, and it was hoped that a few would find work elsewhere in the Group. There was also some hope that test bores elsewhere on the Rubislaw site would prove productive and another quarry could be opened up. This, of course, came to nothing. In May of the following year one notable landmark disappeared as a 120ft crane, which had towered over the site for forty years, was cut down with welders torches. It had been used just two weeks before being dismantled, the dismantling being done by Stewart of Banchory. One other crane still stood, awaiting similar treatment.[34] The quarry finally closed in July 1971. John McLaren thought that the last blocks of Rubislaw granite which were held by John Fyfe were used to clad the plinths for the effigies of Bishop Henry Lichtoun and an unnamed canon in the Cathedral Church of St Machar.

At the end of its life the quarry was 485ft deep; more than 160ft below sea level; the rim meas-ured 900ft by 750ft; the floor measured 600ft by 300ft; and the quarry had been kept dry with a centrifugal pump with a 600ft head.[35] It had reputedly provided around 6 million tons of stone in its long life. According to Sandy Argo at the time it closed it was the same depth as Fyfe's original quarry at Kemnay and the two were thought to be the deepest quarries in Europe.[36]

Student Exploits at Rubislaw

The tower supports for the huge blondin erected in 1928 had dominated the Aberdeen skyline. As noted in the *Evening Express* the year after closure, the cables stretching across the quarry had attracted a number of student pranks.[37] The first was by the daredevil Charles Ludwig, who came from an artistic and musical family of German origin. Ludwig, along with fellow medical student Donald Dawson, had caused a stir in 1931 when the pair placed a pyjama-clad skeleton on top of the Mitchell Tower at Marischal College. Then in December the same year Ludwig crossed the Rubislaw quarry hole hand over hand across the cable. Not content with this feat he later climbed down the quarry face and then back up again. Ludwig joined the RAF in the Second World War and was killed in action in 1942. In March 1951 a student hung a cardboard body wearing a gown from the main cable, 30ft out over the 430ft drop. This was in support of a vote about to be taken to re-introduce the red gown at the University. According to workmen two students had climbed along the cable, the second one bringing a thicker pair of gloves to his friend, the cable being freezing at that time in the morning. The student returned to land to face some abuse from fore-man John Ross. Unfortunately for the intrepid students the weight of the body and gown proved too much for the head and they separated and fell to a ledge below, leaving the head with a trilby dangling on the cable. The *Evening Express* carried dramatic pictures of the event taken by some of the student's supporters.[38] In 1954 an unnamed 24-year-old student, supporter of the Rev. Michael Scott's candidacy for the University Rectorship, dragged a banner in support of Scott along the cable crossing the quarry. Having fixed the banner he was almost back to safety when one end of it came unstuck and he had to return to re-fix it. While there, as his friends took photographs, he lit a cigarette began singing the rectorial song. This feat was repeated three years later and there was also an incidence of a student stringing a hammock from the cable. In 1967, as recounted on the official quarry website, two mountaineers, Bill Jenkins and Adam Watson, climbed across the cable with the effigy of a newly graduated student. They proceeded to drop the 'body' to the bottom of the quarry.

What Do We Do with the Big Hole Now?

That was one of the headlines in the *Press & Journal* when it announced the imminent closure of Rubislaw Quarry on its front page on 28 April 1970. The *Journal* also commented that to restore the ground around the quarry would take years, and if left to nature the quarry would fill with water and 'it is located in a high-amenity, high-value residential district of the city'. As we now know, despite an immense amount of office building on the site, the quarry was left to its own devices and it did fill with water. However, in the many years since it closed there have been a number of ideas for doing something with the quarry.

Just a year after the quarry closed a plan was brought forward to build a small hotel on the site, also to include a conference centre, fifty flats, shops and a tourist centre with a restaurant. Following objections the company pulled out but returned five years later with a plan for the hotel on its own. The hotel plan came to nothing and neither, thankfully, did a suggestion to use it a replacement for the refuse dump at Tullos, though I dare say it could have held an awful lot of rubbish! The Labour group leader on the council provocatively commented, 'the Tories are against the dumping because it is in the middle of bourgeois Rubislaw. They are just unwilling to accept that the West End will have to carry its fair share of the environmental burden of this city.' Among other rather more fanciful suggestions were to lower a redundant oil platform into the quarry and build a revolving restaurant on the top; use a heat pump to produce heating for 10,000 homes; use it as a nuclear bomb shelter; use it as a training centre for climbers and mountain rescue teams; build a jail or remand centre in it!

In 1987 the Aberdeen Construction Group, who still owned the quarry, proposed to spend £40,000 to build a covered granite-clad viewing platform to which visitors would have free access to look down into the quarry. Only if ACG needed to employ a warden would they make a charge for entry to the platform. Alan Chapman, ACG director, commented that the quarry site had been a popular stopping-off point for coach tours for many years but that health and safety issues had led them to fence off the quarry. Now a solution was at hand. Aberdeen Director of Tourism, Gordon Henry, supported the idea and went further, saying that he would ideally like to see a granite museum and even public access to the quarry floor. Inevitably there was a snag - the issue of parking! According to Chapman, ACG had no land available for a car-park but he thought the Council did since they had bought, at huge expense, a piece of land to widen the access road to the Hill of Rubislaw site and the various oil company buildings which had been built there. Chapman stated that part of this land was unused and could be donated by the Council to provide a parking site.

Some on the Council thought that they should not become involved in helping an outside company develop a tourist attraction. The issue was deferred and came to nothing. A similar proposal, to build a viewing platform projecting out above the quarry, was also put forward by one of the oil companies. Again it came to nothing.[39]

More recently, in January 2010, the quarry went up for sale at a starting price of £30,000. In April that year two local men, Hugh Black and Sandy White, bought the quarry. It may not have been their initial aim but Hugh and Sandy soon came to the conclusion that they wanted to not only build a viewing platform at the site but also to create what Gordon Henry had proposed almost 30 years earlier, a heritage centre where the granite story could be told – to locals, to tourists and to school groups. The unveiling of the proposals at the 2012 and 2013 Granite Festivals showed that there was a wave of public affection for the quarry and for what the two men planned to do with it. Hugh and Sandy have the spent the years since talking to interested groups all over the north-east. Sadly Sandy died before any of their dreams could be realised but Hugh has continued to work hard on his own. Initially the plans for a building at the site were opposed by council planners but eventually that obstacle was overcome. However, at the time of writing the Lands Tribunal in Edinburgh has twice turned down a change in the title deeds to allow the centre to go ahead – this despite the panel describing the proposals as a 'bold and imaginative use for a unique site ... with wider public benefits for Aberdeen and the north-east.'[40]

Other Quarries in the Post-War Period and Today

Kemnay and Rubislaw were the only quarries that continued to produce granite stone in any quantity for anything other than aggregate and road material. However, some other quarries did survive for a time and a few are still productive today. In 1955 Manuelle's quarry at Sclattie was taken over by King & Co., Quarrymasters, of Glasgow, and Sclattie survived for a number of years after that. As has already been noted the last quarry worked at Stirlinghill was the old Admiralty one which closed in 1956.

As noted earlier, Breedon Group took over Fyfe's in 2013 and still produces Fyfestone at Kemnay, although the quarry itself is closed. Breedon also owns or operates quarries at Corrennie, Craigenlow, Tom's Forest and Stirlinghill. Corrennie does still have a face where dimensional stone could be taken if required and it also produces decorative aggregate for a variety of uses – driveways, car parks, landscaping etc. Stirlinghill produces aggregate and concrete. Craigenlow is no stranger to huge blasts. In 1955 one exceptional blast brought down 100,000 tons of rock, more than double what had originally been estimated and enough to make the front page of the *Evening Express*![41] The face blasted out was 120ft long by 100ft high and 50ft deep. Six years later this feat was more than repeated when 20 tons of explosive brought down 120,000 tons of stone. At the time it was said to be the largest well-hole blast ever carried out in a granite quarry in Britain with the sound of the explosion heard at least 15 miles away, and with a huge dust cloud travelling miles over the countryside.[42]

Today Craigenlow continues to operate on a scale that would surely astound the old time quarry men. One blast, for example, can dislodge up to 40,000 tons of rock using 16 tons of explosive. This type of blast can take place once a fortnight or once a month, depending on busy they are. A huge array of machines can then reduce the stone as required, right down to the level of dust. One mobile crusher is the largest of its kind in Scotland. As well as aggregate, Craigenlow has a concrete plant and an asphalt plant. It also produces larger stone for civil engineering use and can also supply granite for building cladding as in the Union Street frontage of the Silver Fin office building, opened in 2017. The cutting of the stone for that project was carried out by Fyfe Glenrock at Old Meldrum. Tom's Forest, between Kintore and Kemnay, is even larger than Craigenlow, and produces psammite as well as granite, with granite reserves enough to last several hundred years at current extraction rates. The stone is more fragmented, so it doesn't produce large stones. However, sand and gravel sit on top of the rock and this can be removed, washed and used for concrete sand and drainage stone.

Merger of the Granite Yards and Survival of the Industry

The continuing decline in the number of granite yards in Aberdeen saw a symbolic moment in 1953 when the premises in Constitution Street of the Aberdeen Granite Works, founded by Alexander Macdonald, was sold to a scrap metal dealer. Macdonald's had occupied the site since 1836, although, in fact, granite work had actually ended in 1941.

We have already seen that Henry Hamilton had identified the need for fewer granite yards, with larger units of production more able to invest in new machinery and compete at home and abroad. At the time of the arguments over brick versus granite in the building of the Kincorth Estate in 1954 the City Director of Planning, J. E. Barlow, commented at a conference of Town Planners, 'the granite industry may require gradually to concentrate and further reduce the number of its small individual units if it is to survive economically'.[43] John McLaren echoed these comments when he stated that the big question after the war was how all these relatively small firms could make the advances necessary to survive. The yards were old with no production line planning. They were also hampered in any expansion plans by their locations, most being hemmed in by housing developments and other buildings or enterprises. To re-organise a yard would mean taking down existing buildings and then rebuilding them, and the yards couldn't afford the loss of income this would entail. In addition they didn't have the capital for major investment in buildings or equipment, even for repairs to the latter.[44]

The virtual end of building in granite was undoubtedly inevitable. New methods of construction and new materials seduced architects and builders and they were undoubtedly cheaper. The extension to the Town House in 1975 was not even clad in granite, but rather some mosaic marble effect cladding designed to look like granite. For the quarries competition from abroad was a primary reason for their decline, but so also was the lack of quality stone suitable for monumental work. In the metaphorical sense many of the quarries dried up or became exhausted, those that survived reduced to providing road aggregate and such like. For the monumental yards there were a number of possible causes for the industry's decline. Competition from abroad, cremation and changing customs, inability to attract apprentices to the industry, perhaps stubbornness among the work force when new methods were brought in. All of these played a part but in talking to some of those who ran the granite yards in the 1970s the overriding reasons they give for the closure of so many yards relate to the fact that there were too many yards and they failed to modernise. The two are connected in that many were too small and lacked capital to invest in new machinery and methods. The notable exceptions were A. & J. Robertson (Granite) Ltd and John Fyfe Ltd. As one former granite director said to me, too many of the men running the yards thought that the industry owed them a living and they were not willing to invest or merge to assure their future. Moreover, as we have seen in the chapter on the Granite Association, the owners of the granite yards were stubborn and independent; thrawn is the word we would use in the Scots language.

By 1962 the number of yards in the city had further declined to twenty-three. Looking back on that time Sandy Robertson of Alexander Robertson & Son commented, 'if the whole of the Aberdeen granite industry had been rolled into one company it would still have been a relatively small business in international terms'.[45] Today, as Robertson Granite, they are the only two surviving granite yards in the Aberdeen area. How has it survived where others went to the wall?

In 1936 Alexander Robertson's was the smallest of the Aberdeen granite yards, still doing everything by hand with no machinery, no electricity, not even a telephone.[46] This was the situation when Alexander R. Robertson (Sandy) joined the family business then being run by his father William. From then on Robertson's began to expand, installing electricity and, after the war, expanding into neighbouring premises and introducing new machinery. In 1951 Sandy bought over the small firm of James Taggart and moved his main operation to their premises at 92 Great Western Road.

Amongst the twenty-three yards in 1962 there were two Robertson's – James Robertson & Son and Alexander Robertson & Son. During 1962 Ian McLaren, owner of Bower & Florence, approached various firms regarding a merger and consolidation of their work and sites. Sandy Robertson was involved in the negotiations and at around the same time he was also approached by Bill Robertson of James Robertson & Son to merge with them. In 1962 the larger merger proposed by McLaren fell through, though Bower & Florence did merge with Stewart & Co. two years later. However, the two Robertsons did merge as A. & J. Robertson (Granite) Ltd. The first board meeting of the new company took place on 26 February 1963 and in June they were accepted as members of the AGA. Following the merger Robertson's bought the share capitol of William Edwards & Sons in 1965, with the latter initially continuing to trade under its own name. In 1966 Robertson's acquired Kemp & Co. and Caie & Co. In April 1970 Robertson's bought William Taggart & Son, including the latter's Fraserburgh Monumental Works.[47] It also bought Robert Crofts & Sons in 1971, their premises at Pittodrie Street being next to the former Edward's yard allowing the combined Robertson's business to consolidate at Pittodrie Street/Merkland Road.

While all this was happening the closure of yards continued. We have already seen above that Fyfe's/Aberdeen Construction Group took over a number of businesses. As well as the merger of Bower & Florence and Stewart & Co., 1964 also saw James C. Hogg incorporate with James A. Mitchell, though the combined business ceased trading in 1976. James R.R. Kennedy went out of business completely in 1964. In 1969 Gibb Brothers and James Hadden ceased trading. 1973 saw the Pittodrie Granite Turning Company close down with the business being moved to Glasgow. In December 1975 the St Peter Street works of Charles Dorian & Son closed down with the loss of

Robert Croft's yard at Pittodrie Street in the 1970s at around the time they were taken over by Robertson's.

thirteen jobs. In March 1976 the oldest surviving granite yard in the city, the Royal Granite Works of James Wright & Sons, closed with a loss of twenty-four jobs, it being more profitable to rent out their premises to an oil-related company. Also in 1976 Alexander J. Wilson closed down. The following year Robert Gibb, established in the 1870s, closed. Finally in 1981 D. Ruddiman closed.

There are various factors that contributed to Robertson's success and survival. The merger with James Robertson & Son created a bigger company more able to invest in new machinery from Germany and Belgium, and able to take on a wider range of work. This continued as other firms were taken over. Sandy was also determined to build up a management team to run the business if he or Bill Robertson were no longer there. The *Press & Journal* in 1985 described Robertson's yards as fully automated with modern sophisticated machinery, some of it installed in the last two years. It boasted push-button technology with diamond-tipped and infra-red-light precision cutting.[48] According to Graeme Robertson only now do they have to replace some of the machinery bought at that time.[49]

Another key move that has helped them survive is their network of retail outlets. This began in the period from 1978–84 when they took over five outlets in Scotland This continued in the period from 1985-90 with a further twelve firms which included some in the north of England

Robertson's mason's shed at Merkland Road.

Inside Robertson Granite's new premises at Westhill in 2017.

and the expansion continued in the 1990s with businesses acquired in the south of England.[50] Today around thirty branches are listed on their website, from Orkney to London

Even in 1985 virtually all of Robertson's granite came from abroad. Today most of it comes already cut to size, 70 per cent of it coming ready polished from India, the quality of finished stone from India and China being much better today than it had been in the past, all the company has to do is add the lettering. Some stone also comes from Scandinavian countries and France and this is polished at its premises. In 2017 the company moved from Merkland Road to new custom-built premises at Westhill, 7 miles west of Aberdeen. At the new premises nearly all the machinery is new, with just a couple of polishing machines having been moved from the old premises. With this substantial investment its future seems assured.

Bruce Walker: The Last of the Traditional Granite Sculptors?

In the history of the granite industry Bruce Walker is a rare, if not unique man in that he combines the artistic flair of artists such as Hamilton Buchan and William Macmillan, with the technique and craftsmanship of a granite worker such as James Philip. At his workshop in Kirriemuir Bruce still carves huge blocks of granite largely using hand tools that would be familiar to an Aberdeen mason from a hundred years ago. Although today he is known as a monumental sculptor and glass engraver, he started his working life as an ordinary apprentice in a granite yard.

Bruce was born in 1946 'at the fit o' Bennachie', the croft of Westerton of Braco. His father was a farm servant and two years later the family moved to Gamrie and then on to Rhynie. Bruce went to the village school in Rhynie, where he was interested in art, an interest fostered by Bruce's art teacher, John Runcie. Later on, when both men eventually moved to Aberdeen, they stayed in touch and John remained a friend and a big influence on Bruce all his life. Bruce left school at the age of 15. He tried being a motor mechanic for a few months, and worked on the farm for a few months before, in 1963, he applied for an apprenticeship with the old established granite yard of William McKay & Sons in Holland Street. McKay's employed about 100 people at that time, masons and polishers. As well as being sent to day classes at the Technical College, Bruce also attended evening classes four nights a week at Gray's School of Art, among the last apprentices to receive this art school training. Classes at the art school were a revelation to Bruce and tutors such as Richard (Dickie) Robertson in sculpture, and Sandy Fraser in drawing and painting, both pushed and inspired him. He took classes in life drawing, lettering and design, as well as stone carving.

He credits Bill McKay as an inspiration, Bill placed a great emphasis on training and he realised that Bruce had an artistic talent. Bruce was to be trained as a draughtsman, but Bill 'made me do a year of hard graft first'. John McLaren records that in late 1950s the 'Van Dyne' process was introduced at Bower & Florence via an English company. This was a method of diamond hand engraving on polished granite using existing dentist's drilling equipment with a diamond tipped dentist's drill rotated at high speed. For several years the process was kept secret by Bower & Florence while other yards tried to emulate their work using sand-blasting methods. Eventually other yards adopted the Van Dyne method and McLaren says that McKays were fortunate in

Bruce Walker at work on the Scott/Wilson Monument.

The Elrick Horse. The pink granite commemoration plinth to the right is in Corrennie granite.

unearthing an employee with considerable artistic ability who produced some remarkable work.[51] This was Bruce Walker and from engraving on stone Bruce developed an interest in glass engraving, with Bill McKay getting him some commissions from Aberdeen glass company A.C. Yule. Bruce could see the way things were going in the granite yards with increasing use of machinery, and that was not for him. Moreover, he was making more at the glass engraving than he was for his work in the yard. He left the yard in 1975 and established a business doing glass engraving as well as some stone carving. For more than twenty years he had a studio in the old schoolhouse at Kirkbuddo in Angus. Then in 1997 he moved to Kirriemuir and more recently, in 2012, he established a workshop on the Hillhead Industrial Estate in Kirrie. From there he has been able to work on huge blocks of granite from and Kemnay. His most outstanding work to date has been the Scott-Wilson Memorial, sited at Scott's View in Glen Prosen, Angus, some three miles from Kirriemuir. Depicting Scott and Wilson, as well as two of their huskies and two of their ponies, it was unveiled in 2012 to commemorate the centenary of the Terra Nova Expedition to Antarctica and the South Pole. Captain Robert Falcon Scott and Doctor Edward Wilson had done some of their planning for the expedition in Glen Prosen where Wilson was carrying out some government work. This massive granite monument, carved from a 20-ton block of stone, presented a huge logistical challenge simply in cutting it down and transporting it to Bruce's workshop. For Bruce the challenge was also immense – both technically and physically, as he tried to shape the stone and then carve the detail.

Bruce's latest granite commission, unveiled in November 2017, has been a piece of sculpture outside the new Hampton by Hilton Hotel in Elrick, Westhill, some seven miles west of Aberdeen. This is carved from an 8-ton block of Craigenlow granite, the quarry being just a few miles from Elrick. It features a Clydesdale horse on the side facing the road, modelled on a real horse, and with the interiors of a blacksmith's and joiner's workshops on the reverse side, reflecting the history and heritage of the original village of Elrick. Round the base of the statue Bruce has engraved a verse from north-east poet/educator, J. C. Milne, relating to the Clydesdale. The base of the monument is completed by having polished black granite panels engraved with scenes of the working life of the ploughman, blacksmith and joiner, as well as lines from local writers.

The Scott-Wilson Monument is perhaps the largest figurative granite sculpture in Scotland since the 1920s. With both monuments Bruce's artistic drive has created an incredible achievement, one that men such as Arthur Taylor, James Philip and Robert Warrack Morrison would have admired. Bruce may well be the last person capable of such work, certainly the last trained in the manner of these old time masons.

Postscript

Walking through any of Aberdeen's main graveyards, especially Springbank, Nellfield, Allenvale and St Peter's, you will encounter the graves of many of Aberdeen's granite men, from humble stonecut-ters, masons and polishers, to wealthy granite merchants. Their headstones tend to stand out; often they carved their own stones. The work of these granite men is all around us, not just in Aberdeen and the smaller towns and villages of the north-east, but in high streets, parks, public squares and cemeteries all over the United Kingdom, most notably in London. It can also be found in cemeteries, memorials and great buildings in North America and other parts of the world. Other industries may have brought more income and wealth into Aberdeen but perhaps no other industry gave Aberdeen a world-wide reputation and put it on the world stage. This reputation came not only from the quality of the workmanship of its granite workers but from the city itself being known as The Granite City. For that reason alone the work of the granite men deserves to be acknowledged and remembered.

APPENDIX

SOME GRANITE YARDS AND BUILDERS OF THE NINETEENTH CENTURY

This appendix does not aim to be a comprehensive account of every granite yard and granite builder. Not every granite yard is listed here, some lasted just a few years and little is know about them. The information mostly comes from the *Aberdeen Post Office Directory* which appeared every year from the mid 1820s onwards (referred to below as *Directory*); the Aberdeen Granite Association Minutes and List of Members, and most of the firms associated with the AGA are included; the Aberdeen newspapers listed in the bibliography, especially the obituaries of the granite masters and the Granite Chips column; and publications such as Diane Morgan's books and *Scotland of Today* (see bibliography). For some of the builders there is a list of some of the buildings they worked on. Hopefully this list will be a starting point for anyone who wants to look further into individual yards

Aberdeen Co-operative Granite Co., Ltd, 120 Hutcheon Street
First appeared in the *Directory* in 1912.
Aberdeen Granite Turning Company Ltd, Merkland Road East/King Street
First appeared in the *Directory* in 1905. Several members of the Turning Company were directors of the AGA. Ceased trading in 1919 when their factory and machinery was sold to William G. Edwards, though they did continue to appear in the *Directory* until 1924. For eight of those years it was managed by James Singer and after it closed he went on to manage the Pittodrie Granite Turning Company for many years.
Aberdeen Operative Masons' Building Company Ltd
Formed in 1867 or 1868 at around the time of a major strike by the operatives (see Chapter 12). The first ordinary meeting of shareholders held on 28 October 1868. Although the company seems to have been short-lived among the building they are known to have built are Tarland Parish Church, opened in 1870, and Dyce Parish Church, opened in 1872 but later demolished.
Adamant Stone and Paving Co., Ltd, Dancing Cairns
First appeared in the *Directory* in 1913. See main text for more on them.
James Alexander & Co., Gerrard Street/Kittbrewster Granite Works, 118 Leslie Terrace/Great Northern Road

First appeared in the *Directory* in 1888 as stonecutters, 82 Gerrard Street, then as granite merchants at King's Crescent. They became the Kittybrewster Granite Works in 1898. Last appeared in the *Directory* in 1902, though a James Alexander, stonecutter of Clifton Road, was later listed.

Allan & Lyon *see Lyon and Allan*

Anderson & McKenzie, Constitution Street

First appeared in the *Directory* in 1869. Ceased in 1872 when the yard and machinery was put up for sale. Described then as a large business trading with Glasgow, the rest of the UK and America.

Aeneas and James Anderson/Anderson Brothers, **Providence Granite Works**, Sinclair Road/7 Victoria Road, Torry/Back Hilton Road

Aeneas Anderson senior was born in Aberdeen in 1832 and served a five-year apprenticeship with Macdonald & Leslie, and then worked for them for a number of years. He went to Quincy in America for a season in 1881 and also worked in Shap in Westmorland. The business seems to have been established by his sons, James and Aeneas, and he worked for them. Aeneas junior first appears in the *Directory* in 1888. James spent some time in America before setting up in business with his brother. In 1919 Anderson Brothers moved to Back Hilton Road. James retired from the business around 1931 and died in 1951. The brothers did a considerable amount of export work for America. Taken over by Bridgewater Brothers Holdings Ltd. in 1967.

Angus Brothers, Trinity Works, Park Road

First appeared in the *Directory* in 1921. Angus, Hardie & Co. took over the works of Alexander Burnett in May 1920 and applied for membership of the AGGA. As Angus Brothers they were admitted in August 1920.

Annand & Murray, 30 Great Western Road

First appeared in the *Directory* in 1891. Probably Joseph Annand, both are listed in the 1893 AGA Membership List.

Auchinachie & Burns /W. Auchinachie, St Clair Street

First appeared in the *Directory* in 1911. Not listed in AGA Membership List for 1913. William A. Auchinachie first appeared on his own at the same address in the 1915 *Directory*.

Ebenezer Bain & Son, builders. 209 George Street and 3 Broadford Place

Established 1845 when Bain was described as a wright in the *Directory*. He wasn't called a builder until 1885. Joined by his son in 1887. Last entry in the *Directory* was 1895 Built Mitchell & Muil's premises on Schoolhill, later part of RGU.

Robert Beattie/Robert Beattie & Son, Hutcheon Street West/45 Holland Street, builders, granite merchants and contractors

Beattie had been in partnership with Robert Smith until around 1883. (see under Smith & Beattie). First appeared in the *Directory* on his own in 1884. After the First World War the partners also operated a quarry at Blackhill, Longhaven.

Birnie & Stewart, builders, Crimon Place

First appeared in the *Directory* as Birnie & Stuart, Skene Terrace in 1860. By the 1880s it was just Alex Birnie.

Peter Bisset & Son, builder, Porthill/Gallowgate/Loch Street

Reputedly founded around 1840 but first appeared in the *Directory* in 1846. Founded by Peter H. Bisset and then he was joined by his son James H. probably in 1860 when they first appeared in the *Directory* as & Son. According to John Morgan James Bisset speculated on buying land for feuing including Burnside and Ruthrieston from the trustees of Miss Duthie. The former was sold to the Town Council on Bisset's death for almost double what he had paid. He was succeeded by Peter B. Bisset. Introduced Portland Cement to the north-east, using it for concrete. Built what is now the Tivoli using concrete. Laid out Duthie Park. Built Rosemount Viaduct from South Mount Street to Union Terrace; Gilcomston, Ferryhill and Ruthrieston Free Churches; Rosemount and Mannofield Parish Churches; private chapel at Haddo House; Commercial Bank, 78 Union Street 1888 (later demolished); Holburn Free Church; Salvation Army Citadel 1895; Savings Bank, Union Terrace 1896; Main Post Office, Crown Street/Dee Street 1902–07. Built harbours using Portland cement concrete at Port Errol, Gardenstown, and Cove, as well as foundations for the bridge over the Ythan at Newburgh.

Thomas J. Blann, Advocates Road/Constitution Street/Pittodrie Street

Blann was born in England first came to Aberdeen on a training ship in 1863. After spending some years in the merchant navy he returned to Aberdeen in the 1870s. He spent fifteen years with John Fraser & Co., and then was foreman with W. C. Townsend before setting up his own monumental business, first appearing in the *Directory* in 1887. In August 1898 his new yard was opened by Archibald A. Brown, granite merchant, on a half-acre site at Pittodrie Street. The *Aberdeen Journal* for 30 August described it as having a stone and lime building with a polishing mill fitted with Sangster's four-spindle carriage, three vertical and one pendulum polishing machines. In a separate building two rapid stone saws and 14 HP 'Globe' gas engine. There were also offices, stonecutters' sheds and three cranes.

William Boddie, Offices and polishing works in St Clair Street, show-yard in King Street

Boddie came from Forgue in Aberdeenshire and served his apprenticeship as a building mason in Rhynie. He learned the monumental trade with Fraser & Son. In 1869 he went to America, claiming to be among the first to do so, returning to Aberdeen in 1875. In America he worked on the building of the Boston Post Office. With the money he made there he set up in business with Alexander. Wilson. They first appeared as Boddie & Wilson in the *Directory* for 1876/77. Boddie appeared on his own from 1882. From 1903 he was joined by his son as Willam Boddie & Son. Boddie was one of the prime movers of the Aberdeen Granite Association and its President from 1891–93. He also served several terms on the Town Council. Mainly monumental and architectural work. Supplied material for building fronts in London where he had considerable connection among London architects. Operated one of the Peterhead Quarries and had a branch in Huntly. In 1890 sixty men were employed at St Clair Street. Exhibited at Glasgow International Exhibition. One of the most prestigious monuments he manufactured was the Gladstone Memorial in Glasgow. Elected to Town Council in 1895, retiring in 1904.

Boddie died in 1917 at the age of 79, his sons carried on the business which continued until 1943.

J.M. Bonnyman & Co., Great Western Road

First appeared in the *Directory* as a granite polisher in 1880 at South Bridge, Holburn Street.

Bower & Florence, **Spittal Granite Works,** King's Crescent

Established 1867, (John McLaren says 1862 and Bower's obituary says around 1866), first appearing in the *Directory* in 1869, by James H. Bower and John Florence. A John and Peter Bower had appeared at Spital Road in the 1867 *Directory*. Bower had worked for railway companies in Forfar and Aberdeen before setting up in business with Florence who was a time served stone cutter. Employed upwards of eighty men in 1890 and at that time they had a considerable overseas trade. Bower was a director of a number of companies and chairman of the Aberdeen Ice Company, Culter Paper Mills and the Distillers Utilisation and Cake Feeding Company. He also bought the Pitmurchie Estate at Torphins. Florence died in 1892 at the age of 55 and Bower in 1901 at the age of 70. The latter's eldest son, Haddon A. Bower carried on the business eventually taking John McLaren into partnership. Haddon Bower died in 1927 and McLaren became sole proprietor. McLaren's son, also John, ran the business after the Second World War, John senior dying in April 1945. In the early 1930s McLaren said that there were around sixty men and boys employed at the yard. Registered as a limited company in April 1947. At various times operated quarries at Blackhill and Toadhall, Cruden and also Burnside at Kintore. Amalgamated with Stewart & Co. in 1964. *See also Westland & Florence and John McLaren.*

Thomas Brebner, Millburn Street

William Brebner, Off Kings Crescent/Palmerston Road

First appeared in the *Directory* in 1889. Included in the AGA members list 1893.

Brigson Granite Company Ltd, 45 Holland Street

In 1958 *Directory*.

Bristol Marble & Granite Co., Linksfield Road

First appeared in the *Directory* in 1913.

British Granite and Marble Co., Adelphi/7 St Clair Street

First appeared in the *Directory* in 1906 at the Adelphi. Ceased business at the end of May 1956.

Archibald Brown, **St Nicholas Granite Works**, 10 Jasmine Place/Advocates Road.

Born at Kittybrewster, Brown served his apprenticeship with Bower & Florence and set up on his own with James McIntosh at King Street after only one year as a journeyman. When the partnership was dissolved Brown continued on his own, moving from King Street to Advocates Road. They first appeared separately in 1883 with McIntosh at Gerrard Street. Brown completed a number of large mausoleums for export to America. One interesting monument produced by the company in 1899 was a Latin cross of polished Peterhead granite. It was going to the south of England to be erected to the memory of the hero of Rorke's Drift, Colonel J.R.M. Chard VC. A prominent member of the Aberdeen Granite Association, Brown died in May 1917. A.A. Brown was still in business in 1946.

W.J. Brown & Son

William J. Brown was a quarryman who operated quarries at Tillyfourie and Kemnay. At the time of his death he operated the Dunecht Quarry. Died in October 1938 aged 63.

Brown Brothers, 211 Auchmill Road, Bucksburn

First appeared in the *Directory* in 1920.

W.H. Buchan, 43 Summer Street
First appeared in the *Directory* in 1899. Member of AGA.
James Burgess, quarrier, Birsemore, Aboyne. Also John Burgess & son, Aboyne
Caie & Co., Orchard Granite Works, Pittodrie Place
John Caie came from Fittie in Aberdeen and spent time in America before establishing his own business. At some point Caie & Co. formed a partnership with John O. Rettie as Caie & Rettie, first appearing in the *Directory* in 1908. This partnership was dissolved in 1926 (see separate entry for Rettie). David Knowles Stephen was Caie's representative on the AGA in 1913 and at some point he became his partner, Caie died in April 1940, aged 68, and Stephen carried on the business. Bought over by A. & J. Robertson in 1966.
Alexander Carnie, Clayhills
Originally Morgan & Carnie, first appearing in the *Directory* in 1884. Members of AGA. First appeared on his own in 1892.
James Chalmers, 47 Canal Road/558 King Street
Chalmers & Cooper first appeared at 1A Canal Road in the *Directory* for 1889. Chalmers was on his own at the same address by 1891.
Alexander Cheyne, builder, Ferryhill Terrace/St Swithin Street
Cheyne began as an apprentice with George Fordyce & Co. While with them he worked on Ardoe House. Had a partnership for five years with Baillie John Brown at Clayhills. First appeared on his own in the *Directory* in 1883. Built Episcopal Church at Bucksburn; Free Church Hall, Woodside; houses in Union Terrace; most of Portland Street; warehouses at Waterloo Quay for Aberdeen Steam Navigation Company; Shore Porters Building; Fire Station in King Street; three-storey dairy building in Kemnay; building in Leadside Road for Mr Culter, dairyman; two houses and five shops on the corner of Ashvale Place and Union Glen.
Alexander George Cheyne, 87 Holburn St/Howburn Place
First appeared in the *Directory* in 1904. Member of AGA. From 1913 also known as the Nellfield Granite Works.
Christie, Greig & Co., Trinity Granite Works, Park Road
First appear in the *Directory* in 1896. Francis Christie's father and grand-father were both masons, his father working at Dunecht House and operating the Craigenlow Quarry. Christie worked with his father as Francis Christie & Son before setting up in business with Greig. Produced polished granite fronts for buildings as well as monumental work.
Hugh Cocker/Cocker & McKay *See Inglis*
Cosgrove, Laurie & Lindsay, Pittodrie
As Cosgrove, Lindsay & Co. first appeared in the *Directory* in 1910 at 9 Merkland Road East.
James Cosgrove, Pittodrie Granite Works
First appeared as this in the *Directory* in 1903, though Coutts & Cosgrove were listed the previous year at North Esplanade.
Cotton Street Granite Polishing Works
First appear in the *Directory* in 1872

Charles Coutts, Banks of Dee/22 Bank Street

First appeared in the *Directory* in 1890 at Esplanade. John Coutts died 1932. He had been a partner in George Kemp & Co., but in 1925 set up in business for himself. He was succeeded by sons Charles G. Coutts and John Coutts.

Coutts & Younie, Pittodrie Street

George Younie served his apprenticeship with James Willox, builder, and went to America for several years. On returning he worked for McIntosh & Rae and was first permanent secretary of the Operative Mason's Society. After a few years he set up with William D. Coutts. Younie carved a granite coat of arms for Crathes Castle. He was a prominent member of the Aberdeen Granite Association. Younie died on 6 January 1910 at the age of 47. Coutts & Cosgrove appeared in the *Directory* in 1902 (not clear which Coutts it is). Coutts & Younie appeared the following year.

W.D. Coutts & Sons, St Peter Street

William D. Coutts went into business with his sons in 1921, first appearing in the *Directory* in that year. They also joined the AGA in February that year.

John Craig & Co., Nelson Monumental Works, Park Road

John Craig, stonecutter first appeared in the *Directory* at Nelson Street in 1869. By 1877 they had become John Craig & Co., Nelson Monumental Works, Park Road.

Alexander Cran, monumental works, Station Road, Ellon

Recorded in Granite Chips column of the *Aberdeen Journal*, 22 April 1896.

John Crichton, Eden Place/King Street Road

Came from Turriff and was apprenticed to James Willox. Went to America and then started on his own. First appeared in the *Directory* in 1891. A member of the AGA. Died in 1908. Possibly carried on as John Crichton & Son, Regent Walk.

William J. Crichton, Linksfield Place/King Street/Regent Walk

First appeared in the *Directory* in 1906. On the AGA Membership List for 1910.

Crofts & Flett, Pittodrie Street

Robert Crofts and Henry Morris Flett. First appeared in the *Directory* in 1909. Fined by the AGA in 1910 for infringing the price list. Henry Flett died in January 1922.

Robert Crofts & Sons, Emerald Granite Works, Pittodrie Street/9 Merkland Road

First appeared separate from Flett in 1916 at Merkland Road. Bought Alexander Lambie's yard. Robert Crofts senior died in 1952. Still there in 1958.

Robert D. Cruickshank, Albyn Granite Works, Victoria Bridge, Torry/South Esplanade East

Robert Cruickshank came from the Kintore area and was apprenticed to Macdonald, Field & Co. He spent a few years in America before returning and from 1877–82 he was part of the partnership of Stewart & Cruickshank in Charles Street. They were dissolved around 1885 and Cruickshank went into business on his own and is listed in the 1886 *Directory* at Gerrard Street. He later moved to Torry. Founding member of AGA in March 1888. Upwards of sixty men were employed in 1890. The company did tomb and headstones, crosses, columns and pillars, statue pedestals, shop and house fronts. Cruickshank died in 1890 and his manager James Coutts took over the firm along with William A. Cruickshank, nephew of Robert. Coutts died in 1907 and William Cruickshank died in 1908. One prestigious monument that the company made in 1900 was a red granite pedestal for the statue of Sir William Mackinnon, chief instigator of the Imperial British East Africa Company, in Mombassa in what is now Kenya. 10ft in diameter at the base, it was 12ft in height.

Alex. Davidson, Claremont Street

First appeared in the *Directory* in 1888. Founding member of AGA in March 1888.

J. Davidson, 12 Irvine Place

First appeared in the *Directory* in 1901.

J. & A. Davidson, Raik Road

First appeared in the *Directory* in 1900.

Alexander Dawson/ Dawson & Pope, South Esplanade East/Victoria Bridge.

First appeared in the *Directory* in 1886 at Richmond Street., moving to Torry the following year. Founding members of AGA in March 1888. Pope seems to have set up his own business in 1893. Alexander Dawson & Son still in business in 1951.

George Donaldson, Huxter Row/Park Street

First appeared in the *Directory* in 1849. Last appeared in 1876. Built Town House/Municipal Buildings in the 1860s. One of the builders who worked on Balmoral.

Charles Dorian & Son, St Peter Street

Accepted as members of the AGA in May 1925, also appearing in the *Directory* for the first time that year. Charles Dorian had been in partnership with Alfred Milne since 1920, as James K. Milne, Regent Walk. Charles died in November 1942. Closed in 1975 at which time the work-force numbered thirteen.

Douglas Granite Co., Linksfield Road

Granite merchants and quarry owners they first appeared in the *Directory* in 1910.

George Duguid, builder, Kintore Place.

First appeared in the *Directory* as Duguid & Wilson in 1879, later as George Duguid & Son, possibly George's son John. Duguid was also a councillor. Last appeared in the *Directory* in 1924. Responsible for large block of tenements in Hutcheon Street West, 1896; William Kelly additions to the Royal Infirmary in 1895/96; John Fleming's wood yard, 1896; four-storey block on George Street at its corner with John Street for A.R Duncan, draper. 1899.

Alexander Duncan, Deebank Granite Works

Duncan came from Cluny and served his apprenticeship with Francis Christie at Dunecht House. He then worked with Wright & Sons, John Street before going to America, working in Buffalo and Barre. On returning he set up with James Cowie, first in Rose Street, then around 1907 at Deebank Granite Works, Allenvale. Cowie went to Canada in 1911 and Duncan took his own son George into partnership with him.

John G. Duncan, Advocates Road/Rosebank Granite Works, Rosebank Terrace

Established 1883 by Messrs Smith & Taylor. Succeeded by Duncan in 1887, though Smith & Taylor continue to be listed. He moved to Advocates Road in 1890. Small yard with twelve men in 1890. Sculptural and monumental work. By 1914 Henry Duncan, his son, also appears and they became known as Grampian Granite Co. John transferred the business to Henry in 1922.

Duncan & Cowie, granite merchants, Allenvale

First appeared in the Diretcory in 1902 at Rose Street. In 1907 architect Duncan Hodge built a granite yard for them on land owned by the Hammermen Incorporation. By at least 1922 the yard had been taken over by William Taggart.

Duncan & Greig/ William K. Greig, 232/238 King Street.

Established 1887 as Duncan & Greig. First appeared in the *Directory* in 1888 and Duncan retired the same year. Founding members of AGA in March 1888.

Dunn Brothers, Northern Granite Works, Fraser Road/5–9 Holland Street

David Dunn and John N. Dunn in 1893 AGA Membership list. Whether or not they were sons of Dunn of Dunn & Mitchell is unclear. In 1895 there was a significant investment in their yard with the addition of a slated polishing mill lit by gas. It had a brick chimney stack, a new boiler and a 12hp steam engine. A Jenny Lind was to follow. The engineering work was done by William Grant, engineer of Fraser Road. John Petrie Dunn took over the business from his father David in 1911. One notable building they provided the granite for the street-level storey, 21ft high, of the Capital and Counties Bank in Brighton. The building was at the intersection of two streets, with one side being adjacent to the Royal Pavilion. One side of the building was 55ft long, the other 60ft and the ornate granite doorway was at the corner between the two. The granite was dull polished and came from Dancing Cairns Quarry.

Dunn & Mitchell/James A. Mitchell, 175 North Broadford

Established 1884 by a Mr Dunn. Joined by Mitchell in 1886. Employed between twenty and thirty men in 1890. Sculptor and polished granite. Founding members of AGA in March 1888. Mitchell seems to have gone into business on his own in 1891 (see separate entry).

William Edwards, Nelson Granite Works, St Clair Street/King Street/Pittodrie Street

Established 1878, when they first appeared in the *Directory*, by William Edwards who came from Auchindachy near Keith. When he came to Aberdeen around 1867 he worked for William Boddie and then served his apprenticeship with John Fraser. William spent six years working at Dix Island, Maine. To his apparent surprise when he came back his wife had saved enough for him to start up in business for himself. His first granite yard was in Nelson Street. He then moved to St Clair Street and finally to King Street. Founding members of AGA in March 1888. Employed twenty men in 1890. Around 1900 he was joined by his son, William G. Edwards, and they moved to Pittodrie Street. The elder William, despite very limited schooling, joined the Town Council in 1902 and became a Baillie. He continued on the Council until his death in January 1917 at the age of 71. His son was President of the Granite Manufacturer's Association and director of the Aberdeen Granite Supply Association. He also joined the Town Council in 1920, serving until 1931, becoming City Treasurer in 1929. William G. Edwards died in January 1933. Still in business in 1958. Share capital was bought by A. & J. Robertson in 1965 but they continued trading under their own name. Closed down in 1969.

William Farquharson, builder, Gilcomston Park/Hutcheon Street West/Fraser Road

Camc from Fraserburgh and began his business in Aberdeen *c.*1871, though first appeared in the *Directory* in 1876. Among the buildings he built were Crown Mansions, extension to the Fish Market, Aberdeen Steam Laundry, and additions to Glentanar House. Also responsible for the memorial fountain to commemorate the founders of the Northern Co-operative Company. Unveiled in April 1912, it is 21ft high and 10ft wide, polished Peterhead and fine-axed Kemnay granites. William's son James carried on the business after his death in 1911.

Henry Flett, Pittodrie Street

Initially in partnership with Robert Crofts (*see Robert Crofts*). In 1916 they split up and formed their own yards. In 1931 Henry Morris Flett joined with Alexander Lambie to form Flett & Lambie. Alexander Lambie had been with Caie & Co. The partnership was very short-lived and Lambie appeared in the *Directory* on his own at Pittodrie Street so perhaps Flett had died.

Peter Florence, 15 Nelson Street/251 King Street

First appeared in the *Directory* in 1882, though a John and Peter Florence had appeared in the *Directory* in 1867, presumably the same John who went into business with James Bower. Founding member of AGA in March 1888.

James Forbes & Son, **Ernan Granite Works**, 21 Mounthooly/Froghall Lane

According to Scotland of Today, published *c.* 1890, this business was established by Chalmers & Ewen about 1859, nine years later they were succeeded by Andrew Williamson and then it passed to James Forbes in 1878, though Williamson continued to appear in the *Directory* and Forbes does not appear in his own name until 1881. As a stonecutter he moved quickly from Charles Street to Nelson Street and then in 1884 to Mounthooly. He employed fifteen men in 1890. Founding member of AGA in March 1888. In 1893 he moved to Froghall Lane and in 1896 he seems to have had a house built next to the granite works and he named it Ernan Cottage. (According to Diane Morgan, *The Spital Lands*, this was built because he misinterpreted the feu charter and thought he was required to build a house there. He later moved to No. 8 Erskine Street.) For a time in the early 1900s the works were known as the Ernan Granite Works. James's son Francis (Frank) William served his apprenticeship with his father and took over the business in 1922, James himself dying in 1931. Frank died in December 1938 aged 65, his widow, Annie Duguid Forbes and one his sons, William, carried on the business. James Forbes & Son last appeared in the *Directory* in 1966 when William Forbes took ill and the yard closed. James Forbes, who had the Kincorth Quarries in the late nineteenth/early twentieth centuries, is not the same person.

George Fordyce & Co., builders and contractors, Hutcheon Street West

Established 1871. Fordyce died in the 1880s and the business was carried on by senior partners William Watt and Alexander Anderson.

They built the Free Press Building on Union Street, Ruxton Buildings in Bridge Street; Middle School in the Gallowgate; a four-storey building at Regent's Quay for W. Williams & Sons (1899); and Ardoe House. They also built a house in Rubislaw Den for the architects/surveyors Walker & Duncan.

David Fraser & Son

Operated several quarries in Newhills Parish including Sclattie and Caskieben.

John Fraser & Son, Aberdeen Polishing Granite Works, Fraser Road/81 North Broadford

One of the oldest granite yards who also carried out building work. John Fraser first appeared in the *Directory* at Broadford in 1835. He was later listed as a builder and moved to Charlotte Street on the corner with John Street in the late 1840s. In 1854 he was joined by his son. In 1864 they built a new 5-acre granite polishing yard between North Broadford and Berryden, but they still had their office in John Street. The new premises had an engine house, polishing mill, and boiler house. They were succeeded by J. Whitehead & Sons in 1888.

William Fraser, Abergeldie Road

First appeared in the *Directory* in 1901.

John Fyfe Ltd

As well as running various quarries and acting as building and civil engineering contractors, John Fyfe also operated a granite yard in Aberdeen. Examples of their work can be seen in the heraldic panel for the bridge over the Thames at Kew, detailed in the main text), and Lord Cowdray's monument at Echt Churchyard. The latter, unveiled in 1933, was executed in Kemnay granite with the base and steps using the estate's own granite from Craigenlow an some pink from Hill O'Fare.

Gall & Walker, builder, Richmond Street

First appeared in the *Directory* in 1879 at View Terrace. Built Aberdeen Central Library, Ashley Road, Ferryhill and Broomhill Schools.

John Gammie, Clayhills/22 Ashvale Place/Rosebank Terrace

First appeared in the *Directory* in 1893.

Garden & Co. Victoria Granite Works, 213–233, then 217–251 King Street.

Established 1871 by William and Charles Garden, initially in Gerrard Street where they lived. In the 1874 *Directory* they appear as James Garden & Co. In 1879 they moved to the site at King Street, becoming Garden & Co. in 1882. Founding members of AGA in March 1888. In 1890 their yard covered an acre. Mainly monumental work including polishing. Upwards of 150 men employed in 1890. They won a silver medal at the Paris International Exhibition in 1900. They carried out a lot of work at Dunecht House for Lord and Lady Cowdray. This included Cowdray's coat of arms panel, carved in 1913 in Kemnay granite, erected at Dunecht House. The panel was modelled by the London sculptor William Frith. Garden & Co. last appeared in the Aberdeen *Directory* in 1962/63.

W. Garstin & Sons, granite and marble merchants,

An English company based at Kensal Green but variously listed as London Granite Works, Palmerston Road, King Street Granite Works, 195–201 King Street, and 10 Belmont Street. First appeared in the *Directory* in 1893, members of the AGA the same year. Company seems to have been dissolved in 1901, though they continued in Aberdeen for a few years after this.

Gauld & Third, John Third & Son, Belmont Granite Works, 1 Canal Road

Established 1878 by Andrew Williamson. John Gauld & Co., appeared in the *Directory* at Belmont Road in 1880, the following year as Gauld & Third at Nelson Street. Gauld and Third took over the Belmont Works in 1885 and are listed at Canal Road in that year's *Directory*. Founding member of AGA in March 1888. John Gauld had been a foreman in a granite polishing yard in Peterhead for 30 years before starting his own business with John Third. In 1890 the yard was about an acre and they employed upwards of fifty men. Gauld also acted as a granite agent for several American firms. John Gauld died in 1905, though he had left the business some years before that.

John Third was born in Aberdour in 1835 and was apprenticed to J. & J. Gauld at New Pitsligo. He was foreman on the building of number of railway bridges and in charge of building the aqueduct from Invercannie to Aberdeen His son Henry Webster Third joined him after Gauld left, the firm becoming J. Third & Son. John died in September 1911. Henry died in January 1926 aged 50. Martin Third was President of the AGMA from 1940–42.

Edgar Gauld, builder, 60 Skene Street/28 Gilcomston Terrace

First appeared in the *Directory* at Skene Street in 1856 (presumably the father). Edgar Gauld senior died in 1874 and he has a fine granite headstone in Nellfield Cemetery. The better-known son was born in Lumsden and went into business in Aberdeen along with his father at Gilcomston Terrace. He built a considerable number of buildings in Aberdeen and the surrounding area. As well as housing, these included Mar Lodge, for which he opened up the quarry on Morrone; he also opened a quarry at Campfield, Glassel for granite for the chapel; Garthdee House; Gray's School of Art on Schoolhill; Greyfriars Buildings in Broad Street; Glenkindie House, Cruden Bay Hotel; Kingseat Asylum; Albion Street School; Torry School; Ruthrieston School and Parish Church; Causewayend School; North United Free Church; Episcopal Church in Aboyne; the Mannofield Reservoir; Northern Co-operative Building at Berryden; the north wing and tower of Marischal College; Bon Accord U.F. Church; a six-storey building on the corner of Gaelic Lane and Belmont Street, the front to Belmont Street being Kemnay granite, the gable on Gaelic Lane Persley granite, with the rest of the building of Rubislaw granite; Albion Street School, architect Arthur Clyne; and bridges at Maryculter, Monymusk and Auchedly, Ellon. He also built a mansion house in Aboyne using stone from one of the Hill O'Fare quarries. The carved granite work for the outside of the Masonic Temple in Crown Street was also carried out by Gauld's workforce, after models by the sculptor W.H. Buchan. Gauld was also a nationally known expert in building baker's ovens. Gauld also operated quarries at Blackhill, Peterhead. He died in August 1929, aged 87. One of his sons was William Edgar Gauld, the architect.

John Gauld & Son, Whinhill/Holland Street

First appeared in the *Directory* in 1893. Members of AGA.

Gerrie & Nicol, Claremount Granite Works, Peter Gerrie, **Ferryhill Granite Works**, Clayhills

Peter Gerrie and Alex Nicol first appeared together in the *Directory* in 1891. They were members of AGA. In 1896 they separated with Nicol staying on at Claremont Street and Gerrie moving to Clayhills (*see separate entry under Nicol*).

Robert Gibb. Excelsior Granite Works, King Street.

Reputedly established 1875, first appearing in the *Directory* in 1878. Gibb served his apprenticeship with William Keith jun and then spent eighteen months in America before setting up in business for himself in Nelson Street with only himself and a boy. By 1890 his yard covered around an acre of ground with 640 feet of shedding with a polishing mill 160ft by 40ft and a crane capable of lifting 15 or 20 tons. At that point he was employing upwards of 100 men. Monumental and architectural, exporting all over the world. Gibb was one of the first to import granite from overseas and operated quarries in Norway and elsewhere. He was a founder and director of the Aberdeen Granite Supply Association and a partner and one of the originators of the Aberdeen Iron Grit Company. All of his three sons were associated with the business and carried it on after his death in 1907. Closed *c.*1977.

Gibb Brothers, Roslin Granite Works, Ashgrove Road and Back Hilton Road
Carried on by J.M. Gibb, Alfred Gibb and William Gibb. They first appeared in the *Directory* in 1902 at 377 King Street and Merkland Road East. Alfred Gibb was President of the Aberdeen Granite Association and a director of Mowatt's Pioneer Grit Co., from its founding in 1911. They bought A.H. Wright's business in 1910. J.M. Gibb died in 1916 at the age of 42 and his brothers carried on the business. In the 1930s the firm was one of the largest and best equipped of its kind in the country. The brothers split in 1932. William died in October 1935, his son carrying on the business. Gibb Brothers still around in 1958 at 558 King Street
Monumental and polished architectural work as well as a turning plant for manufacturing rollers. Ceased trading 1969. W.R.H. Gibb died the following year.

Alfred Gibb & Co., **Caledonian Granite Works**, 45 Holland Street
In 1932 Alfred Gibb split from Gibb Brothers and established his own business. As well as being President of the AGA Gibb was also a director of the Aberdeen Granite Supply Association. He died in May 1937 aged 64. Alf Gibb & Co., advertised as staring a business as the Britannia Granite Works, 45 Holland Street in 1938. Alfred Gibb & Co. still around in 1950.

Charles Gordon, builder, Powis Lane
Building in St Paul Street for King & Co., printers; extensions to Royal Lunatic Asylum designed by William Kelly 1899; large block of buildings in Virginia Street for James Wisely, carting contractor. 1896; a large two-storey building at Regent Quay for the Harbour Commissioners 1898.

David Massie Grant (successor to Messrs J .& J. Ogg). **Caledonian Granite Works**, Wellington Road.
Established 1867 at 77 Holburn Street as J. & J. Ogg, 1870 moved to Wellington Road. Taken over by Grant *c*.1890. The yard at Wellington Road was 200ft by 190ft in 1890. As well as monumental and architectural work they also did smaller pieces including curling stones.
Listing in Aberdeen *Directory* stopped in 1893.

John Grant & Sons, **Allenvale Monumental Works**
First appeared in the *Directory* in 1892.

Grant & Watt, Albert Granite Works, Affleck Street/Portland Street/Victoria Street South
Began monumental and polishing work in 1874, at which time they appeared in the *Directory*. In May 1880 they advertised that they had bought the premises of a Mr Robertson in Victoria Street South and were moving there. With increased accommodation and the latest machinery they were able to carry on granite polishing, including all kinds of monumental and architectural work. Founding members of AGA in March 1888.

James Gray, Crimond Place/ 7 St Clair Street
Gray first worked for Gavin Low. He went to America in the early 1870s. On his return he went into partnership with John Burnett in St Clair Street. On Burnett's death Gray carried on the firm, first appearing on his own in 1883. He died in 1910, aged 72. Founding member of AGA in March 1888.

Great North of Scotland Granite Co., Peterhead
Asked to attend the inaugural dinner of the Aberdeen Granite Association in 1888 but their membership of the Association was erratic. Members of the Red Granite Quarriers Association in the 1890s. Operated a quarry at Stirlinghill.

William K. Greig, *see Duncan and Greig*

James Hadden, 37 Powis Place/Imperial Granite Works, Back Hilton Road
Hadden & Reilly first appeared in the *Directory* in 1892 at George Street and Charles Street. Reilly appears on his own in 1893. Hadden first appears on his own in 1900 at Froghall Lane. Involved in a serious dispute with the AGA in 1912 (see Chapter 10). James died in 1919 and business was carried on under the same name by his son Andrew W. Hadden. He was later joined by his son, Andrew J. Hadden. Andrew senior died in 1955, his son having died the year before. The headstone to James and Andrew is in a lovely slightly Art Deco style. The business closed in 1969.

George and Robert Hall, builders, Gilcomston Park
George Hall came from Newhills and had four brothers who also trained as masons. In Aberdeen he served his apprenticeship with George Donaldson, working on Balmoral. According to his obituary he was then foreman for a builder called John Thom, and worked on the Imperial Hotel (now the Carmelite), Benjamin Reid's warehouses in Guild Street, Brebner & Grant's in St Nicholas Street and the Belmont Street United Presbyterian Church. He then went into business for himself and appeared in the 1874 *Directory* at 8 North Charlotte Street. Two years later he was in partnership with one of his brothers, Robert, at Gilcomston Park. Their name, G. & R. Hall, appears prominently on the master mason's granite fountain in Victoria Park. By 1881 Robert was working on his own. George's obituary simply states that at that point he went back to Newhills with his family. He died at Watchman Brae, Newhills in March 1899. Robert had worked in New Zealand and America in his younger days and was involved in recruiting men to go to work on the ill-fated State Capitol in Austin Texas (see Chapter 7). Robert continued the business on his own until around 1887 when he moved to South Africa, dying there in 1917 at the age of 76.
The firm built much of Queen's Terrace as well as other housing in the West End, and Beaconhill House at Murtle.

George Hall, builder, Blenheim Place/Back Hilton Road
Oldest son of James Hall, builder of Ballater. Served his apprenticeship with his uncles, George and Robert Hall, becoming foreman for the latter. He also worked for a time in Edinburgh before setting up in business for himself. By the time of his death his firm was one of the largest in the north of Scotland. First appeared in the *Directory* in 1890 at Mackie Place.
Took over the Upper Persley Quarry before 1900.
Hall died in 1921, aged 65, and the business was then run by Norman Murray who had been resident engineer when Union Bridge was widened. After the First World War he joined the business, succeeding Hall on the latter's death. Murray retired in 1952 but the firm continued until at least 1958. Built premises for the Aberdeen Storage Company in Commerce Street (1896); all the tenements on the east side Wallfield Crescent, 1899 onwards; large block of shops and houses on Rosemount Place, extending from Wallfield Place to Wallfield Crescent, with the demolition of Wallfield House, 1899 onwards; St Clement Street School; Sunnyside School; Unitarian Church, Skene Street (now the Kingdom Hall); Cromar House (now Alastrean House) and Douneside House, both in Tarland Innes House near Elgin; widening of Union Bridge 1905–08; bridge over the Dee at Mar Lodge 1905; mason work for the railway viaduct over the River Dee at Craiginches and over the Tay at Perth; Teacher Training College, St Andrew Street (later part of RGIT/RGU); Wartime work in Invergordon and Longside; the firm also did polished granite fronts for buildings in London.

Henderson and Webster, Affleck Street

First appeared in the *Directory* in 1880, Henderson being Webster's father-in-law. William Webster had been apprenticed to Macdonald, Field & Co., before working for the Imperial Granite Works. By the 1890s Webster was the sole partner doing dressing, turning, sawing and polishing of granite. Employed upwards of sixty men in 1890. Responsible for the granite obelisk in Duthie Park in memory of Gordon Highlanders who died in India, erected in 1899. Also built Aberdeen Savings Bank in Union Terrace. Founding members of AGA in March 1888. In May 1915 all their machinery, plant and a glass and corrugated-iron shed was auctioned at their Affleck Street premises.

Alexander Hendry or Henry, Henry & Adam, builders

Hendry came from Auchterless and was apprenticed as a carpenter. In the 1860s he set up a building business with a Mr Adam, first appearing in the *Directory* as house carpenters in 1867 at Skene Street. By 1871 Henry was on his own as a house carpenter and builder at Gilcomston Park. In 1889 a Mr Keith became his partner. They built schools, an extension to the Royal Lunatic Asylum, and the newer parts of the Royal Infirmary at Woolmanhill. Hendry retired in 1898.

Peter Henry, Whinhill Road

Peter Henry first appeared in the *Directory* in 1911. That same year he was fined by the AGA for infringing the price list. May have become Turner & Henry, because the AGA Minutes records them becoming Peter Henry in 1914.

Heslop, Wilson & Co./Peterhead Granite Polishing Company (see Chapter 5)

Worked quarries at Longhaven, Rora, Bog and Stirlinghill. William Heslop died in May 1899. Andrew Wilson died *c.*1911 and was succeeded by his son Alexander. They survived into the early 1960s, with their last entry in the *Directory* being in 1962.

James C. Hogg Ltd, Glencoe Granite Works, 567 King Street

James Carnie Hogg served his apprenticeship with Charles McDonald. He then spent about ten years in America before returning and setting up his own yard. Following his death in August 1936, at the age of 56, his oldest son carried on the business, though in 1940 his widow, Emily Hogg, took over the AGA membership. Incorporated with J.A. Mitchell (Granite) Ltd. in 1964. Ceased trading in 1976.

James Hunter, Hunter & Robertson Willowdale Place/209 King Street/Merkland Road East/455 King Street.

James Hunter was born *c.*1820 and after his apprenticeship spent nine years as manager of a granite business in Glasgow. He returned to Aberdeen in the early 1860s and set up in business with Alexander Robertson. They separated again after just a few year, Hunter appearing in the *Directory* on his own in 1869. Robertson eventually went to America. Hunter retired *c.*1888 and his son James carried on the business. Founding member of AGA in March 1888. Listed in the 1910 AGA Membership List but not in the 1913 one.

James Hutcheon, 401 King Street, **Cemetery Granite Works/ Hill O'Fare Granite Works,** 71 King Street

James Hutcheon was born in Mintlaw in 1834. Educated at Robert Gordon's Hospital, he was apprenticed to MacDonald & Leslie at the age of 15 and subsequently worked at the building of

Balmoral Castle. At the age of 23 he managed William Keith's yard in King Street before establishing his own business in 1869. He was chairman of the company who opened the Hill o' Fare Quarry *c*.1884. Founding member of AGA in March 1888. His sons Edward and Henry continued the business with Edward taking over the monumental business and Henry the quarrying. In fact Henry objected to Edward being nominate to take over the membership of the AGA by their father's executors. Edward was accepted as member but Henry was also admitted as a quarrier He bought the Hill O' Fare Granite Company and also bought a granite yard at 71 King Street which he re-named the Hill O'Fare Granite Works and it became one of the best equipped in the city. They then bought the old established firm of Alexander MacDonald & Co. when it got into trouble. Edward, who died aged 48 in 1910, was a director of the Aberdeen Granite Supply Company and became a councillor and baillie. Henry carried on the business until his own death in October 1934 aged 67. He was a prominent member of the AGA. His son, Henry jun. then carried on the business and, as Henry Hutcheon Ltd, he was still in business in 1951. They finally closed in 1953.

James Inglis/Inglis & Cocker, Ashgrove Road, **Hugh Cocker**, Back Hilton Road

Inglis & Cocker applied to become became members of the AGA in May 1900, first appearing in the PO *Directory* in 1901. Within a few years they split with Cocker becoming Cocker & McKay at Ashgrove Road and James Inglis at Merkland Road East, first appearing as such in the *Directory* in 1904. James Inglis was still there in 1950.

John Ironside & Sons, 367 King Street/567 King Street

First appeared in the *Directory* in 1904. Members of the AGA. John died c.1912 because in that year his widow nominated her son Alexander George Ironside to take his place as a member of the AGA. From 1917 they were known as Ironside & Co.

George Leslie Jamieson & Co., Crown Granite Works, 13 & 15 North Charlotte Street

A son of George Jamieson of Drumgarth (Jamieson the Jewellers). He first appeared in the *Directory* in 1870. An advertisement in 1871 described them as manufacturers of columns, pedestals, fountains, vases etc. Founding members of AGA in March 1888. The business was put up for sale in October 1890 (see James Rae). Jamieson died in 1900. A fine example of his work is the monument in St Clement's Churchyard to the famous Ogston family of professors and soap manufacturers.

Jones Brothers, Palmerston Road/Rosebank Terrace

First listed in the *Directory* in 1901.

William Keith jun., King Street Granite Works.

William Keith was born *c*.1827 in New Deer. Lived in Peebles for seven years before returning to Aberdeen to work with his father who was a slater in Aberdeen. Established on his own in 1855, first appearing in the *Directory* as a slater and slate merchant. A few years later he added polished granite to the business. He also helped establish the Pitmuxton Brickworks which later moved to Torry and eventually merged with the Seaton Brick and Tile Co. He owned the Blackhall Quarry at Peterhead, producing red granite. As well as monumental work he also supplied stones for large buildings including Jenners in Edinburgh and the burial enclosure at Haddo House designed by Alfred Waterhouse in 1884. An example of their architectural work for London in the same year can be seen in the Royal Commonwealth Society building in Northumberland Avenue (known as the Royal Colonial Institute at the time it was built). The company employed 150 men in 1890, at which time the yard was 1½ acres. Shortly after this Keith retired and his business was taken over by Garstin & Co. He built the ostentatious Rubislaw Den House for himself in 1881, described in his obituary as one of the largest and finest in the city with extravagant gothic and Scots baronial details. A more recent architectural guide comments that the architect (if any) is thankfully unknown! Keith fancied that his family was connected to the Earl Marischals who were also Keiths. A large ornamental sundial was removed from the Earl Marischal's old house in the Castlegate and later came into the possession of Lord Provost Sir Alexander Anderson who erected it at old Rubislaw House. Keith acquired it from the Provost and erected it at Rubislaw Den House. It was later moved to the House of Schivas where it still resides. Keith also had the Earl Marischal's motto carved into a granite panel at his house. Founding members of AGA in March 1888. He died in 1903.

George Kemp & Co., Rosemount Place/ Gilcomston Park

First appeared in the *Directory* in 1891. Member of AGA.

Among the partners were John Coutts and William Forbes. In 1925 Coutts left and set up in business on his own. Forbes was dead by this time.

Bought by A. & J. Robertson in 1966.

James R.R. Kennedy, 10 Summerfield Place

First appeared in the *Directory* in 1893 at 251 King Street. Listed as a granite merchant in the AGA Membership List. Registered as members of the AGA in September 1921, possibly because the founder's son had taken over. James Kennedy died in 1933 and was succeeded by his son Alexander J. Kennedy. The name of the firm remained the same. Ceased trading in 1963.

William M. Kennedy, Quarrier, Playhillock, Longhaven

William King/James King, builder and quarry owner, Hutcheon Street West/11 Fraser Place

First appeared in the *Directory* in 1877 as William King, builder, Hutcheon Street. In 1880 they were J. & W. King, probably his son James. In 1887 James was on his own. From 1911 he operated a quarry at Tyrebagger. From 1913 they had become Wm. King & Co. at Fraser Place.

Large extension to Kilgour & Walker, Berryden Woollen Mills (1895). Curing works in Sinclair Road, Torry for Marshall & Co., Spring Garden, architect George Coutts.

Kinghorn & Scott /David M. Kinghorn, Pittodrie Street

First appeared in the *Directory* in 1907. Only David M. Kinghorn is listed in the 1910 AGA Membership List at Linksfield Road, though the firm is still in the *Directory* as Kinghorn & Scott. David died in 1938 and his son David M. Kinghorn took over. Still in business in 1958.

James Knowles, granite and marble merchant, 55/57 John Street. Seems to have began as a manufacturer of chimney pieces in freestone, marble and slate. First appeared in the *Directory* in 1881/82 at Hutcheon Street West. Presumably succeeded Knowles & Smith, stone cutters on the same street. They first appeared in the *Directory* in 1880/81. Even after the move to John Street James Knowles is still listed as a freestone stonecutter. In 1899 James Knowles opened a new yard at Ashgrove Road, one of the best in the city at the time (see main text). James died in 1918 aged 68.

Alexander Lambie, Pittodrie

Lambie had been in partnership with a Mrs. Kyd as Flett & Lambie when the partnership was dissolved in December 1931. Lambie continued on his own and applied to join the AGA that year. He later sold the yard to Crofts.

Robert Lawrence, **University Granite Works**, Regent Walk/ 63 Nelson Street
First appeared in the *Directory* in 1881 at Nelson Street. Founding members of AGA in March 1888.
Robert Lawrence died in 1914 and his son Charles H. Lawrence took over.

John W. Legge, Windmill Brae/South Bridge Granite Works, 87 Holburn Street
Est 1849 by John Legge, he was succeeded by John W. Legge in 1872. He died in 1880 but the business carried on. The yard covered 1½ acres in 1890 with a polishing mill containing steam-powered
polishing machinery. Founding members of AGA in March 1888.

James Leith. 35A Union Street.
Originally rom Bonnyton, Rayne, Leith began his life in farming but at the age of 15 became a
dystane dyker. A granite merchant and contractor who owned and quarried at Cairncry, and also
leased Persley. He also operated the quarry at Dunecht in the 1890s until around 1906. Employed
upwards of 200 men in 1890. Leith lived at Lower Middlefield House, Woodside, then in 1895
bought Clifton House. Prior to buying Cairncry he did a lot of work for the railways. Subsequently
among the contracts he carried out were Persley Bridge, Trinity Cemetery, a sewer at the Links and
the Riverside Esplanade. The latter included rebuilding the arch at the north end of Wellington
Suspension Bridge (1886) in granite from his Persley Quarry. He got into a spat with fellow mason,
John Morgan, then on the Council, over additional costs for the Esplanade contract. The building
of the bridge over the River Don at the site of the Persley Ferry was a protracted affair. A bridge
had been suggested at the beginning of the nineteenth century but it wasn't until September
1887 that a resolution to build a bridge was passed at a public meeting of Woodside and district
residents. At that meeting a letter was read out from James Leith offering to build the bridge for
£4,000, £3,000 having already been raised. Architect for the bridge was Patrick M. Barnett, Chief
engineer of the GNSR and William Paton of Grandhome was the main contributor to the cost.
Leith installed a blondin to carry excavated earth across the river. The embankment and pier on the
north side were finished before the work was halted for nearly three years. This was due to a legal
dispute between A. Pirie & Sons, Stoneywood Papermill versus James Leith and J. & J. Crombie of
Grandholm Mill, Pirie alleging interference with the cut or channel on the Don from where he
drew his water. An agreement was eventually reached in 1891 and work resumed. The keystone
for the central arch of the bridge was laid on 28 November 1891, the stone having being carried
across from the south side by the blondin. By this time the cost had risen to £6,000. Leith's obituary states that he contributed £1,000. The bridge, of course, would be of considerable advantage
for his Persley Quarry. It was eventually opened by Lord Provost Stewart on the 9 July 1892. James
Leith's 9ft-high monument, made in fine-axed Persley stone by James Gray of St Clair Street, is
in the Grove Cemetery, facing Leith's Persley Quarry. At the time of his death in 1900, at the age
of 61, his son Alexander operated the Persley Quarry and another son, James, had his own carting
and contracting business. At some point James junior took over the family business and at various
times operated Cairncry, Clochandichter and Kincorth quarries, and after the Second World War
they operated the quarry at Burnside near Kintore. By the 1940s Leiths had added public works
contractors to their company designation and, in the 1960s, haulage contracting. The family name
survives today as Leiths Group. Privately owned, they comprise a group of companies covering civil
engineering and construction, quarrying, plant and transport etc. They operate fourteen quarries

throughout Scotland with their headquarters at Cove overlooking one of these quarries which is on the site of one of the original quarries at Cove. As detailed in the main text, in 2017 they took over Fyfe Glenrock, the last remaining company with the famous Fyfe name.

James Littlejohn, Hill o'Fare Quarry, Craigton, Banchory

Low & Hardie, Back Hilton Road

Short-lived firm formed in 1913 by Alexander Hardie and William Low in 1913. ended two years later in bankruptcy and a legal argument over rights to membership of the AGA.

Low & Chalmers, Whitehouse Street

Gavin Low and William Chalmers. Noted by John Morgan as being one of the seven mason contractors in the city when he began in 1862. William Chalmers, builder, first appeared in the *Directory* in 1849. Low & Chalmers first appear in 1850. The Asylum at Elmhill (Elmhill House) in the late 1850s. Education Trust Buildings, King Street.

Lyon & Allan, Linksfield Road/St Peter Street

First appeared in the *Directory* in 1907. John Taylor Lyon at 31 University Road was listed in the 1901 AGA Membership List. In 1916 Lyon & Co. were in the *Directory* at 24 St Peter Street; no mention of Allan.

John McAdam & Sons, carters and contractors, 47–49 Charlotte Street

Had a granite crushing works in Catherine Street. At various times they operated quarries at Old Town, Cummings Park, Hareness and Cove. Road and paving work. Paved the Chanonry in 1896.

Daniel Macandrew, architect and builder, John Street/Loch Street

One of the major builders in Aberdeen in the second half of the nineteenth century. Macandrew studied architecture under William Henderson, architect, and then building under Watson & Robb. He then set up in business on his own in John Street. Due to ill-health he spent some a few years in New Zealand before returning to Aberdeen in 1854, buying the joinery part of the Hendersons' business, then belonging to James Henderson. Around 1887 Macandrew retired and was succeeded by one of his sons, Daniel in association with James A. Smith. Macandrew senior died in 1899 at the age of 78, Daniel having predeceased him by five years as a result of a gas explosion in his house. The firm won the contract for Government Buildings in Aberdeen and around, including Craiginches and Peterhead Prisons; the library at King's College; the anatomical buildings at Marischal College. He also built and laid out numerous buildings and streets around the Spital area including three pioneer concrete buildings at King's Crsecent on the Spital.

Charles Macdonald Ltd., Froghall Granite Works, Jute Street

Est. 1875/1877 in Nelson Street by Charles Macdonald, first appearing in the *Directory* in 1878. Founding members of AGA in March 1888. Macdonald came from Dyce where his father was a crofter but a mason to trade, as were Charles's two brothers. Served his time with George Donaldson, contractor for the Town House, before spending time in America. Returned and set up on his own in Gerrard Street c.1875/77. He moved to Nelson Street and then Jute Street c.1881, building up one of the largest firms in the city, which employed 150 at the time of his death in 1892. The Institution of Mechanical Engineers recorded in 1907 that when he moved to Jute Street power was supplied by steam engine with one 9ih cylinder, soon replaced by a 14in one. Macdonald continued to expand and introduce new machinery and by 1909 they had steam driven saws, travelling and steam derrick-cranes, and pendulum and rotary polishing machines. The company exported all over the world as well as to England. Owned Longhaven Quarry, near Peterhead and were partners in the Kirkmabreck Quarry, Creetown, Kirkcubrightshire. He also tried granite quarrying on Shetland but this proved unsuitable for polishing. Pioneer in importing granite especially from Sweden and Norway. At its height employed around 180 men. After Macdonald's death the firm was run by his trustees, becoming a company around 1903 with the same management. It amalgamated with Rust & Alexander and James Rust became a director in 1916, managing director in 1920. (see Rust & Alexander). In 1972 it was still run by Rust's son, James, and then grandson, Dugald. Eventually taken over by John Fyfe in 1979. (See main text for more on Macdonald especially Chapter 10 for his dispute with the AGA)

Macdonald & Leslie, Macdonald & Field, Macdonald & Co. Aberdeen Granite Works (see Chapter 5) Ceased in 1941. New Post Office, Market Street 1840; building of Market Street 1840; pedestal for statue of Burns in Union Terrace; tombstone for Sir Walter Scott, Dryburgh Abbey.

John McGregor, McGregor & Taggart, Monumental Sculptor 116 Gt. Western Road
John McGregor, monumental mason, first appeared in the *Directory* in 1878 at Woolmanhill. The following year he was at Baker Street and in 1880 was listed as McGregor & Taggart (with James Taggart) at Ashley Place. In 1883 they have separated with McGregor remaining at Ashley Place. Employed around twenty men in 1890 when the yard was 1½ acres. Founding members of AGA in March 1888.

James McIntosh, Gerrard Street
See under Archibald Brown. First appeared separately from Brown in 1883.

James McIntosh/McIntosh & Rae, Lorne Granite Works, Hutcheon Street West
Born in Huntly, James McIntosh came to Aberdeen in 1864. After serving his apprenticeship with Westland & Anderson he worked on the building of the Town House. He spent three years in America and three in Canada. When he returned around 1876, 'his pockets being full of the almighty dollar', he set up his own business. (*Aberdeen Journal*, 16 September 1903) before going into partnership with Rae. Founder members of the AGA in 1888, McIntosh was President from 1896–97. The partnership with Rae was dissolved in 1896 when a dissolution sale of stones was held. Rae set himself up in Park Road. Initially McIntosh remained at the Lorne Works but then he returned to Canada in 1903 where he set up a business with his sons before retiring. Died in Vancouver in 1912.

William McKay & Son, City Granite Works, Holland Street
William McKay was born into a farming family in Rhynie but he became a stone mason. He went into partnership with David B. Morren, first appearing in the *Directory* in 1908–09 as McKay & Morren, 34 Holland Street, shortly after they expanded into No. 32. Later they occupied 32–62 Holland Street. By 1913 the two men had gone their separate ways with Morren forming David Morren & Co., and McKay being joined by his son Walter J. as William McKay & Son. William McKay was a Baillie and was also twice President of the AGMA, from 1926–27, and 1929–30. He did resign in 1927 in a row over the authority of the directors, but was re-elected as director almost immediately. Walter succeeded him and continued in the firm until his death in July 1955. His son,

William J. McKay took over and was President of the AGA in 1974. He died in 1977 when his two sons took over. In 1983 they merged with John Fyfe but the name was still retained.

McRobbie & Milne, builders, Leadside Road and Albert Place

Reputedly established in 1860, though first appeared in the *Directory* in 1867. Survived into the early twentieth century. Among the work they did was on Marischal College, Mar Lodge, Glenkindie House, Kildrummy Castle, Skibo Castle, Blairs College Chapel, Drumtochty Castle, Drumoak Free Church, Torry Free Church, Rubislaw Parish Church.

A. & F. Manuelle

An English company of quarry owners and stone merchants, founded by Charles Manuelle and carried on by his two sons. They first appeared in Aberdeen in the 1830s (see Chapter 3) and at various times owned or operated quarries at Dancing Cairns, Sclattie and Dyce.

Mason & Adam, builders

Block of buildings at junction of Beechgrove Terrace and Midstocket Road.

Alexander Mearns/Mearns & Reid, Leslie Road/Gt. Northern Road

Alexander Reid and Alexander Scott Mearns. First appeared in the *Directory* in 1902 although they joined the AGA the year before. Alexander S. Mearns died in 1923 and his son Douglas A. Mearns took over.

Middleton & Milne, South Constitution Street.

Founding members of AGA in March 1888.

Alexander Milne & Co. /Imperial Granite Works, St Clair Street/ 124 West North Street

Alexander Milne, monumental work, Denburn, first appeared in the *Directory* in 1870. Two years later he was Alexander Milne & Co. Founding members of AGA in March 1888. Last appeared in the *Directory* in 1903.

Alexander Milne, builder

First appeared at Loanhead in 1874, moving to 130 Rosemount Place.

Built most of the houses in the Mile End area.

James K. Milne, University Road/St Peter Street/Regent Walk

First appeared in the *Directory* in 1903. Member of the AGA. In 1920 the partners were Charles Dorian and Alfred Milne. In 1925 Dorian went into business on his own.

Robert Milne, Blaikies Quay

First appeared in the *Directory* in 1900. Member of AGA. Died 1915, appearing in the *Directory* for the last time that year.

Adam Mitchell & Co. Builders/ John Morgan, 53 North Charlotte Street

Mitchell came from Kennethmont where his father had been a substantial farmer until ruined in a failed litigation with the laird. Mitchell himself was apprenticed to Macdonald & Leslie at the age of about 20. As an apprentice he worked on the pedestal for the statue of the Duke of Gordon in Aberdeen (*see Chapter 5*). Supposedly established about 1850, though he doesn't appear in the *Directory* until 1857. John Morgan joined his uncle as an apprentice in 1862 After Mitchell's death in 1877 Morgan ran the business in co-partnership with this uncle's trustees and later in his own right. Both men served on the City Council. Employed upwards of 150 men in 1890. Did a consider-able amount of work outside Aberdeen for John Fyfe including the granite work for the Glasgow

Municipal Buildings, the City Bank at Ludgate Hill in London, the first few floors of the Canadian Life Assurance Company in Toronto the White Stone Shipping Company Offices, Liverpool, the Royal Exchange Insurance Company Building, Liverpool. They built a huge number of prominent Aberdeen buildings, especially under Morgan. These including: Aberdeen Grammar School; Aberdeen Joint Station and the Denburn Railway; Corse House; Glenmuick House; Shannaburn House, Blairs; Kittybrewster School; St Ninian's Church; Marischal College – the greater part; Palace Hotel (later destroyed by fire) Douglas Hotel; Grand Hotel (now the Caledonian); Imperial Hotel (now the Carmelite); Mar Lodge; Melville Carden Place Church; Nazareth House; Northern Assurance Office, corner of Union Terrace; Northern Fire and Life Insurance Company Building; Queen's Cross Church; St James's Church, Union Street/Holburn Junction; spire of St Mary's Cathedral; housing in Queen's Road, Hamilton Place etc.; a block of three shops at ground level with flats above in St Swithin Street (1895); Isle of Man Banking Company; White Stone Shipping Company Offices, Liverpool (with John Fyfe); Royal Exchange Insurance Company Building, Liverpool (with John Fyfe).

James Adam Mitchell, granite merchant, Holland Street

Came from Premnay and served his apprenticeship as a stonecutter with his uncle Adam Mitchell. A cousin of John Morgan. Went to America for three years before going into business with Mr Dunn as Dunn & Mitchell. First listed on his own in the *Directory* in 1891. Involved in a serious dispute with the AGA in 1912 (see Chapter 10). When he died in November 1916 his son Alfred carried on the business. Alfred died in April 1948. J.A. Mitchell (Granite) Ltd., continued and were admitted as a member of the AGA in 1946 with manager James Younie as the representative. Still in business in 1958. Incorporated with James C. Hogg in 1963. Combined company ceased trading in 1976.

J. & J. Mitchell, Turning Co., Willowdale

First appeared in the *Directory* in 1883 at Broadford Place.

John Mitchell, 150 West North Street

First appeared in the *Directory* in 1881. Founding members of AGA in March 1888.

Morgan and Carnie/William Morgan, Clayhills/Portland Street

First appeared in the *Directory* in 1884. Founding members of AGA in March 1888.

Mainly monumental, statues, columns, headstones, shop fronts. Employed upwards of thirty men in 1890 in a yard that was 120ft by 62ft. William Morgan first appeared on his own in 1892. William Morgan died in December 1916, aged 66.

David Morren & Co., 5–9 Holland Street

Formed when Morren split from McKay & Morren c.1913, first appearing in the *Directory* that year. Still in business in 1958.

James Muiry, Clayhills

Muiry served his apprenticeship with J. & J. Ogg's Caledonian Granite Works. He started his own business c.1887, and first appeared in the *Directory* in 1892. The business was sold to John Robb by Muiry's trustees in 1899.

Mutch & Anderson, Claremount Street/Justice Mill Lane

First appeared in the *Directory* in 1887. Founding member of AGA in March 1888.

Alexander Nicol, monumental sculptor, **Claremont Granite Works**, Claremont Street
First appeared in the *Directory* with Peter Gerrie as Gerrie & Nicol in 1891. They separated in 1896 (*see entry under Gerrie*), with Nicol continuing at the original premises. At the time of his death in 1926 the AGA Minutes stated that he was an original member.

Norrie & McLaren, St Peter's Street
John McLaren was born on a croft between Dunecht and Lyne of Skene. Served his time as an apprentice mason and after working abroad joined Bower & Florence. Left to set up with Alec Norrie c.1913. The partnership was quite short-lived before McLaren re-joined Bower & Florence as a partner.

North of Scotland Granite Polishing Works, Peterhead

J. & J. Ogg, Clayhills/ 34 Wellington Road
First appeared in the *Directory* in 1868 at Holburn Street. Founding members of AGA in March 1888. John Ogg senior at Great Western Road, John Ogg, Abergeldie Road in the 1901 *Directory*. John Ogg died in 1909, aged 72. Succeeded by David Grant.

Alexander Petrie & Co., Bon-Accord Granite Polishing Works, Constitution Street
Originally in partnership with James Petrie, Alexander set up his own monumental and polishing works in Constitution Street in 1873. He advertised that year as having first-class machinery and working plant able to execute monumental and architectural work in fine axed or polished red, blue and grey granites. Last appeared in the *Directory* in 1880.

James Petrie & Co., Clayhills Granite Works, Clayhills/50 Wellington Road
James Petrie first appears in the *Directory* in 1850 at Union Bridge, presumably after splitting from James Wright. Shortly after in 1853 the company appears as Petrie & Co. Petrie's advertisement in the *Directory* states that they were established in 1840. Petrie died in 1882 but the firm continued as it was a founding member of AGA in March 1888.

Pittodrie Granite Turning Co. Ltd, 27 Merkland Road East
First appeared in the *Directory* in 1916. with James Singer as managing director. He had formerly been manager of the Aberdeen Granite Turning Company. Admitted as member of the AGMA in July 1947. Ceased trading in Aberdeen in 1973, with operations transferred to Glasgow.

James Pope & Son, Torry Granite Works/Whinhill Road
Pope came from Culsalmond and served his apprenticeship with MacDonald & Field. Spent a few years in America and then seems to have been in business with Alexander Dawson. In 1893 they seem to have separated and Pope established the Torry Granite Works, South Esplanade West. After three years he moved to Whinhill Road. He was later joined by his son James. Elected as Torry's first town councillor in 1891. Died in March 1927 aged 74. The company ceased trading in 1938.

David Porter, builder, St Peter Street
Lower Denburn Viaduct (Union Terrace to Schoolhill) 1889
Building in Canal Road for A. Milne & Sons, Provision Curers. (Porter used stone from his own quarry; *Ab Jo*, 22 April 1896, Granite Chips column.) Warehouse at Gilcomston Mills for J. Strachan & Sons, 1896; villa near New Bridge of Don 1896; Beechwood, 48 Rubislaw Den South for A. Wilson of Wilson & Morrice, Solicitors, 1896 (Brown & Watt architects).

Pringle & Slessor (William Pringle and Robert Slessor)

First appeared in the *Directory* in 1873 as builders at Thistle Lane. They later operated quarries at Tyrebagger and Little Clinterty. Built Holburn Street School; several houses in Rubislaw Den, including two for the architect William Kelly; extensions to Glen Dye House, 1896, using reddish local stone. Later became R. & S. Pringle, builders and granite merchants at 296 Hardgate.

James Rae & Son, Crown Granite Works, Park Road/King's Crescent

Rae served his apprenticeship with Bower & Florence and then set up McIntosh & Rae (see under McIntosh). When this was dissolved in 1887 he initially began on his own in Park Street before moving to King's Crescent where he had a small yard. He may have bought the name and machinery of Leslie Jamieson's Crown Granite Works at Charlotte Street when these were put up for sale in 1890, but he first appeared in the *Directory* in 1897 at King's Crescent. Member of AGA and later a director. He was also a director of Aberdeen Football Club. In 1913 Forbes Y. Rae, his son, was representative on AGA. James Rae died in April 1938. The firm closed in 1956.

Alexander Rainnie (or Rannie), Commerce Street

Thomas Rannie, mason, Thistle Street appeared in the *Directory* of 1825. Alexander Rannie, house carpenter, 10 Prince's Street, was in the 1828 *Directory*. The following year Alexander Rainnie, builder, Commerce Street was in the *Directory*. His name was also sometimes given as Rannie in later volumes of the *Directory*. As well as work outside the city he built many of Archibald Simpson's buildings in Aberdeen including the New Market (1840–42); Marischal College (at the time the largest contract ever undertaken in Aberdeen); East Church of St Nicholas; Mrs Emlsie's Institution (now Harlaw Academy); Woolmanhill Infirmary; Post Office near the top of Market Street (wright, plumbing, glazing and slating work only as Macdonald's did the mason work); North of Scotland Bank; Free Churches in Belmont Street; and the Blind Asylum for John Smith. He died in 1845 and a brief obituary appeared in the *Aberdeen Journal* Wednesday 16 April 1845. As well as listing most of these buildings it stated that he was involved with 'Almost every public edifice of any consequence that has been added to Aberdeen within the last ten years.' The business continued after his death under the same name, later becoming George C. Rainnie. Last appeared in the *Directory* in 1889.

Samuel Ramsay, Craigie Street/ 2 Jopp's Lane

First appeared in the *Directory* in 1880. Founding members of AGA in March 1888.

Nicholas Reilly (or Reilley), St Machar Drive/Great Northern Road

Hadden & Reilly first appeared in the *Directory* in 1892 at George Street and Charles Street. Reilly served his apprenticeship as a monumental mason at the Crown Granite Works, Charlotte Street. Reilly appeared on his own in 1893. Served five years as a councillor, 1905–10, and was also a JP. Known as the tallest man in the city (6ft 7½in). Died at the age of 50 in October 1915.

John O. Rettie/John C. Rettie/Laurelwood Granite Works, Merkland Road East

Rettie came from Rora and served his apprenticeship with George Stalker. He was in business on his own *c.*1913 when he is listed in the AGA Membership List. At some point he formed a partnership with Caie & Co., as Caie & Rettie. This partnership was dissolved in 1926 and Rettie began on his own at Laurelwood Granite Works, Merkland Road East. John died aged 58 in January 1931, and his obituary appeared in the *Press & Journal*. The business was continued by three of his children – Forbes, John and Elizabeth. It closed in 1969.

John Ritchie, Bloomfield Road

First appeared in the *Directory* in 1885. Founding member of AGA in March 1888.

John Robb, Crimon Place/Wellington Granite Works, Wellington Road

Robb came from Peterhead and first appeared in the Aberdeen *Directory* in 1891 at Crimon Place. In 1899 he expanded by buying the machinery and premises of James Muiry, also in Wellington Road. After he died in 1917 his son John carried on the business.

Alexander Robertson & Son/A. & J. Robertson (Granite) Ltd, St Clair Street/Great Western Road/Merkland Road

The full story of Robertson's is told by Diane Morgan in her history of the company. Alexander Robertson spent a brief time in America before establishing a short lived partnership with a Mr Gray in St Clair Street in 1876. After a couple of years Robertson had set up on his own at No. 259 King Street. By the late 1870s he had a second yard in St Clair Street. Alexander died suddenly in 1886, returning from Dancing Cairns Quarry. He was only 45. He was succeeded by his son George; three sons by Alexander's second marriage later also joined the company. Under George they were founding members of the AGA in March 1888. George also died quite young in 1905 at the age of 44, his half-brother William managing the company thereafter. Up to the Second World War the company was very small, with only two employees in 1936, both of them family members. Bought James Taggart in 1951 and moved their headquarters to their premises at 92 Great Western Road. Amalgamated with James Robertson and Son in 1963 to become A. & J. Robertson (Granite) Ltd. The new company was admitted to the AGA in June 1963. Subsequently took over other businesses. Today, as Roberton Granite it is the only surviving granite yard in Aberdeen, albeit just outside the city boundary, with retail branches throughout the country (see Chapter 14).

James Robertson & Son, Holburn Granite Works, Holburn Street/ Hardgate

Established in 1878 by James senior (first appearing in the *Directory* in 1879). Founding members of AGA in March 1888. James junior died in 1921 and was succeeded by his son William James with the name of the firm staying the same. William died in 1955 but the firm continued under his son, also William, and the firm eventually amalgamated with Alexander Robertson & Son in 1963.

Robertson & Hunter, Wellington Road.

Rubislaw Granite Company Limited

Established in 1889 to take over the running of Rubislaw Quarry from the Gibb Family (See Chapter 3). Still in business in 1958.

Ruddiman Brothers, Pittodrie Lane/Merkland Road East, **George Ruddiman jun.**, Claremont Street

Applied to become members of the AGA in February 1900, although they didn't appear in the *Directory* until 1904. Established by George Ruddiman and his brother David. In 1919 they split forming David Ruddiman at Merkland Road East and George Ruddiman & Son at 558A King Street. George visited America several times on granite business. He died in May 1925, aged 57. David Ruddiman still in business in 1951. By 1957 there was just D. Ruddiman Ltd., with J.R. Ruddiman as their representative on the AGA. The AGA Minutes record that the business closed in August 1981, though the company continued to appear in the *Directory* for a few years after that..

Rust & Alexander, Holland Street

James R. Rust was a farmer's son from Danestone. He came to Aberdeen in 1887 at the age of 14, and served his apprenticeship with Alexander Milne of the Imperial Granite Works, where he became foreman. At the age of 30 he became a partner in Rust & Alexander which applied to joint the AGA in March 1902. They later merged with Charles Macdonald Ltd., and Rust became a director and then managing director. He was also President of the Granite Manufacturer's Association. In 1914 he was elected to Aberdeen Town Council and was Lord Provost from 1928-32. He died in 1945.

Adam Scroggie, Spa Street

First appeared in the *Directory* in 1888. Built Skene Square School.

Robert Simpson/North British Granite Works, 237 Holburn Street

Robert Simpson came from Kintore. After serving his apprenticeship he went to America and was present at the building of the New York Post Office. On his return he was foreman for James Hunter. First appeared in the *Directory* at Gerrard Street in 1876. He bought the North British Works at 71 Constitution Street *c*.1881. Founding member of AGA in March 1888. He was elected to the Town Council in 1886. He died in February 1922 aged 75.

Simpson Brothers, 34 Cotton Street

George Simpson served his apprenticeship with James Wright. Went to America and worked on the Brooklyn Bridge. In 1881 he set up in Princes Street in partnership with his brother John. Another brother joined and they moved to Cotton Street. Mainly monumental work. Founding members of AGA in March 1888. John died in 1926.

Robert Singer, Robert Singer Turning Co, Nelson Street/Willowdale Place.

Came from Rayne and served his apprenticeship with James Wright & Son where he operated the new patent granite turning machine. He was said to have been the first man in the north-east to cut an urn using this machine. He stayed with Wright for ten years before setting up his own business with Robert Lawrence in Nelson Street. In 1882 he went into business on his own at Willowdale Place, West North Street. Specialised in urns and kept a note of how many he had made. By 1895 the total was 2,870. Founding members of AGA in March 1888. A small yard with around twelve men employed in 1890. His son Fred took over the business, eventually becoming F.W. Singer, and Robert died in 1903.

Robert Slessor jun., 300 Hardgate

Granite merchant and quarry owner, first appeared in the *Directory* in 1911.

Leslie Smith, builder and contractor, Skene Square.

Born at Couillie, Monymusk and came to Aberdeen *c*. 1877. Model Lodging House, East North Street; Electricity Works, Millburn Street; widening of Union Terrace; work for Caledonian Railway Company; houses in the West End; Peter Jamieson's factory, South College Street. Designed by Kelly & Nicol, architects 1904 (demolished). Died at his home 8 Rubislaw Den South in July 1907 aged 79. His son carried on the business.

Smith & Beattie, builders

Robert Smith was born in Monymusk in 1843 and served his apprenticeship with Francis Christie at Dunecht. He spent a year and a half in America and, on returning, began a business with Robert

Beattie. They first appeared in the *Directory* in 1878. They split up *c*.1886 and Smith carried on by himself. Among the buildings he built were the Free Churches of John Knox, Causewayend and Culter; part of the Marischal College extension; extension to Convent of the Sacred Heart at Queen's Cross; the north side of Hamilton Place West; the mason work for Alexander Wilson's new granite yard in Balmoral Road. Around 1884 Beattie went into business on his own (*see under Beattie*).

Smith & Taylor, Ashvale Place (William Smith and John Taylor)
Established 1884 at 240 King Street, moved to Ashvale Place in 1888. Founding members of AGA in March 1888. Employed upwards of 30 men in 1890 when their polishing mill had three polishing machines powered by gas. Mainly sculptural and monumental. By 1901 Smith was listed on his own at Ashvale Place.

Alexander Snowie, Maberly Street, Whinhill Road/Victoria Buildings, Leadside Road
First appeared in the *Directory* in 1884 at Maberly Street. In the 1893 AGA Membership List.

George M. Stalker see under Wilson & Stalker

Stewart & Co., Bon Accord Granite Works, George Street/35 Charles Street/21–49 Fraser Road. William Stewart came from Portlethen and served his apprenticeship with MacDonald, Field & Co. Spent several years in America before setting up in business as Stewart & Cruickshank in Gerrard Street. In 1885 he started on his own in Charles Street. Later moved to larger premises in Fraser Road. Founding member of AGA in March 1888. In 1915 the company became a private limited one. The company owned the Creetown Quarries in Kirkcudbrightshire. Three of his four sons were involved in the business. He died in June 1925 at the age of 77. William Stewart jun, served his time with his father before spending around six years in America. He died in April 1940 aged 56. They did the granite work for Lloyds Bank in London, the municipal buildings in Dundee and St Andrew's House in Edinburgh. Amalgamated with Bower & Florence, 1964.

James Still & Son, Duff Street
First appeared in the *Directory* in 1888. Founding members of AGA in March 1888.

George Stott/Stott & Warrender, King's Crescent/3 Merkland Road East
Stott & Warrender first appeared in the *Directory* in 1893 and were members of the AGA the same year. By 1896 Stott was listed on his own. Stott died in 1921 and was succeeded by his son Henry W. Stott.

Sutherland, Simpson & Co., Hutcheon Street West
Founding members of AGA in March 1888, though they don't appear in the *Directory* at that time.

James Taggart, 92 Great Western Road
James Taggart was born at Coldwells, Inverurie in 1849. He came to Aberdeen in 1865 and after his apprenticeship with Birnie & Stewart he spent some time in America. Although it is usually stated that he started his own business in 1881 with two or three assistants, in fact from 1880 onwards he is listed in the *Directory* as being in partnership with John McGregor (see separate entry). In 1883 Taggart and McGregor have split and Taggart is at Cuparstone Road. By 1890 he employed forty. The new office opened in 1896 was described as being constructed of rustic-dressed Rubislaw granite picked out with Kemnay granite dressings. In the front are piers in courses of Rubislaw and

Kemnay granite alternately, surrounded by a moulded cornice and pediment. The east gable had a polished slab of Peterhead granite with the Taggart's name and designation cut in large raised letters. An overhead travelling crane ran from one end of the yard to the other, and there was also a travelling crane running the length of the large stone cutting shed. The polishing mill had a Jenny Lind as well as a vertical polisher. The company executed the war memorial in Inver granite, designed by William Kelly, for men on the Balmoral estate at who died during the First World War.

Taggart was elected to the Town Council in 1899 and was Lord Provost from 1914–19. He was knighted in 1918 and died in 1929, his funeral procession being described as the longest ever seen in the city. Shortly before his death his son Harry had taken over the running of the business. Harry sold the business to Alexander Robertson & Son in 1951.

William Taggart & Son, Allenvale Granite Works

Taggart came from Coldwellls, Inverurie and came to Aberdeen at the age of 18. He served his apprenticeship with his uncle, James Taggart and then spent seven years in America before founding his own business in 1901, applying for membership of the AGA that same year. In 1921 his second son John Aberdein Taggart joined him in the business. William died in July 1929 aged 62, with John taking over the business. In 1935 he took his brother Charles Cameron into partnership. Their yard was firstly in Allenvale Road (north side where the cemetery is), then it moved to the Hardgate before returning to the south side of Allenvale Road next to the cemetery. The land was rented from the Town Council but they bought it from the Council in 1933 Still there in 1958.

In 1970 A. & J. Robertson bought the firm including their Fraserburgh Monumental Works. 1972 John Alexander Taggart let the yard at Allenvale to George Cassie & Sons.

Peter Tawse, building contractor

Born in Forfarshire *c.*1855. From 1870–83 he worked on building railways and waterworks, mainly in England. Became associated with Easton Gibb of the family who quarried Rubislaw. Came to Aberdeen in 1883 and was for three years manager of Rubislaw before moving to Kemnay where he was manager for ten years. Began on his own in 1896. Among the major projects he undertook were paving of Schoolhill and Rosemount Viaducts and Union Terrace. He also carried out work on the sewers, the electric subway, and the Torry and Ferryhill tramways. Outside the town he built the Dyce and Waterton Waterworks, and the Peterhead Waterworks. His largest contract was for the Girdleness Outfall Sewerage Scheme which took six years. After his death in 1907 his son William carried on the business.

Arthur Taylor, Jute Street

The business was founded around 1880, first appearing in the *Directory* that year Founding members of AGA in March 1888. It was the first yard to introduce pneumatic tools (see Chapter 4). One of the great granite sculpting yards, where James Philip carved the statue of King Edward VII which stands at the corner of Union Street and Union Terrace in Aberdeen (See Chapter 5). Taylor died in 1930 and Arthur Taylor jun. succeeded his father and carried it on until his death in November 1955. Ferguson Monument, Rothiemay designed by Kelly & Nicol, architects, 1907 Statue of Hygeia in Duthie Park; Peace Statue in Duthie Park's Winter Gardens; Aberdeen's War Memorial lion on Schoolhill; massive 17ft-high pedestal in Kemnay stone for statue (designed by

Alfred Drury) of Queen Victoria in Wellington, N.Z. 1903; even more massive pedestal for the Gladstone Memorial in Liverpool (designed by Sir Thomas Brock). 1903 – 22ft square in Kemnay stone, it was thought at the time to be the largest pedestal ever supplied by an Aberdeen yard.

John Taylor, Whinhill Road/ The Esplanade, Banks of Dee

Taylor came from Drumoak and was apprenticed to Wright & Sons, John Street. Had two spells in Australia, on one of them he engaged in digging for gold. First listed on his own in 1873 at Woolmanhill then Leadside and then at the Reclaimed Ground (in the area of what later became South Market Street/South Esplanade). He twice went to Australia. On returning in 1893 he opened a granite merchant's yard at Woolmanhill and later moved to Whinhill Road. Died in 1908 aged 66. Founding member of AGA in March 1888.

John L. Taylor, Great Western Road/29 Claremount Street

First appeared in the *Directory* in 1899. Member of AGA. Taylor died in 1929.

Taylor & Smith, *see Smith & Taylor*

Third, *see Gauld & Third*

George Thom, Albion Granite Works, Canal Road/39 Jute Street

First appeared in the *Directory* in 1881 at Canal Road, moving to Jute Street where he lived c.1884 Founding member of AGA in March 1888.

W. C. Townsend, Portland Street/Palmerston Road/1 Adelphi

First appeared in the *Directory* in 1886. Townsend was an American who ran a yard in Portland Street. They did a considerable trade with America and he subsequently gave up the yard and had the work done by other merchants. Townsend returned to America and W. Farquhar Pratt, who had started with the business as a junior clerk, became manager and later a partner. Pratt developed their trade with Australia, New Zealand and Canada. He also founded the British Granite and Marble Co., of which Townsend were partners. When a number of smaller merchants grew dissatisfied with the Aberdeen Granite Supply Company and formed a rival organisation, Pratt was managing director while it lasted. He died aged 50 in January 1923.

Watson & Robb Builders. Spring Garden.

Est 1829 by Robert Watson in Nelson Street. Joined by John Robb in 1864. Moved to Spring Garden in 1871. Employed twenty to thirty men in 1890. Worked on a number of castles, including Ballindalloch, Drumuir, Brucklay and Balmoral.

G. M. Watt & Son, Murray Terrace/Esplanade

Appeared in the *Directory* in 1891 as G.M. Watt & Co., at Portland Street. The following year they were at The Esplanade. May have ceased trading in 1896 when the Granite Chips column of 13 May records a sale of their machinery, stones and finished monuments.

David Weir, builder

Weir was from Chapel of Garioch and served his apprenticeship at Pitmedden before going to South Africa. Returned and set up his own business *c.* 1886. Built numerous large tenements and private houses in the city. Also built the Sacred Heart Roman Catholic Church in Torry. Did the mason's work for James Taggart's granite yard on Great Western Road. Member of the Aberdeen Master Masons' and Builders' Incorporation and a director of Aberdeen Football Club. Died in 1911.

Westland & Florence. Spital

John Westland and John Florence. First appeared in the *Directory* in 1865. Short-lived partnership (*see Bower & Florence for John Florence*). Westland became Westland & Anderson in Constitution Street.

Westhall Granite Polishing Works, Oyne

March 1862 sale at Westhall, Oyne, of machinery and other equipment belonging to late John Smith and Westhall Granite Polishing Works, including Bennachie and other polished granite obelisks (*Aberdeen Journal* 26 March 1861).

J. Whitehead & Sons, **The Granite Works**, Fraser Road/Union Chambers, Union Street

Succeeded one of the oldest granite yards, J. Fraser & Son, in 1888. As well as the granite works they had a quarry at Murdoch Head, Cruden and they took over the Overton Quarry at Dyce in the 1890s. Ceased business in 1897 when all their assets, included both quarries, were put up for sale. At the time they employed 300 to 400 men in their various sites. Although short lived a fine example of their work can be seen in the Wilson memorial in Fochabers, erected in 1895 and commemorating Major Allan Wilson who died in the Zulu Wars. The Gothic-style monument stands around 18ft high, in grey and red Peterhead granite.

Alexander G. Will & Son, 22 York Street, Prince Street Granite Works, Prince Street, both Peterhead

On AGA Membership List for 1913. First appears in the *Directory* in 1925. In business in 1958.

Alexander Wilson & Sons, Portland Street/Balmoral Road/Balmoral Granite Works

Established by Alexander Wilson, first appearing in the *Directory* in 1882. It was then taken over by his sons with Alexander jun. the main partner. Founding members of AGA in March 1888. Moved from Portland Street to new premises in 1900. These were described as two parallel buildings 100ft apart, each being 300ft long and 35ft broad. In one building there were two turning lathes, the largest, supplied by J.M. Henderson, capable of turning a column 12ft 6in x 2ft 6in; two polishing pendulums, one supplied by J. A. Sangster; above the lathes and pendulums a 7-ton travelling crane also by Sangster; the steam engine was one of the most powerful in a granite yard in the city, described as being 180hp and capable of carrying a boiler pressure of 100lbs, both the engine and boiler supplied by William McKinnon; for pneumatic tools there was an air compressor supplied by Carrick and Wordale of Gateshead, with attached accumulator supplied by G. & W. Martin, Regent Road, Aberdeen; two Jenny Linds and 13 vertical polishers with a 7-ton travelling crane above them; three polishing carriages, one supplied by McKinnon's having a bed of 24ft; and five granite saws supplied by Sangster's. The other building contained offices and drawing space as well as the dressing, carving and lettercutting shed. The latter contained pneumatic tool plant supplied from the other building. It included nineteen taps for pneumatic hammers, these being supplied by the American Pneumatic Tool Company of New York; five travelling cranes ranging from 2 to 7 tons supplied by Sangster's. Outside there was also a 10-ton steam crane with a 60ft jib, supplied by McKinnon's. The polishing mill and dressing shed were built of stone and lime with corrugated iron fronts and sliding doors. The slated roofs had 5ft-wide windows of thick plate glass to bring light in right along the building. The new works were to be known as the Balmoral Granite Works and employed around 100 men. James Singer was the manager *c.*1904 He would later be the managing director of firstly the Aberdeen Granite Turning Company and then the Pittodrie Granite

Turning Company. Alexander Wilson jun. died in May 1935. He had been a Town Councillor from 1905-1911 and also served on the Harbour Board. One of his sons, also Alexander, worked in the granite business and carried it on after his death. The company was still in business in 1958 at 39 Claremount Street.

Alexander J. Wilson, Regent Walk/Balgownie Granite Works, Merkland Road East /King Street
First appeared in the *Directory* in 1905 at Regent Walk. Members of AGA. On Wilson's death Alexander N. Robb became manager. Moved to 392 King Street *c*.1959. Ceased trading in 1975.

John S. Wilson, Portland Street
First appeared in the *Directory* in 1890 at Wellington Road.

Wilson & Stalker, monumental sculptors and polishers, **St Machar Granite Works**, 215 King Street/Jute Street
George M Stalker and Alexander Wilson. First appeared in the *Directory* in 1882, though Wilson may have been in business earlier. Founding members of AGA in March 1888. Wilson died in 1890 and Stalker carried on under his own name, moving to Jute Street at around the same time. Initially he kept the King Street yard as a show yard. George died in July 1936 but the business continued. Still in business in 1958.

Wishart Brothers/Wishart & Bruce, St Peter Street
First appeared in the *Directory* in 1908 as Wishart Brothers, sculptors, rather than under granite stonecutters (John and Thomas). John is listed in the 1910 AGA Membership List. Moved to Inverurie in 1923 when they left the AGA.

J. Wishart & Son, 1A Canal Road
First appeared in the *Directory* in 1884. Founding members of AGA in March 1888.

John Wood, 367 King Street/ Jasmine Terrace/Merkland Road East
First appeared in the *Directory* in 1879. Founding members of AGA in March 1888.

Alexander Hunter Wright, 90 Crown Street
Born in Aberdeen, Wright was apprenticed to Councillor James Hunter's yard in King Street. Spent six years in America on Dix Island and at Quincy, before returning to work for William Keith. Set up his own business in Windmill Lane, first appearing in the *Directory* in 1888, and moved to Crown Street four years later. Gibb Brothers bought his business from the trustees for his creditors in 1910, though Wright may still have been trading.

James Wright & Sons, John Street Polished Granite & Marble Works/John Street Granite Works/Royal Granite Works
Supposedly established in 1835, I have not been able to confirm this. A John Wright, quarrier, appears in the *Directory* in 1835, as does James Wright of Wright & Petrie, stonecutters, in 1839. (see also under Petrie whose later advertisements state that Petrie's were established in 1840) John Morgan in page 116 of his memoirs named Wright & Petrie as the first granite yard to be established after Macdonald's, and says that they had previously been freestone masons. James Wright first appears on his own in 1850, at John Street, where they would be based for more than 120 years. This date is also given in a letter to the Scotsman in 22 September 1866. Wright exhibited at the Great Exhibition in 1851 and received an honourable mention for a granite headstone. James built himself a lovely cottage-style house on Mount Street, Rosemount. It has polished Stirlinghill gran-

ite round the windows and doors, with two other types of granite, described at the time as unhewn Dyce and Grandholm (probably Persley), though one of them may have been from Sylavethie which they operated from around that time. He would have been within easy walking distance of his works in John Street. James was joined by his two sons William and Frederick in 1876, though James died the same year. They operated the Syllavethie Quarry as well one at Peterhead and two at Stirlinghill. In 1890 the yard site occupied two acres and at the yard and the quarries they employed upwards of 220 men. They had a special appointment to the Queen, they first added *To Her Majesty* to the company name in 1864, becoming the Royal Granite Works in 1885. The firm did monumental and architectural work including contracts in London and elsewhere. One major example of their work in London was the polished granite front for the Union Bank of Australia in Cornhill in 1894. (see Chapter 8) They also supplied granite for the Home and Colonial Office and the Royal Courts of Justice Chambers. In 1927 Frederick Wright was involved in a dispute with the Aberdeen Granite Manufacturers' Association which led to his expulsion. He was readmitted in 1931 (see Chapter 10). Frederick died in 1932, aged 87, and was succeeded by his son Alfred. In 1955 his grandson Michael O'Connor joined the firm eventually becoming Managing Director. He was twice elected as President of the AGA in the 1970s. The firm ceased trading the following year by which time the workforce was twenty-four.

NOTES

Abbreviations

Ab. Jo.	*Aberdeen Journal*
AGA Min.	Aberdeen Granite Association Minutes
AGMA Min.	Aberdeen Granite Manufacturers' Association
Co. Reg.	Aberdeen Council Register
EE	*Aberdeen Evening Express*
FP	*Aberdeen Free Press*
QMJ	*Quarry Managers' Journal*
P&J	*Aberdeen Press and Journal*
RC	Royal Commission
SA	Statistical Account

Endnotes

Introduction

1 In Lallans No. 5, 1975; also quoted in Grampian Hairst, AUP, 1981
2 Knight, p.60
3 Macpherson, 1895, p.72
4 Simpson, Augustinian Priory, p.56
5 Macpherson 1895 p.72

Chapter 1

1 I.e the Provost and Baillies engaged a cassay maker to make and repair all the streets and causeways of the burgh.
2 Stuart, Extracts from the Council Register, p.164
3 Council Register 1603
4 Ibid. 9 June 1731
5 Ibid. 17 August 1741
6 Ibid.
7 Douglas, p.74

8   Robert Gordon's Hospital Annual Accounts 1731–32
9   Diack, *Rise and Progress*, p.26
10   Fenton Wyness, *Spots from the Leopard*, Aberdeen, Impulse Books, 1971, p.136
11   Rettie, p.20
12   Douglas, p.131
13   Keith, p.127
14   Ab. Jo. 4 December 1805
15   Council Register 17 January 1741
16   Ibid. 11 June 1741
17   Ibid. 7 June and 9 June 1788
18   Ab. Jo. 17 May 1791
19   Keith, p.54
20   First SA, Vol. VII, p.203
21   Knight, p.74
22   Council Register 26 March and 27 March 1766
23   David Menzies, letter, 1770
24   First SA, Vol. XIX, pp.157–8
25   Ibid., Vol. VI p.38
26   Ab. Jo. 11 June 1906
27   Patrick Morgan, p.213
28   MS 2253/8, Letter from Robert Mylne to James Forbes, 14 December 1794
29   First SA, Vol. VII p.203
30   Ibid., Vol. XVI p.558, p.614
31   Ibid., Vol. XV p.292-3
32   MS1160/3/13, Account book of James Rankin

Chapter 2

1   Ab. Jo. 16 June 1800
2   Ibid. 27 March 1811
3   Quote by Walmesley, engineer, in a lecture he gave to the Dover Working Men's Institute, repeated in the Granite Chips column of the Ab. Jo., 22 April 1896
4   Fyfe Archive 57/A/30/4
5   Ab. Jo. 6 May 1788
6   Ibid. 22 December 1800
7   *The Times* 15 April 1818
8   *Caledonian Mercury* 16 May 1807
9   Ab. Jo. 30 March 1808
10   *Ipswich Journal* 26 May 1810; *Caledonian Mercury* 13 July 1818
11   McLaren, p.95
12   Harris, p.69
13   Kennedy, Vol. II, p.213
14   Ab. Jo. 17 February 1802
15   Aberdeen Improvements Act 1795
16   Ab. Jo. 31 August 1803
17   Knight, p.66
18   Thom, p.187
19   *Aberdeen Chronicle* 4 March, 7 March, 4 April, 2 May 1818
20   Farmer, p.15
21   G.M. Fraser, *Archibald Simpson*, Chapter VI
22   *Aberdeen Constitutional* 28 August 1840
23   *The Architect*, 1872, reported in Ab. Jo. 3 July 1872
24   Robertson, p.196

Chapter 3

1	From *Building News* quoted in Ab. Jo. 19 December 1866
2	Ab. Jo. 17 September 1845
3	James Skene Archive MS2720/37
4	James Skene Archive MS2720/37, 2720/38
5	James Skene Archive 2720/30
6	James Skene Archive MS 2720/131
7	Minutes of the Proceedings of the ICE, Vol. 10, January 1851, pp.82–5
8	Knight p.57
9	Prospectus of Rubislaw Granite Company, 1889, in Fyfe Archive DD57/B/1
10	Ab. Jo. 16 December 1889
11	F.A. MacDonald Archive MS 2626/1 Box 23.1
12	Ibid.
13	Ibid.
14	Ab. Jo. 26 December 1899
15	Institution of Mechanical Engineers p.829
16	P&J 2 December 1967
17	Harris p.86
18	Ab. Jo. 7 July 1869
19	Douglas W. Gray: *Cove Bay: A History*, Koo Press, 2008, p.124
20	Fyfe Archive DD57/A/16
21	Douglas W. Gray: *Cove Bay: A History*, Koo Press, 2008, p.125
22	P&J 4 February 1927
23	P. Morgan p.213
24	Forbes of Seaton Archive MS 2253/8/29/53
25	Forbes of Seaton Archive MS 2253/8/30
26	Ab. Jo. 28 April 1830
27	Knight p.57
28	Fergusson, letter in Ab. Jo. 9 February 1895
29	Ab. Jo. 19 July 1837
30	Ab. Jo. 1 February and 15 February 1865
31	Ab. Jo. 14 February 1866
32	Harris p.71
33	P&J 12 November 1924
34	EE 21 August 1953
35	P. Morgan p.213
36	Knight p.58
37	Ab. Jo. 12 October 1907
38	Fraser's Notebooks, Vol. 53, p.238
39	Ab. Jo. 27 April 1803
40	Fraser's Notebooks, Vol. 50, p.138
41	P. Morgan p.196
42	Ritchie p.302
43	Ab. Jo. 10 March 1897
44	Diack: *Rise and Progress* p.40
45	Ab. Jo. 11 June 1906
46	Ab. Jo. 10 September 1770
47	Council Register, Vol. 71, 5 December 1826
48	Ab. Jo. 10 December 1798
49	Ab. Jo. 16 June 1800
50	Council Register, November 1826

51   Knight pp.58–9
52   Ab. Jo. 6 November 1906
53   FP 18 January 1861
54   Building News, quoted in Ab. Jo. 19 December 1866
55   Ab. Jo. 24 December 1912
56   Diack: *Rise and Progress* p.40
57   First SA, Vol. 4, p.451
58   Second SA, Vol. 11, p.180
59   Elizabeth M.B. Hay: *Cults: The Evolution of a Village*, SWRI, 1955, pp.19–20
60   Ibid. p.33
61   Council Register 17 December 1767
62   Ab. Jo. 18 March 1788
63   Ibid. 3 October 1810
64   Knight p.64
65   P&J 4 October 1934
66   FP 25 December 1894
67   Ab. Jo. 22 December 1890
68   Ibid. 17 January 1900
69   Grant p.22
70   Ab. Jo. 22 June 1898
71   Personal communication from Sir Archibald Grant, April 2014
72   Fyfe Archive 57/A/6
73   Ab. Jo. 29 July and 8 September 1896
74   Ibid. 29 July 1896
75   Knight p.59
76   Ab. Jo. 15 October 1902
77   Ritchie: *Aberdeen Granite Trade*, p.302
78   Reprinted in Ab. Jo. 6 January 1869
79   Harris pp.73–4
80   Ab. Jo. 2 August 1878 and 12 May 1882
81   Ibid. 1 April 1896
82   Ibid.
83   Ibid. 12 May 1882
84   Ibid. 12 September 1889
85   Ibid. 20 September 1899
86   Ibid. 10 August 1898
87   Ibid. 26 June 1895
88   Ibid. 2 October 1861
89   Ibid. 5 October 1902
90   EE 27 May 1954
91   Ab. Jo. 15 October 1902
92   Personal communication from Dunan Downie
93   Ab. Jo. 12 February 1896
94   Ibid. 12 August 1896
95   Diack: *Rise and Progress*, p.50
96   Knight p.59–60
97   Second SA, Vol XII, p.562
98   Ibid. p.636
99   Ian Carter: 'The Raid on Bennachie' in *Bennachie Again*, A.W.M. Whiteley ed., p.119
100   A G Fordyce: 'The Mystery of the Lintel Quarry' in *Bennachie Again* p.152
101   Personal communication from Sir Archibald Grant, April 2015
102   Second SA, Vol. XII, p.442

103   Ab. Jo. 1 August 1877
104   Ibid. 22 May 1895
105   Grant p.22
106   First SA, Vol. XVI, pp.558, 614
107   Buchan p115–16
108   Grant p.6
109   Knight pp.61–2
110   Pratt p.72
111   Ab. Jo. 30 November 1859
112   *Buchan Observer* 6 January 1903
113   Ab. Jo. 12 July 1865
114   Diack: *Rise and Progress*, p.65
115   FP 25 December 1894
116   Ab. Jo. 23 August 1894
117   Grant p.7
118   Ab. Jo. 23 August 1894
119   Ibid. 10 August 1898
120   EE 2 January 1883 and 6 June 1884
121   Ab. Jo. 23 February 1883
122   Grant p.23
123   P&J 18 August 1923
124   Ibid. 13 February 1928
125   First SA, Vol. XV, pp.292–3
126   Pratt pp.376–7
127   Ab. Jo. 16 February 1803
128   Pratt p.124
129   QMJ, Vol XIV, No. 2, 5 May 1931
130   P&J 27 February 1939
131   Ab. Jo. 3 April 1883

Chapter 4

1   Anderson: *General View*, pp.18–19
2   Wilson: *Granite in its Industrial and Commercial Aspects*, pp.161–2
3   Anderson: *General View*, pp.28–31
4   'The granite quarries and polishing works of Aberdeen', from the *Scotsman*, reprinted in Ab. Jo. 6 January 1869; Harris p.118; Ab. Jo. 13 May 1896)
5   Knight p.67
6   Extract from *The Leisure Hour*, 1 March 1860 in Fyfe Archive 57/A/30/2
7   Knight p.67
8   Ibid pp.66–7; *Saturday Magazine* 2 March 1844
9   Ab. Jo. 25 April 1866
10   Wilson: *Granite in its Industrial and Commercial Aspects*, p.161
11   Knight pp.62–3
12   Ab. Jo. 31 July and 28 October 1886
13   Wilson: *Granite in its Industrial and Commercial Aspects*, p.162
14   Jeffrey p.259
15   P&J 7 May 1924
16   Fyfe Archive 57/A/27/2
17   QMJ April 1926, p.303
18   FP 6 April 1922
19   QMJ October 1933, pp.240–2

20	Harris p.74
21	Donnelly: *Aberdeen Granite Industry*, p.33
22	Diack: *Romance of the Blondin*
23	Ab. Jo. 21 May 1903
24	Ibid. 17 July 1872 and 5 March 1873
25	Wilson: *Granite in its Industrial and Commercial Aspects*, p.163
26	*Elgin Courant* 18 April 1856
27	Ab. Jo. 25 April 1866
28	John Morgan: *Memoirs* p.115
29	FP 1856, reprinted in *Elgin Courant* 18 April 1856
30	Ab. Jo. 25 June 1873
31	*Builder*, Vol. XXXV, No.1810, 13 October 1877, pp.1019–20
32	Wilson: *Granite in its Industrial and Commercial Aspects*, p.164
33	Ab. Jo. 11 October 1896
34	Russell p.35
35	Grant p.7
36	FP 20 December 1888
37	Wilson: *Granite in its Industrial and Commercial Aspects*, p.163
38	FP 10 October 1895
39	Ab. Jo. 28 November 1895
40	Ibid. 8 November 1899
41	Ibid. 24 November 1902
42	Personal communication
43	Ab. Jo. 23 September 1896
44	Ibid. 24 November 1902
45	Allardyce October 1905
46	Ab. Jo. 24 November 1902
47	*People's Journal* 9 September 1905
48	Institution of Mechanical Engineers pp.816–17
49	Ab. Jo. 22 June 1896
50	Ibid. 26 February 1896
51	Ibid. 12 June 1901
52	Ibid. 27 May 1896

Chapter 5

1	Ab. Jo. 16 September 1896
2	First SA, Vol. XVI, p.558
3	Ibid. p.38
4	Knight pp.67–8
5	Ab. Jo. 10 March 1824
6	Obituary in Ab. Jo. 28 March 1860
7	Ab. Jo. 1 October 1894
8	FP 27 and 28 November 1873
9	Gray p.483
10	Marjorie Caygill: *The Story of the British Museum*, 3rd ed., 2002, p.72
11	David M. Wilson: *The British Museum: A History*, 2002
12	Knight pp.71–2
13	James H. Willson: *The Bon Accord Repository*, 1842, pp.176–7
14	Gray pp.483–4
15	John Morgan: *Memoirs* p.173
16	*Aberdeen Herald* 7 November 1846

17   Friends of Norwood Cemetery Newsletter, No. 73, January 2012
18   Ab. Jo. 23 October 1895
19   Pratt pp.376–7
20   *Aberdeen Herald* 23 September 1854
21   Ab. Jo. 17 July 1861
22   *Building News* 1866, quoted in Ab. Jo. 19 December 1866
23   Diack: *Rise and Progress* p.59
24   Ab. Jo. 23 April 1862
25   Ibid. 3 April 1867
26   Fenton Wyness: *Aberdeen: Century of Change*, Impulse Books, 1971, il.150)
27   Harriet Beecher Stowe: *Sunny Memoirs of Sunny Lands*, Letter VI
28   FP 1856, reprinted in *Elgin Courant* 18 April 1856
29   Ab. Jo. 13 May 1896
30   John Morgan: *Memoirs* p.115)
31   William Carnie: *Reporting Reminiscences*, Vol I, AUP, 1902, p.373
32   Obituary in Ab. Jo. 29 December 1884
33   John Morgan: *Memoirs* p.114
34   From *Danbury News*, reprinted in Ab. Jo. 6 January 1875
35   Ab. Jo. 15 May 1895
36   Ibid. 17 July 1861
37   Ibid.
38   Ibid. 23 April 1862
39   Ibid. 22 July 1898
40   *Aberdeen Herald* 11 October 1856
41   *Scotsman* 25 and 29 August and 22 September 1866
42   Ab. Jo. 4 February 1880
43   AGA Min. 29 March 1893
44   Ab. Jo. 18 August 1858
45   Ibid. 7 September 1897
46   Donnelly: *Structural and Technical Change*
47   Ab. Jo. 7 June 189
48   Findlay pp.303–4
49   EE 3 May 1883
50   P&J 28 February 1933
51   Ab. Jo. 4 April 1892
52   *The Times* 16 and 22 January 1935
53   James H. Wilson: *The Bon Accord Repository*, 1842, p.177
54   Ab. Jo. 19 October 1842
55   Bulloch: *Last of his Line*
56   Ab. Jo. 9 February 1895
57   Ibid. 19 October 1842
58   Ibid. 24 April 1844
59   Bulloch: *Last of his Line*
60   Ab. Jo. 25 November 1895
61   Ibid. 14 December 1895
62   Letter to Ab. Jo. 18 December 1895
63   Ab. Jo. 5 March 1906
64   Ibid. 1 July 1909
65   Ibid. 26 July 1910
66   Ibid. 30 March 1911
67   Ibid. 11 December 1911
68   P&J 10 September 1934

69	EE 14 September 1951; *Stone Traders Journal* Sep–October 1941 pp.110–13
70	Ab. Jo. 1 April 1902
71	Ibid. 30 April 1908
72	Ibid. 8 April 1909
73	Ibid. 25 November 1903 and 6 April 1907
74	*Bon Accord* and *Northern Pictorial* 12 April 1930
75	*Bon Accord* 31 August 1929

Chapter 6

1	*The Builder*, Vol XXX, No. 1810, 11 October 1877, p.1019
2	McLaren, p.24
3	RC, Vol. 2, p.5
4	*Bon Accord* 21 May 1953
5	Spence, p.5
6	*Bon Accord* 4 August 1938
7	Ritchie April 1926 p.303
8	Ibid.
9	Ibid.
10	Brian Innes, personal communication
11	RC, Vol. 2, p.2
12	Ab. Jo. 15 March 1826
13	First SA, Vol. VII, p.203
14	Diack: *Rise and Progress*, p.31
15	Ritchie, April 1926, p.302
16	Ibid. p.304
17	Ibid.
18	QMJ December 1934
19	Ibid. November 1933 p.267
20	QMJ 1930–31 p.148–9
21	Fyfe Archive 57/A/27/2
22	McLaren p.7
23	QMJ March 1933 p.401
24	Quoted in *Operative Mason's Journal* August 1901
25	Ab. Jo. 23 October 1895
26	P&J 26 September 1927
27	Morgan: *Memoirs* p.24
28	Ibid.
29	McLaren, p.9–10
30	Quoted in Boddie's obituary in Ab. Jo. 25 April 1917
31	Interviewed in 2009
32	AGA Minutes 30 August 1955
33	*Riverfront Times*, St Louis, 16 August 2000
34	Interviewed January 2015
35	RC, Vol. 2, p.2
36	McLaren, p.21
37	Mackie: *Story with a Picture*
38	Interviewed January 2015
39	Ab. Jo. 8 March 1826
40	Ab. Jo. 7 July 186
41	'The Granite Trade in Aberdeen' in *The Scotsman* 2 August, 25 August, 11 September and 22 September 1866

42   Brian Innes, personal communication
43   EE 22 October 1953
44   Duncan Downie, personal communication
45   Morgan: *The Spital Lands*, p.235
46   Ab. Jo. 19 April 1880
47   AGA Min. May 1889
48   Beveridge, p.490
49   Ab. Jo. 1 June 1895
50   Ab. Jo. 10 October 1892
51   Ibid. 5 May 1895
52   Ibid. 23 October 1895
53   Ibid. 4 November 1863
54   Morgan: *Memoirs*, p.75
55   Ab. Jo. 25 January, 3 February and 29 February 1896
56   Robert Gordon's College Minutes, 30 November 1896, p.7.
57   AGA Min. 3 February, 11 February, 16 June and 14 October 1896
58   Ab. Jo. 20 July 1898
59   Ibid. 26 December 1899
60   Ibid. 20 April 1905
61   Hamilton, p.197
62   McLaren, p.17
63   AGA Min. 16 May 1966, 22 September 1976

Chapter 7

1   Ab. Jo. 27 February 1878
2   *Free Press* 31 December 1884
3   Morgan: *Memoirs* p.72
4   Ab. Jo. 22 February 1879
5   Ibid. 4 February 1880
6   Morgan: *Memoirs* p.51
7   Diack: *Rise and Progress* p.47
8   Fyfe Archive 57/A/19
9   Co. Reg. 1863 pp.179, 181
10   Ab. Jo. 15 May 1877
11   Wilson: *Aberdeen of Auld Lang Syne*, p.61
12   Ab. Jo. 30 April 1877
13   Ibid. 7 May 1877
14   FP 17 May 1877
15   Ab. Jo. 15 May 1877
16   FP 4 May 1877
17   Ab. Jo. 23 May 1877
18   Ibid. 4 July 1881
19   Lord Henry Cockburn: *Circuit Journeys*, Edinburgh, D. Douglas, 1888, p.45
20   Ab. Jo. 15 February 1843
21   *Aberdeen Herald* 14 September 1844
22   *Bradford Observer* 31 October 1844
23   Harriet Beecher Stowe: *Sunny Memoirs of Sunny Lands*, Letter VII
24   *Illustrated London News*, 28 March 1857
25   Ab. Jo. 3 July 1872
26   Ibid. 12 and 19 December 1866
27   Ibid. 18 October 1865

28   From *Danbury News*, reprinted in Ab. Jo. 6 January 1875
29   Ab. Jo. 29 September 1877
30   Ibid. 3 August 1898
31   see Donnelly: *The Aberdeen Granite Industry* p.41, for example
32   FP 1856, reprinted in *Elgin Courant* 18 April 1856
33   From *Danbury News*, reprinted in Ab. Jo. 6 January 1875
34   'New Philadelphia Churches' in *The Art Journal*, Vol. 3 (1877), pp.337–9
35   FP 21 December 1884
36   AGA Min. February/March 1893
37   Ab. Jo. 27 December 1894
38   FP 25 December 1894
39   Ab. Jo. 7 May 1900
40   Ibid. 26 July 1910
41   Ibid. 29 July 1896
42   Ibid. 1 April 1896
43   P&J 17 April 1985
44   EE 13 April 1886
45   Ibid. 17 February 1887
46   Hoffman p.22)
47   Fyfe Archive 57/A/27/2
48   Ab. Jo. 18 December 1895
49   Ibid. 4 February 1880
50   Ibid. 29 December 1888
51   Ibid. 4 April 1888
52   Ibid. 29 December 1888
53   FP 31 December 1884
54   Ibid.
55   Ab. Jo. 8 November 1899
56   Ibid. 1 November 1899
57   Ibid. 15 May 1895
58   Ibid. 27 December 1894
59   EE 3 October 1893
60   Ab. Jo. 27 December 1894
61   Ibid. 22 May 1895
62   Ibid. 4 December 1894
63   Ibid. 26 February 1896
64   McLaren p.26
65   Hamilton p.195
66   McLaren p.18
67   Grant p.9
68   FP 31 December 1884
69   AGA Min., 2 February 1916
70   Ab. Jo. 29 December 1888
71   EE 10 December 1894
72   Ab. Jo. 12 April 1896
73   Ibid. 19 June 1895
74   *Evening Gazette* December 1903
75   Hamilton, p.197
76   *People's Journal* 9 September 1905
77   AGA Min. 17 March 1913
78   Obituary in EE 27 April 1951
79   Hamilton, p.198

80   Diack: *Rise and Progress* p.77
81   Knight p.69
82   Ab. Jo. 19 December 1866
83   Ibid. 23 December 1898 and 26 December 1899
84   'Old Time Mason' in QMJ, Vol. 13, 1930–31, p.148
85   Ab. Jo. 26 December 1899
86   Diack: *Rise and Progress* p.79
87   EE 16 January 1926
88   Ab. Jo. 8 July 1896
89   QMJ, Vol. 13, 1930–31, pp.148–9
90   Diack: *Rise and Progress*, p.80, original quote by Macartney from *Municipal Engineering*, 15 April 1937
91   Ab. Jo. 23 December 1898
92   Ibid. 23 September 1891
93   Ibid. 11 June 1906
94   Ibid. 17 September 1903
95   Ibid. 23 December 1898
96   Ibid. 26 December 1899
97   Ab Jo. 13 July 1907
98   Ibid. 24 December 1912

Chapter 8

1   Ab. Jo. 25 June 1878
2   Ibid. 7 September 1877
3   Ibid. 23 and 27 February 1878
4   Ibid. 3 August 1880
5   Ibid. 7 May 1881
6   Ibid. 3 November 1898
7   Ibid. 19 June 1895
8   Ibid. 2 September 1896
9   Ibid. 21 May 1903
10   Ibid. 24 October 1900
11   Ibid. 24 April 1903
12   Ibid. 6 February 1903

Chapter 9

1   Morgan: *Memoirs* p.2
2   Ibid. p.4
3   Obituary in Ab. Jo. 4 July 1907
4   Morgan: *Memoirs*, p.23
5   Ibid. p.66
6   Ibid. p.240
7   Ibid. p.63
8   *In Memoriam* 1907 pp.109–16
9   Morgan: *Memoirs*, pp.171–2
10   Ibid. p.3
11   John Betjeman, in a talk given on the BBC Third Programme on 28 July 1947, following a visit to Aberdeen in May that year.
12   *The Architect* 30 October 1891
13   Ab. Jo. 21 February 1898
14   FP 24 September 1906

15   Ab. Jo. 17 March 1898
16   Ibid. 12 October 1895
17   Ibid. 17 September 1895
18   In Lys Wyness: *A Celebration of Marischal College*, Aberdeen, 2011, p.57
19   Ab. Jo. 27 September 1899
20   FP 24 September 1906
21   P&J 25 March 1937
22   Ab. Jo. 8 December 1905
23   Ibid. 28 September 1906
24   FP 24 September 1906
25   Quoted in Ab. Jo. 14 September 1906
26   FP 26 September 1906
27   Ab. Jo. 28 August 1906
28   Ibid. 26 June 1937
29   Ibid.
30   *Architect's Journal*, 12 February 1975
31   Ab. Jo. 15 October 1906
32   FP 24 September 1906

Chapter 10

1   Ab. Jo. 4 April 1888
2   AGA Min., December 1887
3   Ibid. June 1891
4   Ibid. 20 May 1892
5   Ibid. July 1891
6   *In Memoriam* 1892 p.157
7   AGA Min. 4 June 1913
8   Ibid. 13 August 1913
9   Ibid. 26 March 1914
10   Ab. Jo. 29 December 1888
11   Ibid. 1 December 1905, 6 and 7 February 1906, 12 May 1906 and 9 August 1906
12   AGA Min. 28 April 1909
13   Ibid. 2 November 1910
14   Ibid. 19 May 1910
15   Ibid. 10 November 1911
16   Ibid. 27 September 1912
17   Ab. Jo. 10 October 1912
18   AGA Min. 16 October 1912
19   Ab. Jo. 26 December 1912
20   Ibid. 1 October 1912
21   AGA Min. 8 January 1913
22   Ibid. 14 January 1913
23   Ibid. 27 November 1913
24   Ibid. 28 January 1925
25   Ibid. 14 May 1925
26   Ibid. 6 August 1925
27   Ibid. 9 January, 11 March and 21 April 1926
28   P&J 24 July and 25 November 1926, and 18 August 1927
29   AGMA Min. 26 October 1927
30   P&J 28 October 1927
31   AGMA Min. 3 September, 2 and 30 October 1936

32	*Bon Accord & Northern Pictorial* 6 January 1938 p.20
33	McLaren, p.32
34	AGA Min. 11 November 1952
35	Ibid. 27 January 1953
36	Ibid. 3 February 1953
37	Ibid. 10 February 1953
38	Ibid. 13 August 1974

Chapter 11

1	Ab. Jo. 24 October 1768
2	Ibid. 16 October 1769
3	Ibid. 3 March 1780
4	Ibid. 17 May 1796
5	Jeffrey, p.260
6	Ab. Jo. 20 April 1827
7	Ibid. 17 November 1884
8	Ibid. 24 November 1869
9	Ibid. 6 September 1876
10	Ibid. 31 July and 28 October 1886
11	Ibid. 22 April and 24 November 1893
12	Ibid. 29 January and 4 April 1890
13	Donnelly: *Aberdeen Granite Industry* p.132
14	Ab. Jo. 20 September 1912
15	P&J 23 August 1929
16	Ibid. 29 August 1935
17	*Elgin and Morayshire Courier*, 9 September 1853
18	McLaren, p. 80
19	Morgan: *Memoirs*, p.214
20	*Stonecutters Journal* October 1910
21	Ab. Jo. 12 July 1871
22	Ibid. 26 February 1868
23	McLaren, p.26
24	Ab. Jo. 27 July 1898
25	AGA Min. 15 June 1913
26	*Royal Commission*, Vol. I, p.252
27	Ibid. p.255
28	AGA Min. 14 April 1939
29	P&J 26 June 1929
30	AGA Min. 16 March 1916
31	Ibid. 6 August 1918
32	Beveridge p.490
33	AGA Min. 12 June 1906
34	Ibid. 2 October 1912
35	*Royal Commission*, Vol. II, p.4
36	Ab. Jo. 8 August 1913
37	AGA Min. 7 January 1914
38	Ab. Jo. 20 December 1913
39	Ibid. 12 July 1918
40	P&J 4 April 1925
41	Ibid. 21 November 1928
42	Ibid. 19 January 1931

43	Ibid. 15 June 1931
44	AGA Min. 20 April 1945
45	Mair, p.479
46	P&J 5 August 1950
47	Ibid.
48	AGA Min. 18 April 1951
49	Ibid. 21 January 1953
50	EE 7 June 1955
51	McLaren p.77
52	EE 16 June 1955
53	McLaren p77
54	AGA Min. 14 November 1956
55	Ibid. 5 July 1963
56	Ibid. 11 March 1965
57	Lloyd Davies p.227

Chapter 12

1	Miller p15
2	Ebenezer Bain: *Merchant and Craft Guilds: A History of the Aberdeen Incorporated Trades*. Aberdeen, Edmond & Spark 1887, p.59 and 118; Munro
3	*The Architect*, 30 December 1877, pp.406–8
4	William Diack: *History of Trades Council*, Aberdeen Trades Council, 1939, p.132
5	Ab Jo. 18 January 1837
6	Diack: *Trades Council*, p.133
7	Ab. Jo. 30 July 1845
8	Ibid. 13 and 20 August 1845
9	P&J 30 July 1934 article by William Diack: 'Masons' Hundred Years of Peace and War'
10	FP 13 October 1868
11	Ibid. 24 November 1868
12	Ibid. 22 December 1868
13	Ibid. 20 November 1868
14	Ab. Jo. 11 November 1868
15	FP 13 October 1868
16	Ibid. 6 November 1868
17	Ibid. 22 December 1868
18	Ibid. 8 December 1868
19	William Carnie: *Reporting Reminiscences*, Vol II, Aberdeen University Press 1904, p.353
20	John Morgan: *Memoirs*, p.50
21	*Aberdeen, Banff and Kincardine People's Journal*, 23 April 1864
22	Ab. Jo. 14 October 1868; 31 August 1870; 13 March 1872
23	Ibid. 15 January 1873
24	Ibid. 23 May 1877
25	Ibid. 28 May 1877
26	Ibid
27	Ibid. 29 May 1880
28	Ibid. 28 May 1877
29	Ibid. 27 June 1877
30	Ibid. 6 June 1877
31	Ibid. 5 June 1877
32	John Morgan: *Memoirs*, p.171
33	FP 21 August 1877

34 Ab. Jo. 22 February 1879
35 Ibid. 26 January 1878
36 Ibid. 19 April 1880
37 R. W. Postgate: *The Builders' History*, London, AUBTW 1923, pp.328–9
38 Ab. Jo. 19 October 1888
39 FP 25 December 1894
40 Ab. Jo. 9 May 1894
41 Ibid. 26 February 1896
42 Ibid. 29 February 1896)
43 Ibid. 23 February 1884
44 John Morgan: *Memoirs*, p.77
45 Ab. Jo. 13 October 1888
46 EE 9 November 1889
47 AGA Minutes, June 1891
48 Ibid. February 1892
49 Ab. Jo. 11 February 1892
50 EE 10 February 1892
51 Ibid.
52 FP 16 February 1892
53 Ab. Jo. 17 February 1892
54 FP 18 February 1892
55 EE 13 September 1893
56 Ab. Jo. 29 February 1892
57 Ibid. 12 August 1896
58 McLaren, pp.21–2
59 Ab. Jo. 3 July 1895
60 QMJ, Vol IV, December 1933, p.318
61 Ab. Jo. 24 December 1912
62 Ab. Jo. 3 and 30 July 1895
63 AGA Minutes, Vol. I, December 1888
64 Ibid. October 1889
65 Ab. Jo. 7 December 1898
66 AGA Minutes, 12 May, 16 August, 23 August 1920
67 Ab. Jo. 20 September 1898
68 Ibid. 13 September 1898
69 Ibid. 21 September 1898
70 AGA Minutes, March 1890
71 Ab. Jo. 22 April 1896
72 Ibid. 4 June 1896
73 Ibid. 20 June 1896
74 QMJ, Vol IV, December 1933, p.318
75 *P&J Business Journal*, 30 October 1985, p.11
76 Ab. Jo. 31 December 1892
77 John Morgan: *Memoirs*, pp.115–6
78 AGA Minutes, 24 November 1903
79 Ibid. 13 September 1907
80 Ibid. 14 September and 5 October 1910
81 Ibid. 17 March 1913
82 Ibid. 29 March 1913
83 Ab. Jo. 2 April 1913
84 Ibid.
85 AGA Minutes 21 and 22 May, and 18 June 1913; Ab. Jo. 24 May 1913

86	P&J 8 November 1948
87	McLaren, p.78
88	P&J 6 May 1955
89	Ibid. 4 May 1955
90	AGA Minutes, 26 April 1955
91	Ibid. 1 April 1960
92	*P&J Business Journal*, 30 October 1985
93	EE 15 November 1985
94	P&J 30 October 1985

Chapter 13

1	AGA Minutes, 5 May 1915
2	Ibid. 2 September 1914
3	Ibid. 4 November 1914
4	EE 22 May 1915
5	AGA Minutes, 26 March 1915
6	Ibid. 23 February 1916
7	Ibid. 2 February 1916
8	Ibid. 7 February 1917
9	Ab. Jo. 24 December 1915
10	AGA Minutes, 8 February 1916
11	Ibid. 3 May 1916
12	Ab. Jo. 27 February 1917; AGA Minutes, 3 October 1917
13	McLaren p.10
14	AGA Minutes, 7 March 1917
15	Ibid. 8 May 1918
16	FP 27 December 1917
17	AGA Minutes, 27 May 1918
18	Ab. Jo. 26 December 1918
19	Ibid.
20	FP 19 December 1919
21	P&J 1 November 1929
22	QMJ Vol XIII, No.4, 5 July 1930, p.147
23	Diane Morgan p18
24	Ab. Jo. 8 September 1920
25	QMJ Vol IV, No. 6, 15 January 1922, p.220
26	Ibid.
27	Ibid. Vol VI, No.9, 5 April 1924, p.2294
28	Ibid. Vol VII, No. 7, 5 February 1925, p.204
29	P&J 21 December 1925
30	Ibid. 21 February 1928
31	Ibid. 4 March 1929
32	QMJ 5 September and 5 November 1927, and 5 January and 5 August 1928
33	P&J 24 September 1929
34	QMJ Vol XIII, No. 6, 5 September 1930, p.70
35	*My Faither Built the Sydney Brig: A Celebration of the Contribution of the North-East Workers to the Construction of the Sydney Harbour Bridge on its 75th Anniversary*, produced by the Local Studies section of Aberdeen Central Library from material donated by Mr Bill Glennie, 2007; Bill Glennie: 'We've come a' the way frae Scotland tae mak a brig' in *Leopard*, April 2013, pp13–15
36	http://www.sydneyharbourbridge.info Accessed January 2017
37	Ab. Jo. 22 December 1911

38	Ab. Jo. 3 January 1920
39	Anderson: *The Granites of Scotland*
40	Diack: *Rise and Progress*, p.31
41	P&J 7 May 1924
42	Hamilton, p.191
43	P&J 21 September 1934
44	Grant p.9
45	P&J 22 December 1926
46	Ibid. 2 November 1936
47	Power, Section 6.0
48	Diack: *Rise and Progress*, p.67
49	P&J 31 December 1929
50	Ibid. 13 March 1931
51	QMJ Vol XIV, No. 10, 5 January 1932
52	P&J 18 March 1933
53	Ibid. 29 March 1935
54	Ibid. 12 September 1938
55	Ibid. 21 December 1938
56	AGMA Minutes, 5 April 1948
57	P&J 27 December 1928
58	Ibid. 29 December 1936
59	Ibid. 21 December 1938
60	Ibid.
61	*Bon Accord & Northern Pictorial* 15 February 1930 pp.1–10
62	P&J 3 March 1930
63	QMJ May 1934, p.57
64	*Bon Accord & Northern Pictorial* 6 January 1938

Chapter 14

1	Hamilton p.207
2	Grant pp.18–20
3	'The granite industry of Scotland: the Aberdeen tradition' in *The Quarry Managers' Journal*, November 1961, pp.433–7
4	Hamilton p.208
5	AGMA Minutes, 24 April 1942
6	McLaren p.40
7	Chapman, sections 131–3
8	Chapman, sections 513–14
9	P&J 18 August 1950
10	Ibid. 13 April 1950
11	McLaren p.44
12	AGMA Minutes, 13 October 1950
13	P&J 11 September 1950
14	AGA Minutes, 2 June 1952
15	Ibid. 11 November 1952
16	EE 6 March 1953; *The Courier and Advertiser* 7 March 1953
17	EE 25 May 1954
18	P&J 21 November 1950
19	EE 26 May 1954
20	Ibid. 25 May 1954
21	Ibid.

22	Ibid. 21 December 1954
23	Personal communication
24	EE 26 May 1954
25	Ibid. 22 July 1953
26	P&J 13 August 1945
27	Ibid. 2 July 1946
28	Ibid. 8 September 1956
29	Fyfe Archive Boxes 3 and 5
30	Ab. Jo. 15 December 1890
31	*The Herald* 16 December 2000
32	McLaren p.94
33	AGA Minutes, 13 February 1970
34	P&J 12 May 1971
35	Spence p.5
36	Personal communication from Sandy Argo
37	EE 15 August 1972
38	Ibid. 12 March 1951
39	P&J 29 April 1987
40	*Lands Tribunal for Scotland*, 5 January 2018. Case Ref; LTS/TC/2016/0035
41	EE 12 May 1955
42	EE 14 December 1961
43	EE 24 May 1954
44	McLaren p.44
45	Diane Morgan p.29
46	Ibid. p.14
47	Allenvale Granite Works Papers AC1440
48	P&J 5 April 1985
49	Interviewed August 2015
50	Diane Morgan pp.62–5
51	McLaren pp.90–1

BIBLIOGRAPHY

Granite is an industry that has attracted numerous writers over the years, more than many comparable industries. These have included academics interested in the geology such as William Knight who was Professor of Natural Philosophy at Marischal College, as well as workers and managers from the industry itself. It had its own journals such as the *The Quarry Managers' Journal* and the *United Operative Masons and Granitecutters' Journal*. There is also a huge amount of material in newspapers, particularly the *Aberdeen Journal*, the *Aberdeen Free Press*, the *Evening Express*, the *Press and Journal* and the *Bon Accord and Northern Pictorial*. The Granite Chips column which started to appear in the *Evening Express*, and then in the *Aberdeen Journal*, in the 1890s gives a good picture of the industry at the time. Also at that time the *Journal* had an end-of-year survey of each industry in Aberdeen including granite. The articles listed below from these newspapers are some of the longer articles as well as some of the early articles, it would be impossible to list everything.

Archival Material

Aberdeen and Aberdeenshire Archives
Aberdeen Council Register
Records of John Fyfe Granite Merchants DD57 incorporating Rubislaw Granite Company Ltd. DD57/B
Papers of Alexander Macdonald of Kepplestone DD391
Allenvale Granite Works Papers 1952–1971 AC1440
Letter of David Menzies to the Magistrates of Aberdeen, concerning destruction of pasture by quarrying at Nigg, August 10th, 1770. CA/8/P/230/2/6

University of Aberdeen
Forbes and Hay families of Seaton, Aberdeenshire: family and estate papers. MS 2253
James Skene of Rubislaw Papers. MS2720
Records of F. A. MacDonald, engineers and surveyors, including James F. Beattie & Sons. MS2626
Account Book of James Rankin, Cairness. MS 1160/3/13

Aberdeen Central Library
Aberdeenshire Valuation Rolls
John Morgan Memoirs (unpublished)
G. M. Fraser Notebooks and Index
In Memoriam: 1890-1914 (Obituaries from Aberdeen newspapers)

Aberdeen Art Gallery & Museums
Aberdeen Granite Association, Minute Books and other material 1887-1983

Other Archival Material
James Wright & Sons Order Book 1869-1872
Aberdeen Post Office Directories, 1824 onwards Full set available in Aberdeen Central Library.
Those from 1824-1912 are also available on-line via the National Library of Scotland at http://
www.nls.uk/family-history/directories/post-office/index.cfm?place=Aberdeen

Books and Reports

Aberdeen Art Gallery, Alexander Macdonald: from mason to Maecenas. Aberdeen, Art Gallery &
    Museums, 1985
Anderson, James, General view of the agriculture and rural economy of the County of Aberdeen.
    Edinburgh, 1794
Anderson, J.G.C., The granites of Scotland. Memoirs of the Geological Survey Special reports on
    the mineral resources of Great Britain .Vol XXXII. Edinburgh, HMSO, 1939
Argo, Alexander C., John Fyfe: One hundred and fifty years 1846–1996. Kemnay, Time Pieces
    Publications, 1996
Bon Accord, Aberdeen Today: a record of the life, thought and industry of the city. Aberdeen, Henry
    Munro, 1907
Buchan, Peter, Annals of Peterhead. Peterhead, P. Buchan, 1819
Chapman, W. D., Granite City: a plan for Aberdeen. London, Batsford, 1952
Riley, Charles F.
Diack, William, Rise and progress of the granite industry in Aberdeen. Quarry Managers' Journal,
    1949
Donnelly, Tom, The Aberdeen granite industry. University of Aberdeen 1994
Douglas, Francis, General description of the East Coast of Scotland, 1782
Farmer, Frank, The early history of Union Street, 1800–1824. Student dissertation at the Scott
    Sutherland School, Robert Gordon University, 1974 (unpublished)
Findlay, James T., A history of Peterhead to 1896. D. Wylie, 1933
Gibb, Sir Alexander, The story of Telford. London, A Maclehose & Co., 1935
Grant, William S., Reminiscences. Bradford–on–Avon, Dotesios Printers, 1949
Harris, George F, Granite and our granite industries. London, Crosby Lockwood, 1888

Hoffman, Frederick L. The problem of dust phthisis in the granite–stone industry. Washington, Government Printing Office, 1922

Institution of Mechanical Engineers, Visit to works in the Aberdeen area, 1907. Including visits to Charles Macdonald, Alexander Macdonald, James Taggart, John Fyfe and the Rubislaw Granite Company. Available on–line from Grace's Guide at www.gracesguide.co.uk Accessed March 2014

Keith, George Skene, A general view of the agriculture of Aberdeenshire. Aberdeen, A. Brown, 1811

Macdonald, Alexander Improvements in the manufacture of columns, pilasters, and other, similar structures of granite, marble, porphyry, jasper, serpentine, sienite, and other stones capable of receiving a high polish, UK, Patent No. 69 (8 January 1857)

McLaren, John, Sixty years in an Aberdeen granite yard: the craft and the men, Aberdeen, University of Aberdeen, 1987

Macpherson, W. M. , Materials for a history of the Church and Priory of Monymusk. Aberdeen, Adelphi Press, 1895

Miller, A. L. , Notes on the early history and records of the Lodge, Aberdeen. Aberdeen, University Press, 1919

Morgan, Diane, A monumental business: the story of A. & J. Robertson (Granite) Ltd 1876–2001. Aberdeen, Denburn Books, 2001

Morgan, Diane, The Villages of Aberdeen; The Spital. Aberdeen, Denburn Books, 1996

Morgan, Diane, The Villages of Aberdeen: The Spital Lands. Aberdeen, Denburn Books, 1997

Morgan, Patrick, Annals of Woodside and Newhills. Aberdeen, David Wylie, 1886

Munro, A. M., The book of the mason craft: in connection with the Aberdeen Masonic Bazaar, 8,9,10 October 1896. Aberdeen, Adelphi Press, 1896

Power, Thomas, Peterhead granite: report of a desk study, June 1994

Pratt, John B, , Buchan. Edinburgh, Blackwood & Sons, 1858

Rae, Lettice M, , The story of the Gibbs. Edinburgh, T & A Constable 1961

Rettie, James, , Aberdeen fifty years ago. Aberdeen, Lewis Smith, 1868

Robertson, Joseph, The book of Bon Accord. Aberdeen, Lewis Smith, 1839

Royal Commission, Minutes of evidence taken before the Royal Commission on Metalliferous Mines and Quarries. London, HMSO, 1912

Russell, William, Aberdeen: industries and attractions (published in connection with the Empire Exhibition). Aberdeen. Mearns Pub., 1938

Scotland of today, Part II: its growth and progress: a review of the industries of Aberdeen. London, Historical Publishing Co, 1890

Simpson, William, Granite quarrying in Aberdeen Today. Bon Accord 1907

Statistical Account, Statistical Account of Scotland, 1st (Old), 2nd (New) and 3rd

Stuart, John, Extracts from the Council Register of the Burgh of Aberdeen,: 1398–1570. Aberdeen, Spalding Club, 1844

Thom, Walter, The history of Aberdeen. 2 Vols, Aberdeen, D. Chalmers, 1811

Watson, John, British and foreign building stones. Cambridge, 1911

Wilson, Charles A, Aberdeen of Auld Lang Syne. Aberdeen, Henry Munro, 1948

Articles and Papers

Anon. Architecture and building in Aberdeen in *The Architect* (reprinted in *Aberdeen Journal*, 3 July 1872)

Anon. The granite industry of Scotland: the Aberdeen tradition in *The Quarry Managers' Journal*, November 1961, pp.433–437

Anon. Granite in the workshop in *The Builder* Vol XXXV, No.1810, 11 October 1877 pp.1019–1010)

Anon. The granite quarries of Aberdeen in *The Saturday Magazine*, 2 March 1844

Anon. The granite trade in Aberdeen in *The Scotsman*, 25 August, 2 August, 11 September, 22 September 1866

Anon. The founder of the polished granite trade in *Aberdeen Evening Express*, 12 May 1896

Anon. Aberdeen pioneer who taught the world in *Press and Journal*, 26 June 1929

Anon. Granite working in Aberdeen in *Illustrated London News*, 28 March 1857

Anon. The granite quarries and polishing works of Aberdeen from the *Scotsman*, reprinted in the *Aberdeen Journal*, 6 January 1869

Anon. Granite in the workshop in *The Builder*, Vol. XXXV, 11 October 1877, pp.1019–1020

Anon. The granite trade in Aberdeen in 1884 in *Daily Free Press* 31 December 1884

Anon. Our granite quarries in *Illustrated London News*, 26 April 1862

Anon. Passing of the Scottish kerb–makers by An Old Time Mason in *The Quarry Managers' Journal*, Vol. 13, 1930–31, pp.148–9

Anon. Romance of polished granite in *Press and Journal*, 26 June 1929

Anon. Something about Aberdeen in *The Builder* (repinted in *Aberdeen Journal,* 18 October 1865)

Allardyce, William , Granite quarrying, past and presence in *United Operative Masons and Granitecutters' Journal*, Vol. V, No.3, July 1905, p.2, continued in the October issue, Vol V, No.6

Anderson, F.S., Granite and granite quarrying in *The Quarry Managers' Journal*, October 1934, pp.200–203

Beveridge, R., On the occurrence of phthisis among granite–masons *in The British Medical Journal*, Vol. 2, No. 824, 14 October 1876, pp.489–490

Bowie, James, The granite industry in *Aberdeen Free Press*, 25 March, 4 April, 15 April, 26 April

Bulloch, J. M., Last of his line: the Duke of Gordon's statue in Granite: the revival of a long lost art in *Aberdeen Free Press*, 21 May 1904

Danbury News, The City of Aberdeen, reprinted in the *Aberdeen Journal*, 6 January 1875

Dey, Michael, Aberdeen Granite Association and the limits of capitalist cooperation in *Northern Scotland*, Vol. 4, 2013, pp.23–42

Diack, William, An artist in granite (James Philip) in *The Stone Trades Journal*, September – October 1941, pp.110–113

Diack, William, Granite polishing has had romantic history in *Press and Journal*, 15 August 1943

Diack, William, Granite: a romance of Scottish industry in Aberdeen Today: a special issue of *Bon Accord*, 1907, pp.99–104

Diack, William, Six decades of aerial cableways in quarries: Blondins sixtieth birthday in *The Quarry Managers' Journal*, October 1933, pp.240–242

Diack, William , The romance of the blondin in *Press and Journal*, 9 August 1929, p.6.

Donnelly, Tom, The Rubislaw Granite Quarries, 1750–1939 in *Industrial Archaeology*, Vol. 11, No. 3, August 1975, pp.225-237

Donnelly, Tom, Structural and technical change in the Aberdeen granite quarrying industry 1830–1880 in *Industrial Archaeology Review* Vol. 3, No. 3, Summer 1979, pp.228–238

Fraser, G. M., Archibald Simpson: Architect and his times in *Aberdeen Weekly Journal*, April–September 1918 (26 Chapters)

Gibb, Alexander, Extracts from a talk on the granite industry to the British Association meeting in Aberdeen in *Aberdeen Journal*, 21 September 1859

Gray, Roderick, On the granite of Aberdeenshire in *Transactions of the Highland and Agricultural Society of Scotland*, Vol. XII, 1839, pp.483–4

Hamilton, Henry, The granite industry, Chapter III, pp.191–208 of *Further Studies in Industrial Organization*, edited by M. P. Fogarty, London, Methuen, 1948

Harper, Marjory, Aberdeen granite workers in the United States in *Leopard Magazine*, April 1989

Harper, Marjory, Transient tradesmen: Aberdeen emigrants and the development of
the American granite industry in *Northern Scotland*, Vol. 9, 1989, pp.53–75

Harper, Marjory, Westward for work and Texan wrath , in *Press & Journal*, 17 April 1985

Hyslop, Ewen and Lott, Graham, Rock of Ages: The story of British Granite, in *The Building Conservation Directory* 2007, http://www.buildingconservation.com/articles/rockofages/rockof-ages.htm (Accessed November 2013)

Jeffrey, J R , The quarrying and manufacturing of engineering and architectural granite in *The Quarry Managers' Journal*, November 1932, pp.258–261

Kelly, William, On work in granite. Text of a paper read to Aberdeen granite workers, 13 December 1898, reprinted in *A tribute offered by the University of Aberdeen to the memory of William Kelly*, Aberdeen University Press, 1949

Knight, William, Account of the granite quarries of Aberdeenshire in *Prize essays and Transactions of the Highland and Agricultural Society of Scotland*, Vol. X, 1835, p.54

Lawrence, Cameron, Granite: the rise and fall of an industry in *The Press & Journal*, 15 and 16 April 1985

Lloyd Davies, T. A., A radiographic survey of monumental masonry workers in Aberdeen in *British Journal of Industrial Medicine*, Issue 30, 1973, pp.227–231

Mackie, Bill, Story with pictures on working at Rubislaw Quarry (text of article supplied by his daughter Judy)

Mair, Alexander, A survey of the granite industry in Aberdeen with reference to silicosis in *Edinburgh Medical Journal*, Vol. LVIII, No.10, October 1951, pp.457–480

Muir, George W., Granite working in *The Journal of the Society of Arts*, Vol. XIV, No. 705, 25 May 1866. pp.470–474

Ritchie, John, Aberdeen granite trade 1860–1928 in *The Quarry Managers' Journal*, April, May, June 1926

Ritchie, John, The granite industry in *The Quarry Managers' Journal*, November 1926, pp.167–169

Robertson, A. R., The granite industry in *Aberdeen University Review*, Vol. XLII, pp.236–273

Robertson, Graeme, A short history of the Aberdeen granite industry. Account of a talk given to the Aberdeen and north–east Scotland Family History Society, 19 May 2007

Simpson, W Douglas, The Augustinian Priory and Parish Church of Monymusk in *Proceedings of the Society of Antiquaries Scotland*, Vol. 59, 1924–25, pp.34–71

Simpson, William, Granite quarrying in Aberdeen Today: a special issue of *Bon Accord*, 1907, pp.107–110

Smith, John, The rise and fall of Aberdeen's granite industry in *Aberdeen University Review*, Vol. 49, 1982, pp.163–167

Spence, William, Notes on granite and Rubislaw Quarry collected by William Spence of William Tawse Limited, 1972 (in Fyfe Archive)

Stevenson, J. J. , The architectural treatment of granite. Paper read at the Art Section of the Social Science Congress 1877, reprinted in the *Aberdeen Journal*, 29 September 1877

Sutherland, Alistair, Notes on the Granite Supply Association (unpublished)

Walker, David, Aberdeen: the planning of the central area in *St Andrews Studies* Vol. IV, 2000, pp.51–67

Wilson, Andrew, Granite in its industrial and commercial aspects in *Transactions of the Buchan Field Club*, Vol. II, 1891–92, pp.156–167

Websites

www.ellisfamilytree.info For information on Boddie & Co., and other granite firms

Other Material

BBC Radio Scotland, *Our Story*: Series 1: Episode 2: Granite, Presented by Mark Stephen, broadcast 8 July 2013

Taggart, Nan, *Sculpture in Granite*. Filmed 1965, released on DVD by Aberdeen City Council, 2006

Personal communications and interviews with Sandy Argo, Hugh Black, Alan Bruce, Fred Cargill, Duncan Downie, Sir Archibald Grant of Monymusk, Michael A. Grant, Brian Innes, Ron McKay, Mary Macrae, Ron Michie, Michael P.S. O'Connor, Robert Taylor, Graeme Robertson, Alistair Sutherland, Bruce Walker, Mary Williamson

INDEX